What Works for Children and Adolescents?

What Works with Children and Adolescents? fulfils the need for a concise, empirically-based study of the types of psychological treatments that may be effective for common psychological problems in childhood and adolescence.

Providing a solid foundation for evidence-based practice in the treatment of children and adolescents, the book offers evidence from over 150 rigorously conducted research trials. Examining problems which are of central concern to practising clinicians – including child abuse, enuresis and encopresis, ADHD, childhood conduct problems, adolescent violence, drug abuse, anxiety and depression, anorexia and bulimia nervosa, paediatric pain, and post-divorce adjustment problems – it also highlights priority areas for future research on the treatment of children and adolescents' psychological problems.

What Works with Children and Adolescents? complements *The Handbook of Child and Adolescent Clinical Psychology* (Carr, 1999), and will be valuable to professionals in training.

Alan Carr is Director of the Doctoral Training Programme in Clinical Psychology at University College Dublin and Consultant Psychologist at the Clanwilliam Institute for Marital and Family Therapy in Dublin. He is the author of *The Handbook of Child and Adolescent Clinical Psychology* (1999).

What Works for Children and Adolescents?

A critical review of psychological interventions with children, adolescents and their families

Edited by
Alan Carr

London and New York

First published 2000 by Routledge
11 New Fetter Lane, London EC4P 4EE

Simultaneously published in the USA and Canada
by Taylor & Francis Inc
325 Chestnut Street, 8th Floor, Philadelphia PA 19106

Routledge is an imprint of the Taylor & Francis Group

Typeset in Times by Graphicraft Limited, Hong Kong
Printed and bound in Great Britain by Biddles Ltd, Guildford and King's
Lynn

British Library Cataloguing in Publication Data
A catalogue record for this book is available from the British Library

Library of Congress Cataloging in Publication Data
A catalogue record for this book has been requested

ISBN 0-415-22113-7 (hbk)
ISBN 0-415-23350-X (pbk)

Brother, the greatest of all virtues is curiosity
and the end of all desire is wisdom.

I might observe, not in order to combat your views but merely to continue
an interesting conversation, that wisdom may not be the end of everything.
Goodness and kindliness are, perhaps, beyond wisdom.

James Stephen (1912) *The Crock of Gold* (pp. 11–12). Dublin: Gill and
Macmillan.

Contents

Figures and Tables

Figures

Tables

Contributors

Joanne Behan, BA (Hons), MA (Applied Psychology), Midland Health Board

Rachel Brosnan, BA (Hons), North Western Health Board

Alan Carr, PhD, Director of the Clinical Psychology Programme, University College Dublin

Coleen Cormack, BA (Hons), MA (Health Psychology), South Eastern Health Board

Jennifer Edgeworth, BA (Hons), MA (Psychology), MSc (Neuroscience), North Eastern Health Board

Kathleen Mitchell, BA (Hons), Dip Couns Psych, MSc (Couns Psych), South Eastern Health Board

Maggie Moore, BSc (Hons), RGN, RMN, North Eastern Health Board

Eddie Murphy, BA (Hons), BSc (Hons), MSc (Health Psychology), RN, Midland Health Board

Margretta Nolan, BA (Hons), MA (Applied Psychology), Dip Stats, Midland Health Board

Maria O'Halloran, BA (Hons), RGN, RSCN, Midwest Health Board

Preface

In this era of increased demands for evidence-based practice and the use of empirically supported psychological interventions there has been a clear need for a concise, empirically based statement of the types of psychological treatments that may be effective for common psychological problems in childhood and adolescence. Our aim in writing this text has been to meet this need. We have set out to honour both of the sentiments expressed by James Stephens' philosophers in the excerpt from *The Crock of Gold* which opens this book. That is to maintain a commitment to curiosity and wisdom on the one hand, and benevolence on the other.

Empirical evidence from rigorously conducted research trials in each of eleven problem areas is reviewed by a team of ten psychologists in this volume. This evidence was culled from thorough literature searches for psychological treatment outcome studies that had been published in English language journals in the twenty-year period from 1977 to 1997. From this enormous body of literature only those studies which met stringent methodological criteria were selected for inclusion in the data base for this book. In all, over 150 well-conducted studies were identified and these contained over 5,000 participants. Thus, the conclusions reached in this volume are based on a solid bedrock of rigorous empirical evidence.

What Works for Children and Adolescents? complements the *Handbook of Child and Adolescent Clinical Psychology* (Carr, 1999, published by Routledge), insofar as it provides a review of the evidence on which the approach to practice described in the *Handbook* is based.

Alan Carr
November 1998

Acknowledgements

We are grateful to the many people who have helped develop the ideas presented in this book. A particular debt of gratitude is due to Professor Ciarán Benson, Dr Patricia Noonan Walsh, Fíona Kelly Meldon and Frances Osborne who have been very supportive during our efforts to write this text. The research on which this book is based has been supported, in part, by a UCD Faculty of Arts Grant to Alan Carr which is gratefully acknowledged. The research was also supported by funds from the Midland Health Board, the North Eastern Health Board, the North Western Health Board, the South Eastern Health Board, and the Midwestern Health Board in the Republic of Ireland. Thanks, too, to Derek Deasy for assistance with a preliminary literature search.

We are grateful to the American Psychiatric Association for permission to reproduce diagnostic criteria previously published in 1994 in the Fourth Edition of the *Diagnostic and Statistical Manual of Mental Disorders* and to the World Health Organization for permission to reproduce diagnostic criteria previously published in 1992 in *The ICD-10 Classification of Mental and Behavioural Disorders. Clinical Descriptions and Diagnostic Guidelines.*

1 Introduction

Alan Carr

Between 10 and 20 per cent of children and adolescents suffer from psychological problems serious enough to warrant psychological treatment (Carr, 1993). For clinical psychologists working with children and adolescents, and for those who use and fund these psychological services, a central concern is what psychological interventions are most effective for which particular problems (Kendall and Chambless, 1998; Paul, 1967). Our book aims to answer this question. Our answer is based on a thorough review of rigorously conducted treatment outcome research.

Early evaluations of psychological interventions

Within modern clinical psychology, the question of the effectiveness of psychological intervention was addressed most poignantly by Eysenck, who in 1952 concluded that traditional forms of psychodynamically based psychotherapy led to no greater improvement in neurotic adults than that which occurred as a result of spontaneous remission. These conclusions were central to Eysenck's broad argument against psychoanalysis and in favour of behaviour therapy. There is little doubt now that Eysenck asked the wrong question and that the data he used to answer it were from methodologically flawed studies. He asked *Does psychotherapy work?* when it would have been more useful to ask *What works for whom?* The data he used to answer the question were of questionable reliability and validity, and none of the studies included in the 1952 paper would receive a high score on the methodological checklist presented later in this chapter. However, the importance of Eysenck's paper is that it opened up a lively (and often caustic) debate between clinicians of various theoretical persuasions and provided an impetus for rigorous research into the effectiveness of psychological interventions (Bergin and Garfield, 1994; Garfield and Bergin, 1971, 1978, 1986; Kendall and Chambless, 1998).

Five years after Eysenck's paper, Levitt (1957) published a review of eighteen studies of psychotherapy with neurotic children and concluded that after therapy, 78 per cent of treated cases showed sustained improvement and that this improvement rate was little different from the 73 per cent of untreated cases who showed spontaneous remission! Levitt's paper, like Eysenck's led to great controversy and contributed to the growth of interest in research on psychotherapy with children (Kazdin, 1988). Like Eysenck, Levitt also asked the wrong question and used unreliable data from methodologically flawed studies to answer it.

However, the debates sparked by the publication of Eysenck's and Levitt's papers highlighted a variety of methodological features that must be built into psychological intervention outcome studies, if valid conclusions are to be drawn from them. For example, cases should ideally be diagnostically homogenous, randomly assigned to groups and reliably assessed before and after a well-specified treatment programme offered by trained therapists. Later in this chapter, a checklist of methodological features which was used to evaluate all of the studies reviewed in this book will be presented. This checklist owes its origins to the Eysenck and Levitt debates. These debates also contributed to a re-evaluation of the question *Does psychotherapy work?* and led Gordon Paul to rephrase it as

> What treatment by whom is most effective for this individual with that specific problem under which set of circumstances?
>
> (Paul, 1967)

Meta-analysis

Traditionally, attempts to summarize and synthesize available evidence on the effectiveness of psychological interventions with adults and children have relied on simple box-score methods and narrative reviews (Garfield and Bergin, 1971, 1978, 1986). With box-scores, the number of cases that improved in treatment groups are summed across studies and compared with the sum of improved cases from control groups. However, data from published studies are often not presented in a manner that allows such analyses to be conducted by reviewers. For example, investigators often only report that following treatment the difference between the means of the treatment and control group differed significantly, without reference to the clinical significance of this statistically significant difference. In such instances, the reviewer may make claims within a narrative review about the degree to which treatments are effective, with which other experts might disagree. One solution to the simplicity of the box-score approach and the danger of reviewer-bias unduly influencing the conclusions of narrative reviews is meta-analysis.

Meta-analysis is a set of quantitative techniques that may be used to synthesize the results of multiple studies which is statistically more sophisticated than the box-score method and less prone to reviewer bias than the narrative review method. With meta-analysis, a group of studies is first selected according to certain criteria, for example, comparative group outcome studies of psychotherapy with children. The results of each of these

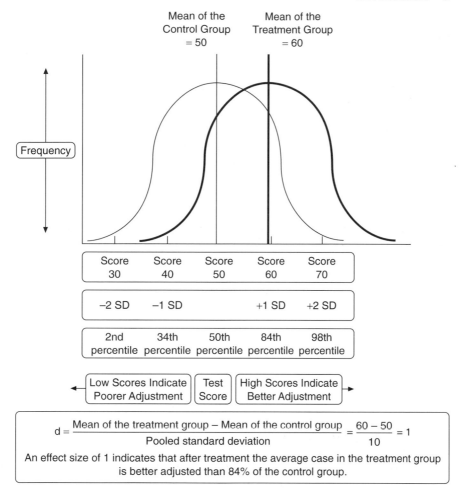

Figure 1.1 Graphic representation of an effect size of 1.

are converted into a common metric (usually effect size, *d*) which indicates the extent to which a treatment group improved following treatment in comparison with a control group. A graphic explanation of effect size is given in Figure 1.1. These effect sizes may then be aggregated across studies and the mean effect size for a group of studies calculated. Various characteristics of each study may also be coded, such as the type of problem studied, the treatment used, the level of training of the therapists, the duration of treatment and so forth. The impact of these characteristics (as independent variables) on effect size (as the dependent variable) may then be determined using routine statistical procedures such as analysis of variance or multiple regression.

Within the psychotherapy field, Smith, Glass and Miller conducted the first meta-analysis and included 475 studies of child, adolescent and adult psychotherapy in their database (Smith and Glass, 1977; Smith *et al.*, 1980). They concluded that following therapy, the average treated cases fared better than more than 70 per cent of untreated cases and that all types of psychological treatments were equally effective. Smith, Glass and Miller's work has been the target for much criticism (Weisz and Weiss, 1993). One important criticism was their failure to analyse the data on psychological interventions with children separately.

Other researchers have since taken up this challenge. In their overview of a number of major meta-analyses of the child psychotherapy literature, Weisz and Weiss (ibid.) concluded that these quantitative syntheses of the results of over 200 studies containing more than 11,000 children and adolescents show that the average treated case is better adjusted following treatment than 76 per cent of untreated cases. Thus, the results of meta-analyses of child and adolescent psychotherapy outcome studies are remarkably similar to the results from meta-analyses of the adult psychotherapy outcome literature.

Such grand meta-analyses, which address the question *Does psychotherapy work?* have given way to those that focus on specific treatment approaches and two of these, which deal with cognitive-behavioural therapy and family therapy deserve particular mention. Durlak *et al.* (1991) in a meta-analysis of 64 studies in which cognitive behavioural procedures were the main treatment method, found that the average treated case fared better at the end of treatment than 71 per cent of untreated controls and these gains were maintained at six-month follow-ups. In this meta-analysis, studies included cases with a range of internalizing, externalizing and mixed behaviour problems and a wide range of predominantly individually focused cognitive-behavioural interventions were used, such as social and problem solving skills training and self-instruction. Shadish *et al.* (1993) in a meta-analysis of 163 randomized trials of marital and family therapy, included 101 studies of family therapy and in many of these studies, the central presenting complaint was a child or adolescent adjustment problem. Overall, the average case treated with any form of family therapy fared better than 68 per cent of untreated cases.

The similarity of the results of these two meta-analyses is quite remarkable. In both individually based cognitive behavioural therapy and family therapy the average treated case, according to these results, fared better than approximately 70 per cent of untreated cases after therapy.

Focused reviews

While the results of meta-analyses reviewed so far may offer justification for using psychological interventions generally in addressing the problems of children and adolescents, they offer little guidance for clinicians on which specific interventions to use in which particular cases. Indeed the extraordinarily consistent and positive results of these meta-analyses underline the importance of conducting a series of tightly focused literature reviews, using both narrative review and meta-analytic methods, to examine the effectiveness of specific interventions with specific problems. This was precisely what we set out to do when we wrote this book.

In setting out to undertake this task, a decision was made about which areas to cover. We decided to address clinical problems commonly seen by clinical psychologists working in routine community, outpatient or hospital settings, on which a number of methodologically sound treatment outcome studies had been conducted. Using these inclusion criteria the following problem areas were selected:

- Child abuse and neglect
- Enuresis and encopresis
- Attention deficit hyperactivity disorder
- Oppositional defiant disorder
- Conduct problems in adolescence
- Drug abuse in adolescence
- Anxiety
- Depression
- Anorexia and bulimia nervosa
- Paediatric pain problems including headaches, recurrent abdominal pain and aversive medical procedures
- Adjustment to divorce

A decision was also made to exclude coverage of communication and learning problems such as developmental language delay (Whitehurst and Fischel, 1994); autism and related disorders (Howlin, 1998); intellectual disability (King and State, 1997; State and King, 1997); and specific learning disabilities (Maughan, 1995). The treatment outcome literature on these problems is sufficiently large to warrant consideration in a separate volume.

Overall review strategy

For each of the eleven problem areas listed in the previous section, the following review strategy was used for the twenty-year period 1977 to 1997.

1 A PsychLit search of English language journals and book chapters was conducted using the core problem term and variations of it combined with the terms *treatment*, *therapy* and related phrases to identify potential treatment outcome studies.
2 A PsychLit search was conducted using the core problem term combined with the term *review*, to identify review papers.
3 The bibliographies of review papers, treatment outcome studies and relevant journals were manually searched.

4   In certain instances investigators were contacted directly to solicit copies of recent articles, although only in exceptional circumstances where very few high quality published studies were available were unpublished studies included in reviews.

5   Studies were selected for inclusion if they met the following stringent methodological criteria: a comparative group outcome design rather than a single case design was used; cases were diagnostically homogenous; cases were randomly assigned to groups; at least five cases were included in each group; and pre- and post-treatment measures were used.

6   If these stringent methodological criteria yielded a particularly small pool of studies, the criteria were relaxed and less methodologically robust studies were included for review. These procedures ensured that for each problem area, a pool of the most methodologically robust available studies containing at least a hundred treated cases were reviewed.

7   For each group of studies four types of tables were drawn up to summarize key features. These tables covered (a) general characteristics; (b) methodological features; (c) effect sizes and outcome rates; and (d) key findings. The structure of these tables and definitions of the terms included in them will be given below.

8   Narrative accounts were written summarizing the main trends in each of the tables, with one section giving an overview of the characteristics of the studies; a further section commenting on their methodological features; and the third section summarizing the substantive findings.

9   In writing sections on substantive findings studies were grouped by problem subtype (e.g. physical abuse, sexual abuse), type of intervention (e.g. family therapy, individual cognitive behaviour therapy), or study design (e.g. active treatment vs. waiting list control, comparison of two active treatments). In outlining substantive findings reference was made to the design, measures and results of each study or each group of similar studies.

10 A summary of the main conclusions and the confidence with which these were drawn were outlined before highlighting the implications for clinical practice, service development and further research.

Strategy for tabulating general characteristics of studies

To provide an overview of the general characteristics of studies reviewed, a table containing the following headings was constructed for problems addressed in each chapter.

- *Authors*
- *Year:* The year of publication was given under this heading.
- *Country:* The country in which the study was conducted was given under this heading.

- *N per group:* The number of cases in each group was given under this heading.
- *Mean age and range*
- *Gender:* The number of males and females was given under this heading.
- *Primary diagnoses:* The name and source of the diagnosis were given under this heading, e.g. DSM III-R Depression.
- *Severity and chronicity:* The numbers of cases with severe and/or chronic primary diagnoses were given under this heading.
- *Co-morbid diagnoses:* The number of children with comorbid problems or diagnoses was given under this heading.
- *Family characteristics:* Descriptions of the structure, size, socio-economic status, parental diagnoses or problems and any other defining family characteristics were given under this heading.
- *Referral characteristics:* Four main types of referrals were distinguished under this heading. These were routine referrals from GPs, schools, etc.; media solicited referrals where clients answered a newspaper advertisement to attend free treatment, usually at a university clinic; school-based group treatment usually conducted by a university clinician with minimal parent involvement; and coercive referrals where social workers, probation officers or other statutory workers arrange for court mandated treatment.
- *Treatment setting:* Distinctions were made between hospital inpatient settings, residential centres, fostercare, community outpatient settings, and university outpatient settings.
- *Duration of treatment:* The average number of sessions or hours of therapy and the time period over which this occurred were given under this heading, e.g. twenty hourly sessions over one year.

Where all studies shared a particular characteristic or where information on a particular characteristic was unavailable for most studies, then a column for categorizing that characteristic was eliminated from the table so as to simplify the overall presentation of information.

Strategy for tabulating methodological features of studies

To provide an overview of the methodological features of studies, a table containing categories listed below was constructed in each chapter and the presence or absence of each methodological feature for each study was noted. These categories collectively constitute a checklist for assessing methodological robustness. The checklist represents a synthesis of other similar checklists (Carr, 1997; Gurman and Kniskern, 1978, 1981; Kazdin, 1988; Kendall and Chambless, 1998). In interpreting tables based on this checklist, attention was paid to both profiles and total scores. Examination of each study's profile on this checklist threw light on its methodological strengths and weaknesses. Greater confidence was place in the results of studies that obtained higher total scores. What follows are definitions of items in the checklist.

- *Control group:* A control group was used.
- *Random assignment:* Cases were randomly assigned to treatment and control groups.
- *Diagnostic homogeneity:* All cases in treatment and control groups had the same diagnosis or psychometric profile.
- *Comparable for co-morbidity:* Cases were assessed for co-morbidity and the results reported showed that the groups were similar in this respect.
- *Demographic similarity:* Cases in treatment and control groups did not differ significantly in terms of the children's age or gender.
- *Pre-treatment assessment:* Cases were assessed before treatment.
- *Post-treatment assessment:* Cases were assessed after treatment.
- *Follow-up assessment:* Cases were assessed at some specified period after the treatment group had completed therapy. Follow-up assessments typically occur at three months, six months or a year after treatment.
- *Children's self-report:* Children's self-report instruments were used to assess children's adjustment before and after treatment.
- *Parents' ratings:* Instruments that yielded parents' ratings of children's adjustment were used to assess children's pre-treatment and post-treatment status.
- *Teachers' ratings:* Teachers' ratings of children's adjustment were used to assess children's pre-treatment and post-treatment status.
- *Therapists' ratings:* Instruments that yielded therapists' ratings of children's adjustment were used to assess children's pre-treatment and post-treatment status.
- *Researchers' ratings:* Instruments that yielded researchers' ratings of children's adjustment were used to assess children's pre-treatment and post-treatment status.
- *Child's symptom assessed:* The core symptom was assessed before and after treatment using a symptom-focused measure such as the Child Behaviour Checklist (Achenbach, 1991).
- *System assessed:* Some important aspect of the wider family or school social system was assessed before and after treatment using a systemic self-report measure such as the Family Assessment Device (Kabacoff *et al.*, 1990) or an observational measure of parent–child interaction, teacher–child interaction or peer group-based behaviour.
- *Deterioration assessed:* Deterioration following treatment was evaluated in those cases where it occurred.
- *Drop-out assessed:* The number of drop-outs from the treatment and control groups was reported.
- *Clinical significance of change assessed:* Cases were classified as clinically improved following treatment using cut-off scores on standardized instruments or Reliable Change Indices (Hageman and Arrindell, 1993;

Jacobson *et al.*, 1984) and the frequency of improved cases in treatment and control groups was compared using appropriate non-parametric statistics.

- *Experienced therapists used for all treatments:* Experienced therapists with formal training or therapy qualifications delivered treatment.
- *Treatments were equally valued by therapists:* Where two treatments were compared, skilled therapists committed to their model of intervention delivered both treatments.
- *Treatments were manualized:* Treatment was guided by a manual that was either flexibly or rigidly adhered to by therapists.
- *Therapy supervision was provided:* All therapists participating in the study received ongoing supervision to ensure that a high quality of therapy was offered to clients.
- *Treatment integrity checked:* The integrity of each active treatment was checked by, for example, audio-taping a selection of sessions and using a checklist to assess the degree to which therapists' behaviour conformed to the guidelines laid down in the treatment manual.
- *Data on concurrent treatment given:* Information was given on whether or not children or other family members were receiving concurrent psychological or pharmacological treatment for the core problem or related difficulties.
- *Data on subsequent treatment given:* Information was given on whether or not children or other family members engaged in further treatment following the intervention assessed in the study.

Strategy for tabulating effect sizes and outcome rates

In tabulating effect sizes and outcome rates, a framework was drawn up which takes account of a number of important distinctions that have been established in the psychotherapy and family therapy treatment outcome literature (Bergin and Garfield, 1994; Gurman and Kniskern, 1978; Kazdin, 1988; Kendall and Chambless, 1998; Pinsof and Wynne, 1995). Distinctions were made between improvements shown immediately following treatment and improvement shown at follow-up. Distinctions were also made between symptomatic improvement in the presenting problem and systemic improvement in important aspects of the child's social context such as family, school or peer relationships. Within the framework, provision was made for reporting both effect sizes and percentages of cases showing clinically significant improvement and deterioration. Finally, provision was made for identifying whether the source of outcome data was a child, parent, teacher, therapist, or researcher. Results, where available, were tabulated in the six domains defined below.

- *Symptomatic improvement after treatment.* This refers to improvement in symptoms or target problems immediately following treatment and was assessed in some studies by scales like the Child Behaviour Checklist (Achenbach, 1991), the Teacher Report Form (Achenbach, 1991), the Childhood Depression Inventory (Kovacs and Beck, 1977), behavioural ratings of the child made by researchers and other scales that measure maladaptive features of children's behaviour, affect or cognition central to their presenting problem. Where possible, data based on children's self-reports, parent ratings, teacher ratings, therapist ratings and researcher ratings were abstracted and in each instance converted to effect sizes using the procedures set out in Table 1.1 (Shadish, 1990).

- *Symptomatic improvement at follow-up.* This refers to improvement in symptoms or target problems at any point more than three months after treatment and was tabulated in the same manner as data on symptomatic improvement after treatment.
- *Systemic improvement after treatment.* This refers to improvement in aspects of the child's social network, particularly the family, school and peer group, immediately following treatment. It was assessed in some studies by self-report instruments such as the Family Assessment Device (Kabacoff *et al.*, 1990), and by interactional rating scales for evaluating parenting skills, parent–child interaction, teacher–child interaction, peer group interaction, and ratings of other aspects of the child's immediate social network. Where possible, data based on children's self-reports, parent ratings, teacher ratings, therapist ratings and researcher ratings were abstracted and in each instance converted to effect-sizes using the procedures set out in Table 1.1 before tabulation.
- *Systemic improvement at follow-up.* This refers to improvement in aspects of the child's social network, particularly the family, school and peer group, at any point more than three months after treatment and was tabulated in the same manner as data on systemic improvement after treatment.
- *Positive clinical outcomes.* This refers to the percentage of cases in the treatment group that were identified as showing clinically significant improvement according to some clearly defined criterion. Such criteria included moving from the clinical to the normal range on a relevant assessment instrument such as the Child Behaviour Checklist (Achenbach, 1991) or demonstrating reliable change as defined by the Reliable Change Index (Hageman and Arrindell, 1993; Jacobson *et al.*, 1984). This information was recorded where possible for the period immediately after treatment and also for any follow-up period three months after treatment.
- *Negative clinical outcomes.* This refers to the percentage of cases in the treatment group that deteriorated from pre-treatment to post-treatment assessment according to a clinically meaningful criterion such as showing a negative change of at least .5 of a standard deviation on the Child Behaviour Checklist (1991). The percentages of cases that dropped out of treatment or went on to engage in further treatment were also recorded in this domain.

Table 1.1 Calculation of effect sizes

	Conditions where suitable	Formula	Definition of terms
1	Means and standard deviations are given	$d = \dfrac{M1 - M2}{SD}$	SD = Standard deviation of the control group or the pooled standard deviation $\text{Pooled } SD = \dfrac{\sqrt{(n1-1)SD1^2 + (n2-1)SD2^2}}{(n1+n2-2)}$ M1 = Mean of the treatment group M2 = Mean of the control group n1 = no. of cases in treatment group n2 = no. of cases in control group SD1 = Standard deviation of treatment group SD2 = Standard deviation of control group
2	Frequency of improved cases in treatment and control groups is given	$d = \ln(AD/CB)\sqrt{3}/\pi$	$\sqrt{3}/\pi = .55$ ln = natural log A = no. of improved treated cases B = no. of unimproved treated cases C = no. of improved untreated cases D = no. of unimproved untreated cases
3	t-test result on raw post-treatment scores is given	$d = t\sqrt{1/n1 + 1/n2}$	t = t value from t-test on raw post-treatment scores n1 = no. of cases in treatment group n2 = no. of cases in control group
4	For two group studies ANOVA F statistic on raw post-treatment scores is given	$d = \sqrt{F(1/n1 + 1/n2)}$	F = F value from t-test on raw post-treatment scores n1 = no. of cases in treatment group n2 = no. of cases in control group

Table 1.1 (cont'd)

	Conditions where suitable	Formula	Definition of terms
5	For studies with more than two group ANOVA F statistic on raw post-treatment scores is given along with means	$d = \dfrac{M1 - M2}{\sqrt{\sum ni(Mi - GM)^2/(k - 1)}\,F}$	M1 = Mean of the treatment group M2 = Mean of the control group ni = no. of cases in group i Mi = mean of group i GM = grand mean k = number of groups F = F statistic
6	ANCOVA F statistic on adjusted post-treatment scores is given	$d = \sqrt{F(1/n1 + 1/n2)(1 - rxx)}$	F = F value from t-test on raw post-treatment scores n1 = no. of cases in treatment group n2 = no. of cases in control group rxx = test–retest correlation of covariate if reported. If not reported assume it is .5
7	Probability level (p < .05 or p < .01), n1 and n2 only are given	$d = t\,(estimated)\sqrt{1/n1 + 1/n2}$	t (estimated) = take from a table of t values for two-tailed tests for the reported p value and df value df = (n1 + n2) – 2 n1 = no. of cases in treatment group n2 = no. of cases in control group
8	Results are described as non-significant and no data are given	$d = 0$	Assume d = 0 if results are reported to be non-significant and no other data are available

Source Adapted from Shadish (1993).

For some clinical problems addressed in chapters 2 to 12 variations on the overall strategy outlined in this section were used, and these are specified in the text where they occur. For example, in Chapter 4 which deals with ADHD (Attention Deficit Hyperactivity Disorder), effect sizes were calculated for performance on laboratory tests of vigilance, since scores on such tests were common dependent variables in treatment studies of this disorder.

Strategy for calculating effect sizes

Where possible, effect sizes were calculated for self-reported ratings, parent ratings, teacher ratings, therapist ratings and researcher ratings in each of the first four domains described in the previous section using the methods set out in Table 1.1 from Shadish's (1993) manual. These were interpreted using Table 1.2.

Where studies contained a single treatment group and a single control group, effect sizes were based on a comparison of the two groups. Where studies contained more than two treatment groups and a control group, effect sizes were calculated for comparisons of each active treatment group with the control group. Where other comparisons were made these are clearly specified in a table of quantitative results in each chapter.

Where studies contained many dependent variables, within each of the six domains outlined in the previous section, effect sizes were calculated and tabulated for variables which specifically assessed the precise symptom, problem or aspect of the child's social system which the treatment aimed to improve. So in a study of the effect of treatment of conduct disorder, for the domain of symptomatic improvement following treatment (parent's rating), if there was a choice between calculating an effect size for the Child Behaviour Checklist total problem scale score (Achenbach, 1991) and the externalizing problem scale score, effect sizes in this instance would be based on the externalizing scale score since this scale specifically measures conduct problems. In a study of depression, for symptomatic improvement at follow-up (children's self-report) if there was a choice between the Child-hood Depression Inventory (Kovacs and Beck, 1977) total score and a total self-esteem score, the Childhood Depression Inventory Score would be chosen since it specifically assesses the problem targeted by the treatment.

Strategy for tabulating key findings

For each study, statistically and clinically significant differences between treatment and control or comparison groups after treatment and at follow-up were tabulated as bullet points. In addition, the performance of the treated group or groups with respect to control or comparison groups was given in shorthand using mathematical symbols. For example, $1 > 2 = 3$ means that following treatment group 1, overall, fared better than group 2 and 3 whose level of improvement was similar.

Table 1.2 Interpretation of effect sizes

An effect size d indicates that	the average treated case was functioning better than	a % of untreated cases
A d of 0.1 indicates that after therapy	the average treated case was functioning better than	54% of untreated cases
A d of 0.2 indicates that after therapy	the average treated case was functioning better than	58% of untreated cases
A d of 0.3 indicates that after therapy	the average treated case was functioning better than	62% of untreated cases
A d of 0.4 indicates that after therapy	the average treated case was functioning better than	66% of untreated cases
A d of 0.5 indicates that after therapy	the average treated case was functioning better than	69% of untreated cases
A d of 0.6 indicates that after therapy	the average treated case was functioning better than	73% of untreated cases
A d of 0.7 indicates that after therapy	the average treated case was functioning better than	76% of untreated cases
A d of 0.8 indicates that after therapy	the average treated case was functioning better than	79% of untreated cases
A d of 0.9 indicates that after therapy	the average treated case was functioning better than	82% of untreated cases
A d of 1.0 indicates that after therapy	the average treated case was functioning better than	84% of untreated cases
A d of 1.1 indicates that after therapy	the average treated case was functioning better than	86% of untreated cases
A d of 1.2 indicates that after therapy	the average treated case was functioning better than	88% of untreated cases
A d of 1.3 indicates that after therapy	the average treated case was functioning better than	90% of untreated cases
A d of 1.4 indicates that after therapy	the average treated case was functioning better than	92% of untreated cases
A d of 1.5 indicates that after therapy	the average treated case was functioning better than	93% of untreated cases
A d of 1.6 indicates that after therapy	the average treated case was functioning better than	95% of untreated cases
A d of 1.7 indicates that after therapy	the average treated case was functioning better than	96% of untreated cases
A d of 1.8 indicates that after therapy	the average treated case was functioning better than	96% of untreated cases
A d of 1.9 indicates that after therapy	the average treated case was functioning better than	97% of untreated cases
A d of 2.0 indicates that after therapy	the average treated case was functioning better than	98% of untreated cases

Reader's guide

Each chapter in this volume closes with a statement of the implications of the results of the studies reviewed within it for clinical practice, service development and further research. From a clinical and service development perspective, our intention has been to provide an empirical basis from which well-founded arguments may be made about the development of services for children and adolescents. While reference is made to the main components of effective treatment programmes, the level of detail concerning treatment procedures is insufficient for psychologists to use this text as a treatment manual. However, references to treatment manuals are given at the end of each chapter, where appropriate.

From a research perspective, the level of detail given throughout the text, particularly in the sections on substantive findings, is sufficient to provide the basis for designing new methodologically robust studies. In pitching the overall level of detail given about studies reviewed within each chapter, we have intentionally opted to give more, rather than less detail, so that this text may be used as a source book for researchers seeking information on the nitty-gritty of designing and conducting studies on the effectiveness of psychological interventions for problems of childhood and adolescence. The text is replete with references to specific intervention programmes, specific assessment instruments, specific approaches to data analysis and detailed consideration of important methodological issues. Hopefully advanced postgraduate students and researchers will find this level of detail helpful and will find it useful to study particular sets of substantive findings in depth.

On the other hand, clinicians and those involved in service development or funding may find it more useful to read the opening and closing sections of each chapter in detail, and skim through the intervening sections on substantive findings. Most readers will find the final chapter of interest, since it offers a summary of the central findings of the entire project.

FURTHER READING

Bergin, A. and Garfield, S. (1994). *Handbook of Psychotherapy and Behavior Change* (Fourth Edition). New York: Wiley.

Kazdin, A. (1988). *Child Psychotherapy: Developing and Identifying Effective Treatments*. New York: Pergamon.

Mash, E. and Terdal, L. (1997). *Assessment of Childhood Disorders* (Third Edition). New York: Guilford.

Nathan, P. and Gorman, J. (1998). *A Guide to Treatments that Work*. New York: Oxford University Press.

Pinsof, W. and Wynne, L. (1995). *Family Therapy Effectiveness: Current Research and Theory*. (Special Edition of *Journal of Marital and Family Therapy*, Volume 21, Number 4). Washington, DC: AAMFT.

Roth, A. and Fonagy, P. (1996). *What Works for Whom. A Critical Review of Psychotherapy Research*. New York: Guilford.

Van Hasselt, V. and Hersen, M. (1998). *Handbook of Psychological Treatment Protocols for Children and Adolescents*. Mahwah, New Jersey: Lawrence Erlbaum.

Weisz, J. and Weiss, B. (1993). *Effects of Psychotherapy with Children and Adolescents*. London: Sage.

2 Child abuse

Jennifer Edgeworth and Alan Carr

Child abuse is now recognized as a problem of significant proportions in most industrialized cultures (Briere *et al.*, 1996). Despite this, few sound empirical treatment outcome studies have been conducted. Thus, the effectiveness of treatments currently used with this clinical population remains largely in question. The aim of this chapter is to draw reliable conclusions about the effectiveness of psychological interventions offered exclusively to abused children and abusive families.

Definitions

Child abuse is a general term which encompasses physical abuse, sexual abuse emotional abuse, neglect and non-organic failure-to-thrive (Briere *et al.*, 1996; Browne, 1995). Physical abuse refers to the intentional injury or poisoning of a child. Sexual abuse refers to the use of a child for sexual gratification. Sexual abuse may vary in intrusiveness (from viewing or exposure to penetration) and frequency (from a single episode to frequent and chronic abuse). A distinction is made between intrafamilial sexual abuse, the most common form of which is father–daughter incest and extrafamilial sexual abuse where the abuser resides outside the family home. Emotional neglect and emotional abuse are two forms of child maltreatment in which particular parenting practices, usually spanning a substantial time period, lead to adverse consequences for the child such as attachment difficulties and non-organic failure to thrive. With neglect, there is a passive ignoring of the child's physical and psychological needs. These include the needs for feeding, clothing and shelter; safety; nurturance; intellectual stimulation, social interaction and conversation; appropriate limit setting and discipline; and age-appropriate opportunities for autonomy and independence. Typically, parents who neglect their children do not do so intentionally. Rather it arises through parents' lack of awareness of their children's needs. In contrast to neglect, emotional abuse involves intentional and frequent rejection, criticism, punishment for minor misdemeanours, discouragement of attachment, blocking the development of appropriate peer relationships and corruption.

Effects of abuse and neglect

Child abuse and neglect is of particular concern because of the devastating effects it can have on the psychological development of the child.

Effects of physical abuse

Physical child abuse has short- and long-term physical and psychological consequences (Cicchetti and Toth, 1995; Malinosky-Rummell and Hansen, 1993). The physical consequences of abuse include scarring, disfigurement, neurological damage, visual or auditory impairment and failure of growth. While the majority of these effects attenuate with time, most persist into adulthood. The short-term psychological consequences include low self-esteem, low self-efficacy, problems with the development of linguistic and cognitive competencies, problems with affect regulation and associated excesses of internalizing and externalizing behaviour problems and relationship difficulties. Longer term psychological consequences include teenage delinquency, aggression, domestic violence, child abuse, substance abuse, self-injury, suicide, anxiety, depression, somatization and difficulties in making and maintaining intimate relationships. The short-term cognitive and language delays which typify many abused children in some cases lead to long-term educational and vocational problems.

Effects of neglect

Children who suffer neglect and whose basic physical and psychological needs are not met develop a range of psychological difficulties including physical, psychomotor, cognitive, linguistic and social developmental delays (Briere *et al.*, 1996). Non-organic failure to thrive and reactive attachment disorder are two specific syndromes associated with neglect (Iwaniec, 1995; Zennah, 1996). With non-organic failure to thrive the child suffers growth retardation and his or her weight falls below the third centile in weight and height. A central difficulty in non-organic failure to thrive is the problematic interactions that occur between the child and parent during feeding. These interactions are often characterized by anxiety and anger and low food intake (Iwaniec, 1995). Reactive attachment disorder is characterized by a profound disruption of normal secure parent–child attachment. The child shows contradictory or ambivalent approach-avoidance social responses during partings and re-unions with parents; emotional disturbance characterized by misery and withdrawal or aggression; and fearfulness and hypervigilance in the presence of parents or other adults or alternatively indiscriminate sociability with marked inability to exhibit appropriate selective attachments (Zennah, 1996).

Effects of sexual abuse

Sexual abuse has profound short- and long-term effects on psychological functioning (Berliner and Elliott, 1996; Kendall-Tackett *et al.*, 1993; Wolfe and Birt, 1995). About two-thirds of sexually abused children develop psychological symptoms. Behaviour problems shown by children who have experienced sexual abuse typically include sexualized behaviour, excessive internalizing or externalizing behaviour problems, school-based attainment problems and relationship difficulties. In the eighteen-month period following the cessation of abuse in about two-thirds of cases behaviour problems abate. Up to a quarter of cases develop more severe problems. About a fifth of cases show clinically significant long-term problems which persist into adulthood.

One of the most useful models for conceptualizing the intrapsychic processes that underpin the behaviour problems or symptoms that arise from sexual abuse is Browne and Finklehor's (1986) traumagenic dynamics formulation. Within this formulation, traumatic sexualization, stigmatization, betrayal and powerlessness are identified as four distinct yet related dynamics that account for the wide variety of symptoms shown by children who have been sexually abused. With traumatic sexualization, the perpetrator transmits misconceptions about normal sexual behaviour and morality to the child. These may lead the child in later life to either engage in oversexualized behaviour or to avoid sex. With stigmatization, the perpetrator blames and denigrates the child and coerces the child into maintaining secrecy. Following disclosure, other members of the family or the network may blame the child for participating in the abuse. The child develops negative beliefs about the self including the ideas of self-blame and self-denigration. These beliefs lead to self-destructive behaviours such as avoidance of relationships, drug abuse, self-harm and suicide. The child may also internalize the abuser's demand for secrecy and dissociate whole areas of experience from consciousness. These may occasionally intrude into consciousness as flashbacks. The dynamics of betrayal begin when the trust the child has in the perpetrator is violated and the expectation that other adults will be protective is not met. These violations of trust and expectations of protection lead the child to believe that others are not trustworthy. This loss of a sense of trust in others may give rise to a variety of relationship problems, to delinquency and to intense feelings of sadness and anger.

The dynamics of powerlessness have their roots in the child's experience of being unable to prevent the abuse because of the perpetrator's use of physical force and psychological coercion. This may be compounded by the refusal of other members of the network to believe the child or take effective professional action. The child, as a result of this experience of being powerless, may develop beliefs about generalized personal ineffectiveness and develop an image of the self as a victim. These beliefs may lead to depression, anxiety and a variety of somatic presentations. The experience of powerlessness may also lead to the internalization of a victim–persecutor internal working model for relationships, which sows the seeds for the child later becoming a perpetrator when placed in a position where an opportunity to exert power over a vulnerable person arises.

Moderating factors

Adjustment to abuse or neglect is moderated by a wide variety of factors including characteristics of the abuse, characteristics of the child's family network and the way the placement and legal proceedings related to the abuse are managed (Briere *et al.*, 1996; Iwaniec, 1995; Malinosky-Rummell and Hansen, 1993; Spaccarelli, 1994). Frequent, severe abuse and the co-occurrence of a number of forms of abuse or neglect are associated with a poorer outcome. The presence of a variety of contextual risk factors including problems with parental adjustment, child adjustment, quality of the parent–child relationship; marital discord; family organizational difficulties; high levels of family stress; and low levels of parental and child social support are all associated with poorer long-term adjustment. Poorer adjustment occurs in cases where there is continued contact with the abuser and the abuser denies the occurrence of the abuse. Poor long-term adjustment is also associated with multiplacement experiences and protracted legal proceedings associated with the abuse.

For all forms of abuse, better adjustment occurs where the abuse is less severe and chronic and where it occurred as a single form of abuse rather than in conjunction with another form of abuse or neglect. For sexual abuse, whether the abuse was perpetrated by a family member or by someone outside the family has a bearing on the degree to which trust was violated, and the less trust was violated the better the child's adjustment following abuse. At a personal level, the specific characteristics and skills of abused children are protective factors. With physical abuse, children who are abused before the age of five and who do not sustain neurological damage tend to be more resilient, as do children with high ability levels, an easy temperament, and the capacity and opportunity to form socially supportive relationships with adults in the extended family and elsewhere despite the abuse. For sexual abuse important protective factors include assertiveness skills, physical strength, and functional coping strategies like seeking social support and using socially supportive relationships as opportunities for catharsis. At a family level, good parental adjustment, at least one good parent–child relationship and minimal exposure to parental conflict are all protective factors for all forms of abuse or neglect. For intrafamilial sexual abuse, a strong supportive relationship with the non-abusing parent is a critical factor for ensuring adjustment following abuse. Within the broader social system, good adjustment following abuse occurs where the child and family have high levels of support, low levels of stress and where children have supportive educational or day-care placements.

Epidemiology

Estimates of the incidence of physical abuse range from less than 1 per cent to more than 60 per cent, depending on the definitions used (Gelles, 1987). One-fifth of children on the British Child Protection Register for the year ending March 1993 were registered solely on the basis of neglect (Brown, 1995). Estimates of prevalence rates for child sexual abuse vary from 2–30 per cent in males and 4–30 per cent in females, depending on the population studied and definitions used (Carr, 1999).

Previous reviews

Two narrative reviews have addressed outcome of the treatment of physical abuse and neglect in childhood (Oates and Bross, 1995; Wolfe and Werkerle, 1993). While all programmes reviewed by Oates and Bross (ibid.) reported some degree of success in specified domains no conclusions were drawn on the differential successes of the various interventions addressed. Wolfe and Werkerle (ibid.) identified cognitive behavioural interventions as being particularly effective in parent-focused treatment programmes. Reeker *et al.* (1997) in a meta-analysis of group treatment outcome studies for sexually abused children reported a mean effect size of d = .79, suggesting that after group treatment the average treated case is functioning better than 78 per cent of untreated controls. All three of these reviews included methodologically heterogeneous studies, with some being well designed and some with serious limitations. In a comprehensive narrative review of treatment for all categories of child abuse, Becker *et al.* (1995) concluded that there was a paucity of well-designed empirical studies conducted in this field and a wide variety of possible intervention modalities and formats.

Treatment outcome studies covered in these reviews may be classified by the type of abuse and the focus of intervention. In terms of type of abuse, some studies are concerned with the treatment of cases of physical abuse only; others deal with neglect or non-organic failure to thrive only; some deal with mixed groups of cases in which both physical abuse and neglect have occurred; and a final group are concerned with sexual abuse only. With respect to focus of intervention, three distinct categories may be identified. Some treatment programmes are predominantly child-focused and aim to ameliorate the effects of abuse or neglect by working primarily with the child. Individual or group psychotherapy, intensive day-care, or residential treatment programmes fall into this category. These programmes provide a context within which children may receive social support and develop skills which may reduce the risk of re-abuse. Other programmes are predominantly parent-focused. They aim to enhance the quality of care available to the child and reduce the risk of re-abuse by working with parents. These programmes include parenting skills training and personal therapy for parents to help them improve their capacity to regulate aggressive or sexual impulses. The third type of programme focuses broadly on the family and the wider social context. These programmes aim to improve the quality of parent–child interactions; the quality of support parents give each other; and the quality of relationships within the wider family system so that overall, more social support is available to the family and the abused child. Ecobehavioural, family therapy and multisystemic programmes fall into this category.

In the present review an attempt was made to identify well-designed controlled studies covering each type of abuse and each focus of intervention described here.

Method

The PsychLit database was searched for the years 1977 to 1997, specifically looking for articles on child abuse where treatment was provided for either parents or children. The terms *abuse, sexual abuse, physical abuse, emotional abuse, neglect* and *non-organic failure-to-thrive*, limited to the term *child*, were combined with terms such as *treatment, intervention* and *therapy*. The bibliography of recent review articles on the topic was also consulted to complement the database literature search. Studies were selected for review if they were comparative group designs with more than five participants in each group; included a fairly homogeneous group of cases; included pre- and post-treatment measures; and offered a clearly defined intervention. From over fifty identified papers, a final set of nineteen published studies were identified as meeting the inclusion criteria.

Characteristics of the studies

The characteristics of the nineteen studies reviewed in this chapter are set out in Table 2.1. Seventeen studies included a no-treatment control group and two studies compared two active treatments. The seventeen no-treatment control studies were classified in terms of the focus of intervention (child-focused, parent-focused or family-focused) and the type of abuse (physical abuse; physical abuse and neglect; NOFTT; and child sexual abuse). Five studies examined child-focused interventions in cases of child abuse and neglect with only one examining child-focused intervention with NOFTT. Two studies examined child-focused interventions with child sexual abuse. Three studies examined parent-focused interventions with child abuse and neglect and two examined this type of intervention in cases of physical abuse. In four studies the impact of family-based intervention with cases of child abuse and neglect was examined.

Of the nineteen studies identified fifteen were conducted in the past ten years. All but one was conducted in the US. All studies included at least eight cases in the treatment group. Aggregating across the seventeen no treatment control studies, 206 children received individual or group-based

Table 2.1 Characteristics of treatment outcome studies for child abuse and neglect

Study no.	Study type	Authors	Year	Country	N per gp	Mean age & range	Gender	Type of abuse	Severity and chronicity	Family characteristics	Treatment setting	Treatment duration
1	CFI-PAN	Elmer	1986	USA	TRC = 17 C1 = 17	17 w 6–31 w	m 55% f 45%	Physical 32% At-risk 68%		Cauc 45% Black 48%	Residential	3 m
2	CFI-PAN	Culp et al.	1987	USA	TDC = 35 C = 35		m 57% f 43%	Physical 20% Neglect 63% A & N 6% At-risk 11%		Cauc 37% Black 63% LI 91%	Community OP	30 h per w over 8 m
3	CFI-PAN	Culp et al.	1991	USA	TDC = 17 C = 17	5 y 4–6 y	m 56% f 44%	Physical 41% Neglect 59%		Cauc 44% Black 56% LI 100%	Community OP	30 h per w over 9 m
4	CFI-PAN	Fantuzzo et al.	1988	USA	Peer = 12 Adult = 12 C = 12	4 y 3–5 y	m 72% f 28%	Physical 23% Neglect 46% At-risk 31%		Cauc 46% LI 100%	University Research Centre	8 × 15 min sess over 4 w
5	CFI-PAN	Fantuzzo et al.	1996	USA	RPT = 25 C = 21	5 y 4–5 y	m 41% f 59%	Physical 32% Neglect 50% A & N 18%	1.4 incidences per child	Black 100% LI 100% SPF 72%	School	15 h over 2 m
6	CFI-NOFTT	Bithoney et al.	1991	USA	MDT = 53 C = 107	2 y	m 56% f 44%	NOFTT 100%		LI 63%	Hospital OP	10 h over 6 m
7	CFI-CSA	Sullivan et al.	1992	USA	CBT = 35 C = 37	12–16 y	m 71% f 29%	CSA 100%	82% severe		Community OP	36 × 2 h sess
8	CFI-CSA	McGain and McKinzey	1995	USA	GT = 15 C = 15	11 y 9–12 y	m 0% f 100%	CSA 100%			Community OP	1 h per w over 9–12 m
9	PFI-PAN	Hornick and Clarke	1986	USA	SHH = 27 C = 28			Physical 36% At-risk 64%			Home	19 h per m variable duration
10	PFI-PAN	Whiteman et al.	1987	USA	CR = 8 RT = 12 PS = 11 CR + RT + PS = 11 C = 13	11 y	m 58% f 42%	Physical 27% High risk 73%		Cauc 22% Black 50% LI 51% SPF 69%	Community OP	6 sess
11	PFI-PAN	Wolfe et al.	1988	USA	PT = 16 C = 14	2 y 1–5 y		At-risk 100%			Community OP	29 sess over 20 w

Table 2.1 (cont'd)

Study no.	Study type	Authors	Year	Country	N per gp	Mean age & range	Gender	Type of abuse	Severity and chronicity	Family characteristics	Treatment setting	Treatment duration
12	PFI-PA	Wolfe et al.	1981	USA	PT = 8 C = 8	5 y 2–10 y		Physical 100%			Community OP	3 h per w over 8 w
13	PFI-PA	Egan	1983	USA	SM. = 11 PT = 11 SM + PT = 9 C = 10	2–12 y		Physical 100%			Community OP	1 h per w over 6 w
14	FBI-PAN	Wesch and Lutzker	1991	USA	Eco = 232 C = 232	7 y	m 53% f 47%	A & N 100%		Cauc 89% LI 80%	Community	
15	FBI-PAN	Rzepnicki et al.	1994	USA	FPS = 49 C = 48			A & N 100%	21% severe	Black 95% LI 33% SPF 54%	Home	90 d
16	FBI-PAN	Gaudin	1991	USA	SNIP = 34 C = 17*			Neglect 100%		Cauc 46% Black 54%	Community	2–23 m
17	FBI-PAN	Nicol et al.	1988	UK	FC = 19 C = 19	5 y 0–14 y		Physical 100%		Cauc 100% LI 87% SPF 69%	Home/School	3 sess per w over 6–8 w
18	CTS	Brunk et al.	1987	USA	MST = 16 PT = 17	8 y	m 55% f 45%	Abusive 55% & Neglectful 45%		Cauc 57%	Community OP	12 h over 8 w
19	CTS	Kolko	1996	USA	CBT = 21 FT = 17	9 y	m 74% f 26%	Physical 100%	13% severe	Cauc 54% LI 58% SPF 63%	Community OP	18 h over 16 w

Key CFI-PAN = Child-focused intervention for physical abuse and neglect. CFI-NOFTT = Child-focused intervention for non-organic failure-to-thrive. CFI-CSA = Child-focused intervention for child sexual abuse. PFI-PAN = Parent-focused intervention for physical abuse and neglect. PFI-PA = Parent-focused intervention for physical abuse. FBI-PAN = Family-based intervention for physical abuse and neglect. CTS = comparative treatment studies. TRC = Therapeutic residential care. TDC = Therapeutic day care. GT = Group therapy. C = Control. MMT = Multimodal therapy. Peer = Peer-initiated supportive interactions. Adult = Adult-initiated supportive interactions. RPT = Resilient peer treatment. MDT = Multidisciplinary team. SHH = Supportive home help. CR = Cognitive restructuring. RT = Relaxation training. PS = Problem solving. PT = Parent training. SM = Stress management. Eco = Ecobehavioural approach. FPS = Family preservation services. SNIP = Social network intervention programme. FC = Focused family casework. MST = Multisystemic therapy. CBT = Cognitive-behaviour therapy. FT = Family therapy. Cauc = Caucasian. LI = Low income. SPF = Single parent family. OP = Outpatient. A & N = Abuse and neglect. d = days. m = months. y = years. sess = sessions.

intervention and 267 were controls. Treatment was offered to 124 parents and 73 were controls. The systems approach was applied to 334 families with 316 families acting as controls. The age of the children across all twenty studies for which data were available ranged from six weeks to sixteen years and 54 per cent of cases were male. Definitions of category of abuse were based on reports of statutory workers or legal definitions. Treatments were offered for physical abuse in 42 per cent of cases for which data were available, for neglect in 23 per cent, sexual abuse in 12 per cent, NOFTT in 6 per cent and as a preventive measure in 15 per cent of cases.

Much of the data on family characteristics were incomplete. In general children came from single parent Caucasian families with an annual income of less than $10,000 or were recipients of state aid. Children were referred for treatment by statutory bodies, one study accepted some self-referrals. In only one case was the treatment of a residential nature. Of the community-based interventions, four were home-based, two were delivered in a school setting, the remainder were delivered on an outpatient basis.

Child-focused interventions for physical abuse and neglect consisted largely of those based on a developmental model. In the two studies of child sexual abuse individual and group therapy were evaluated. Social learning theory provided the theoretical model for the majority of the parent-focused interventions and in these studies cognitive-behavioural treatments were common. Interventions focusing on families used variations of the systems approach including eco-behavioural treatments. The duration of individual interventions ranged from six weeks to twelve months with all participants receiving at least six treatment sessions.

Methodological features

Table 2.2 summarizes the methodological features of all nineteen studies. In fifteen of the nineteen studies a randomly assigned or matched control group was used. In six studies it was possible to establish that cases in both groups had the same basic diagnosis. Only one study assessed comorbidity. Demographic similarity of treatment and control groups was established in eleven studies. In seventeen studies cases were assessed immediately before and immediately following treatment. In two studies, post-therapy testing was conducted some months after treatment. Follow-up data, collected more than three months after the end of treatment, were available for six studies in total. In ten of the nineteen studies outcome measures were based on only one perspective. Parent and researcher ratings were most common (50 per cent), followed by caseworker ratings (35 per cent). Child self-report was used in only two studies. Children's symptoms were assessed in thirteen studies while family and wider system functioning was assessed in fourteen studies. In fifteen studies treatment was manualized or offered according to an explicitly stated treatment protocol. While many authors provided train-ing to psychology graduate therapists prior to intervention, experienced

Table 2.2 Methodological features of studies of child abuse and neglect

Feature	Study number																		
	S1	S2	S3	S4	S5	S6	S7	S8	S9	S10	S11	S12	S13	S14	S15	S16	S17	S18	S19
Control group	1	1	1	1	1	1	1	1	1	1	1	1	1	1	1	1	1	0	0
Random assignment/matched control	0	1	0	1	1	0	0	1	1	0	1	1	1	1	1	1	1	1	1
Diagnostic homogeneity	0	0	0	1	0	1	0	1	1	0	0	1	1	0	0	1	1	0	1
Comparable for comorbidity	0	0	0	0	0	0	0	0	0	0	0	0	0	0	0	0	0	0	0
Demographic similarity	1	1	1	1	1	1	0	1	0	1	1	0	0	1	1	0	0	1	1
Pre-treatment assessment	1	1	1	1	1	1	1	1	1	1	1	1	1	1	1	1	1	1	1
Post-treatment assessment	1	1	1	1	1	1	0	1	1	1	1	1	1	1	1	1	1	1	1
Three months' follow-up assessment	1	0	0	0	0	0	1	0	0	0	1	0	0	0	1	0	0	0	0
Children's self-report	0	0	1	0	1	0	0	0	0	0	0	0	0	0	0	0	0	1	1
Parent's ratings	0	0	0	0	0	0	0	1	1	1	1	1	1	0	1	0	0	0	1
Teacher's ratings	0	0	0	0	1	0	0	0	0	0	0	0	0	0	0	0	0	0	0
Therapist's ratings	0	0	0	0	0	1	0	0	0	0	0	0	1	0	0	0	1	1	0
Caseworker's ratings	0	0	0	0	0	0	1	0	0	0	0	0	1	0	1	0	0	0	0
Researcher's ratings	1	1	1	1	1	1	0	1	0	1	1	1	1	1	0	1	1	0	0
Child's symptom assessed	1	1	1	1	1	1	0	1	1	1	1	0	1	1	1	1	1	1	1
System assessed	1	0	0	1	1	0	0	0	0	1	0	1	0	1	1	1	0	1	1
Deterioration assessed	0	0	0	0	0	1	0	0	0	0	0	0	1	0	0	0	0	0	1
Drop-out assessed	0	0	0	0	0	0	0	0	1	0	0	1	0	0	0	1	1	1	1
Clinical significance of change assessed	0	0	0	0	0	0	1	0	0	1	0	0	0	0	0	0	0	0	1
Experienced therapists used	0	0	1	0	1	1	0	0	0	0	0	0	0	0	0	0	0	1	1
Treatments were equally valued	0	1	0	1	0	0	1	0	0	0	0	1	0	1	1	0	0	1	1
Treatments were manualized	0	1	1	0	1	1	1	0	1	1	1	0	0	1	1	1	1	1	1
Therapy supervision was provided	0	0	0	1	1	0	1	0	1	0	0	0	0	1	0	0	0	0	1
Treatment integrity checked	0	0	0	1	1	1	0	0	0	1	1	0	1	1	1	0	0	1	1
Data on concurrent treatment given	0	0	0	0	0	0	0	0	0	1	0	0	0	0	0	0	0	0	1
Data on subsequent treatment given	0	0	0	0	0	0	0	0	0	0	0	0	0	0	0	0	0	0	0
Total	8	8	8	12	12	9	8	9	9	8	16	15	11	10	9	13	9	14	17

Key: S = study. 1 = design feature was present. 0 = design feature was absent.

therapists were used in six studies. Supervision was provided in eight studies and treatment integrity was checked in five. The statistical significance of treatment gains was reported in all studies, but the clinical significance of such gains was alluded to in just four of these. Drop-out was assessed in nine studies, deterioration in two. Two studies addressed the issue of concurrent treatment. None mentioned subsequent treatment. It may be concluded that overall this was a fairly methodologically robust group of studies.

Substantive findings

Treatment effect sizes for the nineteen studies are given in Table 2.3, and Table 2.4 summarizes in narrative form the key findings of each of the studies.

Studies of child-focused interventions

In eight studies, the effectiveness of child-focused interventions was assessed. In the first five of these reviewed below, the central concern was physical abuse and neglect (Culp *et al.*, 1987, 1991; Elmer, 1986; Fantuzzo *et al.*, 1988, 1996). Non-organic failure to thrive was the principal diagnosis in one study (Bithoney *et al.*, 1991) and two studies were concerned with child sexual abuse (McGain and McKinzey, 1995; Sullivan *et al.*, 1992).

Child-focused intervention for physical abuse and neglect

Residential treatment, therapeutic day care and resilient peer therapy were the child-focused treatments evaluated in the five studies reported in this section. Elmer (1986) evaluated the impact of a child-focused therapeutic residential programme on the adjustment of children who had been physically abused or were at risk of abuse. Abused and high-risk children admitted to a residential centre were matched with a cohort of seventeen children who were eligible to attend the centre on the basis of maltreatment but who received routine community-based services. This group therefore constituted a treatment-as-usual control group. The treatment group received intensive individualized treatment programmes with the goal of promoting optimal development of each infant. Such programmes included infant stimulation and the promotion of high quality parent–child interaction. Parents visited infants several days a week and were coached in infant-care skills. Parents were also able to avail themselves of parent training, counselling and advocacy services. The overriding aim of the programme was to promote the reunification of families so that at-risk or abused children could safely return to their families of origin. Assessments were conducted on admission and discharge from the centre and approximately five months later. Anthropometric measures and the Bayley Scales of Infant Development (Bayley, 1969) were used to assess the child's symptoms while videotapes of mother–child interaction were used to assess the child's social system. In terms of

Table 2.3 Summary of results of treatment effects and outcome rates from studies of child abuse and neglect

Variable	Study type, number and treatment type																								
	CFI-PAN						CFI-NOFTT	CFI-CSA		PFI-PAN						PFI-PA				FBI-PAN				CTS	
	S1 TRC	S2 TDC	S3 TDC	S4 Peer	S4 Adult	S5 RPT	S6 MDT	S7 CBT	S8 GT	S9 SHH	S10 CR	S10 RT	S10 PS	S10 CR+PS+RT	S11 PT	S12 PT	S13 SM	S13 PT	S13 SM+PT	S14 ECO	S15 FPS	S16 SNIP	S17 FC	S18 MST	S19 CBT
	>C	>C	>C	>C	>C	>C	>C	>C	>C	>C	>C	>C	>C	>C	>C	>C	>C	>C	>C	>C	>C	>C	>C	>PT	>FT
Symptomatic improvement after treatment																									
Children's self-report	–	–	–	–	–	–	–	–	–	–	–	–	–	–	–	–	–	–	–	–	–	–	–	–	0.9
Parent's ratings	–	–	0.7	–	–	–	–	–	–	–	–	–	–	–	0.1	0.7	–	–	–	–	0.5	0.9	–	–	0.4
Teacher's ratings	–	–	–	1.5	−0.3	–	–	–	2.1	–	–	–	–	–	–	–	–	–	–	–	–	–	–	–	–
Caseworker's ratings	–	–	–	–	–	–	1.4	–	–	–	–	–	–	–	–	–	–	–	–	0.4	–	0.5	–	0.7	–
Researcher's ratings	–	0.9	–	–	–	–	–	–	–	–	–	–	–	–	–	–	–	–	–	–	–	–	–	–	–
Symptomatic improvement at follow-up																									
Children's self-report	–	–	–	–	–	–	–	–	–	–	–	–	–	–	–	–	–	–	–	–	–	–	–	–	–
Parent's ratings	–	–	–	–	–	–	–	–	–	–	–	–	–	–	1.6	–	–	–	–	–	0.3	–	–	–	–
Teacher's ratings	–	–	–	–	–	1.8	–	–	–	–	–	–	–	–	–	–	–	–	–	–	–	–	–	–	–
Caseworker's ratings	–	–	–	–	–	–	–	1.8	–	–	–	–	–	–	–	–	–	–	–	–	–	–	–	–	–
Researcher's ratings	–	–	–	–	–	–	–	–	–	–	–	–	–	–	–	–	–	–	–	0.0	–	–	–	–	–

Systemic improvement after treatment

Children's self-report	–	–	–	–	–	–	–	–	–	–	–	–	–	–	–	–	–	–	–	1.0	–	–	–	0.8
Parent's ratings	–	–	–	–	–	0.7	–	–	–	–	–	–	–	–	–	–	1.0	1.1	–	–	-0.7	0.0
Teacher's ratings	–	–	–	–	–	–	–	–	–	–	–	–	–	–	–	–	–	–	–	–	–	–
Caseworker's ratings	–	1.4	-0.2	–	–	–	–	–	–	–	–	–	–	–	–	–	1.1	–	–	0.7	–
Researcher's ratings	0.7	1.3	–	0.0	0.0	1.2	0.0	0.0	0.9	0.9	0.0	4.1	0.3	0.0	0.9	0.9	0.7	–

Systemic improvement at follow-up

Children's self-report	–	–	–	–	–	–	–	–	–	–	–	–	–	–	–	–	–	–
Parent's ratings	–	–	–	–	–	–	–	–	–	–	1.2	–	0.3	–	–	–	–
Teacher's ratings	–	–	–	–	–	–	–	–	–	–	–	–	–	–	–
Caseworker's ratings	–	–	–	–	–	–	–	–	–	–	–	–	–	–
Researcher's ratings	0.0	–	–	–	–	–	0.0	–	–	–

Positive clinical outcomes

% improved after treatment	–	–	87%	–	–	–	–	–	–	–	73%
% improved at follow-up	–	–	–	100%	–	–	59% > 24%	–	41%

Negative clinical outcomes

% Deterioration	–	–	0%	–	–	0%	–	–	0%	–	–
% Drop-out	–	0%	26% > 50%	–	2%	0%	–	–	33%	29%	45%	23% > 23%	14% > 6%	0% > 28%
% Engaged in further treatment	–	–	–	–	–	–	–	–	–	–	–

Key CFI-PAN = Child-focused intervention for physical abuse and neglect. CFI-NOFTT = Child-focused intervention for non-organic failure-to-thrive. CFI-CSA = Child-focused intervention for child sexual abuse. PFI-PAN = Parent-focused intervention for physical abuse and neglect. PFI-PA = Parent-focused intervention for physical abuse. FBI-PAN = Family-based intervention for physical abuse and neglect. CTS = comparative treatment studies. TRC = Therapeutic residential care. TDC = Therapeutic day care. C = Control. MMT = Multimodal therapy. Peer = Peer-initiated supportive interactions. Adult = Adult-initiated supportive interactions. RPT = Resilient peer treatment. MDT = Multidisciplinary team. SHH = Supportive home help. CR = Cognitive restructuring. RT = Relaxation training. PS = Problem solving. PT = Parent training. SM = Stress management. Eco = Ecobehavioural approach. FPS = Family preservation services. SNIP = Social network intervention programme. FC = Focused family casework. MST = Multisystemic therapy. CBT = Cognitive-behaviour -herapy. FT = Family therapy.

Table 2.4 Key findings from child abuse and neglect treatment outcome studies

Study no.	Type	Authors	Year	Country	N per gp	Treatment duration	Group differences	Key findings
1	CFI-PAN	Elmer	1986	USA	1. TRC = 17 2. C = 17	3 m	1 > 2	• Compared with untreated controls, cases treated with 3 months' residential therapy showed significant gains in physical growth, psychomotor development and parent–child interaction. • At 6 months' follow-up there were no differences between treatment and control groups.
2	CFI-PAN	Culp et al.	1987	USA	1. TDC = 35 2. C = 35	30 h per w over 8 m	1 > 2	• Compared with untreated controls, cases treated with 8 months of intensive day-care therapy showed significant gains in psychomotor, cognitive, linguistic and social development.
3	CFI-PAN	Culp et al.	1991	USA	1. TDC = 17 2. C = 17	30 h per w over 9 m	1 > 2	• Compared with untreated controls, cases treated with 9 months of intensive day-care therapy showed significant gains in self-esteem.
4	CFI-PAN	Fantuzzo et al.	1988	USA	1. Peer = 12 2. Adult = 12 3. C = 12	8 × 15 min sess over 4 w	1 > 2 = 3	• Children enrolled in a therapeutic day-care programme where planned peer-initiated interaction occurred made greater gains in prosocial behaviour and reduction in behaviour problems than similar cases who received planned adult-initiated interaction or routine interactions with peers and adults.
5	CFI-PAN	Fantuzzo et al.	1996	USA	1. RPT = 25 2. C = 21	15 h over 2 m	1 > 2	• Compared with untreated controls, cases treated with 15 hours of resilient peer therapy in a classroom situation showed significant gains in social behaviour in the classroom and these gains were maintained at 2 months' follow-up.
6	CFI-NOFTT	Bithoney et al.	1991	USA	1. MDT = 53 2. C = 107	10 h over 6 m	1 > 2	• Compared with cases who received routine primary care, children with non-organic failure-to-thrive who received multidisciplinary care showed greater growth.
7	CFI-CSA	Sullivan et al.	1992	USA	1. CBT = 35 2. C = 37	36 × 2 h sess over 9 m	1 > 2	• Compared with matched untreated controls, deaf adolescents who had been sexually abused showed fewer behaviour problems following 72 hours of individual therapy over 9 months.

No.	Code	Authors	Year	Country	Groups (N)	Duration	Outcome	Findings
8	CFI-CSA	McGain and McKinzey	1995	USA	1. GT = 15 2. C = 15	1 h per w over 9–12 m	1 > 2	Compared with matched untreated controls, sexually abused adolescent girls showed fewer behaviour problems following 36 hours of group therapy over 9–12 months.
9	PFI-PAN	Hornick and Clarke	1986	USA	1. SHH = 27 2. C = 28	1½ h per m over 6 m	1 > 2	Following 114 hours of supportive home help over 9 months, parents who had abused or neglected their children showed greater ability to empathize with their children, but no differences on measures of hostility or abuse compared with controls who received routine social work services. • These gains were maintained at 6 months' follow-up. • Only 26% of the treated group dropped out compared with 50% of cases receiving routine services.
10	PFI-PAN	Whiteman et al.	1987	USA	1. CR = 8 2. RT = 12 3. PS = 11 4. CR + RT + PS = 11 5. C = 13	6 sess	4 > 1 = 2 = 3 = 5	Parents who had abused or neglected their children and were treated with a programme of cognitive restructuring, relaxation training and problem-solving therapy showed greater improvement in anger management compared with cases who received only one treatment component or controls who received routine services.
11	PFI-PAN	Wolfe et al.	1988	USA	1. PT = 16 2. C = 14	29 sess over 20 w	1 > 2	Parents who had abused or neglected their children and participated in a 29-session behavioural parent-training programme following treatment and at 3 months' follow-up showed greater improvement in parenting risk and reported fewer child behaviour problems than parents who received routine services.
12	PFI-PA	Wolfe et al.	1981	USA	1. PT = 8 2. C = 8	3 h per w over 8 w	1 > 2	Parents who had physically abused their children and participated in a 24-session behavioural parent-training programme following treatment showed greater improvement in parenting skills and these gains were maintained 2.5 months after treatment. • A year after treatment there were no further incidences of abuse in any of the treated families.

Table 2.4 (cont'd)

Study No	Type	Authors	Year	Country	N per gp	Treatment duration	Group differences	Key Findings
13	PFI-PA	Egan	1983	USA	1. SM. = 11 2. PT = 11 3. SM + PT. = 9 4. C = 10	1 h per w over 6 w	1 > 2 > 3 > 4	• Parents of abused children who received stress management training showed reduced family conflict and improved relationships with their children after treatment. • Parents who received behavioural parent training more frequently used behavioural parenting procedures after treatment. • The combined treatment package was not as effective as each component alone.
14	FBI-PAN	Wesch and Lutzker	1991	USA	1. Eco = 232 2. C = 232		1 > 2	• During a 5-year treatment period abuse occurred in only 13% of cases treated with ecobehavioural methods compared with 25% of cases who received routine services. • After treatment there were no intergroup differences in re-abuse rates.
15	FBI-PAN	Rzepnicki et al.	1994	USA	1. FPS = 49 2. C = 48	90 d	1 > 2	• After 7 months of treatment, compared to families receiving routine services, those who participated in an intensive family preservation programme reported improvements in housing, economic conditions, physical child care and children's conduct. • At 16 months' follow-up families, compared to families receiving routine services, those who participated in an intensive family preservation programme reported improvements in physical child care, children's academic adjustment, and parental coping.
16	FBI-PAN	Gaudin	1991	USA	1. SNIP = 34 2. C = 17	2–23 m	1 > 2	• After 6 months of social network intervention, treated cases showed improvements in the quality of child care and home environment and the amount of social support available to parents compared with cases receiving routine services.

					Groups/n	Duration		Findings
17	FBI-PAN	Nicol et al.	1988	UK	1. FC = 19 2. C = 19	3 sess per w over 6–8 w	1 > 2	• After 12 months of intervention, treated cases maintained gains in the quality of child-care practices and the improvements in parental social support and also showed improvements in parental empathy and expectations of children and discipline practices. • After treatment, compared with cases where children received play therapy, cases receiving focused family casework showed a greater reduction in coercive parent–child interaction and a greater improvement in positive parent–child interaction.
18	CTS	Brunk et al.	1987	USA	1. MST = 16 2. PT = 17	12 h over 8 w	1 > 2	• Both multisystemic therapy and parent training led to reductions in parental adjustment and overall family stress. • Multisystemic therapy led to greater improvements in family problems and parent–child interactions associated with abuse and neglect compared with parent training. • Parent training led to greater improvements in parents' extrafamilial social problems compared with multisystemic therapy.
19	CTS	Kolko	1996	USA	1. CBT = 21 2. FT = 17	18 h over 16 w	1 > 2	• Over the course of treatment, in cases treated with CBT children and parents reported less use of force in parent–child interactions, less parental anger and fewer family problems than parents treated with family therapy. • Children with psychological problems and those with more chronic problems were more likely to be subjected to physical abuse or use of force by their parents.

Key CFI-PAN = Child-focused intervention for physical abuse and neglect. CFI-NOFTT = Child-focused intervention for non-organic failure-to-thrive. CFI-CSA = Child-focused intervention for child sexual abuse. PFI-PAN = Parent-focused intervention for physical abuse and neglect. PFI-PA = Parent-focused intervention for physical abuse. FBI-PAN = Family-based interventions for physical abuse and neglect. CTS = comparative treatment studies. TRC = Therapeutic residential care. TDC = Therapeutic day care. GT = Group therapy. C = Control. MMT = Multimodal therapy. Peer = Peer-initiated supportive interactions. Adult = Adult-initiated supportive interactions. RPT = Resilient peer treatment. MDT = Multidisciplinary team. SHH = Supportive home help. CR = Cognitive restructuring. RT = Relaxation training. PS = Problem solving. PT = Parent training. SM = Stress management. Eco = Ecobehavioural approach. FPS = Family preservation services. SNIP = Social network intervention programme. FC = Focused family casework. MST = Multisystemic therapy. CBT = Cognitive-behaviour therapy. FT = Family therapy. d = days. m = months. y = years. sess = sessions.

systemic change, an effect size of 0.7 was obtained which showed that residential treatment resulted in the average treated case functioning better than 76 per cent of the control group. At follow-up however there were no differences between the groups.

In a series of two studies Culp *et al.* (1987, 1991) examined the impact of therapeutic day-treatment programmes on abused and neglected children. The day-treatment programmes evaluated in both studies were similar in many important respects. Both were cognitive-developmental group milieu programmes with a low child–teacher ratio (between 2 and 4:1). Within each programme, strong child–teacher relationships were fostered. Individual physical therapy, play therapy and speech and language therapy were available for children as required. In addition, parental counselling and education services were provided. The control group in each study comprised a matched cohort of maltreated children who met the eligibility criteria for admission to the day-treatment programmes but for practical reasons were not attending. To assess progress, in the first study (Culp *et al.*, 1987) the Early Intervention Developmental Profile (Bricker, 1982; Schafer and Moesch, 1981) which yielded scores for five developmental areas (fine motor, gross motor, cognitive, social/emotional and language development) was used. In the second study (Culp *et al.*, 1991) the Perceived Competence and Social Acceptance Scale (Harter and Pike, 1984), a self-report instrument, was used to assess symptomatic change. As neither treatment programme had a specific target the average of all subscales was used to calculate effect size in both cases. Effect sizes calculated for the five developmental areas of the Early Intervention Developmental Profile ranged from 0.7 (language development) to 1.0 (cognitive, social/emotional development) with a mean of 0.9. This indicates that following treatment the average treated case was functioning better than 82 per cent of the control group. The Perceived Competence and Social Acceptance Scale is a composite of four subscales whose effect sizes ranged from 0.2 for physical competence to 1.0 for peer acceptance, The mean effect size for the four subscales was 0.7, indicating that following treatment the average treated case was functioning better than 76 per cent of untreated cases.

In a series of two studies Fantuzzo and colleagues (1988, 1996) examined the impact of resilient peer treatment on the social adjustment of withdrawn children who were physically abused, neglected or at risk. The central premise of such programmes is that providing abused children with an opportunity to interact with well-adjusted socially skilled peers who initiate and maintain positive social interactions will have beneficial effects. In the first study children were randomly assigned to peer-initiated or adult-initiated conditions or a control group. In the peer initiation condition children rated high on positive social behaviours by their teachers modelled these behaviours for two treatment children during fifteen-minute play sessions. For the adult initiation group a familiar adult modelled the prosocial behaviours. In the control condition the additional peer or adult responded to the abused or neglected child but did not initiate prosocial behaviours. While this first study (Fantuzzo *et al.*, 1988) was a laboratory-based investigation of a brief intervention (eight fifteen-minute sessions over four weeks) the second study (Fantuzzo *et al.*, 1996) was community based and involved fifteen hours of treatment over two months. Treatment was implemented by preschool teaching staff and parents in the children's own classrooms. There were four treatment conditions: maltreated and non-maltreated children who were randomly assigned to a resilient peer-treatment group or an attention control group. These two treatment conditions were broadly similar to the peer initiation and control conditions of the earlier study. In both studies observational coding systems were used to both select cases for treatment and to assess progress. In addition, in the first study teachers rated psychological adjustment on the Preschool Behaviour Questionnaire (Behar and Stringfield, 1974) and pre-academic progress using the Brigance Diagnostic Inventory of Early Development (Brigance, 1978). In the second study the preschool teacher version of the Social Skills Rating System (Gresham and Elliot, 1990) which contains social skills and problem behaviour subscales was used to assess children at two-month follow-up. In the first study (Fantuzzo *et al.*, 1988) effect sizes of 1.4 and 1.5 were obtained which indicated that the average child in the peer initiation group was functioning better than 93 per cent and 92 per cent of controls in terms of teacher-rated symptomatic and researcher-rated systemic change respectively. For those children in the adult initiation group the corresponding effect sizes were −0.3 and −0.2, indicating that the control group were actually functioning better than the adult initiation group. In the second study (Fantuzzo *et al.*, 1996) results from the observational rating system yielded an effect size of 1.3 which indicated that, on average, the experimental group were interacting better than 90 per cent of the controls following treatment. At follow-up an effect size of 1.8 showed that teachers rated the average treated child as having better interpersonal skills than 96 per cent of control children. The improvement was clinically significant in that, following treatment, significantly more control children fell within the clinical range of the Problem Behaviour subscales than treated children.

From the five studies reviewed in this section it may be concluded that residential treatment, therapeutic day care and resilient peer therapy were effective child-focused treatments in cases of child abuse and neglect insofar as they improved functioning in a number of domains. Residential treatment in which the child was placed in a special unit and visited daily by parents provided a protective, supportive and intellectually stimulating context within which positive parent–child interaction was fostered. Therapeutic day care where intellectual stimulation was provided within the context of supportive child–teacher relationships and good staffing levels promoted cognitive and social-emotional development. Resilient peer therapy, where at-risk children were given structured opportunities to be befriended by socially skilled peers promoted social development.

Child-focused intervention for non-organic failure-to-thrive

Only one well-controlled intervention study for non-organic failure-to-thrive was identified and this examined the impact of multidisciplinary team treatment in a Growth Nutrition Clinic on the development of children with serious growth problems. Bithoney *et al.* (1991) compared children with non-organic failure-to-thrive referred to a multidisciplinary team in a Growth Nutrition Clinic with a retrospective cohort of children who received treatment-as-usual in a primary care clinic. Children entering the study met the criteria of the National Centre for Health Statistics growth chart (Hamill, 1979) for failure-to-thrive and had no definable organic illness to cause the disturbance. The multidisciplinary team at the growth nutrition clinic consisted of a paediatrician, nutritionist, developmental specialist, nurse practitioner, child psychiatrist and social worker. Treatment was intensive and mainly child-focused with an emphasis on helping children develop appropriate feeding patterns. Other interventions were offered to parents and members of the wider system as necessary. Control group patients were routinely assessed by medical staff only, with referrals for social and nutritional care when appropriate. Progress was evaluated using a growth quotient analysis which compares each child's weight gain during a given time period to the expected weight gain for a child of the same age. An effect size of 1.4 showed that after treatment the average treated child had gained more weight than 92 per cent of children in the control group.

This study is important because it was the only empirical study of a well-defined treatment for non-organic failure-to-thrive found in a literature search of the last twenty years. One limitation of the study was that cases were not randomly assigned to treatment and control groups. This shortcoming may have been offset by the fact that children attending the growth clinic had more chronic malnutrition than those in the control group and had proved refractory to treatment in a primary care setting. This makes the positive outcomes of the treatment group particularly impressive.

Child-focused intervention with child sexual abuse

Two studies examined the impact of child-focused psychotherapy on youngsters who had experienced sexual abuse (McGain and McKinzey, 1995; Sullivan *et al.*, 1992).

Sullivan *et al.* (ibid.) used a quasi-experimental design to evaluate treatment outcome of broad-based individual psychotherapy on a group of deaf male and female adolescents. An untreated control group emerged when, for about half the adolescents, parental consent for participation in the treatment study was withheld. McGain and McKinzey (ibid.) evaluated the efficacy of group treatment of sexually abused girls using a waiting list control design. Key features of the treatment programme evaluated in each study were the alleviation of guilt and depression, facilitating the expression of anger, promoting the development of self-esteem, dealing with sexual issues, dealing with victimization issues, assertiveness skills training, and fostering relationship-building skills (Sullivan and Scanlan, 1987). Adjunctive meetings were held with parents of children participating in these studies. A particularly noteworthy feature of these studies is the fact that experienced clinicians conducted the therapy programmes. In Sullivan *et al.*'s (1992) study the Child Behaviour Checklist (Achenbach and Edelbrock, 1983) completed by each child's house parent assessed symptomatology pre-treatment and at follow-up. The Revised Behaviour Problem Checklist (Quay and Peterson, 1987) and Eyberg Child Behaviour Inventory (Eyberg, 1980) were completed by parents and used to assess symptomatic change in McGain and McKinzey's (1995) study. Because sexual abuse can result in internalizing and externalizing problems (Kendall-Tackett *et al.*, 1993) and neither treatment study had a specific symptomatic focus, total scores on these instruments were used to calculate effect sizes. In Sullivan *et al.*'s (1992) study an effect size of 1.8 was obtained which showed that the average treated case was functioning better than over 98 per cent of untreated cases at one-year follow-up. In McGain and McKinzey's (1995) study an effect size of 2.1 was obtained which indicated that following group psychotherapy the average female was functioning better than over 96 per cent of untreated cases. The clinical significance of the improvement was shown by the fact that for 87 per cent of children, their scores on the Eyberg Child Behaviour Inventory dropped from the clinical to the normal range over the course of treatment. From these studies it may be concluded that individual and group therapy formats focusing on abuse-related issues ameliorates behavioural problems for abused adolescents.

Parent-focused interventions

Of the five studies which evaluated the effectiveness of parent-focused interventions, three involved diagnostically heterogeneous groups of cases where physical abuse and/or neglect had occurred or were at risk of occurring (Hornick and Clarke, 1986; Whiteman *et al.*, 1987; Wolfe *et al.*, 1981) and two involved diagnostically homogeneous groups of cases of physical abuse (Egan, 1983; Wolfe *et al.*, 1981).

Parent-focused interventions for physical abuse and neglect

The studies reviewed in this section examined the impact of three parent-focused interventions (supportive home help, parent-focused cognitive behaviour therapy and behavioural parent training) on families where child abuse and/or neglect had occurred or where children were at-risk of their occurrence (Hornick and Clarke, 1986; Whiteman *et al.*, 1987; Wolfe *et al.*, 1981). Hornick and Clarke (ibid.) evaluated the effectiveness of supportive home help by randomly assigning cases to treatment and control groups. In the treatment group, full-time paid supportive home helpers provided support, modelled parenting skills, and coached parents in home-making skills. An effect size of 0.7 was obtained for a measure of parental empathy with children (Clarke and Hornick, 1984). Thus the average case treated with lay therapy fared better than 76 per cent of the control group following treatment. Statutory social workers also spent significantly less time working with the experimental group and there was 24 per cent less attrition in this group.

Whiteman *et al.* (ibid.) examined the impact of training parents of physically abused children or children at-risk of physical abuse in cognitive-behavioural anger reduction strategies (D'Zurilla and Goldfried, 1971; Novaco, 1975). Participants were randomly assigned to four cognitive-behavioural treatment groups and a control group that received routine community-based services. Participants in the cognitive-behavioural treatment groups were trained in either cognitive restructuring, relaxation skills, problem-solving skills or a composite treatment package comprising all three elements. A variety of stimulus materials including hypothetical situations and role play in addition to parental self-description of proneness to anger were used to assess systemic change. From these data, a child-rearing attitudes scale and a parental anger scale were constructed. Effect sizes were calculated for the latter and for the combined treatment package an effect size of 1.2 was obtained. The average case in the combined cognitive-behavioural treatment programme was functioning better than 88 per cent of control group cases. Individually the components of the combined treatment programme did not have a significant effect on parents' capacity to control anger towards their children.

Wolfe *et al.* (1988) evaluated the impact of behavioural parent training on families in which there was a high risk of physical abuse or neglect. Thirty mother–child dyads were randomly assigned to either a behavioural parent training programme (Forehand and McMahon, 1981; Reid, 1985) or a control group. The treatment programme involved training parents to increase positive interaction with their children; to use reward systems and time-out procedures to increase children's compliance with parental directives; and to use specific exercises to promote language and cognitive development. Instruction modelling, rehearsal and video-feedback were used to promote skill development. Parents in the control group attended a routine community-based information programme for parents. Mothers with higher intervention priorities were excluded from the study. Assessments were conducted before and after treatment and at three-month follow-up. Recidivism rates were calculated at one year. The Child Abuse Potential Inventory (Milner, 1986) and the Beck Depression Inventory (Beck *et al.*, 1961) were used to diagnose parents at-risk for inclusion in the study. Children's behavioural problems were assessed with the Pyramid Scales (Cone, 1984) and the Behaviour Rating Scale (Cowen *et al.*, 1970) and effect sizes were calculated for the latter measure as an index of symptomatic change. The dyadic parent–child interaction coding system (Robinson and Eyberg, 1981) and the Home Observation and Measurement of the Environment Scale (Caldwell and Bradley, 1985) provided researcher ratings of systemic functioning. Effect sizes were calculated for the former as an index of researcher ratings of systemic improvement. In addition, the Child Abuse Potential Inventory was re-administered at follow-up and was used to calculate effect size for parents' perception of systemic change. The average child of a treated parent showed fewer behaviour problems following treatment than 54 per cent of children of untreated cases. This figure increased to 95 per cent at follow-up. In terms of researcher-rated systemic functioning there was no difference between the groups immediately following treatment or at follow-up. However, the average treated parent reported less abusive potential than 84 per cent of the control parents at follow-up. One year later 37 per cent of treatment families had their cases closed compared to 14 per cent of the control group.

These three studies of parent-focused intervention showed that supportive home help provided by lay therapists was particularly effective in improving parental empathy with children, reducing the requirement for professional input, and preventing drop-out for families where physical abuse or neglect had occurred or where there was a risk of such abuse occurring. A six-session comprehensive multicomponent cognitive-behavioural treatment programme was effective in improving parental anger management and a twenty-nine-session comprehensive behavioural parent training programme was effective in reducing children's behaviour problems and the risk that parents might physically abuse their children.

Parent-focused interventions for physical abuse

Two studies examined the effects of parent-focused interventions (behavioural parent training and stress management training) in families where physical child abuse had occurred (Egan, 1983; Wolfe *et al.*, 1981). Wolfe *et al.* (ibid.) allocated sixteen families with a substantiated complaint of physical abuse to behavioural parent training (Forehand and McMahon, 1981; Reid, 1985) or a control group. Parent training consisted of instruction on child development, child management skills training, and self-control training. The control group received standard statutory services. Assessments were conducted before and after assessment with a ten-week follow-up assessment and a case review at one year. The Eyberg Child Behaviour Inventory (Eyberg, 1980) was completed by parents to assess symptomatic change. The Parent–Child Interaction Form (Sweitzer and Boyd, 1979), a criterion-based observation system, was used to assess researcher-rated systemic change. A further systemic measure, caseworker ratings of family treatment needs, was collected before and after treatment. Effect sizes were calculated for all three measures. Records for each family were reviewed after one year for recidivism rates. The average child of treated parents performed better on the Eyberg Child Behaviour Inventory than 76 per cent of children in the control group as indicated by an effect size of 0.7. The effect size of 4.1 based on researcher ratings of the child management skills subscale of the Parent–Child Interaction Form showed that the average treated parent performed better than 98 per cent of the untreated group. The effect size of 0.3 based on caseworker ratings of systemic improvement indicated that the average treated case had less severe treatment needs than 62 per cent of untreated cases. Follow-up assessment indicated that the decrement over time was not statistically significant. At one-year follow-up, supervision had been terminated for all eight treatment families compared to six control families.

Egan *et al.* (1983) examined the impact of behavioural parent training and cognitive behavioural stress management on parents in families where physical child abuse had occurred. Cases were randomly assigned to behavioural parent training (Patterson, 1973); stress management training (Meichenbaum, 1985); a combined parent training and stress management programme; and a control group which received treatment-as-usual, i.e. a weekly meeting with a social worker. The behavioural parent training included coaching in the use of reward systems and time-out routines to improve children's compliance with parental directives and increase positive parent–child interaction. Stress management training aimed to improve parental emotional control and included relaxation skills training and cognitive restructuring. Treatment, in all three conditions, was offered on a group basis over six weekly sessions. Greatest changes occurred in the stress management group. The effect sizes for parent-rated systemic change on the conflict dimension of the Family Environment Scale (Moos and Moos, 1981) and researchers rated systemic change from observation of positive parent–child interaction were 0.9, indicating that the average case in this treatment programme fared better than 82 per cent of controls. For the parent training group, the effect sizes for researcher-rated systemic change from observation of parents reinforcing children complying with requests was 0.9, indicating that in this domain the average case in this treatment programme fared better than 82 per cent of controls. Cases in the combined therapy group did not make significant treatment gains.

These two studies show that with cases of confirmed physical child abuse, behavioural parent training and cognitive behavioural stress management training which aims to foster parental mood regulation improved family functioning. These results are consistent with those reported in the previous section for groups of cases which included families at-risk of abuse; families in which neglect had occurred; and families in which physical abuse had occurred.

Family-based treatment for physical abuse and neglect

Four studies examined the effects of family-focused interventions in cases of physical abuse and neglect (Gaudin, 1991; Nicol *et al.*, 1988; Rzepnicki *et al.*, 1994; Wesch and Lutzker, 1991). Wesch and Lutzker (1991) in a retrospective archival study evaluated an eco-behavioural approach to abuse and neglect. Families in Project 12-Ways were matched with a group of families receiving a variety of standard statutory services. Services to Project 12-Ways families included behavioural parent training, stress reduction, problem-solving and assertiveness training and single parent services (Lutzker, 1984). Researcher reports of rates of abuse, neglect or out-of-home placement before, during and after treatment were used to assess systemic change. During the five-year treatment phase further abuse occurred in only 13 per cent of cases treated with ecobehavioural methods compared with 25 per cent of cases that received routine services (and this is recorded in Table 2.4 as an effect size of 0.4). There was no difference between the two groups at follow-up in terms of the rates of abuse, neglect or out-of-home placement.

Rzepnicki *et al.* (1994) randomly assigned abuse and neglect cases to home-based family preservation services or standard services for abusive and neglectful families. Services for the treatment group were similar to those offered in the Project 12-Ways study with additional financial support and material assistance being offered to cases in this group. A structured parental interview about changes in the number and magnitude of problems was the main outcome measure. For symptomatic change as assessed by parental reports of improvements in children's conduct an effect size of 0.5 was obtained after treatment indicating that the average treated case fared better than 69 per cent of controls on this dimension. For systemic change as assessed by parental reports of improved child care following treatment the effect size was 1.0, showing that in this area the average treated case fared better than 84 per cent of controls. At sixteen-month follow-up effect sizes based on the proportion of problems in both of these domains were 0.3. Thus the average treated case fared better than 62 per cent of controls at follow-up.

Gaudin (1991) randomly assigned cases of child neglect to the Social Network Intervention Treatment Programme or a control group which received treatment-as-usual. Cases in the Social Network Intervention Programme received social skills training; self-help support group membership; and support from volunteers and neighbourhood helpers. Effect sizes based on caseworker ratings of neglect on the Child Neglect Severity Scale (Edgington *et al.*, 1980) were 0.5 after six months of treatment and 1.1 at one-year follow-up. Effect sizes based on the empathy scale of the Adult–Adolescent Parenting Inventory (Bavolek and Comstock, 1983) which assesses parents' ability to empathize with their children were 0.9 after six months of treatment and 1.1 at twelve months' follow-up. Thus at twelve months' follow-up both caseworker and parent ratings concurred that the average treated family was functioning better than 86 per cent of untreated cases. In terms of clinical significance, 59 per cent of treated families had their cases closed at termination of the project compared with 24 per cent of control families. Caseworkers reported no deterioration in any of the treated families.

Nicol *et al.* (1988), in the only UK study reviewed in this chapter, randomly assigned families in which physical abuse had occurred to social worker facilitated family-focused casework or an individual child-play therapy control condition. Family casework was a home-based intervention which included behavioural family assessment and feedback followed by a programme of family-focused problem-solving therapy. This included parental instruction in behavioural child management principles, family crisis intervention, and reinforcement of parents for engaging in the casework processes. Following treatment an effect size of 0.7 was obtained for the Family Interaction Coding System (Reid, 1978) which yielded an index of the amount of coercive parent–child behaviour. As a result of the intervention the average treated family was displaying less coercive behaviour than 76 per cent of the untreated families.

It may be concluded from these four studies that family-focused interventions including eco-behavioural programmes, family preservation services, social network enhancement programmes, and focused family casework were effective in improving the functioning of families in which child abuse and/or neglect had occurred and in some instances these gains were maintained at follow-up a year or longer after treatment.

Studies comparing two active treatments

Two studies compared the relative effectiveness of two clearly defined treatments. In each instance a variant of family systems therapy was compared with a behavioural alternative, either parent training or concurrent child and parental cognitive behaviour therapy. Brunk *et al.* (1987) randomly assigned neglectful and abusive families to either multisystemic family therapy or behavioural parent training with the type of maltreatment counterbalanced across conditions. Multisystemic family therapy was based on an assessment of family functioning and involved conjoint family sessions, marital sessions, individual sessions and meetings with members of the wider professional network and extended family as appropriate (Henggeler and Borduin, 1990). Interventions included joining with family members and members of the wider system, reframing interaction patterns and prescribing tasks to alter problematic interaction patterns within specific subsystems. Therapists designed intervention plans on a per-case basis in light of family assessment and received regular supervision to facilitate this process. In the behavioural parent training programme, parents received treatment within a group context. The programme included instruction in child development and the principles of behavioural management including the use of reward systems and time-out routines. Key resources for the programme were *Parents are Teachers* (Becker, 1971) and *Living with Children* (Patterson, 1973). Following treatment both groups showed significant improvement in parental functioning as assessed by the Symptom Checklist-90 (Derogatis *et al.*, 1973) and family stress as evaluated by the Family Inventory of Life Events and Changes (McCubbin *et al.*, 1985). A treatment outcome questionnaire was developed to assess therapists' and parents' perceptions of the severity of family needs. Researchers also used observational procedures to evaluate parental control strategies. Multisystemic therapy was superior to parent training on therapist-rated amelioration of family problems and researcher-rated improvement on all observational measures of parent–child interaction. In both domains effect sizes of 0.7 occurred indicating that the average case treated with multisystemic therapy fared better than 76 per cent of cases who participated in parent training. In contrast participants in parent training reported a greater decrease in social problems.

Kolko (1996) randomly assigned physically maltreated children and their abusive parents to family therapy or concurrent parent and child cognitive behaviour therapy. Most children in these families had disruptive behaviour disorders with ADHD (31 per cent) and Oppositional Defiant Disorder (24 per cent) being the most common diagnoses. Family therapy in this study (Alexander and Parsons, 1982; Robin and Foster, 1989; Szapocznik and Kurtines, 1989) was designed to enhance family functioning and relationships by helping family members identify and alter problematic patterns of family interaction. The protocol consisted of four phases: engagement and assessment; communication and problem-solving skill building; application of skills to specific problems; and disengagement. Individual cognitive behaviour therapy was directed towards teaching intrapersonal and interpersonal skills (Walker *et al.*, 1988). Intrapersonal skills included identifying stressful situations and using relaxation and cognitive coping strategies to manage stress reactions. For parents the emphasis was on anger management and for children the emphasis was on coping with potential parental violence. For children interpersonal skills training emphasized using social supports and assertiveness to minimize risks of harsh punishment. For parents behavioural parent training involving the use of reward systems and time-out routines were the main features of interpersonal skills training. Children and parents in the cognitive behavioural programme had separate therapists. For both the family therapy and the cognitive-behaviour therapy programmes home and clinic sessions were offered. On a weekly basis parents and children completed separate forms which assessed the severity of child and family problems, the severity of parental anger and the use of physical discipline on Likert scales. Compared with cases receiving family therapy, those receiving cognitive-behaviour therapy returned ratings of parental anger with effect sixes of 0.9 for children's ratings and 0.4 for parent ratings. For reductions in family problems cognitive-behaviour therapy cases also fared better with effect sizes of 0.8 for children's ratings but 0.0 for parental ratings. 73 per cent of cases who received cognitive-behaviour therapy abstained from the use of physical force in parent–child interactions compared with only 41 per cent of those who received family therapy. Deterioration occurred in the family therapy but not the cognitive-behaviour therapy group. There was a 28 per cent increase in cases with any physical discipline, force or injury in the family therapy group. In contrast, there was a 16 per cent decrease in such cases in the cognitive behaviour therapy group following treatment. The overall drop-out rate of 10 per cent in this study was very low.

From these two studies it may be concluded that the design of a treatment programme for families where physical abuse has occurred determines those aspects of family functioning that improve following the programme. Programme design also has an impact on risk reduction. Parallel cognitive-behavioural programmes which equip parents and children with the skills for regulating negative emotions and avoiding potentially violent interaction patterns were particularly effective as were multisystemic family therapy programmes which were sufficiently flexible to permit the clinician latitude to work intensively with key social systems that had an impact on risk of further abuse. Such programmes were probably more effective than behavioural parent training which focuses exclusively on child management skills and routine family therapy which inflexibly focuses on restructuring problematic interactions within the nuclear family.

Conclusions

The studies reviewed in this chapter have clear implications for setting up effective treatment programmes and developing services for families where child abuse has occurred. They also suggest targets for future research.

Abused children and their families can benefit from psychological interventions of various types. Clearly, for any particular form of child abuse not all interventions are equally effective. The effectiveness of various interventions and the domains of functioning within which positive changes occur depend in part upon the design of the intervention. Interventions may focus on the child, the parents, or the social system within which the abuse occurs. Combinations of interventions that fall into these three categories are probably synergistic rather than antagonistic in their effects.

For physical abuse and neglect, three child-focused interventions are particularly effective. These are residential treatment, therapeutic day care and resilient peer therapy. Residential treatment in which the child is placed at a special unit and visited daily by parents provides a protective, supportive and intellectually stimulating context within which positive parent–child interaction may fostered. Therapeutic day care where intellectual stimulation is provided within the context of supportive child–teacher relationships and high staffing levels may promote cognitive and social-emotional development. Resilient peer therapy, where at-risk children are given structured opportunities to be befriended by socially skilled peers can enhance social development. For non-organic failure to thrive, which may occur as part of a pattern of neglect, multidisciplinary assessment and an intensive child-focused programme which aims to help the child develop regular and appropriate feeding patterns is effective in promoting growth.

Effective parent-focused interventions for physical abuse and neglect include behavioural parent training which equips parents with child management skills and individual cognitive-behaviour therapy which helps parents develop the skills required for regulating negative emotional states, notably anger, anxiety and depression.

Effective interventions for the family and wider system within which physical child abuse and neglect occurs entail co-ordinated intervention with problematic subsystems based on a clear assessment of interaction patterns that may contribute to abuse or neglect. The aim of such intervention is to restructure relationships within the child's social system so that interaction patterns that may contribute to abuse or neglect will not recur. Significant subsystems requiring intervention may include the child, the parents, the marital subsystem, the extended family, the school system and the wider professional network.

In developing services for families in which physical abuse, neglect or failure-to-thrive has occurred, programmes that begin with a comprehensive assessment and include parallel parent-focused and child-focused components with adjudicative family sessions should be prioritized. Parent-focused programmes should include training in both child management skills and negative mood regulation skills. They should also provide parents with ongoing social support, and so are probably best offered within a group treatment format. Where the core issue is failure-to-thrive, training in feeding practices is essential. Child-focused programmes, in contrast, should foster positive relationships between children and therapists and between the children themselves. There is a strong argument for including well-adjusted peers in such groups and pairing each of these with an abused or neglected child. Within such groups, the focus should be on training in self-regulation and social skills and promoting cognitive and linguistic development. Adjunctive family sessions should be used to help parents and children use their new skills to strengthen parent–child attachment and avoid negative patterns of interaction. Methods for preventing attrition should be built into such programmes. For example, the assistance of lay volunteers might be enlisted to transport parents and children to and from the treatment sessions, or sessions might be scheduled in local community centres within walking distance of clients' homes. To maximize the impact of such a programme, given our current state of knowledge, it would probably need to run over a six-month period with two half-day sessions per week during which parents would attend a parent training and support group and children would concurrently attend a therapeutic play-group. For such programmes to be practically feasible, at least two therapeutically trained staff would be required, an equipped play room and a parent training room along with adequate administrative support and therapeutic supervision.

For children who have been sexually abused, individual or group therapy over twelve to thirty-six sessions is effective in promoting adjustment. Such therapy should aim to help youngsters deal with guilt and depression, abuse-related anger, victimization issues, sexuality issues and low self-esteem. It should also provide a forum within which to develop assertiveness skills and learn relationship-building skills. In planning such a service it would be essential to precede entry to such a programme with comprehensive assessment and to couple the programme with adjunctive family sessions with the non-abusing parents. Where intrafamilial sexual abuse has occurred, it is essential that the offender live separately from the victim until they have completed a treatment programme and been assessed as being at low risk of re-offending.

Further controlled treatment outcome studies, which meet the methodological criteria given in Chapter 1, are required in the field of child abuse and neglect. Studies of NOFTT and sexual abuse should be prioritized, since few studies in these areas have been conducted. For child sexual abuse, family-focused interventions which aim to enhance the relationship between the abused child and the non-offending parent or parents deserves investigation. For child abuse and neglect, integrated programmes containing child-focused, parent-focused and systems-focused interventions required evaluation.

ASSESSMENT INSTRUMENTS

Physical abuse and neglect

Bavolek, S. and Comstock, C. (1983). *Handbook for the Adult–Adolescent Parenting Inventory (AAPI)*. Eau Claire, WI: Family Development Associates.

Behar, L. and Stringfield, S. (1974). *Manual for the Preschool Behaviour Questionnaire*. Chapel Hill: University of North Carolina.

Brigance, A. (1978). *Brigance Diagnostic Inventory of Early Development*. North Billerica, MA: Curriculum.

Caldwell, B. and Bradley, R. (1985). *Home Observation of Measurement of the Environment*. New York: Dorsey Press.

Clarke, M. and Hornick, J. (1984). The development of the Nurturance Inventory: An instrument for assessing parent practices. *Child Psychiatry and Human Development*, 14, 49–63.

Cowen, E., Huser, J. and Beach, D. (1970). Parents perception of young children and their relation to indexes of adjustment. *Journal of Consulting and Clinical Psychology*, 34, 97–103.

Hamill, P. (1979). Physical growth: National Centre for Health Statistics percentiles. *American Journal of Clinical Nutrition*, 32, 607.

Harter, S. and Pike, R. (1984). The pictorial scale of perceived competence and social acceptance for young children. *Child Development*, 55, 1969–82.

Milner, J. (1986). *The Child Abuse Potential Inventory Manual (Revised)*. Webster, NC: Psytec Corporation.

Reid, J. (1978). *A Social Learning Approach to Family Interventions. Volume 2. Observations in Home Settings*. Eugene, OR: Castalia.

Robinson, E. and Eyberg, S. (1981). The dyadic parent–child interaction coding system: Standardization and validation. *Journal of Consulting and Clinical Psychology*, 29, 245–50.

Saunders, B. and Becker-Lausen, E. (1995). The measurement of psychological maltreatment: Early data on the Child Abuse and Trauma Scale. *Child Abuse and Neglect*, 19, 315–23.

Straus, M. (1979). Measuring intrafamilial conflict and violence: The Conflict Tactics (CT) Scale. *Journal of Marriage and the Family*, 41, 75–88.

Sexual abuse

Friedrich, W., Grambsch, P., Damon, L., Hewitt, S., Koverola, C., Lang, R., Wolfe, V. and Broughton, D. (1992). Child Sexual Behaviour inventory. *Psychological Assessment*, 4, 303–11.

Putnam, F., Helmers, K. and Trickett, P. (1993). Development, reliability and validity of a child dissociation scale. *Child Abuse and Neglect*, 17, 731–42.

Wolfe, V., Gentile, C., Michienzi, T., Sas, L. and Wolfe, D. (1991). Child Impact of Traumatic Events Scale. A measure of post-sexual-abuse PTSD symptoms. *Behavioural Assessment*, 13, 359–83.

TREATMENT MANUALS AND RESOURCES

Physical abuse and neglect

Alexander, J. and Parsons, B. (1982). *Functional Family Therapy*. Monterey, CA: Brooks Cole.

Becker, W. (1971). *Parents are Teachers*. Champaign, Ill: Research Press.

Dale, P. (1986). *Dangerous Families: Assessment and Treatment of Child Abuse*. London: Tavistock.

Donohue, B., Miller, E., Van Hasselt, V. and Hersen, M. (1998). An ecobehavioural approach to child maltreatment. In V. Van Hasselt and M. Hersen (eds), *Handbook of Psychological Treatment Protocols for Children and Adolescents* (pp. 279–358). Mahwah, NJ: Lawrence Erlbaum.

Forehand, B. and McMahon, R. (1981). *Helping the Non-compliant Child: A Clinician's Guide to Parent Training*. New York: Guilford.

Henggeler, S. and Borduin, C. (1990). *Family Therapy and Beyond: A Multisystemic Approach to Treating the Behaviour Problems of Children and Adolescents*. Pacific Grove, CA: Brooks Cole.

Iwaniec, D. (1995). *The Emotionally Abused and Neglected Child: Identification, Assessment and Intervention*. Chichester: Wiley.

Meichenbaum, D. (1985). *Stress Inoculation Training. A Clinical Guidebook*. New York: Pergamon.

Novaco, R. (1975). *Anger Control*. Lexington, MA: D.C. Heath.

Patterson, G. (1973). *Living with Children*. Champaign, Ill: Research Press.

Pearce, J. and Pezzot-Pearce, T. (1997). *Psychotherapy of Abused and Neglected Children*. New York: Guilford.

Robin, A. and Foster, S. (1989). *Negotiating Parent-Adolescent Conflict: A Behavioural Family-Systems Approach*. New York: Guilford.

Szapocznik, J. and Kurtines, W. (1989). *Breakthroughs in Family Therapy With Drug Abusing Problem Youth*. New York: Springer.

Walker, C., Bonner, B. and Kaufman, K. (1988). *The Physically and Sexually Abused Child: Evaluation and Treatment*. New York: Pergamon.

Sexual abuse

Deblinger, A. and Heflinger, A. (1996). *Treating Sexually Abused Children and their Non-offending Parents: A Cognitive Behavioural Approach*. Thousand Oaks, CA: Sage.

Friedrich, W. (1995). *Psychotherapy with Sexually Abused Boys: An Integrated Approach*. Thousand Oaks, CA: Sage.

Furniss, T. (1991). *The Multiprofessional Handbook of Child Sexual Abuse: Integrated Management, Therapy and Legal Intervention*. London: Routledge.

Hansen, D., Hecht, D. and Futa, K. (1998). Child sexual abuse. In V. Van Hasselt and M. Hersen (eds), *Handbook of Psychological Treatment Protocols for Children and Adolescents* (pp. 153–75). Mahwah, NJ: Lawrence Erlbaum.

3 Enuresis and encopresis

Eddie Murphy and Alan Carr

Definitions

The development of bladder and bowel control occurs in a stage-wise manner in most children during the first five years of life (Buchanan, 1992; Fielding and Doleys, 1988; Shaffer, 1994). Enuresis and encopresis – the absence of bladder and bowel control by the age of four or five years – have a negative impact on children's social and educational development and so may be a focus for clinical intervention. Children with elimination problems may be excluded from school, ostracized by their peers and they may develop conflictual relationships with their parents. This in turn can lead to the development of academic attainment problems, low self-esteem, and secondary emotional or conduct problems.

Enuresis and encopresis constitute a heterogeneous group of disorders and any classification system must take account of a number of important distinctions (Butler, 1998b; Gontard, 1998). First, both wetting and soiling may occur exclusively during the day; exclusively during the night; or at any time. Second, with primary enuresis and encopresis, incontinence has been present from birth, but with secondary enuresis or encopresis, there has been a period of bowel or bladder control which at some point broke down. Third, with secondary enuresis and encopresis, a distinction may be made between cases where the wetting or soiling is intentional and those where it is unintentional. Fourth, with encopresis, at a symptomatic level, soiling may occur either with or without constipation and overflow incontinence. Fifth, elimination problems may occur as monosymptomatic presentations or as cases characterized by both faecal and urinary incontinence. Sixth, elimination problems may occur as an uncomplicated one- or two-symptom presentation or as part of a wider set of adjustment problems primarily related to a chaotic, stressful or abusive psychosocial environment; or as one aspect of a developmental disability or medical condition.

From Figure 3.1 it may be seen that within ICD 10 and DSM IV, many of these features have been taken into account in describing elimination disorders, but few have been taken into account in subclassification. In ICD 10, a distinction is made between enuresis and encopresis, but no attempt is

	DSM IV	ICD 10
Enuresis	A. A repeated voiding of urine into bed or clothes (whether involuntary or intentional). B. The behaviours clinically significant as manifested by either a frequency of twice a week for at least 3 consecutive months or the presence of clinically significant distress or impairment in social, academic (occupational) or other important areas of functioning. C. Chronological age of at least 5 years (or equivalent developmental level). D. The behaviour is not due exclusively to the direct physiological effect of a substance (e.g. a diuretic) or a general medical condition such as spina bifida. Specify type: Nocturnal only. Diurnal only. Nocturnal and Diurnal.	A disorder characterized by the involuntary voiding of urine, by day and/or by night, which is abnormal in relation to the individual's mental age and which is not a consequence of a lack of bladder control due to any neurological disorder, to epileptic attacks, or to any structural abnormality of the urinary tact. The enuresis may have been present from birth or it may have arisen following a period of acquired bladder control. The later onset variety usually begins at the age of 5 to 7 years. The enuresis may constitute a monosymptomatic condition or it may be associated with a more widespread emotional or behavioural disorder. Emotional problems may arise as a secondary consequence of the distress or stigma that results from enuresis, the enuresis may form part of some other psychiatric disorder, or both the enuresis and the emotional/behavioural disturbance may arise in parallel from related etiological factors. There is no straightforward way of deciding between these alternatives.
Encopresis	A repeated passage of faeces into inappropriate places (e.g. clothing or floor) whether involuntary or intentional. B. At least one such event per month for at least 3 months. C. Chronological age is at least 4 years (or equivalent developmental level). D. The behaviour is not due exclusively to the direct physiological effect of a substance (e.g. a laxative) or a general medical condition except through the mechanism of constipation. Specify type: With constipation and overflow incontinence. Without constipation and overflow incontinence.	Repeated voluntary or involuntary passage of faeces, usually of normal or near normal consistency in places not appropriate for that purpose in the individual's own sociocultural setting. There are three main etiological patterns. First, the condition may represent a lack of adequate toilet training, with the history being one of continuous failure ever to acquire adequate bowel control. Second, it may reflect a psychologically determined disorder in which there has been normal physiological control over defecation but, for some reason a reluctance, resistance, or failure to conform to social norms in defecation in acceptable places. Third, it may stem from physiological retention, involving impaction of faeces, with secondary overflow. Such retention may arise from parent–child battles over bowel training or from withholding faeces because of painful defecation as a consequence of an anal fissure or gastrointestinal problem. In some instances the encopresis may be accompanied by smearing of faeces over the body or over the external environment and there may be anal fingering and masturbation. In such instances it usually forms part of a wider emotional or behavioural disorder.

Figure 3.1 Diagnostic criteria for elimination disorders in DSM IV and ICD 10.
Source Adapted from DSM IV (APA, 1994) and ICD 10 (WHO, 1992, 1996).

made to further subclassify elimination problems with different features. In DSM IV encopresis is subclassified into a type characterized by constipation and overflow incontinence and a type where this feature is absent. With enuresis, three subtypes are recognized depending upon the time of day when wetting typically occurs: diurnal, nocturnal and both.

Epidemiology

Encopresis is not diagnosed until four years of age. At five years of age the prevalence of encopresis is about 1 per cent (APA, 1994). Encopresis accounts for 25 per cent of all visits to paediatric gastroenterology clinics and 3 per cent of all visits to general paediatric clinics (Levine, 1991). Enuresis is not diagnosed until five years of age. The prevalence of enuresis among five year olds is 7 per cent for males and 3 per cent for females. At ten years of age the prevalence is 3 per cent for males and 2 per cent for females. At eighteen, 1 per cent of males have enuresis and fewer females suffer from the condition. This gradual reduction in the prevalence of elimination disorders with increasing age is illustrated in Figure 3.2. Secondary elimination problems most commonly occur between five and eight years. The male:female ratio for elimination disorders is about 2:1. Approximately 80 per cent of neurotic children have primary enuresis as they have never attained at least six months of continuous night-time continence and 20 per cent have secondary enuresis (Houts *et al.*, 1994). For treated cases of enuresis, motivation and adherence to behavioural treatment programme regimes are the best predictors of positive outcome (Buchanan, 1992; Kaplan and Busner, 1993). The number of first degree relatives with bedwetting problems is the single most accurate predictor of a poor prognosis for

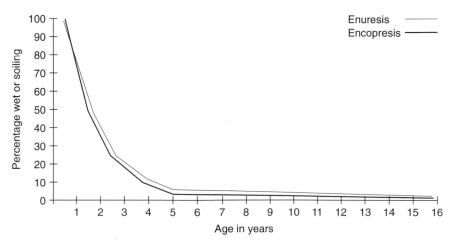

Figure 3.2 Prevalence of wetting and soiling from birth to adolescence.
Source Based on Buchanan (1992) and Houts *et al.* (1994).

enuretics (Barclay and Houts, 1995). With encopresis a poor prognosis has been found in cases characterized by highly coercive or intrusive parent–child interaction (Kelly, 1996).

Previous reviews

A review by Houts *et al.* (1994) of seventy-eight studies of the psychological and pharmacological treatments for enuresis found that children benefited more from psychological interventions compared to pharmacological treatments. Sixty-six per cent of children who are treated with a urine alarm programme, where the child was awoken immediately wetting began by a bell activated by a urine trigger pad, ceased bedwetting following treatment, and at follow-up some months later 51 per cent had not relapsed. In comparison, medications such as imipramine and desmopressin led to no more than 46 per cent of cases becoming dry following treatment, and at follow-up only 22 per cent had not relapsed. There was no evidence that supplementing a urine alarm programme with other behavioural interventions significantly improved post-treatment outcome or relapse rates at follow-up. Such interventions include contingency management, where the child is rewarded for not wetting or for waking to urinate; cleanliness training, where the child is required to change sheets following bedwetting; retention control training, where the child is rewarded for postponing urination while awake after drinking fluid; overlearning, where the child, who has achieved night-time dryness consumes extra liquid before sleeping; and stop-start training, where the child learns sphincter control by practising stopping the urine flow after it has started. Various combinations of these elements have been collated into treatment packages such as Dry Bed Training and Full Spectrum Home Training (Butler, 1998). Treatment-resistant cases of enuresis remain an unresearched subgroup and paediatric examination is recommended in such cases (Gontard, 1998).

Thapar *et al.* (1992) reviewed literature on the effectiveness of verbal psychotherapy; behaviour therapy; physical treatment; and multimodal treatment programmes for encopresis. While noting a paucity of well-designed studies, they concluded that combined behavioural therapy and laxative use was the most effective treatment for children with soiling problems. Behaviour therapy packages in such instances involved contingency management and stimulus control where children were helped to develop a toileting routine. There was also some evidence for the effectiveness of sphincter biofeedback.

These previous reviews of the literature on the effectiveness of psychological treatments for enuresis and encopresis have been wide-ranging and included many studies, some with major methodological limitations. The aim of this chapter is to identify and review a representative group of ten of the better controlled treatment effectiveness studies for enuresis and encopresis.

Method

In order to locate appropriate studies, an extensive literature search of English language journals covering the years 1977 to 1997 was undertaken. The major databases PsychLit, CINALH and MEDLINE were searched using the terms *enuresis* and *encopresis* (and their synonyms) combined with general terms such as *treatment, intervention* and *therapy* and specific terms such as *urine alarms, biofeedback* and *behaviour therapy*. This search was complemented by a manual search of the indexes of review articles and relevant journals. Over fifty studies of the treatment of enuresis identified in this search were very well designed with homogeneous cases assigned to treatment and control with reliable and valid pre- and post-treatment measures. Five exemplar studies were selected from this pool of articles. All five studies contained a number of treatment groups including a urine alarm group and/or a control group. The identification of well-designed studies of the treatment of encopresis was more problematic. Only two well-designed comparative treatment outcome studies were located. Three single group outcome studies were also selected for inclusion in the review. Selected studies included treatment approaches previously identified as promising, i.e. behaviour therapy and biofeedback.

Characteristics of the studies

An overview of the characteristics of the ten studies is given in Table 3.1. All of the studies were published between 1983 and 1997. Two of the enuresis studies were conducted in the USA, one in the UK, one in the Netherlands and one in Israel. All of the encopresis studies were conducted in the USA. Each of the enuresis studies contained three or more active treatment conditions and treatment group sizes ranged from six to 45. There were more than 40 participants in each of the enuresis studies. Aggregating across all five studies there were 348 participants. Two of the encopresis studies were comparative group outcome studies, while three were single group outcome studies. Treatment group sizes ranged from seven to 59 and aggregating across all studies there was a total of 154 participants. In all studies there were more boys than girls. The studies of wetting focused largely on children with primary rather than secondary enuresis. In the studies of encopresis, all cases were chronic and unresponsive to standard medical advice. In the enuresis studies, there was a mixture of self-referred and media-solicited cases on the one hand and physician-referred cases on the other. In contrast, all encopresis cases were referred by physicians. All studies were conducted in community outpatient settings. Five of the enuresis studies and three of the encopresis studies involved behaviour therapy. In two of the encopresis studies biofeedback treatments were used and in one of the encopresis studies family therapy was used.

Table 3.1 Characteristics of treatment outcome studies for enuresis and encopresis

Study no.	Author	Year	Country	N per gp	Mean age & range	Gender	Primary diagnosis	Severity & chronicity	Comorbid diagnosis	Family characteristics	Referral	Treatment setting	Treatment duration
1	Van Londen et al.	1995	Netherlands	UA = 41 UA + ICM = 41 UA + DCM = 45	9 y 6–12 y	m 70% f 30%	87% Primary enuresis 13% Secondary enuresis				Self-referred	Community OP	
2	Ronen et al.	1992	Israel	UA = 19 CBT = 20 CM = 20 C = 18	10 y 7–14 y	m 51% f 49%	100% Primary enuresis				Self-referred	Community OP	
3	Fournier et al.	1987	USA	UA = 7 Imp = 7 IUA + Imp = 8 UA + P = 7 Imp + Ra = 8 Ra + P = 8 P = 6 Ra = 8	8 y 6–11 y	m 72% f 28%	76% Primary enuresis 24% Secondary enuresis	>2 wet nights per week over 6 months	Excluded encopresis, psychopathology, and previous UA treatment	SES II, III and IV most highly represented. SPF 14%	Referred by paediatrician	Community OP	6 w
4	Houts et al.	1986	USA	UA = 9 UA + RCT = 16 UA + RCT + OL = 9 C = 11	9 y 5–13 y	m 78% f 22%	100% Primary enuresis				Media-solicited and paediatric referrals	Community OP	1 h group session Follow-up at 3 m, 6 m & 1 y
5	Bennett et al.	1985	UK	UA = 9 SST = 12 DBT = 14 C = 9	9 y 5–12 y	m 63% f 37%	100% Primary enuresis	Wet 6 nights out of 14	Excluded encopresis, and previous behaviour therapy for nocturnal enuresis		Referred by GP and paediatrician	Community OP	10 sess over 10 w

No.	Author	Year	Country	Groups (n)	Age	Gender	Condition	Inclusion	Exclusion	SES/IF	Referral	Setting	Treatment
6	Stark et al.	1990	USA	BT = 18	8 y 4–11 y	m 83% f 17%	Encopresis	Unresponsive to SMC		SES1 = 28% SES 2, 3 = 45% SES 4, 5 = 27%	Paediatrician	Community OP	6 × 1 h sess over 6 w Follow-up at 1 & 6 m
7	Stark et al.	1997	USA	BT = 59	8 y 3–13 y	m 69% f 31%	Encopresis (retentive)	Unresponsive to SMC		IF = 75% SES 1 = 18% SES 2, 3 = 54% SES 4, 5 = 28%	GP or paediatrician	Community OP	6 × 1 h sess over 6 w
8	Cox et al.	1994	USA	BF = 13 SMC = 13	8 y 4–16 y	m 69% f 31%	Encopresis	Unresponsive to SMC	Excluded ID neuromuscular or gastro-intestinal dysfunction		Paediatrician	Community OP	2 × 1 h sess over 1 m Follow-up at 16 m
9	Cox et al.	1996	USA	BF = 14 BT = 14 SMC = 18	9 y 6–15 y	m 77% f 23%	Encopresis (DSM IV)	Unresponsive to SMC. Encopresis present for more than 1 y	Excluded ID neuromuscular or gastro-intestinal dysfunction	IF = 95% Predominantly SES 2, 3	GP	Community OP	3 × 1 h sess over 2 w Follow-up at 3 m
10	Protinsky and Kersey	1983	USA	FT = 7	8 y 6–10 y	m 100%	Encopresis	Unresponsive to SMC				Community OP	12 × 1 h sess Follow-up at 6 m

Key UA = Urine alarm. CM = Contingency management. ICM = Immediate contingency management. DCM = Delayed contingency management. DBT = Dry bed training. SST = Stop-start training. RCT = Retention control training. OL = Overlearning. CBT = Cognitive behavioural therapy. BT = Behaviour therapy. FT = Family therapy. BF = Biofeedback. C = Control group. SMC = Standard medical care. Imp = Imipramine. P = Placebo. Ra = Random awakening. OP = Outpatient. ID = Intellectual disability. IF = Intact family. SPF = Single parent families. SES = Socio-economic status. d = day. w = week. m = month. y = year.

Methodological features

Methodological features of the ten studies are given in Table 3.2. Seven of the investigations were comparative group outcome studies with a control group and in four studies cases were randomly assigned to groups. In eight of the ten studies cases were diagnostically homogeneous and in two studies cases in treatment and control groups were shown to be demographically similar. In seven studies they were similar in terms of co-morbidity. In all ten studies pre- and post-treatment assessments were conducted and in seven a follow-up assessment was conducted. In all ten studies the core symptom (either enuresis or encopresis) was assessed, whereas in none of the studies was some aspect of the child's social system evaluated. Deterioration was assessed in seven studies and drop-out in five. In two studies information was given on engagement in further treatment. Parent ratings were the principal source of data in this group of studies. Nine studies relied on parent reports, one on child self-report and one on therapist and researcher ratings. Data on the clinical significance of change were given in nine studies. Experienced therapists offered treatment in nine of the studies and in six, where comparisons were made, treatments were equally valued by therapists. Treatment manuals were used in only two studies and checks for treatment integrity were made in only one study. Supervision was offered to therapists in only one study. Data on engaging in subsequent treatment following the completion of the study were given in three studies and data on engagement in concurrent treatment during the study were given in only one report. Overall this was a fairly well-conducted group of studies from a methodological perspective.

Substantive findings

Effect sizes and improvement rates for the ten studies are given in Tables 3.3 and 3.4. What follows is a synopsis of each of the studies and their substantive findings.

Enuresis

The five enuresis studies all involved the comparison of routine urine alarm programmes with other types of behavioural or drug treatments. In Van Londen *et al.*'s (1995) study 110 children with primary enuresis and seventeen children with secondary enuresis were assigned to three urine alarm treatment programmes: a routine programme; a programme that involved immediate contingency management when the alarm sounded; and a programme with delayed contingency management where the child was reinforced or suffered response costs the morning after the alarm sounded. Stickers were given as reinforcers or taken away as response costs in this study. Ronen *et al.* (1992) allocated children with primary enuresis to a

Table 3.2 Methodological features of treatment outcome studies for enuresis and encopresis

Feature	Study number									
	S1	S2	S3	S4	S5	S6	S7	S8	S9	S10
Control group	1	1	1	1	1	0	0	1	1	0
Random assignment	0	0	1	1	1	0	0	0	1	0
Diagnostic homogeneity	0	1	0	1	1	1	1	1	1	1
Comparable for comorbidity	1	1	1	1	1	0	0	1	1	0
Demographic similarity	0	0	1	0	0	0	0	0	1	0
Pre-treatment assessment	1	1	1	1	1	1	1	1	1	1
Post-treatment assessment	1	1	1	1	1	1	1	1	1	1
Follow-up assessment	1	1	1	1	1	1	0	0	0	1
Children's self-report	0	1	0	0	0	1	0	0	0	0
Parent's ratings	1	0	1	1	1	1	1	1	1	1
Teacher's ratings	0	0	0	0	0	0	0	0	0	0
Therapist's ratings	0	0	0	0	0	0	1	0	0	0
Researcher's ratings	0	0	0	0	0	0	1	0	0	0
Child's symptom assessed	0	1	1	1	1	1	1	1	1	1
System assessed	0	0	0	0	0	0	0	0	0	0
Deterioration assessed	1	1	0	0	0	1	1	0	1	1
Drop-out assessed	1	1	0	1	0	0	1	0	1	1
Clinical significance of change assessed	1	1	0	1	1	1	1	1	1	1
Experienced therapists used	0	1	1	1	1	1	1	1	1	1
Treatments were equally valued	1	1	1	1	1	0	0	0	1	0
Treatments were manualized	1	0	0	0	1	0	1	0	0	0
Therapy supervision was provided	0	0	0	0	0	0	0	0	0	0
Treatment integrity checked	0	0	0	0	0	0	0	0	0	0
Data on concurrent treatment given	0	0	0	0	0	0	1	0	0	0
Data on subsequent treatment given	0	0	0	1	0	1	1	0	0	0
Total	12	13	11	15	11	10	14	10	13	10

Key S = study. 1 = design feature was present. 0 = design feature was absent.

Table 3.3 Summary of results of treatment effects for enuresis and encopresis

Variable	Enuresis															Encopresis					
	Study 1			Study 2			Study 3			Study 4			Study 5			Study 6	Study 7	Study 8	Study 9		Study 10
	UA + ICM	UA + DCM	UA	UA	CM	CBT	UA	IMP	IMP + UA	UA	UA + RCT	UA + RCT + OL	UA	UA + SST	UA + DBT	BT	BT	BF	BF	BT	FT
Symptomatic improvement after treatment																					
Children's self-report	–	–	–	–	–	–	–	–	–	–	–	–	–	–	–	–	–	–	–	–	–
Parent's ratings	–	–	–	1.9	1.5	1.8	–	–	–	–	–	–	2.8	1.3	2.5	–	–	.7	.7	.7	–
Teacher's ratings	–	–	–	–	–	–	–	–	–	–	–	–	–	–	–	–	–	–	–	–	–
Therapist's ratings	–	–	–	–	–	–	–	–	–	–	–	–	–	–	–	–	–	–	–	–	–
Researcher's ratings	–	–	–	–	–	–	–	–	–	–	–	–	–	–	–	–	–	–	–	–	–
Symptomatic improvement at follow-up																					
Children's self-report	–	–	–	–	–	–	–	–	–	–	–	–	–	–	–	–	–	–	–	–	–
Parent's ratings	–	–	–	–	–	–	2.3	2.3	1.3	–	–	–	2.9	1.1	1.9	–	–	–	.5	.6	–
Teacher's ratings	–	–	–	–	–	–	–	–	–	–	–	–	–	–	–	–	–	–	–	–	–
Therapist's ratings	–	–	–	–	–	–	–	–	–	–	–	–	–	–	–	–	–	–	–	–	–
Researcher's ratings	–	–	–	–	–	–	–	–	–	–	–	–	–	–	–	–	–	–	–	–	–
Positive clinical outcomes																					
% improved after treatment	73%	98%	84%	79%	70%	90%	–	–	–	60%	87%	60%	44%	17%	50%	89%	86%	–	–	–	86%
% improved at follow-up	72%	92%	77%	40%	40%	85%	–	–	–	56%	38%	89%	–	–	–	100%	–	79%	64%	71%	71%
Negative clinical outcomes																					
% Deterioration	18%	8%	13%	15%	60%	15%	–	–	–	20%	15%	27%	–	–	–	11%	14%	–	30%	30%	28%
% Drop-out	0%	0%	0%	60%	30%	10%	–	–	–	20%	13%	13%	–	–	–	–	12%	–	–	–	14%
% Engaged in further treatment	–	–	–	–	–	–	–	–	–	100%	33%	100%	–	–	–	11%	3%	–	–	–	–

Key UA = Urine alarm. ICM = Immediate contingency management. CM = Contingency management. DCM = Delayed contingency management. CBT = Cognitive behavioural therapy. Imp = Imipramine. RCT = Retention control training. OL = Overlearning. SST = Stop-start training. DBT = Dry bed training. BT = Behaviour therapy. BF = Sphincter biofeedback. FT = Family therapy.

Table 3.4 Summary of key findings from treatment outcome studies for enuresis and encopresis

Study no.	Diagnosis	Author	Year	Country	N per Group	No of sessions	Group differences	Key findings
1	Enuresis	Van Londen et al.	1995	Netherlands	1. UA = 41 2. UA + ICM = 41 3. UA + DCM = 45	6	2 > 3 > 1	• 92% of cases who were treated with immediate contingency management following awakening by a urine alarm were continent at 2.5 years' follow-up compared with 77% of cases who received delayed contingency management and 72% of cases who were treated with a urine alarm programme only.
2	Enuresis	Ronen et al.	1992	Israel	1. UA = 19 2. CBT = 20 3. CM = 20 4. C = 18	14	Following treatment 1 = 2 > 3 > 4 6-month follow-up 2 > 1 = 3 > 4	• 90% of cases who received cognitive behavioural self-control training were dry or improved following treatment compared with 79% of cases who received delayed contingency management and 70% of cases who were treated with a urine alarm programme only. • Six months after treatment 85% of cases who received cognitive behavioural self-control training were dry or improved following treatment compared with 40% of cases who received delayed contingency management and 40% of cases who were treated with a urine alarm programme only.
3	Enuresis	Fournier et al.	1987	USA	1. UA = 7 2. Imp = 7 3. UA + Imp = 8 4. UA + P = 7 5. Imp + Ra = 8 6. Ra + P = 8 7. P = 6 8. Ra = 8	6	Following treatment 1 = 2 = 3 = 4 = 5 > 6 = 8 > 7 3-month follow-up 1 = 2 = 3 = 4 > 6 = 8 > 5 > 7	• Following treatment and at 3 months' follow-up greatest improvements were shown by cases treated with a urine alarm programme or imipramine or a combination of both of these. • At 3 months' follow-up cases treated with a urine alarm programme or imipramine alone had less than one wet night per week.
4	Enuresis	Houts et al.	1986	USA	1. UA = 15 2. UA + RCT = 15 3. UA + RCT + OL = 15 4. C = 11	1	Following treatment 2 > 1 = 3 > 4 3-month follow-up 3 > 1 > 2 > 4	• 87% of cases were dry following treatment with a urine alarm programme coupled with retention control training compared with 60% of cases treated with a urine alarm programme only or a urine alarm programme with retention control training and over-learning. • At 3 months' follow-up only 11% of cases in the full spectrum home-training programme which included a urine alarm programme with retention control training and overlearning had relapsed compared with 62% of cases treated with a urine alarm programme coupled with retention control training compared and 44% of cases treated with a urine alarm programme only.

Table 3.4 (cont'd)

Study no.	Diagnosis	Author	Year	Country	N per Group	No of sessions	Group differences	Key findings
5	Enuresis	Bennett et al.	1985	UK	1. UA = 9 2. SST = 12 3. DBT = 14 4. C = 9	10	1 = 2 = 3 > 4	• Following treatment 50% of cases treated with dry bed training, 44% of cases treated with a urine alarm and 17% of cases treated with stop-start training were continent.
6	Encopresis	Stark et al.	1990	USA	BT = 18	6	Follow-up > Baseline	• Following treatment 89% of cases were recovered and at follow-up 100% of cases were recovered. • There was a significant increase in intake of dietary fibre from baseline to follow-up.
7	Encopresis	Stark et al.	1997	USA	BT = 59	6	Follow-up > Baseline	• Following treatment 86% of cases were recovered and at follow-up 100% of cases were recovered. • There was a significant increase in intake of dietary fibre from baseline to follow-up.
8	Encopresis	Cox et al.	1994	USA	1. BF = 13 2. SMC = 13	2	1 > 2	• 16 months following treatment 79% of cases treated with external anal sphincter biofeedback reported no further soiling compared with 49% of cases receiving standard medical care. • Treated cases showed demonstrable improvements in sphincter control and also reduced rates of constipation and painful bowel movements.
9	Encopresis	Cox et al.	1996	USA	1. BF = 14 2. BT = 14 3. SMC = 18	3	1 = 2 > 3	• 3 months following treatment 64% of cases treated with biofeedback and 71% of cases treated with behaviour therapy showed clinically significant improvement in their encopresis compared with 19% of cases treated with standard medical care which included laxatives and advice. • Failure to respond to treatment in the first 2 weeks predicted eventual treatment failure.
10	Encopresis	Protinsky and Kersey	1983	USA	FT = 7	12	Follow-up > Baseline	• Following treatment 86% of cases receiving family therapy were improved and at 6-month follow-up 71% maintained treatment gains.

Key: UA = Urine alarm. CM = Contingency management. ICM = Immediate contingency management. DCM = Delayed contingency management. DBT = Dry bed training. SST = Stop-start training. RCT = Retention control training. OL = Overlearning-CBT = Cognitive-behavioural therapy. BT = Behaviour therapy. FT = Family therapy. BF = Biofeedback. C = Control group. SMC = Standard medical care. Imp = Imipramine. P = Placebo. Ra = Random awakening.

urine alarm programme, a contingency management programme, a multi-component cognitive behaviour programme and a control group. Fournier *et al.* (1987) randomly allocated 45 children with primary enuresis and fourteen children with secondary enuresis to a urine alarm programme, an imipramine programme, a combined urine alarm and imipramine programme and five other conditions which involved random awakening, or a placebo either alone or in combination with the two active treatments. Houts *et al.* (1986) randomly assigned cases to a control group; a urine alarm programme; a urine alarm programme with retention control training; and full spectrum home training which involved a urine alarm, retention control training and overlearning. For retention control training children drank eight ounces of fluid and delayed micturition for an increasing amount of time. For overlearning, following fourteen dry nights the child drank six-teen ounces of water during the hour before bedtime (Houts and Liebert, 1984). Bennett *et al.* (1985) randomly assigned cases to a control group, a urine alarm programme, stop-start training, or dry bed training.

In all five studies continence diaries in which bedwetting behaviour was recorded were used to assess progress. In Ronen *et al.*'s (1992) study the diary was kept by the children, but in all other studies parents recorded progress.

In Van Londen *et al.*'s (1995) study after treatment 97 per cent of children in the urine alarm programme which was supplemented with immediate contingency management were continent compared with 84 per cent in the group that received delayed contingency management and 73 per cent in the group that received a routine urine alarm programme. Two and a half years following treatment the continence rates for the immediate contingency management, the delayed contingency management and the routine urine alarm groups were 92 per cent, 77 per cent and 72 per cent respectively. Of all five studies reviewed here, the outcome rate for the urine alarm programme combined with immediate contingency management was by far the best. The deterioration rate of 8 per cent for this group was also the lowest across all five studies.

In Ronen *et al.*'s study (1992) the multimodal cognitive behavioural programme was more effective than the routine urine alarm or contingency management programmes. Ninety per cent of cases were improved after treatment and 85 per cent were continent six months after treatment. Seventy-nine per cent of cases in the urine alarm programme and 70 per cent of cases in the contingency management programme were improved after treatment and only 40 per cent of these remained continent at follow-up. Fifteen per cent or fewer in the cognitive-behavioural condition dropped out or deteriorated compared with drop-out and deterioration rates of 30–70 per cent for the other two conditions.

In Fournier *et al.*'s (1987) study, effect sizes for urine alarm programmes and treatment with imipramine of 2.3 were obtained following treatment, indicating that after treatment, the average treated case fared better than

98 per cent of untreated cases. In contrast those that received combined urine alarm and imipramine treatments returned an effect size of 1.3, indicating that the average treated case fared better than 90 per cent of untreated cases. These results were all based on the status of cases three months after treatment.

Houts *et al.* (1986) found that full spectrum home training was no more effective than a routine urine alarm treatment programme in helping youngsters achieve continence following treatment. However, the improvement rate for the full spectrum home training increased from 60 to 89 per cent in the three months following treatment. This increase in improvement did not occur for cases in the routine urine alarm programme or in the urine alarm programme with supplementary retention control training.

Bennett *et al.* (1985) found little difference between the effectiveness of a urine alarm programme and a dry bed training programme, but both were more effective than a urine alarm programme with supplementary stop-start training.

Taken together these studies show that urine alarm programmes supplemented with immediate contingency management, retention control training, overlearning and multimodal cognitive-behavioural treatment are probably the treatment of choice for enuresis. Improvement in more than 85 per cent of cases may be expected with this clinical approach.

Encopresis

The five encopresis studies all involved participants who had failed to respond to previous standard medical interventions which typically included laxative use and advice on developing toileting routines. Behaviour therapy, biofeedback and family therapy were the main approaches to treatment investigated in these studies. Stark *et al.* (1990, 1997) in a series of two uncontrolled studies investigated the efficacy of behaviour therapy for the treatment of encopresis. In the first study, eighteen cases received manualized group treatment for six hourly sessions over a period of seven weeks. In the second study, 59 cases were treated with combined medical management, increased intake of dietary fibre and group behaviour therapy. Cox *et al.* (1994, 1996) examined the efficacy of biofeedback in a series of two studies. In the first, biofeedback was compared with standard medical care and in the second, an additional behaviour therapy group which received enhanced toilet training was added to the design. Protinsky and Kersey (1983) examined the efficacy of Haley's (1976) strategic family therapy model in a small uncontrolled trial. In all five studies, diaries or structured child or parent reports were used to assess progress and measures of soiling frequency were used to calculate effect sizes.

For active treatments (behaviour therapy, biofeedback and family therapy) in all five studies, improvement rates following treatment were greater than

80 per cent and at follow-up improvement rates between 64 per cent and 100 per cent were obtained for biofeedback and family therapy. For family therapy, six months after treatment 71 per cent of cases remained continent. Across all three forms of treatment deterioration and drop-out rates ranged from 11 to 30 per cent. In Cox's comparative study of biofeedback and behaviour therapy, treatments did not differ in effectiveness and effect sizes of .5 to .6 were obtained across end of treatment and follow-up assessments, indicating that the average treated case fared better than 69 to 73 per cent of cases that received standard medical care.

Conclusions

From the evidence reviewed in this chapter it may be concluded that urine alarm-based programmes were the most effective treatment for enuresis. Parents were centrally involved in the implementation of these programmes in which children learned bladder control by being awakened each time they bedwet by a urine-activated alarm system. Effective urine alarm programmes additionally included a psychoeducational component in which a rationale for treatment and treatment procedures were explained; a contingency management programme where children received immediate rewards for avoiding bedwetting and were not inadvertently reinforced for wetting at night; retention control training; and some procedure for ensuring that sufficient trials of waking when the bladder was full occurred to ensure that sufficient opportunities for learning occurred.

For encopresis, successful treatment approaches were family-based and multimodal. They involved standard medical care (laxative use and increasing the intake of dietary fibre) coupled with behaviour therapy involving shaping and maintaining toileting routines through contingency management where the child was rewarded for engaging in such routines; and anal sphincter biofeedback which facilitated learning sphincter control.

Effective programmes for elimination problems were typically offered on an acute care basis over a period of between one and twelve one-hour sessions by multidisciplinary teams within input from paediatric medicine or nursing and clinical psychology.

Improvement in up to 80 per cent of cases may be expected with these clinical approaches.

Future research should focus on the development of manualized multicomponent treatment packages for treatment-resistant cases.

ASSESSMENT

Morgan, R. and Young, G. (1975). Parental attitudes and the conditioning treatment of childhood enuresis. *Behaviour Research and Therapy*, 13, 197–9.

TREATMENT RESOURCES

Buchanan, A. (1992). *Children Who Soil. Assessment and Treatment.* Chichester: Wiley.

Herbert, M. (1996). *Toilet Training, Bedwetting and Soiling.* Leicester: British Psychological Society.

TREATMENT RESOURCES FOR CLIENTS

Adams, J. (1990a). *You and Your Alarm.* Bristol: Enuresis Resource and Information Centre (ERIC, 65 St Michael's Hill, Bristol BS2 8DZ. Phone 0117-9264920).

Adams, J. (1990b). *Your Child's Alarm.* Bristol: Enuresis Resource and Information Centre (ERIC, 65 St Michael's Hill, Bristol BS2 8DZ. Phone 0117-9264920).

Azrin, N. and Besalel, V. (1979). *A Parent's Guide to Bedwetting Control.* New York: Simon and Schuster.

Butler, R. (1998). *Overcoming Bedwetting.* Dr Richard Butler, Leeds Community and Mental Health Services, High Royds Hospital, Menston, Ickley, West Yorkshire LS29 6AQ. Phone 01943–876151.

Clayden, G. and Agnarsson, V. (1992). *Constipation in Childhood: Information Booklet for Children and Parents.* In Appendix A of A. Buchanan (1992). *Children Who Soil. Assessment and Treatment.* Chichester: Wiley.

Houts, A. and Liebert, R. (1984). *Bedwetting: A Guide for Parents and Children.* Springfield, Ill: Charles C. Thomas.

4 Attention deficit hyperactivity disorder

Margretta Nolan and Alan Carr

Definitions

Attention deficit hyperactivity disorder, attention deficit disorder, hyperkinetic disorder, hyperkinesis and minimal brain dysfunction are some of the terms used for a syndrome characterized by persistent overactivity, impulsivity and difficulties in sustaining attention (Barkley, 1990; Hinshaw, 1994; Taylor, 1994). Throughout this chapter preference will be given to the term attention deficit hyperactivity disorder (ADHD) since this is currently the most widely used term. In Figure 4.1 the DSM IV(APA, 1994) diagnostic criteria for ADHD and the ICD 10 (WHO, 1992) criteria for Hyperkinetic Disorder are presented. The most noteworthy feature of the syndromes described in the two widely used classification systems is their similarity. Historically, a narrow definition of ADHD has been used in the UK and defined in the ICD classification system, with great emphasis being placed on the stability of the overactivity problems across home and school contexts. In contrast, in the US, this cross-situation stability has not been a core diagnostic criterion within previous editions of the DSM (Hinshaw, 1994). In view of this historical difference, it is particularly noteworthy that currently in both the North American DSM IV and the European ICD 10, it is stipulated that symptoms must be present in two or more settings such as home and school for a positive diagnosis to be made.

Historically the following features have been used to subtype ADHD:

- The pervasivness of the problem
- Presence or absence of both inattention and hyperactivity
- Co-morbidity with conduct disorder

The occurrence of the symptoms both within and outside the home, presence of both inattention and overactivity, and the presence of conduct disorder are all associated with a more serious condition which is less responsive to treatment and which has a poorer outcome (McArdle *et al.*, 1995). Both DSM IV and ICD 10 distinguish between subtypes of ADHD depending upon the patterning of symptomatology or the presence of co-morbid conditions.

DSM IV Attention deficit hyperactivity disorder	ICD 10 Hyperkinetic disorders
A. Either 1 or 2. 1. Six or more of the following symptoms of inattention have persisted for at least 6 months to a degree that is maladaptive and inconsistent with developmental level. **Inattention** a. Often fails to give close attention to details or makes careless mistakes in schoolwork, work or other activities b. Often has difficulty sustaining attention in tasks or play activities c. Often does not seem to listen when spoken to directly d. Often does not follow through on instructions and fails to finish schoolwork, chores or work duties e. Often has difficulty organizing tasks and activities f. Often avoids or dislikes tasks that require sustained mental effort g. Often loses things necessary for tasks or activities h. Is often easily distracted by extraneous stimuli i. Is often forgetful in daily activities 2. Six or more of the following symptoms of **hyperactivity-impulsivity** have persisted for at least 6 months to a degree that is maladaptive and inconsistent with developmental level. **Hyperactivity** a. Often fidgets with hands or feet or squirms in seat b. Often leaves seat in classroom or in other situations in which remaining seated is expected c. Often runs about or climbs excessively in situations in which it is inappropriate d. Often has difficulty playing or engaging in leisure activities quietly e. Is often on the go or acts as if driven by a motor f. Often talks excessively **Impulsivity** g. Often blurts out answer before questions have been completed h. Often has difficulty awaiting turn i. Often interrupts or intrudes on others B. Some of these symptoms were present before the age of 7 years C. Some impairment from the symptoms is present in **two or more settings** (e.g. home and school) D. Clinically significant impairment in social, academic or occupational functioning E. Not due to another disorder Specify: *Combined type* if inattention and overactivity-impulsivity are present; *Inattentive type* if overactivity is absent; *Hyperactive-impulsive type* if inattentivness is absent	The cardinal features are impaired attention and overactivity. Both are necessary for the diagnosis and should be evident in **more than one situation** (e.g. home or school). **Impaired attention** is manifested by prematurely breaking off from tasks and leaving activities unfinished. The children change frequently from one activity to another, seemingly losing interest in one task because they become diverted to another. These deficits in persistence and attention should be diagnosed only if they are excessive for the child's age and IQ. **Overactivity** implies excessive restlessness, especially in situations requiring relative calm. It may, depending upon the situation, involve the child running and jumping around, getting up from a seat when he or she was supposed to remain seated, excessive talkativeness and noisiness, or fidgeting and wriggling. The standard for judgement should be that the activity is excessive in the context of what is expected in the situation and by comparison with other children of the same age and IQ. This behavioural feature is most evident in structured, organized situations that require a high degree of behavioural self-control. The characteristic behaviour problems should be of early onset (before the age of 6 years) and long duration. Associated features include disinhibition in social relationships, recklessness in situations involving some danger, impulsive flouting of social rules, learning disorders, and motor clumsiness. Specify: *Hyperkinetic disorder with disturbance of activity and attention* when antisocial features of conduct disorder are absent; *Hyperkinetic conduct disorder* when criteria for both conduct disorder and hyperkinetic disorder are met

Figure 4.1 Diagnostic criteria for attention and hyperactivity syndromes in DSM IV and ICD 10.

Source Adapted from DSM IV (APA, 1994) and ICD 10 (WHO, 1992).

In DSM IV the main distinctions are between cases where inattention and overactivity are present or absent whereas co-morbid conduct problems are the basis for subtyping in ICD 10.

Evidence summarized by Hinshaw (1994) indicates that the inattentive and overactive subtypes of ADHD have distinct profiles. Children with the inattentive subtype of ADHD are described clinically as sluggish, apathetic daydreamers who are easily distracted and have difficulty completing assigned tasks within school because of learning difficulties. Within their family history there is a preponderance of learning disorders and emotional disorders such as anxiety and depression. Those with the hyperactive-impulsive subtype of ADHD are characterized by extreme overactivity, oppositional and aggressive behaviours. Conduct problems are their most notable school-based difficulties and they have a high rate of school suspension and special educational placement. Within their family history they have a preponderance of antisocial problems such as drug abuse and criminality and children with the hyperactive-impulsive profile are at risk for long-term antisocial behaviour problems and poor social adjustment. Children with both the inattentive and hyperactive-impulsive subtypes of ADHD have significant relationship difficulties with peers, school staff and family members and both respond to psychostimulant treatment although the inattentive subtype tends to respond to a lower dosage.

The primary distinction made in the ICD 10 system is between hyperkinetic conduct disorder, where a co-morbid conduct disorder is present, and cases where such co-morbidity is absent. Hinshaw (1994) in a review of differences between these two subgroups concluded that those children with co-morbid conduct disorder show greater academic problems and suffer more extreme relationship difficulties with peers, teachers and family members. While they show some response to psychostimulant treatment, they rarely respond to psychosocial individual and family interventions.

ADHD with co-morbid emotional disorders such as anxiety or depression, is not subclassified as a distinct condition within either ICD 10 or DSM IV. Children with such co-morbid profiles have been found to have a later onset for the disorder, fewer learning and cognitive problems and to be less responsive to stimulant medication than youngsters without co-morbid anxiety (Taylor, 1994).

ADHD is a particularly serious problem because youngsters with the core difficulties of inattention, overactivity and impulsivity may develop a wide range of secondary academic and relationship problems (Cantwell, 1996; Gaub and Carlson, 1997; Hinshaw, 1994). Attentional difficulties may lead to poor attainment in school. Impulsivity and aggression may lead to difficulties making and maintaining appropriate peer relationships and developing a supportive peer group. Inattention, impulsivity and overactivity make it difficult for youngsters with these attributes to conform to parental expectations and so children with ADHD often become embroiled in chronic conflictual relationships with their parents. In adolescence, impulsivity may lead to excessive risk taking with consequent complications such as drug abuse, road traffic accidents and dropping out of school. All of these risk-taking behaviours have knock-on effects and compromise later adjustment. As youngsters with ADHD become aware of their difficulties with regulating attention, activity and impulsivity and the failure that these deficits lead to within the family, peer group and school, they may also develop low self-esteem and depression. In light of the primary problems and secondary difficulties that may evolve in cases of ADHD, it is not surprising that for some the prognosis is poor (Hinshaw, 1994). For two-thirds of cases, the primary problems of inattention, impulsivity and hyperactivity persist into late adolescence and for some of these the primary symptoms persist into adulthood. Roughly a third develop significant antisocial behaviour problems in adolescence including conduct disorder and substance abuse and for most of this subgroup, these problems persist into adulthood leading to criminality. Occupational adjustment problems and suicide attempts occur in a small but significant minority of cases.

Epidemiology

Reviews of epidemiological studies of ADHD report overall prevalence rates varying from 1 to 19 per cent depending upon the stringency of the diagnostic criteria applied and the demographic characteristics of the populations studied (Cantwell, 1996; Cohen *et al.*, 1993; Gaub and Carlson, 1997; Hinshaw, 1994; McArdle *et al.*, 1995). Using DSM IV criteria a prevalence rate of about 3–5 per cent has been obtained. The prevalence of ADHD varies with gender and age. ADHD is more prevalent in boys than girls and in preadolescents than in late adolescents. Co-morbidity for conduct disorder and ADHD is about 20 per cent in community populations and possibly double this figure in clinic populations. Co-morbidity for emotional disorders, such as anxiety or depression, and ADHD is about 10 per cent in community populations. In clinical populations the co-morbidity rate may be twice this figure. Virtually all children with ADHD have attainment problems. However, co-morbid severe specific learning difficulties have been estimated to occur in 10 to 25 per cent of cases. A proportion of youngsters with ADHD have co-morbid developmental language delays and elimination problems although reliable epidemiological data are unavailable.

Previous reviews

Historically, individually oriented play therapy based on psychodynamic or client-centred theories was widely used as a treatment for children with ADHD. This tradition has yielded little empirical research and those studies that have been conducted, while promising, have not employed control groups. For example, Fonagy and Target (1994) found that of 69 per cent

of 93 cases who had disruptive behaviour disorders, after a year of psychodynamic treatment showed clinically significant improvement. Children with
oppositional defiant disorder were most likely to improve, those with conduct disorder were least likely to improve and those with ADHD showed
improvement rates that fell between these two groups.

Working within the cognitive-behavioural tradition, Meichenbaum and
Goodman (1971) developed an individual approach to treatment – self-
instructional training – where children with ADHD were coached in the use
of self-instructions to control the way in which they deployed their attention and controlled their impulses to engage in high levels of activity.
Researchers within this tradition have expanded Meichenbaum's original
treatment package to include other elements, notably social as well as
academic problem-solving skills training, and therapy-based contingency
management. However, the development of self-control through training
in the use of self-instructions remains the core feature of this treatment
approach. Extensive reviews of this literature have concluded that while
self-instructional training may have some effects on parent or teacher rated
behaviour problems, these effects are minimal and do not constitute clinically significant improvement (Abikoff, 1991; Hinshaw and Erhardt, 1991).
From their meta-analysis of this literature, Baer and Nietzel (1991) concluded that self-instructional training is maximally effective if therapy focuses
on both academic and social tasks and involves therapy-based contingency
management.

Within the behavioural tradition, a contingency-management approach
to the treatment of children with ADHD emerged from the seminal work
of Patterson (1965). This involved therapy-based contingency management
implemented directly by therapists within therapy sessions or laboratory-
based specialist classrooms. Children with ADHD were reinforced for
deploying their attention in a focused appropriate way and for reduced
inappropriate activity levels. Response-cost systems were used where children lost points for engaging in inappropriate behaviour. Such systems
have typically involved intensive schedules of reinforcement with therapists
or teachers prompting children to engage in appropriate behaviours and
administering reinforcement with high levels of frequency and immediacy.
While such approaches had the potential to strongly influence children's
behaviour, they ran the risk of leading to low generalizability (DuPaul and
Eckert, 1997). That is, they entailed the possibility that treatment effects
would be confined to treatment sessions or specialist classrooms.

Behavioural parent training and school-based contingency management
were developed to deal with this problem (Braswell and Bloomquist, 1991).
In these approaches parents or teachers were trained by therapists in contingency management procedures. They then implemented these contingency
management programmes to modify and normalize the behaviour of children
with ADHD in their home or classroom contexts. Typically parents and
teachers were trained to prompt and reinforce appropriate target behaviours

and to use response cost and time-out methods to reduce the frequency of target negative behaviours. Typically such training procedures have been referred to as behavioural parent training. While these programmes had the benefit of increasing the possibility of generalization of appropriate behaviour to home and school contexts, they ran the risk of reduced potency since typically reinforcement was delivered with lower levels of frequency and immediacy than therapy or special class-based contingency management programmes. Parents and teachers, due to other demands, were unable to offer frequent prompts and to be available to administer reinforcement immediately and frequently. In a review of studies of contingency management approaches for the treatment of children with ADHD, Hinshaw *et al.* (1998) concluded that programmes implemented by therapists in treatment sessions or specialist classrooms have profound immediate effects but these are short-lived and do not generalize beyond the classroom setting to the home or normal school context. Contingency management programmes implemented by parents and teachers, in contrast, have in a limited number of studies led to sustained clinically significant benefits.

Following the serendipitous discovery by Bradley (1937) of the positive effects of stimulants on the conduct and academic performance of disturbed children, more than a hundred controlled studies of the effects of stimulants on children with attention and hyperactivity problems have been conducted. Early studies examined the effects of dextroamphetamine, but the bulk of recent studies have focused on methylphenidate.

Following a thorough review of this literature, Greenhill (1998) concluded that stimulant therapy is effective in 70 per cent of cases in reducing the core symptoms of ADHD. Stimulants have a greater effect on behaviour than academic achievement. The effects of stimulants are short term and evidence for their long-term effectiveness has not been established.

The idea that combined psychological and pharmacological therapies might have synergistic effects has led to studies of the impact of combined treatment packages. Typically these studies have evaluated the effects of stimulant therapy combined with self-instructional training, behavioural parent training and school- or therapy-based contingency management. In these studies the effects of combined therapy packages have been compared with those of psychological treatments, stimulant therapy and/or various control conditions. Such control conditions have included placebo pills, psychological support groups for children which have acted as attention placebo conditions, and waiting list control groups. In a review of such studies Hinshaw *et al.* (1998) concluded that the short-term effects of stimulant therapy are greater than those of behavioural parent training and contingency management programmes. While contingency management interventions add little incremental value to the short-term impact of high dosage (.6–.8 mg/kg body weight) stimulant therapy, they may reduce the requirement for high dosages by 50 per cent and they may lead to long-term maintenance of treatment gains.

Method

The aim in this chapter was to review well-designed studies of the effects of psychological interventions or combined psychological and pharmacological interventions for children and adolescents with ADHD. A computer-based literature search of the PsychLit database was conducted. Terms that defined the disorder, such as *attention deficit hyperactivity disorder, hyperactivity, impulsiveness, inattention* and *hyperkinesis* were combined with terms that defined interventions such as *treatment, therapy, intervention, contingency management, behavioural parent training, self-instructional training, social skills training, behaviour therapy, cognitive-behaviour therapy, family therapy, methylphenidate* and *stimulant therapy*. The search, which was confined to English language journals, covered the period 1977 to 1997 inclusively. A manual search through bibliographies of all recent review papers on psychological interventions for ADHD was also conducted. Treatment outcome studies were selected for inclusion in this review if they contained a psychological or psychological and pharmacological treatment condition or group and a control or comparison condition or group; if at least five cases were included in the active treatment group; and if reliable and valid pre- and post-treatment measures were included in the design of the study. Single-case designs and studies reported in dissertations or convention papers were not included in the review. Using these inclusion and exclusion criteria twenty studies were selected.

Characteristics of the studies

Characteristics of the studies are set out in Table 4.1. All of the studies were conducted between 1978 and 1993 and all were conducted in either the USA or Canada. Of the twenty studies eleven evaluated the effects of psychological interventions and nine examined the effects of combined psychological and pharmacological interventions. Eighteen studies employed comparative group designs and two used repeated measures designs where the same group of cases participated in two or more different treatment conditions sequentially. One thousand and ninety-six children were contained in the 66 treatment groups or conditions of the twenty studies. Of these 1096 children 862 were in treatment groups and 234 were in control conditions. Participants' ages ranged from three to eighteen years. For the sixteen studies where gender data were given, 87 per cent of cases were male and 13 per cent were female. Co-morbidity data were reported in only eight studies and for these, oppositional defiant disorder and conduct disorder were the most commonly reported co-morbid conditions. For the ten studies where referral information was given, schools and physicians were the principal referring agents. Cognitive and/or behavioural treatment interventions were evaluated in all of the studies selected. All of the programmes were conducted on an outpatient basis with two in community

Table 4.1 Characteristics of treatment outcome studies for ADHD

Study no.	Study type	Authors	Year	N per gp	Mean age & range	Gender	Co-morbid diagnosis	Referral	Treatment setting	Treatment duration
1	PI	Kendall and Finch	1978	SIT + TB-CM = 10 C = 10	11 y	m 80% f 20%	90% IBP		Hospital OP	6 sess
2	PI	Kendall and Wilcox	1980	SIT-CON + TB-CM = 11 SIT-ABS + TB-CM = 11 C = 11	11 y 8–13 y	m 76% f 24%			School	12 sess over 3 w
3	PI	Kendall & Braswell	1982	SIT-ABS + TB-CM = 9 TB-CM = 9 C = 9	10 y 8–13 y	m 85% f 15%		School	School	12 sess over 6 w
4	PI	Frankel et al.	1997	SST = 49 C = 24	9 y 6–13 y	m 77% f 23%	38% ODD	Physicians School	Hospital OP	12 sess over 12 w
5	PI	Pisterman et al.	1992	BPT = 23 C = 22	4 y 3–6 y	m 91% f 9%		Physicians	Hospital OP	12 sess
6	PI	Anastopoulos et al.	1993	BPT = 19 C = 15	6–11 y	m 74% f 26%	41% ODD 6% IBP		University, OP	9 sess over 8 w
7	PI	Barkley et al.	1992	BPT = 20 PS + CT = 21 FT = 20	12–18 y				Hospital OP	10 sess over 10 w
8	PI	Horn et al.	1987	BPT + SIT = 7 BPT = 6 SIT = 6	10 y 7–12 y			Physicians School	Community OP	16 sess over 8 w
9	PI	Abikoff and Gittleman	1984	BPT + SB-CM = 28 C = 28	9 y 6–13 y	m 96% f 4%		School	School	15 weeks
10	PI	Horn et al.	1990	BPT + SIT + SB-CM = 11 BPT = 12 SIT = 11	9 y 7–11 y	m 81% f 19%	67% CD 24% ODD		University OP	27 sess over 12 w
11	PI	Bloomquist et al.	1991	BPT + SB-CM + SIT = 11 SB-CM = 12 C = 13	9 y	m 69% f 31%	35% ODD	School	School	29 sess over 10 w
12	PI-ST	Cohen et al.	1981	SIT + ST = 6 SIT = 6 ST = 8 C = 4	6 y	m 88% f 12%			School	20 sess over 10 w
13	PI-ST	Brown et al.	1985	SIT + ST = 10 SIT = 10 ST = 10 C = 10	11 y 6–12 y	m 100%		Physicians School	University OP	24 sess over 12 w

No.	Type	Author	Year	Design / Groups	Age	Gender	Comorbidity	Setting	Location	Sessions
14	PI-ST	Hinshaw et al.	1984	SIT + ST = 11 SIT + P = 10	8–13 y	m 100%		Physicians School	Community OP	6 sess over 3 w
15	PI-ST	Abikoff and Gittleman	1985	SIT + ST = 21 ST + SUP = 14 ST = 15	10 y 6–13 y	m 90% f 10%			School University OP	32 sess over 16 w
16	PI-ST	Brown et al.	1986	SIT + ST = 9 SIT + P = 10 ST + SUP = 8 SUP + P = 8	9 y 5–14 y	m 85% f 15%	15% CD	Physicians School	University OP	22 sess over 12 w
17	PI-ST	Firestone et al.	1986	BPT + ST = 30 BPT + P = 21 ST = 22	5–9 y			Physicians	Hospital OP	9 sess
18	PI-ST	Carlson et al.	1992	SB-CM + Hi-ST = 24 SB-CM + Lo-ST = 24 SB-CM + P = 24 SB – Hi-ST = 24 Lo-ST = 24 P = 24	9 y 6–13 y	m 100%	29% CD 50% ODD		Summer day programme	40 sess over 8 w
19	PI-ST	Pelham et al.	1993	Repeated measures design SB-CM + Hi-ST = 31 SB-CM + Lo-ST = 31 SB-CM + P = 31 Hi-ST = 31 Lo-ST = 31 P = 31	8 y 5–10 y	m 100%	50% CD 30% ODD		Summer day programme	40 sess over 8 w
20	PI-ST	Horn et al. Ialongo et al.	1991 1993	Repeated measures design BPT + SIT + SB-CM + hi-ST = 16 BPT + SIT + SB-CM + lo-ST = 16 BPT + SIT + SB-CM + P = 16 Hi-ST = 16 Lo-ST = 16 P = 16	7–11 y		8% CD 16% ODD		University OP	27 sess over 12 w

Key PI = A study of psychological intervention only. PI-ST = A study of combined psychological intervention and stimulant treatment. BPT = Behavioural parent training. SIT = Self-instructional training. SIT-CON = Concrete self-instructional training. SIT-ABS = Abstract self-instructional training. TB-CM = Therapy-based contingency management. SB-CM = School-based contingency management. PS & CT = Problem solving and communication skills training. SST = Social skills training. FT = Family therapy. ST = Stimulant therapy with ethylphenidate between 10 and 40 mg per day in a divided dose and based on .3–.4 mg/kg body weight. Lo-ST = 0.3–0.4 mg/kg, bid of methylphenidate. Hi-ST = 0.6–0.8 mg/kg, bid of methylphenidate. C = Control group. CD = Conduct disorder. ODD = Oppositional defiant disorder. IBP = Internalizing behavioural problems. OP = Outpatient. d = day. w = week. m =month. y = year. sess = sessions.

settings; five in hospitals, six in university outpatient clinics, six in schools and two in school-based summer treatment programmes. The number of sessions of treatment ranged from six to 40 sessions over three to sixteen weeks.

Methodological features

Methodological features of the twenty studies included in this review are presented in Table 4.2. All of the studies included in this review contained control or comparison groups or conditions. All studies contained diagnostically homogeneous groups which were assessed before and after treatment on reliable and valid measures. In 60 per cent of studies parent ratings of improvement were recorded and in 75 per cent of studies teacher ratings of behavioural changes were made. Parent- and teacher-rated symptomatic improvement after treatment and at follow-up were commonly assessed with the Conners Parent Rating Scale or the Conners Teacher Rating Scale (Conners, 1990), both of which contain a specific hyperactivity factor score. Researcher-rated improvements, which were conducted in sixteen studies, were based on observations of specific classroom behaviours such as on-task and off-task behaviour or disruptive behaviour. Improvements in relationships within the child's family system and social network were conducted in only two of these twenty studies, but self-esteem was assessed in four studies, attentional deployment in eleven, and academic achievement in eight. *The Piers-Harris Children's Self-Concept Scale* (Piers and Harris, 1969) was commonly used to assess self-esteem and the *Wide Range Achievement Test* (Wilkinson, 1993) to assess academic performance. To assess children's capacity to deploy attention in a sustained manner a range of laboratory test were used and these included the Matching Familiar Figures Test (Kagan, 1966), the *Continuous Performance Test* (Conners, 1995) and the Porteus Mazes (Porteus, 1955). In 70 per cent of studies cases were randomly assigned to conditions. In 40 per cent of studies cases within conditions were matched for co-morbidity. In 75 per cent of studies, groups were demographically similar. In 50 per cent of studies follow-up assessments were conducted two or more months following the end of treatment. In 50 per cent of studies deterioration was assessed and in 80 per cent, drop-out rates were reported. In 20 per cent of studies information on engagement in further treatment was given. In 45 per cent of studies information on both statistical and clinical significance of treatment gains was reported. Experienced therapists were used in 50 per cent of studies and in eight of the fourteen studies (57 per cent) where two or more treatments were compared, information given in the reports suggested that treatments were equally valued by the research team. In 75 per cent of studies treatments were manualized but in only 35 per cent of studies was information on supervision given. In 55 per cent of studies treatment integrity was checked. Different treatments compared were equally valued. In 80 per cent of studies information on concurrent treatment was given but in only 10 per cent of studies

Table 4.2 Methodological features of ADHD studies

Feature	Study number																			
	S1	S2	S3	S4	S5	S6	S7	S8	S9	S10	S11	S12	S13	S14	S15	S16	S17	S18	S19	S20
Control or comparison group or condition	1	1	1	1	1	1	1	1	1	1	1	1	1	1	1	1	1	1	1	1
Random assignment	1	1	1	1	1	0	0	1	0	0	0	1	1	1	1	1	1	0	0	1
Diagnostic homogeneity	0	1	1	1	1	1	1	1	1	1	1	1	1	1	1	1	1	1	1	1
Comparable for co-morbidity	0	0	0	1	0	1	0	1	1	1	1	0	0	0	0	1	0	0	0	0
Demographic similarity	1	1	1	1	1	1	1	1	1	0	1	1	1	0	1	1	0	1	1	1
Pre-treatment assessment	1	1	1	1	1	1	1	1	1	1	1	1	1	1	1	1	1	1	1	1
Post-treatment assessment	1	1	1	1	1	1	1	1	1	1	1	1	1	1	1	1	1	1	1	1
Two-month follow-up assessment	1	1	1	0	0	0	1	0	0	1	0	0	1	1	0	1	1	0	0	0
Children's self-report	1	1	1	1	0	0	0	0	0	1	1	0	1	0	0	0	0	1	0	1
Parent's ratings	0	0	1	1	0	0	0	1	0	1	0	0	1	0	0	1	0	0	0	1
Teacher's ratings	0	1	1	1	0	0	1	1	0	1	1	1	1	0	0	1	0	0	0	0
Therapist's ratings	1	1	1	0	0	1	0	0	0	0	0	0	0	1	1	0	1	1	1	1
Researcher's ratings	1	1	1	0	1	1	1	1	1	1	1	1	1	1	1	1	1	1	1	1
Child's symptom assessed	1	1	1	0	1	1	1	1	1	0	1	1	1	0	1	1	1	1	1	1
System assessed	0	0	1	0	0	1	0	1	0	1	0	1	0	0	0	1	0	0	0	0
Deterioration assessed	0	0	1	0	0	0	0	1	1	1	1	0	0	0	1	1	1	0	0	0
Drop-out assessed	1	0	1	1	0	1	0	1	1	0	1	0	1	0	0	1	1	1	0	1
Clinical significance of change assessed	0	0	0	1	0	1	0	1	1	1	1	0	0	0	0	1	0	0	0	1
Experienced therapists used	0	0	0	0	0	0	1	1	1	0	0	0	0	0	0	1	1	0	1	1
Treatments were equally valued	0	1	1	0	1	0	0	1	0	1	0	0	0	1	1	1	0	0	1	1
Treatments were manualized	1	1	1	0	1	1	1	1	1	1	1	1	1	1	1	1	1	1	0	1
Therapy supervision was provided	0	0	0	0	0	0	0	1	0	1	1	1	0	0	1	0	0	0	0	1
Treatment integrity checked	0	0	1	1	0	0	0	1	1	1	1	0	1	1	1	1	1	1	1	1
Data on concurrent treatment given	1	0	0	1	0	0	1	1	1	1	0	0	1	1	1	1	1	1	1	1
Data on subsequent treatment given	0	0	0	0	0	0	0	1	0	0	0	1	0	0	1	0	0	0	0	0
Total	15	13	19	12	15	16	15	20	13	19	17	15	13	11	19	20	15	12	12	19

Key: S = study. 1 = design feature was present. 0 = design feature was absent.

was information on engagement in further treatment given. Overall this was a methodologically robust group of studies.

Substantive findings

Effect sizes and other outcome results of the eleven studies which focused exclusively on the effects of psychological treatments of ADHD are given in Table 4.3. Results of studies of combined psychological and pharmacological interventions are given in Table 4.4. A narrative summary of key findings from all twenty studies is presented in Table 4.5. What follows is a summary of these studies.

Psychological treatment

Eleven studies in this review examined the effects of psychological treatment on ADHD in children and adolescents. Three of these studies were concerned primarily with the effects of self-instructional training combined with therapy-based contingency management (Kendall and Braswell, 1982; Kendall and Finch, 1978; Kendall and Wilcox, 1980); one evaluated a social skills training programme (Frankel *et al.*, 1997); three assessed the effects of behavioural parent training (Anastopoulos *et al.*, 1993; Barkley *et al.*, 1992; Pisterman *et al.*, 1992); and four examined the effects of multicomponent programmes involving behavioural parent training, self-instructional training and school-based contingency management (Abikoff and Gittleman, 1984; Bloomquist *et al.*, 1991; Horn *et al.*, 1987, 1990).

Self-instructional training and social skills training

In Kendall's series of three investigations of self-instructional training, the first study (Kendall and Finch, 1978) evaluated the effects of routine self-instructional training. The six-session treatment programme involved Meichenbaum and Goodman's (1971) self-instructional approach combined with a response-cost procedure. In the self-instructional training the therapist demonstrated how to use increasingly covert self-instructions from speaking aloud to engaging in covert self-talk to guide completing particular tasks such as finishing a picture. There were five steps in this self-instructional protocol: problem definition, problem approach, focusing attention, selecting an answer and self-reinforcing for correct performance. For this training, a standard set of materials was used over the six sessions covering the areas of conceptual thinking, attention to detail, recognition of identities, sequential recognition, visual closure and visual reproduction. For example, with sequential recognition children had to work out *what comes next* in a sequence from an array of alternatives. For the response-cost procedure, children were given ten poker chips and informed that they could buy items from a reinforcement menu with the chips after the session but could lose chips for making mistakes during the session. Cases in the control group covered the six-session curriculum but did not receive self-instructional training or undergo response-cost procedures.

In Kendall's second study (Kendall and Wilcox, 1980), similar self-instructional and response-cost therapy techniques and teaching materials were used over twelve sessions, but for one group, concrete self-instructions which focused on the specific task at hand were used whereas for the second treatment condition, children were coached in using abstract self-instructions. For example, children in the concrete self-instructional training group were taught to use task-specific self-instructions such as 'I'm to find the picture that doesn't match; I must look at the pictures'. In contrast, children in the abstract self-instructional training programme used more general, conceptually based self-instructions such as 'My first step is to make sure that I know what I'm supposed to do; I should think about only what I am doing right now'.

In Kendall's third study (Kendall and Braswell, 1982) the self-instructional training procedure initially helped the child to develop concrete self-statements but later, more general abstract self-instructions were taught. In addition, a broader curriculum was used which covered social as well as academic problem solving. This treatment, combined with the response-cost procedure used in the other two studies, was compared with a programme that employed the use of response cost alone and a control condition where neither self-instruction nor response-cost procedures were used.

For the self-instructional training programmes combined with therapy-based response-cost procedures evaluated in these three studies, effect sizes based on teacher-reported improvements ranged from 0.8 to 1.3, with the highest effect size occurring in the group that received the abstract or conceptually based self-instructional training. This indicates that from teachers' perspective, the average child who participated in these programmes fared better after treatment than 79 to 90 per cent of cases in the control group. At four to twelve weeks' follow-up, excluding the group who received concrete rather than abstract self-instructional training and who all relapsed, effect sizes based on teacher-reported improvements ranged from 0.7 to 1.3. Thus, four to twelve weeks following treatment, the average treated cases fared better than 76–90 per cent of cases in the control group on teacher-rated improvements.

Effect sizes for therapist-rated improvement following treatment ranged from 1.8 to 2.0 and at four to twelve weeks' follow-up in the third study the effect size based on therapists' ratings was 1.8. These results indicate that from therapists' perspective the average treated case fared better after treatment and at follow-up than 96 per cent of untreated cases.

Effect sizes for self-rated improvement, parent-rated improvement, self-esteem, and reading achievement both following treatment and at follow-up were small and ranged from −0.3 to 0.5. Effect sizes for performance on laboratory tests of vigilance and attentional deployment following treatment

Table 4.3 Summary of results of effects of psychological treatments for ADHD

Variable	Study number and condition																
	Study 1	Study 2		Study 3		Study 4	Study 5	Study 6	Study 7		Study 8		Study 9	Study 10		Study 11	
	SIT + TB-CM	SIT-CON + TB-CM	SIT-ABS + TB-CM	SIT-ABS + TB-CM	TB-CM	SST	BPT	BPT	BPT > PS & CT	BPT > FT	BPT + SIT > SIT	BPT + SIT > BPT	BPT + SB-CM	BPT + SB-CM > SIT	BPT + SIT + SB-CM > BPT	BPT + SIT + SB-CM	SB-CM
Symptomatic improvement after treatment																	
Children's self-report	0.0	0.3	0.1	–	–				–	–	–	–	–	–	–	–	–
Parent's ratings	–	–	–	–0.3	–0.1	1.1	–	–	–	–	0.2	0.9	–	0.6	0.6	–	–
Teacher's ratings	0.8	0.8	1.3	0.8	0.0	1.0	–	1.3	–	–	–0.3	–0.6	–	–0.2	–0.4	–0.1	–0.1
Therapist's ratings	–	1.8	2.0	1.8	0.9	–	–	–	–	–	–	–	–	–	–	–	–
Researcher's ratings	–	–	–	–	–	–	0.5	–	–	–	–	–	0.7	–	–	>2.0	<2.0
Symptomatic improvement at follow-up																	
Children's self-report	0.0	–0.1	0.0	–	–				–	–	–	–	–	–	–	–	–
Parent's ratings	–	–	–	–0.2	0.0	–	–	–	–	–	–1.0	.4	–	.6	.7	–	–
Teacher's ratings	1.3	–0.1	0.8	0.7	–2.0	–	–	–	–	–	–0.1	–.3	–	.5	–.5	0.4	0.1
Therapist's ratings	–	–	–	1.8	0.9	–	–	–	–	–	–	–	–	–	–	–	–
Researcher's ratings	–	–	–	–	–	–	0.7	–	–	–	–	–	–	–	–	>2.0	>2.0

Measure	Values (by treatment column, left → right)
Systemic and cognitive improvement after treatment	
Parent–child interaction	1.3 – – – – – 1.2 0.6 – – – – 0.9 0.7 – – – – – –
Children's self-esteem	– 0.5 0.9 0.4 –0.3 0.5 –0.2 0.7 0.3 –1.0 –0.2 0.5 0.4
Performance on lab tests	1.3 0.1 0.4 0.5 0.6 –0.2 –0.4 0.5 0.3 –0.7
Reading achievement	– 0.1 0.5 0.2 0.5 0.2 –0.5
Systemic and cognitive improvement at follow-up	
Parent–child interaction	0.8 – – – – – 1.3 – – – 1.1 – – –
Children's self-esteem	– 0.2 –0.4 0.2 –0.4 0.2 0.3 0.7 0.3 –1.0 0.3 0.0 –0.4
Performance on lab tests	0.0 1.0 0.2 0.6 0.4 0.2 0.7 0.3 –0.3
Reading achievement	– 0.2 0.7 0.3 –0.3
Positive clinical outcomes	
% improved after treatment	83% 65% 64% 20% (>19%) 20% (>5%) 51% 36% (>9%) 36% (>17%)
% improved at follow-up	65% 68% 73% (>27%) 73% (>25%)
Negative clinical outcomes	
% Deterioration	15% 10% (>0%) 10% (>0%)
% Drop-out	15% 21% 5% 5% 15% (>15%) 23% (>15%) 23% (>20%)

Key BPT = Behavioural parent training. SIT = Self-instructional training. SIT-CON = Concrete self-instructional training. SIT-ABS = Abstract self-instructional training. TB-CM = Therapy-based contingency management. SB-CM = School-based contingency management. PS & CT = Problem solving and communication skills training. SST = Social skills training. FT = Family therapy. ST = Stimulant therapy with methylphenidate between 10 and 40 mg per day in a divided dose and based on .3–.4 mg/kg body weight. Lo-ST = 0.3–0.4 mg/kg, bid of methylphenidate. Hi-ST = 0.6–0.8 mg/kg, bid of methylphenidate. S = Improvement was significant at $p < .05$ but insufficient data were provided to calculate.

Table 4.4 Summary of results of effects of combined psychological intervention and stimulant therapy for ADHD

Variable	Study 12		Study 13		Study 14	Study 15	Study 16		Study 17		Study 18	Study 19	Study 20
Treatment condition (Study number and treatment condition)	SIT + ST > SIT		SIT + ST > SIT	SIT + ST > ST	SIT + ST > SIT + P	SIT + ST > ST	SIT + ST > SIT + P	SIT + ST > SUP	BPT + ST > BPT + P	BPT + ST > ST	SB-CM + Hi-ST / SB-CM + lo-ST / Hi-ST > SB-CM + P / Lo-ST	SB-CM + Hi-ST / SB-CM + lo-ST / Hi-ST > SB-CM + P / Lo-ST	BPT + SIT + SB-CM + Hi-ST / BPT + SIT + SB-CM + lo-ST / Hi-ST > BPT + SIT + SB-CM + P / Lo-ST
Symptomatic improvement after treatment													
Children's self-report	–	–	0.3	0.1	–	–	–	–	–	–	0.4	–	0.0
Parent's ratings	0.2	–0.9	1.4	0.2	–	0.0	0.9	0.0	0.7	0.0	–	–	0.0
Teacher's ratings	0.8	0.1	0.9	0.0	–	0.4	0.2	–0.7	0.8	0.0	–	0.6	0.6
Therapist's ratings	–	–	–	–	–	–	–	–	–	–	–	–	–
Researcher's ratings	–	–	–	–	S	–	–	–	–	–	0.5	0.6	–
Symptomatic improvement at follow-up													
Children's self-report	–	–	2.4	0.3	–	–	–	–	–	–	–	–	0.0
Parent's ratings	–	–	0.8	–0.4	–	0.3	–0.5	–0.6	–0.4	0.0	–	–	S
Teacher's ratings	–	–	0.7	0.0	–	–0.3	0.1	–0.1	0.0	0.2	–	–	0.0
Therapist's ratings	–	–	–	–	–	–	–	–	–	–	–	–	–
Researcher's ratings	–	–	–	–	–	–	–	–	–	–	–	–	–

Systemic and cognitive improvement after treatment

Parent–child interaction	0.8	–	–	–	–	–	–	–	–	–
Children's self-esteem	0.6	–	0.6	1.0	–	–0.9	–	0.6	–	–
Performance on lab tests	–	–	0.0	0.0	0.0	–0.3	–	0.0	–	–
Reading achievement	–	0.2	–0.2	0.1	0.1	–	0.3	–	–	–

Systemic and cognitive improvement at follow-up

Parent–child interaction	–	–	–	–	–	–	–	–	–	–
Children's self-esteem	–	–	–	0.9	–	0.0	–	0.9	–	–
Performance on lab tests	–	–	0.9	0.2	0.4	0.0	–	0.3	–	–
Reading achievement	–	0.5	–0.3	–0.1	0.4	–0.5	–	0.4	–	–

Positive clinical outcomes

% improved after treatment	–	–	–	–	–	–	–	–	57% > 45%	–
% improved at follow-up	50% > 50%	50% > 50%	–	–	–	–	–	–	–	–

Negative clinical outcomes

% Deterioration	–	–	–	–	–	13%	–	–	–	–
% Drop-out	–	0%	0%	–	85%	13%	–	–	18%	–
% Engaged in further treatment	–	–	–	–	–	–	–	–	–	–

Key BPT = Behavioural parent training. SIT = Self-instructional training. SIT-CON = Concrete self-instructional training. SIT-ABS = Abstract self-instructional training. TB-CM = Therapy-based contingency management. SB-CM = School-based contingency management. PS & CT = Problem solving and contingency management. FT = family therapy. ST = Stimulant therapy with methylphenidate between 10 and 40 mg per day in a divided dose and based on .3–.4 mg/kg body weight. Lo-ST = 0.3–0.4 mg/kg, bid of methylphenidate. Hi-ST = 0.6–0.8 mg/kg, bid of methylphenidate. S = Improvement was significant at p < .05 but insufficient data were provided to calculate.

Table 4.5 Summary of main findings of twenty treatment outcome studies of ADHD

Study no.	Study type	Authors	Year	N per gp	No. of sessions	Group differences	Key findings
1	PI	Kendall and Finch	1978	1. SIT + TB-CM = 10 2. C = 10	6	1 > 2	• The SIT + TB-CM group improved in teacher-rated impulsivity, MFFT, but not self-reported impulsivity or teacher-rated conflicts.
2	PI	Kendall and Wilcox	1980	1. SIT-CON + TB-CM = 11 2. SIT-ABS + TB-CM = 11 3. C = 11	12	2 > 1 > 3	• Both SIT-ABS and SIT-CON groups improved on teacher-rated impulsivity but the SIT-ABS group showed greatest improvement. • No improvement on self-reported impulsivity or tests of attentional deployment (MFFT and Porteus Mazes) occurred.
3	PI	Kendall and Braswell	1982	1. SIT-ABS + TB-CM = 9 2. TB-CM = 9 3. C = 9	12	1 > 2 > 3	• Overall the SIT-ABS treatment was superior to the TB-CM treatment. • Teachers' ratings of child's self-control post-treatment were higher for the SIT-ABS + TB-CM group but this difference washed out at 1 month follow-up. • Therapist's ratings of improvement were greatest for the SIT-ABS – TB-CM group. • Both treatments led to improvements in teacher-rated hyperactivity. • Performance on matching familiar figures test; reading, spelling and arithmetic subtests of the WRAT; self-esteem and parent-rated control and hyperactivity for both conditions were the same as those shown by the control group.
4	PI	Frankel *et al.*	1997	1. SST = 49 2. C = 24	12	1 > 2	• Children in the SST group showed improvements in parent-reported self-control and assertion and teacher-rated withdrawal, likeability and aggression.
5	PI	Pisterman *et al.*	1992	1. BPT = 23 2. C = 22	12	1 > 2	• For preschoolers with ADHD children whose parents received group-based BPT increased compliance with parental requests and parent–child interaction also improved. • 65% of cases improved clinically and remained improved at 3-month follow up.
6	PI	Anastopoulos *et al.*	1993	1. BPT = 19 2. C = 15	9	1 > 2	• Children in the BPT group improved on the ADHD rating scale.

							Findings
7	PI	Barkley et al.	1992	1. BPT = 20 2. PS + CT = 21 3. FT = 20	10	1 = 2 > 3	• At a systemic level the BPT group improved on the parent and child domains of the parenting stress index and the parents also improved on an index of parenting self-efficacy. • For adolescents with ADHD, BPT was as effective as PS + CT and a little better than FT with about 20% showing clinically significant improvement.
8	PI	Horn et al.	1987	1. BPT + SIT = 7 2. BPT = 6 3. SIT = 6	16	3 > 1 = 2	• Overall the outcome for children receiving SIT was slightly superior to that of children receiving BPT or a combined treatment package which included both treatments. • At one-month follow-up children in the SIT group obtained lower hyperactivity scores on the CPRS and in this way SIT was superior to the other two approaches. • The outcome for cases receiving SIT, BPT and the combined package was similar after treatment and at one-month follow-up on all other parent- and teacher-rated symptoms, child self-concept, child performance on lab tests which assessed attentional deployment (MFFT) and achievement tests (WRAT). • Improvement was associated with the following factors: level of social support available for parents; children's capacity to reflect on their problems and children's locus of control.
9	PI	Abikoff and Gittleman	1984	1. BPT + SB-CM = 28 2. C = 28	15w	1 > 2	• Children who received the BPT + SB-CM package showed significant reductions in aggression, but not hyperactivity and inattention.
10	PI	Horn et al.	1990	1. BPT + SIT + SB-CM = 11 2. BPT = 12 3. SIT = 11	27	1 > 2 = 3	• When cases were classified on the CBCL externalizing scale as improved or not following treatment, the combined treatment (BPT + SIT + SB-CM) led to more improvement than either BPT or SIT. • All three treatments led to parent- and teacher-rated improvements in behaviour from pre- to post-test on the CBCL and the CTRS. • None of the treatments led to teacher-rated improvements on the CTRS at follow-up. • None of the treatments had a significant effect on achievement test (WRAT) scores, lab tests of attentional deployment (CPT), or self-concept.

Table 4.5 (cont'd)

Study no.	Study type	Authors	Year	N per gp	No. of sessions	Group differences	Key findings
11	PI	Bloomquist et al.	1991	1. BPT + SB-CM + SIT = 11 2. SB-CM = 12 3. C = 13	29	1 > 2 > 3	• The multicomponent programme (BPT + SB-CM + SIT) was more effective than the SB-CM programme in improving on-task behaviour in school but at one-month follow-up this effect washed out. • The programmes had no effects on teacher or child ratings of adjustment.
12	PI-ST	Cohen et al.	1981	1. SIT + ST = 6 2. SIT = 6 3. ST = 8 4. C = 4	20	1 = 2 = 3 = 4	• For kindergarten children with AHD all three treatment packages were no more effective than no treatment on parent and teacher ratings on the Conners' scales, lab tests of attentional deployment (MFFT), and self-concept.
13	PI-ST	Brown et al.	1985	1. SIT + ST = 10 2. SIT = 10 3. ST = 10 4. C = 10	24	1 = 2 > ST > 4	• For pre-adolescent boys with ADHD, combined SIT and ST treatment was no better than ST alone and both were better than SIT. • Improvements for parent and teacher ratings on the Conners scales occurred for the SIT + ST and ST groups. • SIT + ST and ST groups improved their scores on lab tests of attentional deployment (MFFT). • None of the groups improved on measures of academic achievement (WRAT).
14	PI-ST	Hinshaw et al.	1984	1. SIT + ST = 11 2. SIT + P = 10	6	1 > 2	• The SIT + ST package produced optimal effects. Decreases in the intensity of behaviour when provoked occurred as a result of the ST component and increases in the use of self-control strategies when provoked occurred as a result of SIT.
15	PI-ST	Abikoff and Gittleman	1985	1. SIT + ST = 21 2. ST + SUP = 14 3. ST = 15	32	1 = 2 = 3	• Following treatment there were no differences between the three conditions on parent or teacher behaviour ratings, lab tests of attentional deployment (MFFT) or achievement tests (WRAT).

16	PI-ST	Brown et al.	1986	1. SIT + ST = 9 2. SIT + P = 10 3. ST + SUP = 8 4. SUP + P = 8	• After treatment children ceased medication for one month and 85% of children resumed medication due to exacerbation of symptomatology, indicating that SIT does not give children with ADHD skills required for relapse prevention. • Overall this study showed that SIT and ST alone and combined are ineffective in treating ADHD. • In this study, ST was discontinued for a week before post-testing which revealed no group differences for parent- or teacher-rated hyperactivity, attentional deployment (MFFT) or achievement (WRAT).
				$1 = 2 = 3 = 4$	
17	PI-ST	Firestone et al.	1986	1. BPT + ST = 30 2. BPT + P = 21 3. ST = 22	• After treatment ST alone and in combination with BPT was superior to BPT in improving teacher-rated hyperactivity, parent-rated conduct problems and attentional deployment in laboratory tests (delayed reaction time), but not achievement test scores. • At two-year follow-up, intergroup differences washed out, so the benefits of ST were short term.
				$1 = 3 > 2$	
18	PI-ST	Carlson et al.	1992	1. SB-CM + Hi-ST = 24 2. SB-CM + Lo-ST = 24 3. SB-CM + P = 24 4. Hi-ST = 24 5. Lo-ST = 24 6. P = 24 Repeated measures design	• The overall finding of this study was that high or low dose ST combined with CB-CM had a positive impact on classroom behaviour, while only ST (regardless of the dosage) had a positive impact on academic performance. • For classroom observations of on-task behaviour and disruptive behaviour three conditions produced the best results: the high ST condition alone and in combination with SB-CM and the Low ST condition in combination with SB-CM. The low ST condition and the SB-CM + P treatment packages were less effective than these three conditions but were more effective than the placebo control condition. • For academic achievement and children's self-reports of rule following and academic adjustment all four conditions involving ST led to more improvement than the conditions where ST was not employed.
				For class behaviour $1 = 2 = 4 = 5 > 3 = 6$ For on-task behaviour $1 = 2 = 4 > 3 = 5 > 6$ For achievement $1 = 2 = 4 = 5 > 3 = 6$	

Table 4.5 (cont'd)

Study no.	Study type	Authors	Year	N per gp	No. of sessions	Group differences	Key findings
19	PI-ST	Pelham et al.	1993	1. SB-CM + Hi-ST = 31 2. SB-CM + Lo-ST = 31 3. SB-CM + P = 31 4. Hi-ST = 31 5. Lo-ST = 31 6. P = 31 Repeated measures design	40	1 = 4 > 2 = 5 > 3 > 6	• The overall finding of this study was that both SB-CM and ST improved classroom behaviour and academic performance, but the impact of ST was twice that of SB-CM. • For the low ST condition the incremental value of increasing the ST dosage from .3 to .6 mg/kg or of combining it with SB-CM was negligible. • Adding low or high dose ST to SB-CM made a substantial difference to classroom behaviour and academic performance.
20	PI-ST	Horn et al. Ialongo et al.	1991a 1993	1. BPT + SIT + SB-CM + hi-ST = 16 2. BPT + SIT + SB-CM + lo-ST = 16 3. BPT + SIT + SB-CM + P = 16 4. Hi-ST = 16 5. Lo-ST = 16 6. P = 16	27	For class behaviour 1 = 2 = 4 > 3 = 5 > 6 For on-task behaviour & achievement 1 = 2 = 4 = 5 > 3 > 6	• After treatment, cases that received low dose ST with SIT and SB-CM were as improved as those that received high dose ST alone on teacher- (but not parent-) rated hyperactivity. • Cases that received medication (regardless of whether this was combined with psychological intervention) made improvements on researcher-rated off-task behaviour, self-concept, laboratory measures of attentional deployment (CPT), achievement tests (WRAT-R reading scale). • At nine-month follow-up some of these gains were lost, notably those for researcher ratings and laboratory measures of attentional deployment. • From post-test to nine-month follow-up cases that received combined ST and SB-CM treatments made improvements on parent-rated behaviour whereas those that received ST only did not.

Key: PI = A study of psychological intervention only. PI-ST = A study of combined psychological intervention and stimulant treatment. BPT = Behavioural parent training. SIT = Self-instructional training. SIT-CON = Concrete self-instructional training. SIT-ABS = Abstract self-instructional training. TB-CM = Therapy-based contingency management. SB-CM = School-based contingency management. FT = Family therapy. ST = Stimulant therapy with methylphenidate between 10 and 40 mg per day in a divided dose PS & CT = Problem solving and communication skills training. SST = Social skills training. Hi-ST = 0.6–0.8 mg/kg, bid of methylphenidate. C = Control group. Lo-ST = 0.3–0.4 mg/kg, bid of methylphenidate. Hi-ST = 0.6–0.8 mg/kg, bid of methylphenidate. C = Control group. and based on .3–.4 mg/kg body weight. Lo-ST = 0.3–0.4 mg/kg, bid of methylphenidate.

ranged from 0.1 to 0.5 and at follow-up from 0.1 to 1.3. The high level of variability in these results makes it difficult to draw firm conclusions about the impact of treatment on attentional deployment.

Frankel *et al.* (1997) examined the effects of social skills training on children with ADHD. In the training sessions children were taught conversation and telephone skills; group entry skills for joining in peer activities; procedures for managing play-dates where children visit a youngster's home; skills for the management of peer rejection or teasing; negotiation skills for managing conflicts of interest; and skills for managing confrontations with adults. Didactic input, modelling, rehearsal and therapy-based contingency management were used throughout this social skills training programme. Children were also directly coached in play skills. In dyads, therapists used prompting and contingency management to facilitate the development of rule-following and turn-taking behaviours. Concurrently, parents received psychoeducation on the development of social skills in children. Following treatment, effect sizes for parent- and teacher-rated improvement were 1.1 and 1.0 indicating that the average treated child fared better after treatment than 84 to 86 per cent of untreated cases.

The results of these four studies of child-focused psychological interventions for ADHD allow a number of conclusions to be drawn. First, both self-instructional training and social skills training have positive effects on pre-adolescent school-aged children with ADHD. Self-instructional training where children learn both specific and general self-instructions combined with therapy-based contingency management over six to twelve sessions is probably effective in reducing school- and clinic-based behaviour problems, but not achievement problems, behavioural problems in the home or attention deployment as assessed by laboratory tests of vigilance. However, caution in drawing these conclusions is warranted because Kendall's studies on which these conclusions are based were conducted before the introduction of stringent criteria for the diagnosis of ADHD were routinely used in selecting cases for inclusion in treatment trials. A second conclusion is that social skills training conducted over twelve sessions supplemented with therapy-based contingency management and parental psychoeducation is probably effective in reducing home- and school-based behaviour problems. The studies reviewed in this section provide evidence for the short-term effectiveness of self-instructional and social skills training, but do not address the issue of long-term improvement.

Behavioural parent training

Three studies included in this review examined the effects of behavioural parent training offered as a self-contained treatment package (Anastopoulos *et al.*, 1993; Barkley *et al.*, 1992; Pisterman *et al.*, 1992). Pisterman *et al.* (ibid.) evaluated the effects of a twelve-session behavioural parent training programme for preschool children with ADHD. The programme offered parents training in shaping and reinforcing compliance with parental requests and on-task behaviour, and using time-out procedures for dealing with non-compliance (Forehand and McMahon, 1981). Psychoeducation, modelling, rehearsal and video-feedback were used in parent training. Anastopoulos *et al.* (1993) examined the effects of a similar nine-session parent training programme for pre-adolescent school-age children (Barkley, 1987, 1990). Following treatment, in Pisterman's programme 65 per cent of cases showed clinically significant change on researcher ratings of on-task behaviour and in Anoustopoulos' study 64 per cent of cases showed clinically significant change on the ADHD rating scale (DuPaul, 1991). At follow-up in both studies these gains were maintained. In Pisterman's study there were substantial improvements in parent–child interaction. Treated cases fared better than 88 per cent of untreated cases following therapy and at follow-up. In Anastopoulos' study the parent–child system of the average treated case fared better than those 73 per cent of untreated cases. Combined deterioration and drop-out rates for both studies ranged from 20 to 21 per cent. These two studies provide evidence for the efficacy of behavioural parent training in leading to improvements in behaviour and parent–child relationships for preschoolers and pre-adolescent children with ADHD.

In contrast to Pisterman and Anastopoulos, who were concerned with children under twelve years of age, Barkley *et al.* (1992) studied the impact of behavioural parent training with adolescents. They compared the effectiveness of behavioural parent training with a programme of problem solving and communication skills training and a programme of structural family therapy. In each programme, ten sessions of therapy were offered. Clinically significant gains were made by 20 per cent of cases receiving behavioural parent training; nineteen of cases in the problem solving and communication skills training programme; and only 5 per cent of cases who engaged in structural family therapy. Deterioration occurred in 10 per cent of the behavioural parent training cases but not in the other two conditions.

From these three studies it may be concluded that nine to twelve sessions of behavioural parent training is an effective treatment for a proportion of children and adolescents from three to eighteen years old with ADHD. Behavioural parent training leads to short-term positive changes in home-based behavioural problems and parent–child relationships. These studies provide no evidence for the long-term effectiveness of behavioural parent training or its impact on attentional deployment, academic performance or school-based behaviour.

Multicomponent treatment packages

In four studies the effects of behavioural parent training combined with self-instructional training and/or school-based contingency management were examined (Abikoff and Gittleman, 1984; Bloomquist *et al.*, 1991; Horn *et al.*, 1987; Horn *et al.*, 1990). Horn *et al.* (1987) compared the effects of combined behavioural parent training and self-instructional training with self-instructional training alone and behavioural parent training alone. The behavioural parent training programme was similar to those described earlier in this section and was based on Patterson's (1976) approach. The self-instructional training programme was similar to those described in the previous section and was based on the approaches developed by Meichenbaum (1977) and Camp and Bash (1981). In all there were nine-teen treatment sessions: eight for behavioural parent training, eight for self-instructional training and three for school-based contingency management. Abikoff and Gittleman (1984) evaluated the effects of a combined beha-vioural parent training programme (Becker, 1971; Patterson, 1975) and school-based contingency management programme (O'Leary and O'Leary, 1972) in normalizing hyperactive children's behaviour. In all there were approximately fifteen sessions in this programme with eight devoted to parent training and several devoted to school-based contingency manage-ment. Horn *et al.* (1990) compared the efficacy of combined behavioural parent training, self-instructional training and a school-based contingency management programme with a behavioural parent training programme and a self-instructional training programme. The behavioural parent training programme was based on Barkley (1981), Patterson (1976) and Forehand and McMahon's (1981) manuals. The self-instructional training programme was based on the clinical practices outlined in Camp and Bash (1981), Kendall and Braswell (1985) and Meichenbaum's (1977) texts. The school-based contingency management programme involved consultations with teachers and the use of a daily report card system (Ayllon *et al.*, 1975). In all there were 27 sessions: twelve for behavioural parent training, twelve for self-instructional training and three for school-based contingency management. Bloomquist *et al.* (1991) compared the effects of a combined programme of behavioural parent training, self-instructional training and school-based contingency management with a school-based contingency management programme alone using treatment procedures detailed in Braswell and Bloomquist (1991). In all there were 29 treatment sessions: seven for behavioural parent training, twenty for self-instructional training and two for school-based contingency management.

Across these four studies, for improvements in parent-reported behaviour following treatment, effect sizes ranged from 0.2 to 0.6 and at follow-up they ranged from −0.1 to 0.7. The largest sustained effects occurred in Horn *et al.*'s (1990) study where the multicomponent treatment package, when compared with the behavioural parent training and the self-instructional training programmes after treatment and at follow-up yielded effect sizes that ranged from 0.6 to 0.7, indicating that the average case receiving the combined package fared better than 73–76 per cent of cases who received single component treatments. The worst results for combined treatments compared to single component treatments occurred in Horn *et al.*'s earlier (1987) study where they found an effect size of −1.0 at one-month follow-up on parent-rated behaviour. This showed that the average case receiving a combined behavioural parent training and self-instructional training package was worse off than 84 per cent of cases who received self-instructional training alone.

For teacher-rated behavioural improvement comparing combined treatments with single treatments, effect sizes ranged from −0.6 to −0.1 following treatment across the four studies. These results show that none of the combined treatment packages were any better than single component approaches in modifying school-based behaviour in the period immediately following treatment. In fact they were marginally worse. At four to twelve weeks' follow-up, effect sizes for teacher-rated behaviour ranged from −0.5 to 0.5, with the worst and the best results occurring in Horn *et al.*'s later (1990) study. The average case in the multicomponent programme fared better at follow-up than 69 per cent of cases in the self-instructional training programme and worse than 69 per cent of cases in the behavioural parent training programme.

Across the four studies, effect sizes for researcher ratings of children's behaviour ranged from 0.7 to above 2.0, with the largest effect sizes occurring in Bloomquist's (1991) study. The average case receiving a combined programme of behavioural parent training, self-instructional training and school-based contingency management fared better than 98 per cent of untreated controls.

For children's self-esteem, effect sizes across the four studies concerned with the impact of combined treatments ranged from −0.2 to 0.9 following treatment and from −1.0 to 1.1 at follow-up. Both the largest and smallest effect sizes occurred in studies where a combined treatment package was compared with self-instructional training. In Horn *et al.*'s earlier (1987) study, effect sizes of 0.9 and 1.1 were obtained post-treatment and at follow-up from a comparison of a combined progamme of behavioural parent training and self-instructional training with self-instructional training alone. In contrast, in Horn *et al.*'s later (1990) study, an effect size of −1.0 was obtained after treatment and at follow-up from a comparison of a combined programme of behavioural parent training, self-instructional training and school-based contingency management with self-instructional training alone. These conflicting findings make it difficult to draw firm conclusions in this domain.

For laboratory tests of attentional deployment, effect sizes across the four studies concerned with the impact of combined treatments after therapy and at follow-up ranged from −0.7 to 0.4. These results suggest that, compared with single component treatments, combined treatments did not enhance attentional deployment and vigilance for children with ADHD.

For academic achievement tests of reading skills, effect sizes across the four studies concerned with the impact of multicomponent programmes after therapy and at follow-up ranged from −0.5 to 0.7. Both the largest and smallest effect sizes occurred in studies where a multicomponent treatment package was compared with behavioural parent training. In Horn *et al.*'s earlier (1987) study, effect sizes of 0.5 and 0.7 were obtained after therapy and at follow-up from a comparison of a multicomponent programme with behavioural parent training alone. In contrast, in Horn *et al.*'s later (1990) study, effect sizes of −0.5 and −0.3 were obtained after treatment and at follow-up from a comparison of a multicomponent programme with behavioural parent training alone. These conflicting findings make it difficult to draw firm conclusions in this domain.

In studies of multicomponent treatment programmes after therapy 36–51 per cent of cases were classified as having made clinically significant improvements or being indistinguishable from children without ADHD and at follow-up these figures improved to 73 per cent. Caution is required in interpreting this follow-up figure since it is based on a single study. In comparison, 9–25 per cent of cases who received single component treatments made clinically significant improvements. The drop-out rate for combined treatment packages was 23 per cent and for single component treatments, drop-out rates ranged from 15–20 per cent.

In summary, the studies reviewed in this section suggest that multicomponent treatment packages may be more effective than single component packages in reducing home-based behaviour problems and researcher-rated behaviour problems. For school-based behavioural and achievement problems, self-esteem and attentional deployment as assessed by laboratory tests of vigilance there was no compelling evidence that multicomponent treatment packages were any better than single component treatments. Effective multicomponent treatment packages included behavioural parent training, self-instructional training and in some instances school-based contingency management and spanned 17 to 29 sessions over eight to twelve weeks.

Combined psychological and pharmacological treatment

Nine studies in this review examined the effects of combined psychological and pharmacological treatments. Five of these involved self-instructional training combined with stimulant therapy (Abikoff and Gittleman, 1985; Brown *et al.*, 1985, 1986; Cohen *et al.*, 1981; Hinshaw *et al.*, 1984). Four involved stimulant therapy combined with either behavioural parent training, or school-based contingency management or multicomponent psychological interventions (Carlson *et al.*, 1992; Firestone *et al.*, 1986; Horn *et al.*, 1991; Pelham *et al.*, 1993).

Self-instructional training and stimulant therapy

Cohen *et al.* (1981) compared the outcome for kindergarten children with ADHD who received self-instructional training combined with stimulant therapy to that of children who received either of the treatment components alone and a control group. The self-instructional training was based on the protocols of Meichenbaum and Goodman (1971), Camp and Bash (1981) and Douglas *et al.* (1976). Stimulant therapy involved 10–20 mgs per day of methylphenidate. Children began medication one to two weeks before the first assessment and remained on medication for the post-treatment assessment. Brown *et al.* (1985), using a similar four-group research design to that of Cohen *et al.* (1981), examined the effects of self-instructional training combined with stimulant therapy with school-aged children. The self-instructional training programme was based on the work of Meichenbaum and Goodman (1971) and Douglas *et al.* (1976). Stimulant therapy involved 5–15 mgs per day of methylphenidate administered in a divided dose and children remained on medication for post-treatment assessment. Hinshaw *et al.* (1984) compared the effects of self-instructional training combined with stimulant therapy to that of the same psychological treatment combined with a pill placebo. The self-instructional training addressed the management of academic problems and socially provocative situations (Meichenbaum, 1977; Spivack and Shure, 1974; Douglas *et al.*, 1976; Kendall and Braswell, 1985). Stimulant therapy dosages of methyl-phenidate ranged from 4–40 mgs. Abikoff and Gittleman (1985) compared the effects of self-instructional training combined with stimulant therapy to those of stimulant therapy alone or in combination with an attention placebo psychological support treatment. The self-instructional training addressed the management of academic and social problems (Douglas *et al.*, 1976; Meichenbaum, 1977; Spivack and Shure, 1974). Stimulant therapy included up to 80 mgs of methylphenidate, 50 mgs of dextroamphetamine or 50 mgs of pemoline per day given in a divided dose. Following sixteen weeks of treatment, all cases on stimulant medication alone and 50 per cent of those in the combined treatment group were placed on placebo pills and subsequently, their requirement for further stimulant treatment assessed regularly for a one-month period. Brown's team in a four-group design compared the effects of combined self-instructional training and stimulant therapy with those of stimulant therapy combined with an attention placebo psychological support treatment; self-instructional training combined with a pill placebo; and a placebo control group (Brown *et al.*, 1985; Brown, Borden *et al.*, 1986; Brown, Wynne *et al.*, 1986).

Self-instructional training followed Meichenbaum and Goodman's (1971) protocol and stimulant treatment involved 10–40 mgs of methylphenidate per day in a divided dose.

Across these five studies, for combined self-instructional training and stimulant therapy compared with self-instructional training alone or with a placebo pill, effect sizes for improvements in parent-rated behaviour ranged from 0.2 to 1.4 after treatment and the average effect size was 0.8, indicating that for parent-rated behaviour problems the average case receiving the combined treatment fared better than 79 per cent of cases treated with self-instructional training alone. However, these parent-rated behavioural gains were not maintained at three months' follow-up in all studies, where effect sizes ranged from −0.5 to 0.8.

For combined self-instructional training and stimulant therapy compared with self-instructional training alone or with a placebo pill, effect sizes for improvements in teacher-rated behaviour ranged from 0.2 to 0.9 after treatment and the average effect size was 0.6, indicating that for teacher-rated behaviour problems the average case receiving the combined treatment fared better than 73 per cent of cases treated with self-instructional training alone. These teacher-rated behavioural gains, however, were not maintained at three months' follow-up in all studies, where effect sizes ranged from −0.3 to 0.7.

For combined self-instructional training and stimulant therapy compared with self-instructional training alone or with a placebo pill, effect sizes for improvements in self-rated behaviour ranged from 0.1 to 0.3 after treatment and from 0.3 to 2.4 at follow-up. Cases treated with the combined treatment made negligible progress compared with cases treated with self-instructional training alone over the course of treatment, but in one study at follow-up substantial gains were made. However, the variability in results precludes firm conclusions being drawn in this domain.

For combined self-instructional training and stimulant therapy compared with self-instructional training alone or with a placebo pill, effect sizes for improvements in attentional deployment as assessed by laboratory tests range from −0.9 to 1.0 after treatment and from −1.0 to 0.9 at follow up. Once again, as with the results on self-reported behavioural improvements, those for attentional deployment have such a wide variability that drawing firm conclusions about the benefits of combined self-instructional training and stimulant therapy compared with self-instructional training alone in this domain is not possible.

For combined self-instructional training and stimulant therapy compared with self-instructional training alone or with a placebo pill, effect sizes for improvements in academic achievement as assessed by standardized reading tests ranged from 0.1 to 0.2 after treatment and from −0.3 to −0.1 at follow-up. These results suggest that combined self-instructional training and stimulant therapy probably have few advantages over self-instructional training alone in this domain.

In one study (Hinshaw *et al.*, 1984) compared with self-instructional training alone or with a placebo pill, combined self-instructional training and stimulant therapy led to significant gains in researcher-rated behaviour when faced with interpersonal provocations in a laboratory situation.

Let us now consider the combined self-instructional training and stimulant therapy compared with stimulant therapy alone or with an attention placebo psychological support intervention. Across the four studies that made such comparisons effect sizes for parent-rated, teacher-rated and self-rated behavioural improvements ranged from −0.9 to 0.4 after treatment and at follow-up. These results suggest that combined self-instructional training and stimulant therapy probably has few advantages over stimulant therapy alone in facilitating behavioural improvements at home or at school. Effect sizes for attentional deployment and academic achievement ranged from −0.5 to 0.6 after treatment and at follow-up. These results suggest that combined self-instructional training and stimulant therapy probably have few advantages over stimulant therapy alone in facilitating improved attention and academic achievement.

In summary, compared with self-instructional training alone or with a placebo pill, combined self-instructional training and stimulant therapy led to short-term improvements in parent- and teacher-rated behaviour, but such gains were not always maintained at follow-up. For self-reported behavioural improvement, attentional deployment as assessed by laboratory tasks requiring sustained vigilance, and for academic achievement as assessed by standardized reading test, there was no firm evidence that combined self-instructional training and stimulant therapy were routinely more effective than self-instructional training alone or with a placebo pill. Combined self-instructional training and stimulant therapy probably had few advantages over stimulant therapy alone in facilitating behavioural improvements at home or school or in facilitating improved attention and academic achievement. Self-instructional training programmes examined in these studies involved six to 32 sessions over three to sixteen weeks and were offered on an outpatient basis. Stimulant therapy commonly involved a daily divided dose of 5–40 mgs of methylphenidate.

Behavioural parent training, school-based contingency management and stimulant therapy

Four studies included in this review investigated the effects of stimulant therapy combined with either behavioural parent training, or school-based contingency management or multicomponent psychological intervention programmes (Carlson *et al.*, 1992; Firestone *et al.*, 1986; Horn *et al.*, 1991; Pelham *et al.*, 1993). Firestone *et al.* (ibid.) compared the effects of nine sessions of behavioural parent training based on Patterson's (1975) approach combined with stimulant therapy, with behavioural parent training combined with a placebo pill. Children receiving stimulant treatment were given 10–30 mgs of methylphenidate per day in a divided dose.

For combined behavioural parent training and stimulant therapy compared with behavioural parent training plus a placebo pill, effect sizes for improvements in parent- and teacher-rated behaviour were 0.7 and 0.8 after treatment, indicating that the average case receiving the combined treatment fared better than 76 per cent of cases treated with behavioural parent training and a placebo at home and better than 79 per cent at school. However, these gains were not maintained when cases were followed up three months later and effect sizes of −0.4 and 0.0 were obtained for sustained improvements in parent- and teacher-rated behaviour respectively.

For attentional deployment on laboratory tests of vigilance an effect size of 0.6 was obtained following treatment and this increased to 0.9 at three months' follow-up. Thus, the average case receiving combined behavioural parent training and stimulant therapy fared better on tests of attentional deployment three months after treatment than 82 per cent of cases who received behavioural parent training plus a placebo pill. Effect sizes for performance on academic reading achievement tests following treatment and three months later were 0.1 and 0.3, indicating that the differences between groups were negligible. At two years' follow-up, differences between cases who received combined behavioural parent training and stimulant therapy and cases who received behavioural parent training plus a placebo pill were negligible on all variables. Following treatment and at three months' and two years' follow-up, differences between cases who received combined behavioural parent training and stimulant therapy and cases who received stimulant therapy only were negligible on all variables. Thus it may be concluded from Firestone's study that combined behavioural parent training and stimulant therapy were more effective than behavioural parent training without stimulant therapy in reducing parent- and teacher-rated behaviour problems and in improving attentional deployment in the short term but not the long term. However, the combined therapy was no more effective in the short term than stimulant therapy alone and neither had a significant impact on academic performance.

Carlson *et al.* (1992) compared the effects of school-based contingency management combined with high and low doses of stimulant therapy, with school-based contingency management combined with a placebo pill. In addition, groups that received high and low doses of stimulant therapy and a group that received a placebo pill without contingency management were included in the six condition repeated measures design. Children received treatment within the context of a summer day programme with 40 daily sessions conducted over an eight-week period. There were twelve children per class. The contingency management programme included a high level of classroom structure, rules posted on classroom walls and teacher feedback on performance; a token and social reinforcement system; time out; an honour roll system; and a daily home–school report card. High dose methylphenidate stimulant therapy was based on 0.6 mg per kg body weight and low dose therapy was based on 0.6 mg per kg body weight. Stimulant therapy was given in a divided daily dose and the first dose was given within two hours of the treatment sessions. Pelham *et al.* (1993) used a similar design, contingency management treatment procedures and stimulant medication dosages for their study. They report that the for low stimulant therapy the range was 5–15 mgs and for the high dose condition the range was 10–23 mgs.

In these two studies, for researcher ratings of on-task behaviour and disruptive behaviour three conditions produced the best results: the high stimulant therapy condition alone and in combination with school-based contingency management and the low stimulant therapy condition in combination with school-based contingency management. When these three conditions were compared with the low stimulant therapy condition and the school-based contingency management plus placebo conditions, the average effect size of 0.55 indicated that the average case in the top three conditions fared better than approximately 70 per cent of cases in the other two conditions. In Pelham *et al.*'s study (1993) 57 per cent of cases in the high stimulant therapy condition alone and in combination with school-based contingency management and the low stimulant therapy condition in combination with school-based contingency management showed clinically significant improvement. In contrast only 46 per cent of cases in a low stimulant therapy condition and the school-based contingency management plus placebo conditions made such improvements. Thus, it may be concluded that the addition of school-based contingency management to a low dose of stimulant therapy made it as effective in improving classroom behaviour as a high dose of stimulant therapy.

Horn *et al.* (1991) compared the effects of a multicomponent treatment package containing behavioural parent training, self-instructional training and school-based contingency management combined with high and low doses of stimulant therapy, and the multicomponent treatment package combined with a placebo pill. In addition, groups that received high and low doses of stimulant therapy and a group that received a placebo pill without the contingency management programme were included in the six-group design. The behavioural parent training was based on manuals by Patterson (1976), Forehand and McMahon (1981), Barkley (1981) and Becker (1971). The self-instructional training component was based on protocols developed by Kendall and Braswell (1985), Camp and Bash (1991) and Meichenbaum (1977). The school-based contingency management programme involved a daily home-school report card system such as that described by Ayllon *et al.* (1975). In all there were 27 treatment sessions: twelve of behavioural parent training, twelve of self-instructional training and three of school-based contingency management. High dose methylphenidate stimulant therapy was based on 0.8 mg per kg body weight and low dose therapy was based on 0.4 mg per kg body weight. Nine-month follow-up data following the withdrawal of stimulant medication was published in a second paper (Ialongo *et al.*, 1993).

In this study, for teacher-rated behavioural improvement following treatment, three conditions produced the best results: the high-stimulant therapy condition alone and in combination with multicomponent treatment package and the low-stimulant therapy condition in combination with the multicomponent treatment package. When these three conditions were compared with the low-stimulant therapy condition and the multicomponent treatment package plus placebo conditions, the average effect size of 0.6 indicated that the average case in the top three conditions fared better than approximately 73 per cent of cases in the other two conditions. From post-test to nine-month follow-up, cases that received combined treatments made improvements on parent-rated behaviour whereas those that received stimulant treatment only did not.

In summary, the following conclusions may be drawn from the four studies addressed in this section. Combined behavioural parent training and stimulant therapy was more effective than behavioural parent training without stimulant therapy in reducing parent- and teacher-rated behaviour problems and in improving attentional deployment in the short term but not the long term. However, the combined therapy was no more effective in the short term than stimulant therapy alone and neither had a significant impact on academic performance. The addition of school-based contingency management or a multicomponent psychological intervention package to a low dose of stimulant therapy made it as effective in improving classroom behaviour as a high dose of stimulant therapy in the short term. Combined stimulant therapy and a multicomponent psychological intervention treatment package was more effective in leading to sustained improvements over a nine-month period in home-based behaviour problems than stimulant therapy alone.

Conclusions

From this review of twenty well-conducted studies, two broad conclusions may be drawn about the effectiveness of psychological treatments alone or in combination with pharmacological treatments for ADHD. First, a range of psychological interventions have positive short-term effects on ADHD symptomatology and related problems. These psychological treatments include child-focused interventions (social skills training, self-instructional training, therapy-based contingency management), family-based interventions (behavioural parent training, problem solving and communications training, family therapy), school-based interventions (school-based contingency management), and multisystemic interventions where child, family and school-focused interventions are combined into a multicomponent treatment package. Second, the effects of these interventions may be enhanced when they are combined with stimulant therapy. In addition to these broad conclusions, a series of specific conclusions may be drawn from this review about the effectiveness of particular interventions on particular features of ADHD symptomatology and related clinical features. A consideration of these follows.

Social skills training and self-instructional training were the principal child-focused psychological interventions for ADHD addressed in this review and the following conclusions concern these interventions. First, social skills training conducted over twelve sessions supplemented with therapy-based contingency management and parental psychoeducation is probably effective in reducing home- and school-based behaviour problems in the short term. Second, self-instructional, where children learn both specific and general self-instructions combined with therapy-based contingency management over six to twelve sessions is probably effective in reducing school- and clinic-based behaviour problems, but not home-based behaviour problems, achievement problems or attention deployment problems. Third, combined self-instructional training spanning six to 32 sessions over three to sixteen weeks and stimulant therapy involving a daily divided dose of 5–40 mgs of methylphenidate is probably more effective than self-instructional training alone in leading to short-term improvements in home- and school-based behaviour problems but no more effective than self-instructional training alone in improving achievement problems and attention deployment difficulties. Fourth, combined self-instructional training and stimulant therapy probably have few advantages over stimulant therapy alone in facilitating behavioural improvements at home or school.

Behavioural parent training was the principal family-based psychological intervention for ADHD addressed in this review and the following conclusions concern these interventions. First, behavioural parent training conducted over nine to twelve sessions probably leads to short-term positive changes in home-based behavioural problems and parent–child relationships for children and adolescents from age three to eighteen with ADHD. Second, behavioural parent training has little impact on attentional deployment, academic performance or school-based behaviour. Third, behavioural parent training is probably as effective as problem solving and communication skills training and structural family therapy with adolescents. Fourth, combined behavioural parent training and stimulant therapy is probably more effective than behavioural parent training without stimulant therapy in reducing home- and school-based behaviour problems and in improving attentional deployment in the short term. Fifth, combined behavioural parent training and stimulant therapy are probably no more effective than stimulant therapy alone.

From this review, the following conclusions about the effectiveness of multicomponent treatment packages may be drawn. First, multicomponent treatment packages that include behavioural parent training, self-instructional training and school-based contingency management and span seventeen to 29 sessions over eight to twelve weeks are probably more effective than single component packages in reducing home-based behaviour problems in the short term. Second, multicomponent psychological intervention packages combined with a low dose (0.3 mg/kg) of methylphenidate stimulant therapy are probably as effective as a high dose therapy (0.6 mg/kg) alone in improving school-based behaviour problems in the short term. Third, multicomponent psychological intervention treatment packages combined with stimulant therapy are probably more effective in leading to sustained improvements in home-based behaviour over a nine-month period than stimulant therapy alone.

In drawing out the implications of these conclusions for clinical practice, service development and further research, it is important to keep in mind the risks associated with psychological and pharmacological interventions. Currently there are no sound reasons to suspect that any of the psychological interventions addressed in this review have serious short- or long-term negative effects on children's health or development. In contrast stimulant therapy has a number of well-documented side-effects, but unfortunately there is little information on the long-term negative effects of protracted stimulant therapy. In the short term methylphenidate may lead to insomnia (59 per cent), decreased appetite (55 per cent), stomach aches (33 per cent), headaches (30 per cent), and dizziness (12 per cent), motor and vocal tics (1 per cent) and there is also some evidence that stimulant therapy may lead to a reduction in growth velocity (Greenhill, 1998). These negative effects of stimulant therapy warrant a cautious approach to the routine use of high dosages.

The conclusions of this review suggest that in clinical practice for effective short-term treatment of ADHD, multisystemic interventions involving multicomponent treatment packages combined with low dose stimulant therapy are the treatments of choice. Multicomponent treatment packages should include behavioural parent training, self-instructional training and school-based contingency management elements and span seventeen to 29 sessions over eight to twelve weeks. Low dose methylphenidate stimulant therapy should be based on 0.3 mg/kg body weight.

For effective long-term treatment, it is probable that a chronic care model of service delivery is required. Children with ADHD and their families, within such a model of service delivery, would be offered the option of infrequent but sustained contact with a psychological and paediatric service over the course of childhood and adolescence. It is likely that at transitional points within each yearly cycle (such as entering new school classes each autumn) and at transitional points within the life cycle (such as entering adolescence, changing school, or moving house) increased service contact would be required. Two of the studies reviewed in this chapter (Carlson *et al.*, 1992; Pelham *et al.*, 1993) underscore the value of intensive summer school day programmes as an option for service delivery and such annual programmes could well form part of a chronic care model of service delivery.

This review highlights the need for well-controlled large-scale long-term studies to examine the effectiveness of multicomponent treatment packages alone and in combination with low dose stimulant therapy offered within the context of a chronic care model. Of course it would be essential for such studies to take account of the design features outlined in Chapter 1 and in addition to include measures of classroom behaviour, academic achievement, attention deployment and stimulant therapy side-effects. Within the context of such studies there is also a need to examine the effects of withdrawing stimulant therapy following normalization of behaviour and achievement. Currently two such studies are nearing completion (Hechtman and Abikoff, 1995; Richters *et al.*, 1995) but more are required.

ASSESSMENT

Atkins, M., Pelham, W. and Licht, M. (1988). The development and validation of objective classroom measures for the assessment of conduct and attention deficit disorders. In R. Prinz (ed.), *Advances In Behavioural Assessment Of Children And Families* (Vol. 4, pp. 3–33). New York: Guilford.

Cairns, E. and Cammock, T. (1978). Development of a more reliable version of the Matching Familiar Figures Test. *Developmental Psychology*, 18, 555–60.

Conners, C. (1990). *The Conners' Rating Scales*. North Tonawanda, NY: Multi-Health Systems.

Conners, C. (1995). *The Conners' Continuous Performance Test*. North Tonawanda, NY: Multi-Health Systems.

Conners, C. (1996a). *Conners' Abbreviated Symptom Questionnaire*. Odessa, FL: PAR. Available from PAR, PO Box 998, Odessa, Florida, USA. Phone +1-800-331-8378.

Conners, C. (1996b). *Conners' Rating Scales Computer Programme*. Available from PAR, PO Box 998, Odessa, Florida, USA. Phone +1-800-331-8378.

DuPaul, G. (1991). Parent and teacher ratings of ADHD symptoms: Psychometric properties in a community based sample. *Journal of Clinical Child Psychology*, 20, 245–53.

DuPaul, G. and Barkley, R. (1992). Situational variability of attention problems: Psychometric properties of the revised Home and School Situations Questionnaires. *Journal of Clinical Child Psychology*, 21, 178–88.

Gilliam, J. (1996). *Attention Deficit Hyperactivity Disorder Test*. Odessa, FL: PAR. Available from PAR, PO Box 998, Odessa, Florida, USA. Phone +1-800-331-8378.

Ullmann, R., Sleator, E. and Sprague, R. (1984). A new rating scale for diagnosis and monitoring of ADD children. *Psychopharmacology Bulletin*, 20, 160–4.

Wilkinson, G. (1993). *WRAT-3: Wide Range Achievement Test* (Third Edition). Wilmington, Delaware: Wide Range Inc.

TREATMENT MANUALS AND RESOURCES

American Academy of Child and Adolescent Psychiatry (1991). Practice parameters for the assessment and treatment of ADHD. *Journal of the American Academy of Child and Adolescent Psychiatry*, 30, i–iii.

Barkley, R. (1987). *Defiant Children: A Clinician's Manual for Parent Training*. New York: Guilford.

Barkley, R. (1990). *Attention Deficit Hyperactivity Disorder: A Handbook for Diagnosis and Treatment* (Second Edition). New York: Guilford.

Becker, W. (1971). *Parents are Teachers: A Child Management Programme*. Champaign, Ill: Research Press.

Braswell, L. and Bloomquist, M. (1991). *Cognitive Behavioural Therapy for ADHD Children: Child, Family and School Interventions*. New York: Guilford.

Camp, B. and Bash, M. (1981). *Think Aloud: Increasing Social and Cognitive Skills: A Problem Solving Program for Children*. Champaign, Ill: Research Press.

Cantwell, D.P. (1994). *Therapeutic Management of Attention Deficit Disorder: Participant Workbook*. New York: Guilford.

Feindler, E. and Ecton, R. (1985). *Adolescent Anger Control: Cognitive-Behavioural Techniques*. New York: Pergamon.

Forehand, R. and McMahon, R. (1981). *Helping the Non-compliant Child: A Clinician's Guide to Parent Training*. New York: Guilford.

Gordon, M. (1995). *How to Operate an ADHD Clinic or Subspecialty Practice*. Odessa, FL: PAR.

Kendall, P. and Braswell, L. (1985). *Cognitive Behavioural Therapy for Impulsive Children*. New York: Guilford.

Meichenbaum, D. (1977). *Cognitive Behaviour Modification. An Integrative Approach*. New York: Plenum.

O'Leary, K. and O'Leary, S. (1972). *Classroom Management: The Successful Use of Behaviour Modification*. New York: Pergamon.

Patterson, G. (1975). *Families: Applications of Social Learning to Family Life*. Champaign, Ill: Research Press.

Patterson, G. (1976). *Living with Children: New Methods for Parents and Teachers*. Champaign Ill: Research Press.

Pelham, W. (1994). *Attention Deficit Hyperactivity Disorder: A Clinician's Guide*. New York: Plenum.

Robin, A. and Foster, S. (1989). *Negotiating Parent–Adolescent Conflict*. New York: Guilford.

FURTHER READING FOR PARENTS

Barkley, R. (1995a). ADHD: What do we know?; ADHD: What can we do?; ADHD in the classroom: Strategies for teachers. These videos are available from PAR Inc., PO Box 998, Odessa, Florida, USA. Phone +1-800-331-8378.

Barkley, R. (1995b). *Taking Charge of ADHD: The Complete Authoritative Guide for Parents*. New York: Guilford.

Ingersoll, B. (1988). *Your Hyperactive Child; A Parent's Guide to Coping with Attention Deficit Disorder*. New York: Doubleday.

Patterson, G. (1976). *Living with Children: New Methods for Parents and Teachers*. Champaign, Ill: Research Press.

Wender, P. (1987). *The Hyperactive Child, Adolescent and Adult. Attention Deficit Disorder Through The Lifespan*. New York: Oxford University Press.

5   Oppositional defiant disorder

Joanne Behan and Alan Carr

Oppositional defiant disorder refers to a pattern of conduct problems characterized chiefly by tantrums and defiance. It is confined largely to the family, school and peer group and does not include violations of the law occurring in the wider community. Diagnostic criteria for oppositional defiant disorder from DSM IV (APA, 1994) and ICD-10 (WHO, 1992) are given in Figure 5.1. A distinction is made between oppositional defiant disorder and conduct disorder. Oppositional defiant disorder is a less pervasive disturbance and is recognized as a possible developmental precursor of conduct disorder. However, it is not a trivial condition and entails a persistent pattern of behaviour which has endured for more than six months. In this respect it is distinguished from transient adjustment reactions characterized by defiance and tantrums.

While oppositional defiant disorder is primarily a disturbance of conduct, it has distinctive cognitive and affective features and is associated with particular social difficulties (Kazdin, 1997). With respect to cognition, there is a limited internalization of social rules and norms and a hostile attributional bias where the youngster interprets ambiguous social situations as threatening and responds with aggressive retaliative behaviour. With respect to affect, anger and irritability are the predominant mood states. With respect to social adjustment, the main relationship difficulties occur with parents and centre on the child's defiance of parental instructions to conform to rules for appropriate behaviour on the one hand and a difficulty in maintaining a warm and positive parent–child relationship on the other. Relationships with teachers may be problematic because of the child's defiance and problems with peer relationships may occur because of the child's aggression.

From a developmental perspective, the onset of oppositional defiant disorder typically occurs during the preschool years and for a proportion of children it evolves into conduct disorder in adolescence and antisocial personality disorder in adulthood (Loeber and Stouthamer-Loeber, 1998). Three classes of risk factors increase the probability that childhood oppositional defiant disorder will escalate into later life difficulties, i.e. child characteristics, parenting practices, and family organization problems (Lehmann and Dangel, 1998). Difficult temperament, aggressiveness, impulsivity and

DSM IV	ICD 10
A. A pattern of negativistic, hostile and defiant behaviour lasting at least six months, during which four or more of the following are present: 1. Often loses temper 2. Often argues with adults 3. Often actively defies or refuses to comply with adults requests or rules 4. Often deliberately annoys people 5. Often blames others for his or her mistakes or misbehaviour 6. Is often touchy or easily annoyed by others 7. Is often angry or resentful 8. Is often spiteful or vindictive. B. The disturbance in behaviour causes clinically significant impairment in social, academic or occupational functioning. C. The behaviours do not occur exclusively during the course of a psychotic or a mood disorder. D. Criteria are not met for conduct disorder or antisocial personality disorder.	The essential feature of this disorder is a pattern of persistently negativistic, hostile, defiant, provocative and disruptive behaviour which is clearly outside the normal range of behaviour for a child of the same age in the same sociocultural context and which does not include the more serious violations of the rights of others associated with conduct disorder. Children with this disorder tend frequently and actively to defy adult requests or rules and deliberately to annoy other people. Usually they tend to be angry, resentful, and easily annoyed by other people whom they blame for their own mistakes and difficulties. They generally have a low frustration tolerance and readily lose their temper. Typically their defiance has a provocative quality, so that they initiate confrontations and generally exhibit excessive levels of rudeness, uncooperativeness and resistance to authority. Frequently this behaviour is most evident in interactions with adults or peers whom the child knows well, and signs of the disorder may not be present during clinical interview. The key distinction from other types of conduct disorder is the absence of behaviour that violates the law and the basic rights of others such as theft, cruelty, bullying, assault and destructiveness.

Figure 5.1 Diagnostic criteria for oppositional defiant disorder in DSM IV and ICD 10.

Source Adapted from DSM IV (APA, 1994) and ICD 10 (WHO, 1992, 1996).

inattention are the main personal characteristics of children that place them at risk for long-term conduct problems. Ineffective monitoring and supervision of children, providing inconsistent consequences for rule violations, and failing to provide reinforcement for prosocial behaviour are the main problematic parenting practices that place children at risk for long-term conduct difficulties. The family organization problems associated with persistence of conduct problems into adolescence and adulthood are parental conflict and violence, a high level of life stressors, a low level of social support and parental psychological adjustment problems such as depression or substance abuse.

Epidemiology

Preadolescent children who present with oppositional behaviour, temper tantrums, defiance and non-compliance constitute a third to a half of all referrals to child and family psychology clinics (Kazdin, 1995). Cohen *et al.* (1993) found that with oppositional defiant disorder for both boys and girls there was a gradual increase from preadolescence to adolescence and a decline as adulthood was entered. The rates for boys were 14.2 per cent in preadolescence, 15.4 per cent in mid-adolescence and 12.2 per cent in late adolescence. For girls the rates were 10.4 per cent, 15.6 per cent and 12.5 per cent for the same periods. There is considerable co-morbidity between oppositional defiant disorder, conduct disorder and ADHD although precise figures are unavailable (Kazdin, 1995).

Previous reviews

In a wide-ranging review of the effectiveness of a variety of psychosocial treatments for children and adolescents with disturbances of conduct including oppositional defiant disorder and conduct disorder, Kazdin (1998) identified four classes of interventions for which there was good empirical support. These were behavioural parent training, child-focused problem-solving skills training, functional family therapy, and multisystemic therapy. Of these, behavioural parent training was identified as a particularly promising approach for the treatment of preadolescent children with conduct problems. No other treatment approach to preadolescent conduct problems has generated such a wealth of empirical research. Serketich and Dumas (1996) in a meta-analysis of over a hundred published and unpublished studies of behavioural parent training concluded that for childhood conduct problems it was a highly effective treatment. In light of the findings of these previous reviews, in this chapter the focus will be on a review of well-conducted studies of behavioural parent training in cases of preadolescent disturbances of conduct.

Behavioural parent training rests on the assumption that if parents can be trained to use specific behavioural skills in managing their children within the home environment on a day-to-day basis, then the youngsters' behaviour will change. One set of skills is routinely monitoring specific positive and negative target behaviours and recording observations of the frequency, intensity and duration of these behaviours, the situations within which they occur and the typical consequences they elicit in a systematic way. A second set of skills is altering the child's environment so as to reduce the number of situations that evoke negative target behaviours and increase the number of situations that precipitate positive target behaviours. A third set of skills is using positive reinforcement to increase the frequency of positive target behaviours and ignoring or using time-out from reinforcement to reduce the frequency of target negative behaviours. Parent training may also include guidance on the use of contingency contracting and negotiation skills.

Pioneers of behavioural parent training conducted treatment with a single family at a time (rather than with groups of parents) (e.g. Hanf and Kling, 1973; Patterson *et al.*, 1975). Typically parents and their children attended treatment sessions and parents were coached by therapists to use behavioural parenting skills when interacting with their children during treatment sessions. Instruction, modelling, shaping and reinforcement were used by therapists to coach parents. In some instances, therapists would observe parents interacting with their children through a one-way viewing screen and give instructions and verbal reinforcement through a 'bug in the ear' communication system. Parents were assigned homework tasks which typically included monitoring and recording particular target behaviours and using specific parenting skills such as reinforcing positive behaviours or giving time-out from reinforcement for negative behaviours.

One problem with this elaborate individually based approach to behavioural parent training was its high cost in terms of therapist time. A concern with the cost-effectiveness of individually based behavioural parent training was one factor that gave rise to group-based approaches (e.g. Cunningham *et al.*, 1994). With group-based approaches, parents from a number of different families attended a series of sessions without their children. Behavioural parenting skills were taught in a tutorial-like situation. In each session parents would both learn new skills, but also review progress and discuss their experiences of trying to apply behavioural parenting skills with their own children between training sessions.

While individually based and group-based behavioural parent training programmes helped many parents acquire new parenting skills, not all parents were equally successful in applying these new skills consistently with their children. High life stress and low levels of social support were found to characterize non-responders. In many instances mothers found themselves in distressed marriages or relationships, where their partners offered little support or actively undermined attempts at implementing behavioural parenting skills. In other situations, single parents found themselves socially isolated with little support from their extended family and social network. Such isolation reduced the energy and resolve they had available to consistently use behavioural parenting skills in managing their children. To address the problems raised by these types of clients, behavioural parent training programmes that included a component which aimed to increase the level of available support to primary caregivers (usually mothers) were developed (e.g. Dadds *et al.*, 1987).

Two further developments occurred in the evolution of behavioural parent training programmes and deserve mention. The first was the use of video-modelling and the second was the inclusion of a child-focused social problem-solving skills component into the overall behavioural parent training treatment package. With the move from individual to group programmes, the observation of parent–child interactions within treatment sessions and discussion of the degree to which specific interactions approximated the correct application of behavioural parenting principles no longer occurred. There was a risk that the effectiveness of treatment would be lessened because of the lack of such observable parent–child interactions. This concern underpinned the development of behavioural parent training programmes which incorporated video-modelling as a central feature. In such programmes, parents and therapists observed videotaped vignettes of parent–child interactions (e.g. Webster-Stratton, 1981). In some of these vignettes parents used behavioural parenting skills appropriately and in others they did not. Discussion in these sessions focused on the differences between such situations and ways in which clients might apply this knowledge to their interactions with their own children.

The fact that poorly developed social problem-solving skills have been found to characterize many children with conduct problems provided an impetus for developing programmes to target this deficit and combining them with behavioural parent training treatment packages (e.g. Kazdin *et al.*, 1992).

Method

One aim of this chapter was to review a selection of well-designed studies of the effects of behavioural parent training for preadolescent children who would qualify for a diagnosis of oppositional defiant disorder. In particular we wished to identify good examples of studies which evaluated each of the five types of parenting programmes outlined in the previous section. A computer-based literature search of the PsychLit database was conducted. Terms that defined the disorder, such as *oppositional defiant disorder, conduct disorder* and *behavioural problems* were combined with terms that defined behavioural parent training interventions such as *parent training, parent management training, behavioural treatment* and *behavioural family therapy*. The search, which was confined to English language journals, covered the period 1977 to 1997 inclusively. A manual search through bibliographies of all recent review papers on psychological interventions for oppositional defiant disorder and conduct disorder was also conducted. Treatment outcome studies were selected for inclusion in this review if they contained cases of predominantly preadolescent children with behavioural problems which would probably warrant a diagnosis of oppositional defiant disorder; evaluated some form of behavioural parent training; contained a control or comparison condition or group; if at least five cases were included in the active treatment group; and if reliable and valid pre- and post-treatment measures were included in the design of the study. Single-case designs and studies reported in dissertations or convention papers were not included in the review. Using these inclusion and exclusion criteria 24 studies were selected.

Characteristics of the studies

The 24 studies selected for review fell into five main categories. The first category included eight studies which focused on individually based behavioural parent training (Bernal *et al.*, 1980; Kent and O'Leary, 1976; McNeil *et al.*, 1991; Olson and Roberts, 1987; Patterson *et al.*, 1982; Peed *et al.*, 1977; Wells and Egan, 1988; Zangwill, 1983). The second category contained four studies which evaluated group-based behavioural parent training (Christensen *et al.*, 1980; Cunningham *et al.*, 1995; Hamilton and MacQuiddy, 1984; Karoly and Rosenthal, 1977). Included in the third category were four studies that evaluated behavioural parent training which incorporated a component designed to increase social support available to the target child's primary caregiver (Dadds *et al.*, 1987, Dadds and McHugh, 1992; Firestone *et al.*, 1980; Martin, 1977). The fourth category included five studies of video-modelling-based behavioural parent training (Spaccarelli *et al.*, 1992; Webster-Stratton, 1984, 1990, 1992; Webster-Stratton *et al.*, 1988). Three studies which combined child-focused problem-solving skills training with behavioural parent training were contained in the final category (Kazdin *et al.*, 1987, 1992; Webster-Stratton and Hammond, 1997).

Twenty of the 24 studies were conducted in the USA. Two were conducted in Australia and two in Canada. All were published between 1977 and 1997. The 24 studies included 1179 cases, with 846 in active treatment groups and 333 in control groups. Target children of parents who received behavioural parent training ranged in age from three to fourteen years although the majority of cases were under eleven years of age. Seventy-five per cent of target children were boys and 25 per cent were girls. Averaging across sixteen studies where data was provided, 48 per cent of cases were single parent families. In fourteen studies rates of father involvement in parent training were provided and these ranged from 0 to 100 per cent. In nine of these fourteen studies in 50 per cent or more cases fathers were involved in parent training. In these 24 studies cases were referred for treatment from many sources. In eleven studies, cases came from multiple sources including health professionals, schools and self-referrals. In five studies the bulk of cases were referred by physicians. In four studies cases were predominantly solicited through the media. In two studies cases were referred by schools. In one study cases were screened in a school setting and in one study cases were self-referred. Treatment sessions in the majority of the programmes addressed in this chapter were typically offered on a weekly basis with individual sessions being of about an hour's duration and group sessions running closer to 90 minutes or two hours. Across the 24 studies, therapy duration spanned six to 41 sessions over two to ten months.

Methodological features

Cases in all studies were diagnostically homogeneous and were judged on the basis of the information given to approximate the criteria for opposi-

Table 5.1 Characteristics of treatment outcome studies of children with oppositional defiant disorder

Study no.	Study type	Authors	Year	Country	N per group	Mean age & range	Gender	Single parent families	Referral	Fathers involved in therapy	Treatment duration
1	I	Patterson et al.	1982	USA	BPT-I = 10 C = 9	3–12 y		53%	Multiple sources		17 sess
2	I	Zangwill	1983	USA	BPT-I = 5 C = 6	2–8 y	m 91% f 9%	73%	Multiple sources	0%	14 sess
3	I	Peed et al.	1977	USA	BPT-I = 6 C = 6	5 y	m 67% f 33%		Multiple sources	0%	10 sess
4	I	McNeil et al.	1991	USA	BPT-I = 10 C = 10	2–7 y	m 76% f 24%		Schools		14 sess
5	I	Wells and Egan	1988	USA	BPT-I = 9 FT = 10	4 y 3–8 y			Physicians		12 sess
6	I	Bernal et al.	1980	USA	BPT-I = 12 SUP = 12 C = 12	8 y 5–12 y	m 86% f 14%		Multiple sources		10 sess
7	I	Olson and Roberts	1987	USA	BPT-I = 12 BPT-I + FSST = 12 FSST = 12	5 y 2–10 y	m 69% F = 31%		Physicians	0%	4 sess
8	I	Kent and O'Leary	1976	USA	BPT-I + SB-CM = 16 C = 16	7–9 y			Schools		20 sess
9	G	Karoly and Rosenthal	1977	USA	BPT-G = 9 C = 8	7 y 3–14 y	m 82% f 18%	35%	Self-referred		10 sess
10	G	Christensen et al.	1980	USA	BPT-G = 12 BPT-I = 12 C = 12	4–12 y	m 78% f 22%	31%	Media solicited	69%	10 sess
11	G	Cunningham et al.	1995	Canada	BPT-G = 48 BPT-I = 46 C = 56	4 y		52%	Screening	?	12 sess
12	G	Hamilton et al.	1984	USA	BPT-G-A-SS = 9 BPT-G-A-S = 9 C = 9	2–7 y	m 67% f 33%		Media solicited	50%	6 sess
13	S	Firestone et al.	1980	Canada	BPT-G-F = 6 BPT-G = 6 C = 6	3–11 y	m 100%	100%	Physicians	50%	12 sess
14	S	Martin	1977	USA	BPT-I-F = 14 BPT-I = 14 C = 15	6–11 y	m 63% f 37%		Screening	50%	5 sess

No.	Type	Study	Year	Country	Groups (N)	Age	Sex	%	Recruitment	%	Sessions
15	S	Dadds et al.	1987	Australia	BPT-I-F = 6 BPT-I = 6 BPT-I-F-D = 6 BPT-I-D = 6	4 y	0%	0%	Multiple sources	50%	6 sess
16	S	Dadds and McHugh	1992	Australia	BPT-I-S = 11 BPT-I = 11	5 y	100%	100%	Media solicited	0%	6 sess
17	V	Webster-Stratton	1984	USA	BPT-G-V = 13 BPT-I = 11 C = 11	5 y	m 68% f 32%	54%	Multiple sources	71%	9 sess
18	V	Webster-Stratton et al.	1988	USA	BPT-G-V = 48 BPT-V = 49 BPT-G = 47 C = 50	5 y 3–8 y	m 69% f 31%	30%	Multiple sources	70%	12 sess
19	V	Webster-Stratton	1990	USA	BPT-I-V = 16 BPT-V = 17 C = 14	5 y 3–8 y	m 79% f 21%	40%	Multiple sources	60%	10 sess
20	V	Webster-Stratton	1992	USA	BPT-V = 59 C = 41	5 y 3–8 y	m 72% f 28%	34%	Multiple sources	62%	10 sess
21	V	Spaccarelli et al.	1992	USA	BPT-G-V + PSST-P = 21 BPT-G-V + SUP = 16 C = 16	6 y	m 59% f 11%	43%	Media solicited	15%	10 sess
22	P	Kazdin et al.	1986	USA	BPT-I + PSST-C + IPC = 20 C + IPC = 14	7–12 y	m 78% f 22%	55%	Physicians		BPT: 13 sess PSST: 20 sess
23	P	Kazdin et al.	1992	USA	BPT-I + PSST-C-I = 37 BPT-I = 31 PSST-C-I = 29	10 y 7–13 y	m 78% f 22%	39%	Physicians		BPT & PSST: 41 BPT: 16 PSST: 25
24	P	Webster-Stratton and Hammond	1997	USA	BPT-G-V + PSST-C-G-V = 22 BPT-G-V = 26 PSST-C-G-V = 27 C = 22	6 y 4–8 y	m 74% f 26%	32%	Multiple sources	73%	BPT: 15 sess PSST: 20 sess

Key I = Study focusing on individually based behavioural parent training. G = Study of group-based behavioural parent training. S = Study of behavioural parent training with explicit inclusion of member of the mother's social system, either the father or another. V = Study of behavioural parent training involving video-modelling. P = Study including a child-focused problem-solving skills training component. BPT-I = Individually based behavioural parent training. BPT-G = Group-based behavioural parent training. BPT-G-A-SS = Individually based behavioural parent training with audiotape instructions and a time-out signal seat that buzzes when the child leaves it without permission. BPT-G-A-S = Individually based behavioural parent training with audiotape instructions and a signal when left without permission. FSST = Family-based social skills training. SB-CM = School-based contingency management. BPT-G-F = Group-based behavioural parent training with father involvement. BPT-I-F = Individually based behavioural parent training with father involvement. BPT-I-F-D = Individually based behavioural parent training with cases where there is marital discord. BPT-I-D = Individually based behavioural parent training with cases where there is marital discord. BPT-I-S = Group-based behavioural parent training with socially supportive network member involved. BPT-I-V = Individually based behavioural parent training with video-modelling. BPT-G-V = Group-based behavioural parent training with video-modelling and minimal therapist contact. BPT-V = Behavioural parent training with video-modelling. PSST = Problem-solving skills training for parents. PSST-C-I = Individually based problem-solving skills training for children. PSST-C-G-V = Group-based problem-solving skills training for children with video-modelling. FT = Family therapy. IPC = Inpatient care. SUP = Supportive therapy, discussion group or attention placebo control group. C = Control group. sess = sessions. w = weeks. m = months. y = years.

Table 5.2 Methodological features of studies of oppositional defiant disorder

Feature	S1	S2	S3	S4	S5	S6	S7	S8	S9	S10	S11	S12	S13	S14	S15	S16	S17	S18	S19	S20	S21	S22	S23	S24
Control or comparison group or condition	1	1	1	1	1	1	1	1	1	1	1	1	1	1	1	1	1	1	1	1	1	1	1	1
Random assignment	1	1	1	1	1	1	1	1	1	1	1	1	1	1	1	1	1	1	1	1	1	1	1	1
Diagnostic homogeneity	1	1	1	1	1	1	1	1	1	1	1	1	1	1	1	1	1	1	1	1	1	1	1	1
Comparable for co-morbidity	0	0	0	0	0	0	0	0	0	0	0	0	0	0	1	1	0	0	0	0	0	1	1	1
Demographic similarity	1	1	1	1	1	1	1	1	1	1	1	1	1	1	1	1	1	1	1	1	1	1	1	1
Pre-treatment assessment	1	1	1	1	1	1	1	1	1	1	1	1	1	1	1	1	1	1	1	1	1	1	1	1
Post-treatment assessment	1	1	1	1	1	1	1	1	1	1	1	1	1	1	1	1	1	1	1	1	1	1	1	1
Two-month follow-up assessment	0	0	0	0	0	1	0	1	0	1	1	1	1	1	1	1	1	0	0	1	1	1	1	1
Children's self-report	0	0	0	0	0	0	0	0	0	0	0	0	0	0	0	0	0	0	0	0	0	0	0	0
Parent's ratings	1	1	0	0	0	0	1	0	0	1	1	0	0	1	1	0	1	1	1	0	1	1	1	1
Teacher's ratings	0	0	0	1	0	0	0	1	1	0	0	0	0	0	0	0	1	0	0	1	0	1	1	1

	S	S	S	S	S	S	S	S	S	S	S	S	S	S	S	S	S	S	S	S	S	S	S	S	S
Therapist's ratings	0	0	0	0	0	0	0	0	0	0	0	0	0	0	0	0	0	0	0	0	0	0	0	0	0
Researcher's ratings	1	1	1	1	1	1	1	1	1	0	1	1	0	0	1	1	1	1	1	0	1	0	1	1	1
Child's symptom assessed	1	1	1	1	1	1	1	1	1	1	1	1	1	1	1	1	1	1	1	1	1	1	1	1	1
System assessed	0	1	1	0	0	1	0	0	1	0	1	0	0	0	1	1	1	1	1	1	1	1	0	1	1
Deterioration assessed	0	0	0	0	0	0	0	0	0	0	0	0	0	0	0	0	0	0	0	0	0	0	0	0	0
Drop-out assessed	0	1	1	1	1	1	1	0	1	0	0	0	0	0	1	1	0	0	1	0	0	0	0	1	0
Clinical significance of change assessed	1	0	0	0	0	0	0	0	0	1	0	0	0	0	0	1	1	1	1	0	1	1	1	1	1
Experienced therapists used	1	0	0	0	1	1	0	1	1	1	1	1	1	1	1	1	1	1	1	1	1	1	1	1	1
Treatments were equally valued	0	0	0	1	0	0	0	1	0	1	1	1	1	1	1	1	1	1	1	1	0	0	1	1	1
Treatments were manualized	1	1	1	1	1	1	1	1	1	1	1	1	1	1	1	1	1	1	1	1	1	1	1	1	1
Therapy supervision was provided	1	1	1	1	1	1	1	1	1	1	1	1	1	1	1	1	1	1	1	1	1	1	1	1	1
Treatment integrity checked	0	0	0	1	0	0	0	0	0	0	0	0	0	0	0	1	0	0	1	0	0	0	0	1	1
Data on concurrent treatment given	0	0	0	0	0	0	0	0	0	0	0	0	0	0	0	0	0	0	0	0	0	0	0	0	0
Data on subsequent treatment given	0	0	0	0	0	0	0	1	0	1	0	0	0	0	0	0	0	1	0	0	0	0	0	0	1
Total	13	13	12	11	13	15	11	15	11	17	14	13	13	13	13	17	17	18	16	14	16	14	16	21	20

Key S = study. 1 = design feature was present. 0 = design feature was absent.

tional defiant disorder. All 24 studies contained treatment and control or comparison conditions and cases were randomly assigned to these groups or conditions. In all studies treatment and comparison or control groups were demographically similar, but in only five studies was there evidence that cases were comparable for co-morbidity. In all studies cases were evaluated before and after treatment on reliable and valid assessment instruments. In fifteen studies follow-up data were collected between two months and one year following treatment. One-year follow-up data were reported in six studies (Bernal *et al.*, 1980; Kazdin *et al.*, 1987, 1992; Webster-Stratton, 1984, 1992; Webster-Stratton and Hammond, 1997). Kent and O'Leary (1976) followed up cases for nine months after treatment. Six-month follow-up results were given in five studies (Cunningham *et al.*, 1995; Dadds *et al.*, 1987; Dadds and McHugh, 1992; Martin, 1977; Spaccarelli *et al.*, 1992). In three studies follow-up data for brief periods of two to four months were available (Christensen *et al.*, 1980; Firestone *et al.*, 1980; Hamilton and MacQuiddy, 1984). In most studies data were obtained from multiple informants. Parent ratings were obtained in twenty studies; independent researcher ratings in seventeen studies, teacher ratings in seven studies and children's self-report ratings in one study. In all studies evaluations of children's behavioural problems or symptoms were made and in fifteen studies data on some aspect of the child's social system were collected. Across the 24 studies a variety of assessment instruments were used. For example, to evaluate parental perceptions of a wider range of child behaviour problems in a number of studies Achenbach's (1991) Child Behaviour Checklist, Eyberg and Ross' (1978) Child Behaviour Inventory or the Becker (1960) Bipolar Adjective Checklist were used. To evaluate parental accounts of specific behaviour problems on a daily basis the Parental Daily Report (Chamberlain and Reid, 1987) was used in a number of studies. Researcher ratings of children's behaviour problems and parent–child interaction were made using systems such as Reid's (1978) family interaction coding system or Robinson and Eyberg's (1981) dyadic parent–child interaction coding system. While the statistical significance of intergroup differences in outcomes was reported in all studies, data on the clinical significance of treatment gains were given in only ten studies. Drop-out rates were reported in only ten studies also. In seventeen studies experienced rather than novice therapists engaged clients in treatment. In fifteen of the sixteen studies where two or more treatment modalities were compared, it was judged that the researchers valued the treatment packages equally and arranged for different treatments to be offered in potent ways. In all of the studies treatments were either manualized or delivered following clearly articulated guidelines and in all studies therapy was regularly supervised. However, explicit reference to attempts to check and control treatment integrity in a systematic way was made in only four studies. Data on concurrent treatment that clients received during the experimental treatment were not given in any of the reports but in three studies information on treatment which occurred after the study was offered. Overall, this group of 24 studies were methodologically rigorous by current standards. Considerable confidence may therefore be placed in their results.

Substantive findings

A summary of treatment effects and outcome rates for the 24 studies of behavioural parent training is presented in Tables 5.3 and 5.4. A narrative account of key findings is given in Table 5.5. The substantive findings contained in these tables will be discussed below in five sections, with each section dealing with one of the five types of studies outlined earlier, i.e. studies of individually based programmes; studies of group-based programmes; studies of programmes which included a social support component; studies of video-modelling-based programmes; and studies of programmes which included a child-focused problem-solving training component.

Individually based behavioural parent training

Eight studies evaluated individually based behavioural parent training (Bernal *et al.*, 1980; Kent and O'Leary, 1976; McNeil *et al.*, 1991; Olson and Roberts, 1987; Patterson *et al.*, 1982; Peed *et al.*, 1977; Wells and Egan, 1988; Zangwill, 1983). In all eight studies the core programme involved meeting with mothers and their children on a regular weekly basis over a period of ten to twenty weeks and training them in behaviourally based parenting skills in the manner outlined earlier (Forehand and McMahon, 1981; Hanf and Kling, 1973; Patterson *et al.*, 1975). Some of the programmes included interesting features worthy of comment. Kent and O'Leary (1976) trained parents to help their children with school work and also included a school-based contingency management component in their programme. Children's teachers were coached in the use of behavioural methods to manage school-based behaviour problems and foster positive behaviour in the school setting. Olson and Roberts (1987) used family-based problem-solving skills training as an adjunctive treatment in one of their treatment groups and this component alone in a comparison group. Structural family therapy (Minuchin, 1974) was the treatment offered to cases in the comparison group in the Wells and Egan (1988) study.

Effect sizes based on parent, teacher and researcher ratings of children's behaviour problems or symptoms immediately following treatment ranged from 0 to 1.8. The unweighted mean effect sizes for parent ratings was 1.2, for teacher ratings 1.0 and for researcher ratings 1.0. Thus, following treatment the average case treated with behavioural parent training fared better than 84 to 88 per cent of cases in control or comparison groups. In two studies, rates of clinical improvement were given and these were based on children's behaviour falling within the normal range following treatment. Averaging the results of these, 56 per cent of treated cases showed clinically

Table 5.3 Summary of results of effects of psychological treatments for oppositional defiant disorder from studies of individually based and group-based behavioural parent training

Study number and condition

Variable	Studies of individually based BPT								Studies of group-based BPT						
	Study 1	Study 2	Study 3	Study 4	Study 5	Study 6	Study 7	Study 8	Study 9	Study 10		Study 11		Study 12	
	BPT-I > C	BPT-I > C	BPT-I > C	BPT-I > C	BPT-I > FT	BPT-I > SUP	BPT-I > FSST	BPT-I + SB-CM > C	BPT-G > C	BPT-G > C	BPT-G > BPT-I	BPT-G > C	BPT-G > BPT-I	BPT-G-A-SS > C	BPT-G-A-S > C
Symptomatic improvement after treatment															
Children's self-report	–	–	–	–	–	–	–	–	–	–	–	–	–	–	–
Parent's ratings	0.6	1.8	1.0	–	–	1.1	1.4	–	–	0.5	0.4	0.2	0.3	2.1	1.2
Teacher's ratings	–	–	–	0.8	–	–	–	1.1	–	–	–	–	–	–	–
Therapist's ratings	–	–	–	–	–	–	–	–	–	–	–	–	–	–	–
Researcher's ratings	0.8	1.3	1.0	1.5	1.8	0.0	–	1.1	1.4	–	–	–	–	–	–
Symptomatic improvement at follow-up															
Children's self-report	–	–	–	–	–	–	–	–	–	–	–	–	–	–	–
Parent's ratings	–	–	–	–	–	–	–	0.0	–	0.8	0.0	0.1	0.2	–	–
Teacher's ratings	–	–	–	–	–	–	–	–	–	–	–	–	–	–	–
Therapist's ratings	–	–	–	–	–	–	–	–	–	–	–	–	–	–	–
Researcher's ratings	–	–	–	–	–	–	–	0.0	–	0.2	-0.5	–	–	–	–

	BPT-I	BPT-G	BPT-G-A-S	BPT-G-A-SS	FSST	FT	SB-CM	SUP	C
Systemic and cognitive improvement after treatment									
Parent–child interaction	–	>2.0	1.0	–	1.8	–	0.5	0.2	–
Children's self-esteem	–	–	–	–	–	–	–	–	–
Performance on lab tests	–	–	–	–	–	–	–	–	–
Reading achievement	–	–	–	–	–	0.0	–	–	–
Systemic and cognitive improvement at follow-up									
Parent–child interaction	–	–	–	–	0.5	–	0.8	0.3	0.0
Children's self-esteem	–	–	–	–	–	–	–	–	–
Performance on lab tests	–	–	–	–	–	–	–	–	–
Reading achievement	–	–	–	–	–	0.8	–	–	–
Positive clinical outcomes									
% improved after treatment	70% > 33%	–	–	–	41% > 17%	–	88% > 70% 75%	88% > 100% 75%	–
% improved at follow-up	–	–	–	–	–	–	33% > 70%	–	–
Negative clinical outcomes									
% Drop-out	38%	–	20%	–	12%	0%	22%	22%	–

Key BPT-I = Individually based behavioural parent training. BPT-G = Group-based behavioural parent training. BPT-G-A-SS = Individually based behavioural parent training with audiotape instructions and a time-out signal seat that buzzes when the child leaves it without permission. BPT-G-A-S = Individually based behavioural parent training with audiotape instructions and a time-out seat that does not give a signal when left without permission. FT = Family therapy. FSST = Family-based social skills training. SB-CM = School-based contingency management. SUP = Supportive therapy group. C = Control group.

Table 5.4 Summary of results of effects of psychological treatment for oppositional defiant disorder from studies of behavioural parent training involving a social support component for the primary caregiver, video-based modelling and child-focused problem-solving skills training

Variable	Study type, number and condition																			
	Studies of BPT with social support component								Studies of BPT with video-modelling							Studies of BPT with child-focused PSST				
	Study 13		Study 14		Study 15	Study 16	Study 17		Study 18		Study 19	Study 20	Study 21		Study 22	Study 23		Study 24		
	BPT-G-F > C	BPT-G > C	BPT-I-F > C		BPT-I-F-D > BPT-I-D	BPT-I-S > BPT-I	BPT-G-V > C	BPT-G-V > BPT-I	BPT-G-V > C	BPT-G-V > BPT-G	BPT-I-V > C	BPT-V > C	BPT-G-V + PSST-P > C	BPT-G-V + SUP-P > C	BPT-I + PSST-C > C	BPT-I > PSST-C	BPT-I + PSST-C > BPT-I	BPT-G-V + PSST-C-G-V > C	BPT-G-V + PSST-C-G-V > BPT-G-V	BPT-G-V + PSST-C-G-V > PSST-C-G-V
Symptomatic improvement after treatment																				
Children's self-report	–	–	–		–	–	–	–	–	–	–	–	–	–	–	0.6	0.3	1.3	0.1	0.5
Parent's ratings	1.3	0.0	1.0		0.5	0.2	0.7	0.1	0.5	0.6	0.5	0.8	1.1	1.1	1.4	0.4	0.5	–	–0.2	0.1
Teacher's ratings	–	–	–		–	–	–	–	–	–	–	–	–	–	0.8	0.3	0.2	–	–0.2	–
Researcher's ratings	–	–	–		0.5	0.6	0.7	0.0	0.0	0.5	0.6	0.3	–	–	–	0.6	0.6	0.2	–0.2	–0.3
Symptomatic improvement at follow-up																				
Children's self-report	–	–	–		–	–	–	–	–	–	–	–	–	–	–	1.2	0.4	–	–	–
Parent's ratings	–	–	–		1.9	0.1	0.2	0.0	–	–	–	–	–	–	2.6	1.1	0.8	–0.2	–0.2	0.1
Teacher's ratings	–	–	–		–	–	–	–	–	–	–	–	–	–	1.4	0.1	0.1	–0.3	–0.3	–0.3
Therapist's ratings	–	–	–		–	–	–	–	–	–	–	–	–	–	–	–	–	–	–	–
Researcher's ratings	–	–	–		>2.0	0.6	0.2	0.2	–	–	–	–	–	–	–	0.8	0.7	0.5	0.5	0.4

Systemic and cognitive improvement after treatment															
Parent–child interaction	0.9	0.5	0.7	0.7	0.7	—	—	—	—	0.7	0.4	0.7	0.7	0.4	0.0 / 0.0
Children's self-esteem	—	—	—	—	—	—	—	—	—	—	—	—	1.0	0.8 / —	0.0
Performance on lab tests	—	—	—	—	—	—	—	—	—	—	—	—	—	—	—
Reading achievement	—	—	—	—	—	—	—	—	—	—	—	—	—	—	—
Systemic and cognitive improvement at follow-up															
Parent–child interaction	>2.0	0.4	—	0.3	—	—	—	—	—	0.6	0.5	—	0.1	0.2	—
Children's self-esteem	—	—	—	—	—	—	—	—	—	—	—	—	—	—	—
Performance on lab tests	—	—	—	—	—	—	—	—	—	—	—	—	0.4	0.4	0.0
Reading achievement	—	—	—	—	—	—	—	—	—	—	—	—	—	—	—
Positive clinical outcomes															
% improved after treatment	66%	—	—	—	—	—	—	—	35%	60%	60%	60%	60%	60%	60%
% improved at follow-up	>33% 100%	>54%	93%	>73%	10% 10%	77%	—	>7% 27%	>18% 50%	>27% 50%	>55%	>73% 95%	>73% 95%	>73% 95%
Negative clinical outcomes															
% Drop-out	>0%	>0% 46%	>0% 73%	10% 10%	>0% 9%	>21% 29%	21%	>21% 13%	60%	60%	74%

Key BPT-I = Individually based behavioural parent training. BPT-G = Group-based behavioural parent training. BPT-G-F = Group-based behavioural parent training with father involvement. BPT-I-F = Individually based behavioural parent training with father involvement. BPT-I-D = Individually based behavioural parent training with cases where there is marital discord. BPT-I-F-D = Individually based behavioural parent training with father involvement with cases where there is marital discord. BPT-I-S = Group-based behavioural parent training with socially supportive network member involved. BPT-V = Behavioural parent training with video-modelling. BPT-I-V = Individually based behavioural parent training with video-modelling. BPT-G-V = Group-based behavioural parent training with video-modelling. PSST-P = Problem-solving skills training for parents. PSST-C-I = Individually based problem-solving skills training for children. PSST-C-G-V = Group-based problem-solving skills training for children with video-modelling. C = Control group.

Table 5.5 Summary of key findings from treatment outcome studies of children with oppositional defiant disorder

Study No	Study type	Authors	Year	N per Group	No of sessions	Group differences	Key findings
1	I	Patterson et al.	1982	1. BPT-I = 10 2. C = 9	17	1 > 2	• Following treatment 70% of cases in BPT were clinically improved.
2	I	Zangwill	1983	1. BPT-I = 5 2. C = 6	14	1 > 2	• Following treatment there was a significant improvement in both child behaviour and parenting skills in the BPT group.
3	I	Peed et al.	1977	1. BPT-I = 6 2. C = 6	10	1 > 2	• Following treatment there was a significant improvement in both child behaviour and parenting skills in the BPT group.
4	I	McNeil et al.	1991	1. BPT-I = 10 2. C = 10	14	1 > 2	• Following treatment there was a significant improvement in school-based child behaviour problems in the BPT group.
5	I	Wells and Egan	1988	1. BPT-I = 9 2. FT = 10	12	1 > 2	• After treatment greater improvements in parenting practices and child behaviour problems occurred in the BPT group compared to the structural family therapy group.
6	I	Bernal et al.	1980	1. BPT-I = 12 2. SUP = 12 3. C = 12	10	1 > 2 > 3	• Following treatment, parents in the BPT group reported fewer child behaviour problems and greater satisfaction. • After treatment and at 6, 12 and 24-month follow-up both groups showed similar outcomes on parent-reported child behavioural problems.
7	I	Olson and Roberts	1987	1. BPT-I = 12 2. BPT-I + FSST = 12 3. FSST = 12	4	1 = 2 > 3	• After treatment, cases treated with the combined programme or the behavioural parent training programme fared better then the group that received social skills training only.
8	I	Kent and O'Leary	1976	1. BPT-I + SB-CM = 16 2. C = 16	20	1 > 2	• Following treatment, the treatment group showed greater behavioural improvement than the control group and at 9 months' follow-up they showed greater academic achievement.
9	G	Karoly and Rosenthal	1977	1. BPT-G = 9 2. C = 8	10	1 > 2	• Following therapy, treated cases showed improvements in children's behaviour problems and family cohesion.

		Authors	Year	Conditions		Outcome	Findings
10	G	Christensen et al.	1980	1. BPT-G = 12 2. BPT-I = 12 3. C = 12	10	1 = 2 > 3	• Following treatment and 2 months later the individual and group-based BPT programmes led to improvements in problem behaviour in over 70% of cases compared with 33% of controls.
11	G	Cunningham et al.	1995	1. BPT-G = 48 2. BPT-I = 46 3. C = 56	12	1 > 2 > 3	• After treatment and at 6-month follow-up parents in the group-based BPT programme reported fewer child behaviour problems. • More at-risk families enrolled in group than individual BPT. • Group-based programme was 6 times more cost-effective than individual BPT programmes.
12	G	Hamilton and McQuiddy	1984	1. BPT-G-A-SS = 9 2. BPT-G-A-S = 9 3. C = 9	6	1 > 2 > 3	• Following treatment and 2 months later significant improvement in children's behaviour problems occurred in both groups with the greatest improvements being shown by the group in which the signal seat was used in treatment.
13	S	Firestone et al.	1980	1. BPT-G-F = 6 2. BPT-G = 6 3. C = 6	12	1 = 2 > 3	• Following treatment and 4 months later, treated cases showed greater improvement in children's behaviour problems than untreated cases.
14	S	Martin	1977	1. BPT-I-F = 14 2. BPT-I = 14 3. C = 15	5	1 = 2 > 3	• Following treatment and 6 months later both treatment groups showed greater improvements in behaviour problems than the control group.
15	S	Dadds et al.	1987	1. BPT-I-F = 6 2. BPT-I = 6 3. BPT-I-F-D = 6 4. BPT-I-D = 6	6	1 = 2 = 3 > 4	• After treatment and at 6-month follow-up, for distressed couples, greater improvements in parenting practices, child behaviour problems and marital satisfaction occurred in the group treated with combined BPT and partner support training.
16	S	Dadds and McHugh	1992	1. BPT-I-S = 11 2. BPT-I = 11	6	1 = 2	• After treatment and at 6-month follow-up similar improvements in parenting practices and child behaviour problems occurred in both groups. • Treatment responders reported higher levels of social support.
17	V	Webster-Stratton	1984	1. BPT-G-V = 13 2. BPT-I = 11 3. C = 11	1	1 = 2 > 3	• Following treatment and a year later group-based BPT with video-modelling and individual BPT both led to significant improvements in children's behaviour. • The group-based BPT with video-modelling was more cost-effective.

Table 5.5 (cont'd)

Study No	Study type	Authors	Year	N per Group	No of sessions	Group differences	Key findings
18	V	Webster-Stratton et al.	1988	1. BPT-G-V = 48 2. BPT-V = 49 3. BPT-G = 47 4. C = 50	12	1 > 2 = 3 > 4	• After treatment group-based BPT with video-modelling was slightly more effective than the other two treatments.
19	V	Webster-Stratton	1990	1. BPT-I-V = 16 2. BPT-V = 17 3. C = 14	10	1 > 2 > 3	• After treatment individually based BPT with video-modelling was more effective than BPT that was completely video-based.
20	V	Webster-Stratton	1992	1. BPT-V = 59 2. C = 41	10	1 > 2	• Following treatment and a year later the treatment group showed greater improvement in parenting practices and child behaviour. • For mothers, being a single parent, being depressed and having a low mental age were associated with poorer outcome. • For fathers, high life stress, depression and low mental age were associated with poorer outcome.
21	V	Spaccarelli et al.	1992	1. BPT-G-V + PSST-P = 21 2. BPT-G-V + SUP = 16 3. C = 16	10	1 > 2 > 3	• After treatment, both programmes led to improvements in parenting skills and target child behaviour problems. • After treatment, the group-based parent training programme with video-modelling and parental problem-solving skills training group led to improvement in a wide range of non-target behaviour problems and parental attitudes to their children and the parenting role. • At 6-month follow-up both groups maintained most treatment gains, but there were no intergroup differences.

22	P	Kazdin et al.	1986	1. BPT-I + PSST-C + IPC = 20 2. C + IPC = 14	BPT: 13 PSST: 20	1 > 2	• Following treatment 35%, and a year later 27%, of treated cases showed clinically significant improvement compared with 7% of controls.
23	P	Kazdin et al.	1992	1. BPT-I + PSST-C-I = 37 2. BPT-I = 31 3. PSST-C-I = 29	41 16 25	1 > 2 = 3	• After treatment and at 1-year follow-up, 50–60% of cases in the combined treatment showed clinically significant improvements in child behaviour problems at home and school compared with 10–27% of cases in the other 2 treatment groups.
24	P	Webster-Stratton and Hammond	1997	1. BPT-G-V + PSST-C-G-V = 22 2. BPT-G-V = 26 3. PSST-C-G-V = 27 4. C = 22	BPT: 15 PSST: 20	For behaviour problems 1 > 2 > 3 > 4 For children's problem solving skills 1 > 3 > 2 > 4	• Following treatment and a year later all 3 programmes led to improvements in behaviour problems, parenting practices and children's skills. • The combined programme was the most effective with 95% of cases showing clinical improvement at follow-up. • The BPT programme led to improvements in parenting while the children's programme led to improvements in problem-solving skills.

Key I = Study focusing on individually based behavioural parent training. G = Study of group-based behavioural parent training. S = Study of behavioural parent training with explicit inclusion of member of the mother's social system, either the father or another. V = Study of behavioural parent training involving video-modelling. P = Study including a child-focused problem-solving skills training component. BPT-I = Individually based behavioural parent training. BPT-G = Group-based behavioural parent training. BPT-G-A-SS = Individually based behavioural parent training with audiotape instructions and a time-out signal seat that buzzes when the child leaves it without permission. BPT-G-A-S = Individually based behavioural parent training with audiotape and a time-out seat that does not give a signal when left without permission. FSST = Family-based social skills training. SB-CM = School-based contingency management. BPT-G-F = Group-based behavioural parent training with father involvement. BPT-I-F = Individually based behavioural parent training with father involvement. BPT-I-D = Individually based behavioural parent training with cases where there is marital discord. BPT-I-S = Group-based behavioural parent training with socially supportive network member involved. BPT-V = Behavioural parent training with video-modelling and minimal therapist contact. BPT-I-V = Individually based behavioural parent training with video-modelling. BPT-G-V = Group-based behavioural parent training with video-modelling. PSST-C-G-V = Group-based problem-solving skills training for children. PSST-C-I = Individually based problem-solving skills training for parents. PSST-P = Problem-solving skills training for children. PSST-C-G-V = Group-based problem-solving skills training for children with video-modelling. IPC = Inpatient care. FT = Family therapy. SUP = Supportive therapy, discussion group or attention placebo control group. C = Control group.

significant improvement after treatment compared with 25 per cent of cases in control and comparison groups.

Effect sizes based on measures of parent–child interaction following treatment ranged from 1.0 to greater than 2.0, so the average treated case showed more improvement in parent–child relationships and parenting skills than upwards of 84 per cent of cases in control groups.

In Kent and O'Leary's (1976) study, which included a school-based contingency management component, positive effects on academic achievement at nine months' follow-up were noted. The effect size here was 0.8 showing that the average treated case fared better academically than 79 per cent of untreated cases nine months after the completion of the programme.

Bernal *et al.* (1980) found that at six, twelve and 24-month follow-up outcomes for cases in the behavioural parent training group and the supportive therapy programme converged and in the long term the outcome for both groups was the same:

Drop-out rates ranged from 0–38 per cent and the average drop-out rate was 23 per cent.

From a review of these eight studies it may be concluded that in the short term, individually based behavioural parent training spanning ten to twenty sessions was more effective than no treatment or less clearly focused family interventions. In particular, for children with oppositional defiant disorder, individually based behavioural parent training reduced home- and school-based behavioural problems and improved parenting skills and parent–child relationships.

Group-based behavioural parent training

Four studies evaluated group-based behavioural parent training programmes (Christensen *et al.*, 1980; Cunningham *et al.*, 1995; Hamilton and MacQuiddy, 1984; Karoly and Rosenthal, 1977). Within these programmes parents received treatment in groups without their children. They were instructed in the use of behaviourally based parenting skills and invited to complete homework assignments as described earlier. Programmes ranged in duration from six to twelve sessions, and typically sessions were held weekly. Groups ranged in size from six to 27 members. In all groups, even the larger ones, parents were given opportunities to discuss the application of behavioural parenting skills to their particular children's behaviour problems and to discuss their progress. In some groups reading material and specialized parenting aids to facilitate the use of behavioural parenting skills were provided. For example, Hamilton and MacQuiddy (1984) gave parents booklets, audiotapes and time-out seats. In one condition the time-out seat contained a signal buzzer which was activated if the child left the seat without permission while in time-out. To test the effectiveness of this particular device, parents in a comparison group received a seat which did not contain a signal buzzer and were asked to use it for timing out their children for misbehaviour.

When the outcome for cases that received group-based behavioural parent training was compared with the outcome for untreated control groups, effect sizes ranging from 0.2 to 1.4 were found for parent and researcher ratings of children's behaviour problems following treatment. When these data were averaged, the mean effect size immediately following treatment was 1.1, indicating that the average treated case fared better than 86 per cent of untreated cases in the control groups. At two to six months' follow-up, effect sizes for children's behaviour problems ranged from 0.1 to 0.8, with the mean effect size being 0.4, showing that treatment gains dissipated with even a brief lapse of time.

For changes in parent–child relationships following treatment, when the outcome for cases that received group-based behavioural parent training was compared with the outcome for untreated controls, an effect size of 0.5 was obtained in a single study. At two to six months' follow-up effect sizes for variables assessing parent–child relationships ranged from 0.5 to 0.8, which when averaged gave a mean effect size of 0.7. Thus, two to six months following treatment, the average treated case fared better than 76 per cent of untreated controls in terms of improvements in parent–child relationships.

When the outcome for cases that received group-based behavioural parent training was compared with the outcome for cases treated with individually based parent training, effect sizes ranging from –0.5 to 0.4 were found for parent and researcher ratings of children's behaviour problems and parent–child relationships following treatment and at follow-up. These data show that differences in the outcome for the two treatment formats was negligible.

Christensen *et al.* (1980) in the only study in this section reporting outcome rates based on stringent criteria for clinically significant improvement, found that two months after treatment 70 per cent of cases receiving individually based programmes and 75 per cent of cases in group-based programmes maintained improvement compared with 33 per cent of untreated controls.

From a review of these four studies it may be concluded that group-based behavioural parent training programmes were as effective as individually based programmes and so may be a more cost-effective alternative to individually based treatment.

Social support and behavioural parent training

Four studies evaluated behavioural parent training programmes which incorporated a component designed to increase social support available to the target child's primary caregiver (Dadds *et al.*, 1987; Dadds and McHugh, 1992; Firestone *et al.*, 1980; Martin, 1977). The rationale for the development of such programmes was that a lack of support within the primary caregiver's marriage, extended family or social network may compromise her capacity to consistently manage her children's behavioural difficulties using behavioural parenting skills. In all four studies the programme that included a social support component was compared to a similar programme which did not include a social support component and in two studies (Firestone *et al.*, 1980; Martin, 1977) a no-treatment control group was also included. In Firestone *et al.*'s (ibid.) study, training was offered on a group basis, whereas in the other three studies it was offered on an individual basis. In three of the studies (Firestone *et al.*, 1980; Dadds *et al.*, 1987; Martin, 1977) the social support component involved explicitly including fathers and mothers in the training session. However, in one study (Dadds and McHugh, 1992) single parents were invited to include a potentially supportive member of their social network in the treatment programme.

When the outcome for cases that received behavioural parent training with the father involved was compared with the outcome for untreated control groups, effect sizes ranging from 1.0 to 1.3 were found for parent ratings of children's behaviour problems following treatment. When these data were averaged, the mean effect size immediately following treatment was 1.2, indicating that the average treated case fared better than 88 per cent of untreated cases in the control groups.

In contrast to this finding, a comparison of the outcome for cases that received behavioural parent training which included a social support component with the outcome for programmes that did not include such a component, in three out of four instances effect sizes were negligible, indicating that the addition of the social support component added little to the effectiveness of treatment. However, Dadds *et al.* (1987) found that for maritally distressed couples the addition of a social support component made a significant difference to treatment effectiveness. A comparison of maritally distressed cases that did and did not receive the programme containing the component designed to increase social support yielded an effect size for researcher-rated improvements greater than 2.0 at six months' follow-up. This showed that the average case in the programme containing the support component fared better than 99 per cent of cases in the regular behavioural parent training programme. In terms of clinically significant improvement, at six months' follow-up 100 per cent of cases in the programme containing the support component were judged to be clinically improved across a range of criteria compared with 0 per cent of cases in the routine programme. An interesting finding in Dadds and McHugh's (1992) study of single mothers was that the availability of social support was the best predictor of a good response to treatment.

From a review of these four studies it may be concluded that in cases where comprehensive assessment showed that a primary caretaker was receiving limited social support from her partner, then the most effective treatment for oppositional defiant disorder was behavioural parent training combined with a component to enhance the social support provided by the partner. In other instances, the addition of a treatment component to increase social support was of little additional value.

Video-modelling-based behavioural parent training programme

Five studies incorporated the use of video-modelling into behavioural parent training programmes (Spaccarelli *et al.*, 1992; Webster-Stratton, 1984, 1990, 1992; Webster-Stratton *et al.*, 1988). Four of these were conducted by Webster-Stratton's group at the Department of Parent and Child Nursing, University of Washington and in all five studies Webster-Stratton's training videotapes were used.

Compared with no-treatment control groups, the effect sizes presented in Table 5.3 suggest that group-based video-modelling programmes alone or with therapist-led discussion or adjunctive parental problem-solving training were highly effective. Mean effect sizes of 0.9, 0.7 and 0.7 occurred for parent-rated child behaviour problems, researcher-rated child behaviour problems and measures of parent–child interaction respectively. The average treated case fared better than 76–82 per cent of untreated controls.

Effect sizes based on comparisons of group-based video-modelling programmes with traditional individually based programmes for parent, teacher and researcher ratings of children's behaviour problems ranged from 0 to 0.2. Thus the outcome for both of these types of programmes were similar.

Compared with no-treatment control groups, video-modelling programmes with minimal therapist contact were somewhat effective with mean effect sizes of 0.7, 0.3 and 0.5 for parent-rated child behaviour problems, researcher-rated child behaviour problems and measures of parent–child interaction respectively. The average treated case fared better than 62–76 per cent of untreated controls.

From these studies it may be concluded that group-based video-modelling-based behavioural parent training programmes were as effective as individually based behavioural parent training programmes and that both of these were more effective than video-modelling behavioural parent training programmes that involved minimal therapist contact. However, the latter types of programmes were quite effective.

Child-focused problem-solving skills training and behavioural parent training

Three studies evaluated child-focused problem-solving skills training combined with behavioural parent training (Kazdin *et al.*, 1987, 1992; Webster-Stratton and Hammond, 1997). In one of these video-modelling was used for both the behavioural parent training and the child-focused training components (Webster-Stratton and Hammond, 1997).

Compared with no-treatment control groups, programmes that combined child-focused problem-solving skills training with behavioural parent training were very effective with mean effect sizes of 1.4 for parent-rated child behaviour problems after treatment. At one-year follow-up this effect size increased to 2.6 in Kazdin *et al.*'s (1987) first study.

Thus the average treated case fared better than 92 per cent of untreated cases after treatment and better than 99 per cent of untreated cases a year later on parent-rated child behaviour problems. Improvements in teacher-rated behaviour were less consistent across studies.

Both Kazdin *et al.* (1992) and Webster-Stratton and Hammond (1997) classified cases as showing clinically significant improvement at one-year follow-up and in both of these particularly well-designed studies, it was found that programmes which combined child-focused problem-solving skills training with behavioural parent training led to better outcomes than programmes that included only one of these two treatment components. Kazdin *et al.* (1992) found that 50 per cent of cases in the combined programmes compared with 9 per cent of cases in the parent training and 13 per cent of cases in the child-focused programme moved from the clinical to the normal range on both the parent and teacher versions of the Child Behaviour Checklist (Achenbach, 1991). Webster-Stratton an Hammond (1997) found that 95 per cent of cases in the combined treatment programme, 60 per cent of cases in the parent training programme and 74 per cent of cases in the child-focused programme were clinically improved a year after treatment. Clinical improvement was based on researcher ratings of a 30 per cent reduction in deviant child behaviour in home observation sessions.

A review of these three studies shows that in both the short term and a year after treatment programmes which combined child-focused problem-solving skills training with behavioural parent training led to better outcomes than no treatment and to programmes that included only one of these two treatment components.

Conclusions

From this review of 24 studies it may first be concluded that behavioural parent training combined with child-focused problem-solving skills training is a particularly effective intervention for preadolescent children with conduct problems of the type which lead to a diagnosis of oppositional defiant disorder. Such programmes entail 35 to 40 sessions. Depending upon the stringency of the outcome criterion, between 50 per cent and 95 per cent of cases treated with the combined treatment package show clinically significant improvement at home and at school a year after the conclusion of treatment. Second, combined programmes are more effective than either behavioural parent training alone or child-focused problem-solving skills training alone. Third, group-based behavioural parent training programmes that include video-modelling are clinically as effective and more cost-efficient than individually based behavioural parent training programmes. Typically both types of programme involve six to twenty sessions. Fourth, group-based behavioural parent training programmes which do not incorporate video-modelling and programmes that involve video-modelling with minimal therapist contact are quite effective but less so than group-based behavioural parent training programmes that include video-modelling or individually based behavioural parent training programmes. Fifth, in cases where a primary caretaker (typically a mother) is receiving little social support from her partner, then including a component to enhance the social support provided by the partner into a routine behavioural parent training programme may greatly enhance the programme's effectiveness. Sixth, child-focused problem-solving skills training over fifteen to twenty sessions is effective in the treatment of some cases of oppositional defiant disorder.

The conclusions of this review have implications for clinical practice and service development. First, services should be organized so that comprehensive child and family assessment is available for cases referred where preadolescent conduct problems are the central concern. Second, where it is clear that cases have circumscribed oppositional defiant disorder without other difficulties, group-based behavioural parent training with video-modelling may be offered to parents and child-focused problem-solving training may be offered to children. Each programme should involve ten to twenty sessions over a period of three to six months. Where there is evidence of marital discord both parents should be involved in treatment with the focus being on one parent supporting the other in implementing parenting skills in the home situation. Where parents are single and have poor social support networks, it may be advisable for them to include a potentially supportive member of their social network in the behavioural parenting programme. Where parents cannot engage in treatment, children may be offered child-focused problem-solving training on its own. Where service demands greatly outweigh available resources, cases on the waiting list may be offered video-modelling-based behavioural parent training with minimal therapist contact as a preliminary intervention. Following this intervention, cases should be reassessed and if significant behavioural problems are still occurring they should be admitted to a combined 40-session programme of group-based behavioural parent training with video-modelling and child-focused problem-solving training.

With respect to future research, it is probably best to focus future evaluation studies on combined group-based programmes that offer concurrent parent training and child-focused training. Future studies should evaluate different types of video-modelling packages and programmes of different durations and intensities. A second important area for study is the evaluation of programmes which specifically aim to increase parental support in cases where this is a central difficulty. The two subgroups deserving attention are families characterized by marital discord and single parent families.

A third area for future research is evaluation of the impact of co-morbidity on responsivity to treatment. Many children with oppositional defiant disorder have additional problems, notably specific learning difficulties, and it is unclear how this impacts on their response to treatment. It would be desirable to build an educational component or school-based contingency management component into such programmes, since research on ADHD, discussed in Chapter 4, suggests that this may be valuable when co-morbid school-based problems are present.

ASSESSMENT

Abidin, R. (1983). *Parenting Stress Index – Manual*. Charlottesville, VA: Pediatric Psychology Press.

Achenbach, T. (1991). *Integrative Guide for the 1991 CBCL/4–18, YSR and TRF Profiles*. Burlington, VT: University of Vermont Department of Psychiatry.

Barkley, R. and Edelbrock, C. (1987). Assessing situational variations in children's problem behaviours: the home and school situations questionnaires. In R.J. Prinz (ed.), *Advances In Behavioural Assessment of Children and Families* (Volume 3, pp. 157–76). New York: JAI Press.

Becker, W. (1960). The relationship of factors in parental ratings of self and each other to the behaviour of kindergarten children rated by mothers, fathers and teachers. *Journal of Consulting Psychology*, 24, 507–27.

Behar, L. (1977). The Preschool Behaviour Questionnaire. *Journal of Abnormal Child Psychology*, 5, 265–75.

Budd, K., Riner, L. and Brockman, M. (1983). A structured evaluation system for clinical evaluation of parent training. *Behavioural Assessment*, 5, 373–90.

Chamberlain, P. and Reid, J. (1987). Parent observation and report of child symptoms. *Behavioural Assessment*, 9, 97–109.

Eyberg, S. (1980). Eyberg Child Behaviour Inventory. *Journal of Clinical Child Psychology*, 9, 29.

Eyberg, S. and Robinson, E.A. (1983). Dyadic Parent–Child Interaction Coding System: A Manual. *Psychological Documents*, 13, Ms. No. 2582. (Available from Social and Behaviour Sciences Documents, Select Press, P.O. Box 9838, San Rafael, CA 94912.)

Futterbunk, B. and Eyberg, S. (1989). Psychometric characteristics of the Sutter-Eyberg Student Behaviour Inventory: A school behaviour rating scale for use with preschool children. *Behavioural Assessment*, 11, 279–313.

Gesren, E. (1976). A Health Resources Inventory: The development of a measure of the personal and social competence of primary grade children. *Journal of Consulting and Clinical Psychology*, 44, 775–86.

Johnston, C. and Mash, E. (1989). A measure of parenting satisfaction and efficacy. *Journal of Clinical Child Psychology*, 18, 167–75.

Kazdin, A. and Esveldt-Dawson, K. (1986). The Interview for Antisocial Behaviour: Psychometric characteristics and concurrent validity with child psychiatric inpatients. *Journal of Psychopathology and Behavioural Assessment*, 8, 289–303.

Kendall, P. and Wilcox, L. (1979). Self-control in children: The development of a rating scale. *Journal of Consulting and Clinical Psychology*, 47, 1020–30.

Quay, H. and Peterson, D. (1987). *Manual for the Revised Behaviour Problem Checklist*. Coral Gables, FL: University of Miami, Department of Psychology.

Reid, J. (1978). *A Social Learning Approach To Family Intervention. Volume 2. Observation In Home Settings*. Eugene, OR: Castalia Press.

Robinson, E. and Eyberg, S. (1981). The dyadic parent–child interaction coding system: Standardization and validation. *Journal of Clinical Child Psychology*, 9, 22–8.

Wahler, R., House, A. and Stambaugh, E. (1976). *Ecological Assessment of Child Problem Behaviour. A Clinical Package for Home, School and Institutional Settings*. New York: Pergamon.

TREATMENT MANUALS AND RESOURCES

Cunningham, C., Bremner, R. and Secord-Gilbert, M. (1994). *A School Based Family Systems Oriented Course For Parents Of Children With Disruptive Behaviour Disorders: Leaders Manual*. Unpublished manuscript.

Dangle, R. and Polstner, R. (1988). *Teaching Child Management Skills*. New York: Pergamon.

Forehand, R. and McMahon, R. (1981). *Helping the Non-compliant Child: A Clinician's Guide to Parent Training*. New York: Guilford.

Hanf, C. and Kling, F. (1973). *Facilitating Parent–Child Interaction: A Two-Stage Training Model*. Unpublished manuscript, University of Oregon Medical School, Eugene.

Herbert, M. (1987a). *Behavioural Treatment of Children With Problems*. London: Academic Press.

Herbert, M. (1996a). *ABC of Behavioural Methods*. Leicester: British Psychological Society.

Herbert, M. (1996b). *Banishing Bad Behaviour*. Leicester: British Psychological Society.

Kendall, P. and Braswell, L. (1985). *Cognitive Behavioural Therapy for Impulsive Children*. New York: Guilford.

Patterson, G., Reid, J., Jones, R. and Conger, R. (1975). *A Social Learning Approach To Family Intervention: Volume 1: Families With Aggressive Children*. Eugene, OR: Castalia Press.

Patterson, G. (1975). *Families: Applications Of Social Learning To Family Life*. Champaign, Ill: Research Press.

Sanders, M. and Dadds, M. (1993). *Behavioural Family Intervention*. New York: Pergamon Press.

Webster-Stratton, C. (1986). *Parent And Children Series Videocassette Program*. Eugene, OR: Castalia Press.

Webster-Stratton, C. (1987). *Parents And Children: A 10 Program Videotape Parent Training Series With Manuals*. Eugene, OR: Castalia Press.

Webster-Stratton, C. (1991). *Dinosaur Social Skills And Problem-Solving Training Manual*. Unpublished manuscript.

Webster-Stratton, C. and Herbert, M. (1994). *Troubled Families, Troubled Children*. Chichester: Wiley.

FURTHER READING FOR PARENTS

Forehand, R. and Long, N. (1996). *Parenting the Strong-Willed Child: The Clinically Proven Five Week Programme for Parents of Two to Six Year Olds*. Chicago, Ill: Contemporary Books.

Herbert, M. (1989). *Discipline: A Positive Guide For Parents*. Oxford: Basil Blackwell.

6 Adolescent conduct problems

Rachel Brosnan and Alan Carr

Conduct problems constitute a third to a half of all clinic referrals and chronic conduct problems are the single most costly disorder of adolescence for three reasons (Kazdin, 1995). First, they are remarkably unresponsive to traditional individual approaches to treatment. Positive outcome rates for routine treatments range from 20–40 per cent. Second, about 60 per cent of adolescents with conduct problems have a poor prognosis. Adolescents with chronic conduct disorder turn to adult criminality and develop antisocial personality disorders, alcohol-related problems and a variety of psychological difficulties. They also have more problems with health, educational attainment, occupational adjustment, marital stability and social integration. The third reason for the high cost of conduct problems is the fact that they are intergenerationally transmitted. Adults with a history of conduct disorder rear children with a particularly high prevalence of conduct difficulties.

Diagnostic criteria for conduct disorder from DSM IV (APA, 1994) and ICD 10 (WHO, 1992) are given in Figure 6.1. The main behavioural feature of conduct disorder is a pervasive and persistent pattern of antisocial behaviour which extends beyond the family to the school and community; involves serious violations of rules; and is characterized by defiance of authority, aggression, destructiveness, deceitfulness and cruelty. Adolescents with conduct disorder show a limited internalization of social rules and norms and a hostile attributional bias where the youngster interprets ambiguous social situations as threatening and responds with aggressive retaliative behaviour. Anger and irritability are the predominant mood states. Problematic relationships with significant members of the child's network typify children with conduct disorder. Negative relationships with parents and teachers typically revolve around the youngster's defiant behaviour and with peers the problems typically centre on aggression and bullying which is guided by the hostile attributional bias with which conduct-disordered youngsters construe many of their peer relationships. With conduct disorders there may also be problematic relationships with members of the wider community if theft or vandalism has occurred. Multi-agency involvement with juvenile justice or social work agencies is common. Also, because conduct disorder is associated with family disorganization, parental criminality

DSM IV	ICD 10
A. A repetitive and persistent pattern of behaviour in which the basic rights of others or major age-appropriate societal norms or rules are violated as manifested by the presence of 3 or more of the following criteria in the past 12 months with at least one criterion present in the past 6 months:	Conduct disorders are characterized by a repetitive and persistent pattern of dissocial, aggressive or defiant conduct. Such behaviour, when at its most extreme for the individual should amount to major violations of age-appropriate social expectations, and is therefore more severe than ordinary childish mischief or adolescent rebelliousness.
Aggression to people and animals 1. Often bullies, threatens or intimidates others 2. Often initiates physical fights 3. Has used a weapon that can cause serious physical harm to others 4. Has been physically cruel to people 5. Has been physically cruel to animals 6. Has stolen while confronting a victim 7. Has forced someone into sexual activity	Examples of the behaviours on which the diagnosis is based include the following: excessive levels of fighting or bullying; cruelty to animals or other people; severe destructiveness to property; firesetting; stealing; repeated lying; truancy from school and running away from home; unusually frequent and severe temper tantrums; defiant provocative behaviour and persistent and severe disobedience. Any one of these categories, if marked, is sufficient for the diagnosis, but isolated dissocial acts are not.
Destruction of property 8. Has deliberately engaged in firesetting 9. Has deliberately destroyed others' property	
Deceitfulness or theft 10. Has broken into someone's house, building or car 11. Often lies to obtain goods or favours or avoid obligations 12. Has stolen items without confronting the victim	Exclusion criteria include serious underlying conditions such as schizophrenia, hyperkinetic disorder or depression.
Serious violation of rules 13. Often stays out late at night despite parental prohibitions (before 13 years of age) 14. Has run away from home overnight at least twice while living in parental home or once without returning for a lengthy period 15. Is often truant from school before the age of 13	The diagnosis is not made unless the duration of the behaviour is 6 months or longer. Specify: CD confined to family context where the symptoms are confined to the home
B. The disturbance in behaviour causes clinically significant impairment in social, academic or occupational functioning.	Unsocialized CD where there is a pervasive abnormality in peer relationships
C. In those over 18 years, the criteria for antisocial personality disorder are not met. Specify childhood onset (prior to 10 years) or adolescent onset. Specify severity (mild, moderate or severe).	Socialized CD where the individual is well integrated into a peer group.

Figure 6.1 Diagnostic criteria for conduct disorder in DSM IV and ICD 10.
Source Adapted from DSM IV (APA, 1994) and ICD 10 (WHO, 1992, 1996).

and parental psychological adjustment difficulties, professionals from adult mental health and justice systems may be involved.

A distinction may be made between transient adjustment disorders involving circumscribed conduct problems on the one hand and more pervasive long-standing conduct problems on the other. This is a useful clinical distinction to make and in this chapter our main concern will be with long-standing pervasive disruptive externalizing behaviour problems. A second distinction is that made between oppositional defiant disorder and conduct disorder with the former reflecting a less pervasive disturbance than the latter. In a proportion of cases oppositional defiant disorder is a developmental precursor of conduct disorder (Loeber and Stouthamer-Loeber, 1998).

As with oppositional defiant disorder, three classes of risk factors increase the probability that adolescent conduct problems will escalate into later life difficulties, i.e. child characteristics, parenting practices, and family organization problems (Kazdin, 1995). Difficult temperament, aggressiveness, impulsivity, inattention and educational difficulties are the main personal characteristics of adolescents that place them at risk for long-term conduct problems. Ineffective monitoring and supervision of adolescents, providing inconsistent consequences for rule violations, and failing to provide reinforcement for prosocial behaviour are the main problematic parenting practices that place adolescents at risk for the development of long-term antisocial behaviour patterns. The family organization problems associated with persistence of conduct problems into adulthood are parental conflict and violence, a high level of life stressors, a low level of social support and parental psychological adjustment problems such as depression or substance abuse.

Epidemiology

Overall prevalence rates for conduct disorder vary from 4–14 per cent depending upon the criteria used and the population studied (Cohen *et al.*, 1993). Conservative estimates of prevalence range from 2–6 per cent (Kazdin, 1995). Conduct disorder is more prevalent in boys than in girls with male/ female ratios varying from 4:1 to 2:1. Comorbidity for conduct problems and other problems, such as ADHD or emotional disorders, is quite common, particularly in clinic populations (McConaughy and Achenbach, 1994). The comorbidity rate for conduct disorder and ADHD in community populations is 23 per cent. The comorbidity rates for conduct disorder and emotional disorders in community populations are 17 per cent for major depression and 15 per cent for anxiety disorders.

Previous reviews

Reviews of evidence for the effectiveness of treatment programmes for adolescent conduct disorders highlight the ineffectiveness of peer group-based outpatient or residential programmes and the relative effectiveness of family-based approaches (e.g. Mulvey *et al.*, 1993). Kazdin (1997), in a review of empirically supported intervention for conduct disorders, concluded that behavioural parent training, functional family therapy and multi-systemic therapy were among the more promising treatments available for adolescents with conduct problems. Chamberlain and Rosicky (1995), in their review concluded on the basis of evidence from a small number of empirical studies that treatment fostercare may be the most effective intervention for cases of conduct disorder where outpatient family-based approaches have failed. This viewpoint is consistent with conclusions drawn in two other important reviews of the treatment fostercare outcome literature (Hudson *et al.*, 1994; Reddy and Pfeifer, 1996). Given the conclusions of previous authoritative reviewers of the field, this chapter is confined to a consideration of well-designed studies which evaluate the effectiveness of behavioural parent training, family therapy, multisystemic therapy and treatment fostercare in the management of severe adolescent conduct problems.

Behavioural parent training

In behavioural parent training, it is assumed that if parents are empowered to change the reinforcement contingencies that maintain the adolescent's deviant behaviour, then the youngster's conduct problems will abate (e.g. Dishion and Andrews, 1995). Behavioural parent training aims to help parents use specific behavioural skills based on learning theory in managing their adolescents' behaviour on a day-to-day basis. It is conceptually similar to similar programmes used with children but there are a number of practical differences to take account of developmental differences between children and adolescents. In behavioural parent training programmes for the parents of adolescents, parents learn to observe, in a systematic way, their adolescents; to monitor specific positive and negative target behaviours; and to record observations of the frequency, intensity and duration of these behaviours, the situations within which they occur and the typical consequences they elicit. They also learn to modify the adolescent's behaviour using methods such as contingency contracting. With contingency contracts, adolescents may earn points by engaging in target positive behaviours and lose points by engaging in target negative behaviours.

Positive behaviours may include completing chores, homework, or following house rules. Negative behaviours may include aggression, destructiveness or breaking house rules. Points have reinforcement value because they may be exchanged on a daily or weekly basis for privileges which the youngster values highly. The target positive and negative behaviours and the points earned or lost may be displayed in the child's home in a prominent place. In behavioural parent training, parents are coached in communication skills so that they can listen and talk to their adolescents effectively. They need to be able to listen closely to their youngsters' needs and wishes, so that the list of privileges they establish are maximally reinforcing. They need to be able to communicate clearly with their adolescents so that the contingency contract with its target behaviours and points system is clearly articulated. In behavioural parent training for families with adolescents, parents are coached in liaising closely with schools so that contingency contracts may cover both school and home environments and points may be earned or lost for behaviour carried out within the school context. Parent training may be conducted on an individual or group basis, with or without the aid of video-modelling.

Functional family therapy

Within functional family therapy it is assumed that if family members can collectively be helped to alter their problematic communication patterns and if the lack of supervision and discipline within the family is altered, then the youngster's conduct problems will improve (Alexander and Parsons, 1982). This assumption is based on the finding that the families of delinquents are characterized by a greater level of defensive communication and lower levels of supportive communication compared with families of non-delinquent youngsters (Alexander, 1973), and also have poorer supervision practices. With functional family therapy, all family members attend therapy sessions conjointly. Initially family assessment focuses on identifying patterns of communication, beliefs about problems and solutions, and reinforcement contingencies that maintain the youngster's conduct problems. Within the early therapy sessions parents and adolescents are facilitated in the development of communication skills, problem-solving skills and negotiation skills. There is extensive use of relabelling and reframing to reduce blaming and to help parents move from viewing the adolescent as intrinsically deviant to someone whose deviant behaviour is maintained by situational factors. In the later stages of therapy there is a focus on the negotiation of contingency contracts similar to those described for parent training.

Multisystemic therapy

In multisystemic therapy it is assumed that if conduct problem-maintaining factors within the adolescent, the family, the school, the peer group and the wider community are identified, then interventions may be developed to alter these factors and so reduce problematic behaviour (Henggeler and Borduin, 1990). Following multisystemic assessment where members of the adolescent's family and wider network are interviewed, a unique intervention programme is developed which targets those specific subsystems which are largely responsible for the maintenance of the youngster's difficulties.

In the early stages of contact the therapist joins with system members and later interventions focus on reframing the system members' ways of understanding the problem or restructuring the way they interact around the problems. Interventions may focus on the adolescent alone, the family, the school, the peer group or community. Individual interventions typically focus on helping youngsters develop social and academic skills. Improving family communication and parents' supervision and discipline skills are common targets for family intervention. Facilitating communication between parents and teachers and arranging appropriate educational placement are common school-based interventions. Interventions with the peer group may involve reducing contact with deviant peers and increasing contact with non-deviant peers.

Treatment fostercare

Treatment fostercare aims to modify conduct problem-maintaining factors within the child, family, school, peer group and other systems by placing the child temporarily within a foster family in which the fosterparents have been trained to use behavioural strategies to modify the youngster's deviant behaviour (Chamberlain, 1994). Treatment fosterparents are carefully selected and trained in the principles of behavioural parent training, as outlined above. Children in treatment fostercare typically receive a concurrent package of multisystemic interventions to modify problem-maintaining factors within the adolescent, the natural family, the school, the peer group and the wider community. These are similar to those described for multisystemic therapy and invariably the natural parents complete a behavioural parent training programme so that they will be able to continue the work of the treatment fosterparents when their adolescent visits or returns home for the long term. A goal of treatment fostercare is to prevent the long-term separation of the adolescent from his or her biological family so that as progress is made the adolescent spends more and more time with the natural family and less time in treatment fostercare.

From this cursory account of these four approaches to the treatment of adolescent conduct problems, it may be seen that they fall along a continuum of intensity of the intervention (Chamberlain and Rosicky, 1995). Parent training focuses largely on the parenting subsystem. Family therapy in contrast addresses the wider family system. Multisystemic therapy targets not only the family system but its individual and dyadic subsystems and the wider social context within which the adolescent resides including the school, the peer group and other systems within the community. Treatment fostercare addresses all of these systems and introduces the youngster into a new and powerfully pro-social system: the treatment foster family. The aim of the present review was to identify well-designed studies which evaluated the effectiveness of each of these approaches to the treatment of adolescent conduct problems.

Method

A computer-based literature search of the PsychLit data base was conducted. Terms that defined the disorder such as *conduct disorder, delinquent* and *young offender* were combined with terms that defined interventions such as *treatment, therapy, intervention, behavioural therapy, parent training, family therapy, multisystemic therapy*, and *treatment fostercare*. The search, which was confined to English language journals, covered the period 1973 to 1997 inclusively. A manual search through bibliographies of all recent review papers was also conducted. Treatment outcome studies were selected for inclusion in this review if they focused on the treatment of twelve to eighteen year olds with conduct disorders or behavioural problems severe enough to warrant such a diagnosis; if the main intervention was behavioural parent training, family therapy, multisystemic therapy or treatment fostercare; if the design included a control or comparison group; if at least five cases were included in the active treatment group; and if reliable and valid outcome measures were included in the design of the study. Studies were excluded if participants were predominantly ADHD, drug abusers, or victims of sexual abuse. Single-case designs and studies reported in dissertations or convention papers were not included in the review. Of the 30 relevant treatment outcome papers identified fifteen qualified for inclusion under these criteria.

Overview of studies

The characteristics of the fifteen studies selected for review are given in Table 6.1. The group of studies included two on parent training (Bank *et al.*, 1991; Dishon and Andrews, 1995); four on family therapy (Alexander and Parsons, 1973; Gordon *et al.*, 1988; Parsons and Alexander, 1973; Stuart *et al.*, 1976); six on multisystemic therapy (Borduin *et al.*, 1995a, 1995b; Henggeler *et al.*, 1986, 1992, 1993; Mann *et al.*, 1990; Scherer *et al.*, 1994); and three on treatment fostercare (Chamberlain, 1990; Chamberlain and Reid, 1991; Kirgin *et al.*, 1982). All were conducted in the USA and published within the past 25 years. Aggregating across all fifteen studies there were 1102 cases and of these 597 received one of the four active treatments of interest to this review while 505 were in control or comparison groups. Eighty-five cases received behavioural parent training; 113 cases received functional or behavioural family therapy; 233 received multisystemic therapy; and 166 received treatment fostercare. For behavioural parent training treatment ranged from twelve sessions in total to 45 hours per month over a number of months. For family therapy it ranged from eight to 36 hours. For multisystemic therapy it ranged from fourteen sessions in total to twenty hours per month over two to 47 months. Treatment fostercare ranged from five to twelve months. Ages of participants across the studies ranged from twelve to eighteen years

Table 6.1 Characteristics of treatment outcome studies for adolescents with conduct problems

Study no.	Study type	Authors	Year	N per gp	Mean age & range	Gender	Family characteristics	Referral	Treatment duration
1	PT	Bank et al.	1991	BPT = 28 C = 27	14 y	m 100	Predominantly low SES SPF 61%	Repeat offenders on probation referred by juvenile court	45 h per m
2	PT	Dishion and Andrews	1995	BPT = 26 PSST = 32 BPT + PSST = 31 P = 29 C = 39	12 y	m 53% f 47%	Predominantly low SES	Self-referred cases with CBCL > 62	12 sess over 3 m
3	FT	Stuart et al.	1976	BFT = 30 P = 30	14 y 12–15 y	m 50% f 50%		Severe conduct problems referred by school	36 h over 9 m
4	FT	Parsons and Alexander	1973	FFT = 10 P = 10 C = 20	15 y	m 45% f 55%	Middle SES	Offenders referred by juvenile court	8 h over 4 w
5	FT	Alexander and Parsons	1973	FFT = 46 CFT = 19 PFT = 11 C = 10	13–16 y	m 44% f 56%	Middle SES	Offenders referred by juvenile court	8 h over 4 w
6	FT	Gordon et al.	1988	FFT = 27 C = 27	15 y	m 70% f 30%	Low SES 80% SPF 60%	Offenders on probation referred by juvenile court	16 sess
7	MST	Henggeler et al.	1986	MST = 57 C = 23	15 y	m 84% f 16%	Low SES 75% SPF 38%	Repeat offenders on probation referred by juvenile court	20 h per m over 2–47 m

8	MST	Mann et al.	1990	MST = 27 C = 18	15 y 13–17 y	m 83% f 17%	Predominantly low SES	Repeat offenders on probation referred by juvenile court	29 h per m
9	MST	Henggeler et al.	1992 1993	MST = 43 C = 41	15 y	m 77% f 23%	Predominantly low SES	Repeat offenders on probation referred by juvenile court with 58% violent crime and 71% incarcerated	33 sess over 3 m
10	MST	Scherer et al.	1994	MST = 28 C = 27	15.2 y 12–17 y	m 78% f 18%	African-American 78% SPF 77%	Repeat offenders on probation referred by juvenile court	14 sess over 4 m
11	MST	Borduin et al.	1995	MST = 8 C = 8	14 y	m 100%	Predominantly lower SES	Repeat offenders who had at least one sexual offence on probation referred by juvenile court	37 sess
12	MST	Borduin et al.	1995a 1995b	MST = 70 C = 56	15 y 12–17 y	m 67% f 33%	Low SES 68%	Repeat offenders on probation referred by juvenile court	24 sess
13	TFC	Kirgin et al.	1982	TFC = 140 C = 52	14 y	m 65% f 35%	White 76%	Repeat offenders on probation referred by juvenile court	12 m
14	TFC	Chamberlain	1990	TFC = 16 C = 16	15 y 13–18 y	m 63% f 37%	Predominantly lower SES SPF 100%	Repeat offenders on probation referred by juvenile court with 69% previous felony charge 2.5% dangerous	5 m
15	TFC	Chamberlain and Reid	1991	TFC = 10 C = 10	14 y	m 40% f 60%	Predominantly lower SES SPF 100%	Hospital referrals of cases with severe conduct problems and psychological difficulties	

Key FT = Family therapy. PT = Parent training. MST = Multisystemic therapy. TFC = Treatment fostercare. FFT = Functional family therapy. CFT = Client-centred family therapy. PFT = Psychodynamic family therapy. BFT = Behavioural family therapy. BPT = Behavioural parent training. PSST = Problem-solving skills training. P = Attention placebo condition. P = Problem-solving skills training for adolescents. C = Control group receiving routine services or no treatment. SES = socio-economic-status. SPF = Single parent family. y = year. m = month. d = day. sess = sessions.

and 68 per cent of participants were male. In ten of the studies sufficient information was given to deduce that cases were from predominantly low socio-economic groups, whereas in two studies cases were from middle-class backgrounds. In five of the six studies where information was given on family structure, the majority of youngsters were living in single parent families. In nine studies cases were repeat offenders; in three they were first-time offenders; in one study they were severe psychiatric hospital referrals; in one they were severe school referrals; and in one study they were self-referred with Child Behaviour Checklist total behaviour problem T-scores above 62, the recognized clinical cut-off (Achenbach, 1991).

Methodological features

Methodological features of the fifteen studies are summarized in Table 6.2. All studies contained control or comparison groups and in eleven studies cases were randomly assigned to treatment and control or comparison groups. In fourteen of the fifteen studies cases were diagnostically and demographically homogenous but in no studies were sufficient data given to make reliable judgements about the similarity of cases in terms of co-morbidity. With the exception of a single study that reported recidivism rates only, in all studies pre- and post-treatment assessments were reported. In ten studies follow-up data collected one year or longer after the completion of treatment were reported. In seven studies children's self-report data were presented; parent ratings were included in eight; teacher ratings in two; therapist ratings in one; and recidivism ratings in ten. In twelve studies the data on the child's conduct problems were reported and in ten information on the functioning of the child's family and social system was given. Drop-out rates were reported in eight studies. Experienced therapists provided treatment in thirteen studies and in nine studies manuals or explicit treatment protocols were used. Supervision was provided to therapists in ten studies and in seven the integrity of treatment was checked. Where two or more experimental treatments were being evaluated, in fourteen studies the treatments were equally valued. However, in many instances routine services were provided to comparison group cases and these services were probably not as highly valued by the research team as the experimental treatment. Overall, the fifteen studies included in this review were methodologically fairly robust and so considerable confidence may be placed in conclusions drawn from them.

Substantive findings

A summary of the effect sizes and outcome rates for the fifteen studies is given in Table 6.3 and a narrative summary of key findings is contained in Table 6.4.

Table 6.2 Methodological features of adolescent conduct problems treatment outcome studies

Feature	Study number														
	S1	S2	S3	S4	S5	S6	S7	S8	S9	S10	S11	S12	S13	S14	S15
Control group	1	1	1	1	1	1	1	1	1	1	1	1	1	1	1
Random assignment	1	1	1	1	1	0	0	1	1	1	1	1	0	0	1
Diagnostic homogeneity	1	1	1	1	1	1	1	1	1	1	1	1	1	1	0
Comparable for co-morbidity	0	0	0	0	0	0	0	0	0	0	0	0	0	0	0
Demographic similarity	1	1	0	0	1	1	1	0	1	1	1	1	1	1	1
Pre-treatment assessment	1	1	1	1	1	1	1	1	1	1	1	1	1	1	1
Post-treatment assessment	1	1	1	1	1	1	1	0	1	1	0	1	1	1	1
1-year follow-up assessment	1	1	0	0	1	1	0	0	1	1	1	1	1	1	1
Children's self-report	0	1	1	0	0	1	0	1	0	0	0	1	0	0	1
Parent's ratings	0	1	1	0	0	0	0	0	1	1	0	1	1	0	1
Teacher's ratings	0	1	1	0	0	0	0	1	0	0	0	1	0	0	0
Therapist's ratings	0	0	1	0	0	0	0	0	1	0	0	0	0	0	0
Recidivism ratings	1	0	0	0	1	1	1	0	1	0	1	1	1	1	1
Child's symptom assessed	1	1	1	1	0	0	1	1	1	1	1	1	1	1	1
System assessed	1	1	1	1	1	0	1	1	1	1	0	1	0	0	0
Drop-out in treatment assessed	0	0	1	1	0	0	1	1	0	1	1	0	0	1	1
Clinical significance of change assessed	0	0	0	0	0	0	0	0	0	0	0	0	0	0	0
Experienced therapists used	1	1	1	0	1	1	1	1	1	1	0	0	0	1	1
Treatments were equally valued	1	1	1	1	0	1	1	1	1	1	1	1	1	1	0
Treatments were manualized	1	1	0	1	1	1	0	0	1	1	0	1	1	0	0
Therapy supervision was provided	1	1	1	1	1	1	0	0	1	1	1	1	1	0	0
Treatment integrity checked	1	1	0	0	0	1	0	0	0	0	1	0	0	0	0
Data on concurrent treatment given	0	0	0	0	0	0	0	0	0	0	0	0	0	0	0
Data on subsequent treatment given	0	0	0	0	0	0	0	0	0	0	0	0	0	0	0
Total	15	17	15	10	14	12	10	13	17	14	12	18	12	11	13

Key S = study. 1 = design feature was present. 0 = design feature was absent.

Table 6.3 Summary of results of treatment effects and outcome rates for adolescent conduct problem treatment outcome studies

Variable	PT				FT			MST						TFC		
	S1 BPT	S2 BPT	S2 BPT +PSST	S3 BFT	S4 FFT	S5 FFT	S6 FFT	S7 MST	S8 MST	S9 MST	S10 MST	S11 MST	S12 MST	S13 TFC	S14 TFC	S15 TFC
	> C	> C	> C	> C	> C	> C	> C	> C	> C	> C	> C	> C	> C	> C	> C	> C
Symptomatic improvement after treatment																
Children's self-report	–	–	–	0.6	–	–	–	–	1.7	0.6	–	–	–	3.8	–	–
Parent's ratings	–	0.3	–0.1	0.6	–	–	–	0.7	–	0.3	0.5	–	1.5	–	–	–
Teacher's ratings	–	0.1	0.4	0.7	–	–	–	–	–	–	–	–	–	0.8	–	–
Therapist's ratings	–	–	–	0.7	–	–	–	–	–	–	–	–	–	–	–	–
Recidivism ratings	0.7	–	–	–	–	–	–	–	–	0.5	–	–	–	0.8	1.0	–
Symptomatic improvement at follow-up																
Children's self-report	–	–	–	–	–	–	–	–	–	–	–	–	–	–	–	0.0
Parent's ratings	–	–0.2	0.0	–	–	–	–	–	–	–	–	–	–	–	–	1.4
Teacher's ratings	–	–0.3	–0.2	–	–	–	–	–	–	–	–	–	–	–	–	–
Therapist's ratings	–	–	–	–	–	–	–	–	–	–	–	–	–	–	–	–
Recidivism ratings	0.1	–	–	–	–	1.0	1.5	–	–	0.5	–	1.7	1.4	0.2	1.5	0.7

Systemic improvement after treatment

	FT	PT	MST	TFC	FFT	CFT	PFT	BFT	BPT	PSST	P	C
Children's self-report	—	—	—	—	—	—	—	—	—	—	—	—
Parent's ratings	—	0.1	0.4	—	—	0.6	0.3	—	—	0.4	0.4	—
Teacher's ratings	—	—	—	—	—	—	—	—	—	—	—	—
Therapist's ratings	—	—	—	—	—	—	—	—	—	—	—	—
Researcher's ratings	0.5	0.6	0.5	0.9	1.1	0.7	1.8	—	0.9	0.9	0.4	—

Systemic improvement at follow-up

	FT	PT	MST	TFC	FFT	CFT	PFT	BFT	BPT	PSST	P	C
Children's self-report	—	—	—	—	—	—	—	—	—	—	—	—
Parent's ratings	—	—	—	—	—	—	—	—	—	—	—	—
Teacher's ratings	—	—	—	—	—	—	—	—	—	—	—	—
Therapist's ratings	—	—	—	—	—	—	—	—	—	—	—	—
Researcher's ratings	0.5	—	—	—	—	—	—	—	—	—	—	—

Positive clinical outcomes

	FT	PT	MST	TFC	FFT	CFT	PFT	BFT	BPT	PSST	P	C
% improved after treatment	—	—	—	—	—	—	—	—	—	—	—	—
% improved at follow-up	—	—	—	—	—	—	—	—	—	—	—	—

Negative clinical outcomes

	FT	PT	MST	TFC	FFT	CFT	PFT	BFT	BPT	PSST	P	C
% Recidivism after treatment	3% > 7%	—	26% > 50%	11% > 67%	—	42% > 62%	—	—	—	—	52% > 83%	25% > 69%
% Recidivism at follow-up	—	—	—	—	—	61% > 80%	—	25% > 75%	22% > 71%	42% > 60%	50% > 94%	—
% Attrition	—	—	4%	—	25%	23%	—	37%	20%	25%	42%	25%
% Engaged in further treatment	—	—	—	—	—	6%	—	—	—	—	60%	25%

Key FT = Family therapy. PT = Parent training. MST = Multisystemic therapy. TFC = Treatment fostercare. FFT = Functional family therapy. CFT = Client-centred family therapy. PFT = Psychodynamic family therapy. BFT = Behavioural family therapy. BPT = Behavioural parent training. PSST = Problem-solving skills training for adolescents. P = Attention placebo condition. C = Control group receiving routine services or no treatment.

Table 6.4 Key findings of treatment outcome studies for adolescents with conduct problems

Study no.	Study type	Authors	Year	N per gp	Treatment duration	Group differences	Key findings
1	PT	Bank *et al.*	1991	1. BPT = 28 2. C = 27	45 h per m	1 > 2	• Compared with cases that received routine community services, those treated with parent training showed a more rapid reduction in offence rates. Cases in the parent training group showed a drop in offence rates during the first year of treatment but cases in the control group did not show a reduction until the year after treatment. • Cases in the parent training group spent an average of 97 days incarcerated compared with control group cases who spent 152 days incarcerated during the 2 years following treatment. • Over the course of treatment cases in the parent training group showed a reduction in parent-reported conduct problems.
2	PT	Dishion and Andrews	1995	1. BPT = 26 2. PSST = 32 3. BPT + PSST = 31 4. P = 29 5. C = 39	12 sess over 3 m	Conduct probs at home 1 = 2 = 3 = 4 = 5 School conduct probs 1 > 4 = 5 > 2 = 3 For conflict in lab 1 = 3 > 2 > 4 = 5 For conflict at home 3 > 1 = 2 = 3 = 4	• Following treatment all groups showed a reduction in parent-reported conduct problems and these gains were maintained a year after treatment. • Following treatment the parent training group showed a reduction in teacher-reported conduct problems compared to controls, but by 1-year follow-up controls had also improved but the combined treatment group and the problem-solving skills group had deteriorated. • Following treatment cases in the behavioural parent training group and the parent training and adolescent problem-solving skills training group showed a reduction in parent–child conflict in a lab problem-solving task. • Following treatment cases in the parent training and adolescent problem-solving skills training group showed a reduction in parent reported parent–child conflict at home compared to the other 4 groups. • Following treatment and at 1-year follow-up both groups that received adolescent-focused problem-solving skills training showed a marked increase in tobacco use compared with other groups.
3	FT	Stuart *et al.*	1976	1. FT = 30 2. P = 30	36 h over 9 m	1 > 2	• Compared with cases in the attention placebo group, cases treated with behavioural family therapy showed improvements in behaviour at school and home as rated by teachers, counsellors and parents. • The recidivism rate was 3% for the treatment group compared with 7% for the control group immediately following treatment.

							Findings
4	FT	Parsons and Alexander	1973	1. FFT = 10 2. P = 10 3. C = 20	8 h over 4 w	1 > 2	• Compared with controls or the placebo discussion group, families in the functional family therapy group showed improvements in communication. They talked more fluently, members permitted each other more equal amounts of talk time and more frequent interruptions (a characteristic of normal family communication).
5	FT	Alexander and Parsons	1973	1. FFT = 46 2. CFT = 19 3. PFT = 11 4. C = 10	8 h over 4 w	1 > 3 > 4 > 3	• The recidivism rate at 6–18-month follow-up in the functional family therapy group was 26% compared with 47% in the client-centred group, 50% in the control group and 73% in the psychodynamic group. • The functional family therapy group showed greater improvements in communication than the other three groups. Specifically they showed greater fluency, more equal talk time and more frequent interruptions (a characteristic of normal family communication).
6	FT	Gordon et al.	1988	1. FFT = 27 2. C = 27	16 sess	1 > 2	• 2.5 years after treatment the recidivism rate in the functional family therapy group was 11% compared with 67% in the comparison group.
7	MST	Henggeler et al.	1986	1. MST = 57 2. C = 23	20h per m over 2–47 m	1 > 2	• Compared with cases receiving routine community services, cases treated with multisystemic therapy following treatment showed improvements in parent-rated behaviour problems and lab-based observations of adolescents' communication with their mothers and fathers. Communication was warmer and more affectionate and adolescents contributed more to exchanges with their parents.
8	MST	Mann et al.	1990	1. MST = 27 2. C = 18	21 h	1 > 2	• Compared with control group cases who received routine individual counselling, adolescents, mothers and fathers in the multisystemic therapy group showed improvements in self-reported psychological symptoms. • Cases treated with multisystemic therapy also showed a decrease in the level of conflict and an increase in the level of supportiveness between adolescents and their fathers and between mothers and fathers on laboratory tasks. • Improvements in adolescents' and fathers' symptoms were specifically associated with improvements in the quality of the mother–father relationship.
9	MST	Henggeler et al.	1992 1993	1. MST = 43 2. C = 27	33 sess over 3 m	1 > 2	• A year following referral compared with control group cases who received routine services, adolescents who received multisystemic therapy had fewer arrests, reported fewer offences and spent 10 fewer weeks, on average, incarcerated. • A year following referral re-incarceration rates were 20% for the multisystemic group and 68% for controls.

Table 6.4 (cont'd)

Study no.	Study type	Authors	Year	N per gp	Treatment duration	Group differences	Key findings
							• A year following referral youths who received MST spent on average 73 fewer days incarcerated. • A year following referral families who received multisystemic therapy reported that adolescents had fewer behaviour problems and that there was greater family cohesion compared with controls. • A year following referral recidivism rates were 42% for the multisystemic therapy group and 62% for controls. • A 2.4-year follow-up showed the recidivism rate was 61% for cases treated with multisystemic therapy and 80% for controls.
10	MST	Scherer et al.	1994	1. MST = 28 2. C = 41	14 sess over 4 m	1 > 2	• Compared with cases who received routine services, adolescents who received multisystemic therapy showed reductions in aggression and psychological symptomatology. • Mothers of cases in the multisystemic group showed improvements in psychological adjustment and parental monitoring of adolescent behaviour.
11	MST	Borduin et al.	1995a	1. MST = 8 2. C = 8	37 sess	1 > 2	• For these sexual offending delinquents 3 years following treatment recidivism rates for sexual offences were 13% for cases treated with multisystemic therapy and 75% for controls who received routine individual counselling services. • 3 years following treatment recidivism rates for non-sexual offences were 25% for the multisystemic group and 50% for controls.
12	MST	Borduin et al.	1995b	1. MST = 70 2. C = 56	24 sess	1 > 2	• Following treatment, compared with controls who received routine individual counselling services, cases treated with multisystemic therapy showed reductions in adolescents' conduct problems and parental psychological symptoms. • Following treatment, families in the multisystemic group reported increases in cohesion and adaptability and in lab tests showed decreases in conflict and increases in supportiveness in relationships between adolescents, mothers and fathers. • 4 years after treatment recidivism rates were 22% for cases who completed multisystemic therapy and 71% for cases who completed routine individual counselling. • Recidivists from the multisystemic group were involved in fewer and less serious crimes and fewer violent crimes than controls.

							Findings
13	TFC	Kirgin *et al.*	1982	1. TFC = 140 2. C = 52	12 m	1 > 2	• During treatment only 52% of cases in treatment fostercare reoffended compared with 83% of controls who were in routine foster homes. • At 1-year follow-up the recidivism rate for treatment fostercare cases was 42% compared with 60% of controls. • Adolescents and their teachers were more satisfied with the treatment fostercare programmes than the control programmes. • Adolescents' ratings of treatment fostercare staff on fairness, concern, effectiveness and pleasantness correlated with reductions in offending during treatment. The better the ratings on these dimensions the lower the offending rate.
14	TFC	Chamberlain	1990	1. TFC = 16 2. C = 16	6 m	1 > 2	• 71% of treatment fostercare cases completed treatment compared with 31% of controls who receivedcare in group homes or residential units. • 7% of treatment fostercare cases ran away compared with 44% of controls before completing treatment. • 18% of treatment fostercare cases were incarcerated compared with 25% of controls before completing treatment. • During the year following treatment 38% of treatment fostercare cases were incarcerated compared with 88% of controls. • During the second year following treatment 43% of treatment fostercare cases were incarcerated compared with 62% of controls. • During the first year following treatment on average treatment fostercare adolescents spent 86 days incarcerated compared with 160 for controls. • During the second year following treatment on average treatment fostercare adolescents spent 44 days incarcerated compared with 69 for controls. • After 2 years of follow-up 50% of treatment fostercare cases had been re-incarcerated at least once compared with 94% of controls. • The more days cases spent in treatment fostercare, the fewer days they spent incarcerated following treatment. No such relationship existed for controls.
15	TFC	Chamberlain and Reid	1991	1. TFC = 10 2. C = 10	1 y	1 > 2	• Cases allocated to treatment fostercare left hospital more quickly and took up placement sooner than controls who were allocated to regular fostercare or residential settings. • Cases in treatment fostercare showed a more rapid reduction in problem behaviour than controls.

Key FT = Family therapy. MST = Multisystemic therapy. TFC = Treatment fostercare. FFT = Funcional family therapy. CFT = Client-centred family therapy. PFT = Psychodynamic family therapy. BPT = Behavioural parent training. PSST = Problem-solving skills training for adolescents. P = Attention placebo condition. C = Control group receiving routine services or no treatment. SES = socio-economic status. SPF = Single parent family. y = year. m = month. d = day. sess = sessions.

Parent training

Two studies evaluated the effectiveness of parent training in cases of
adolescent conduct disorder (Bank *et al.*, 1991; Dishion and Andrews, 1995).
Bank *et al.* (ibid.) compared the effectiveness of parent training with that
of routine services provided by the juvenile court and community agencies
in cases of chronically offending delinquents who had a minimum of two
recorded offences at least one of which was a non-status offence. Sixty
cases were randomly assigned to either the Oregon Social Learning Centre
behavioural parent training programme or the community control group.
The parent-training programme, which was similar to that described above,
was manualized (Dishion and Kavanagh, 1989; Forgatch and Patterson,
1989; Patterson and Forgatch, 1987). The programme involved 45 hours
of contact, about 50 per cent of which occurred by telephone. Recidivism
rates and time spent incarcerated based on official offence records were
used to calculate effect sizes. Following a year of treatment the effect size
for recidivism rates was 0.7 indicating that the average case treated with
parent training fared better than 76 per cent of cases in the control group.
However, at three years' follow-up intergroup differences in offence rates
were negligible. The effect size at this point was 0.1. Following a year of
treatment and three years later, effect sizes based on time spent incarcerated
were both 0.5 indicating that the average treated case spent less time incarcerated than 69 per cent of controls during treatment and during the three-
year period following treatment.

   Dishion and Andrews (1995) compared the effectiveness of a parent training
programme alone and in combination with group-based problem-solving
skills training for adolescents with group-based problem-solving skills training for adolescents alone, an information-pack placebo condition and a
waiting list control group. Cases, which were screened using the clinical
cut-off T-score of 62 on the total behaviour problem scale of the Child
Behaviour Checklist (Achenbach, 1991), were solicited through newspaper
and community advertising and randomly assigned to treatment and control groups. The parent training programme, which was similar to that
described above, involved twelve weekly 90-minute sessions. The problem-
solving skills training group programme for adolescents aimed to help
adolescents acquire skills for self-regulation and for the development of
pro-social peer relationships. Both the parent and adolescent training programmes were manualized (Dishion *et al.*, in press). Effect sizes based on
the externalizing scale of the Child Behaviour Checklist and the Teacher
Report Form (Achenbach, 1991) following treatment and a year later ranged
from −0.2 to 0.4 indicating that gains made by cases treated with parent
training either alone or in combination with adolescent-focused problem-
solving skills training compared with no-treatment controls were clinically
negligible. Effect sizes based on research-rated parent–adolescent interaction during a laboratory family problem-solving task following treatment

were 0.5 and 0.6 for the combined treatment group and the group that received parent training only. Thus the average treated case fared better than between 69 per cent and 73 per cent of untreated control group cases in terms of joint parent–adolescent problem solving. In this study cases that received adolescent-focused group-based problem-solving skills training either alone or in combination with parent training showed an increase in tobacco usage compared with all other cases. This suggests that group-based interventions for adolescents may promote antisocial activity.

From these two studies it may be concluded that for repeat adolescent offenders intensive behavioural parent training with frequent telephone contact amounting to 45 hours over a one-year period reduced recidivism during active treatment and reduced incarceration following treatment. However, for adolescents at-risk for offending with significant conduct problems, less intensive treatment of only twelve sessions over three months had little impact on conduct problems at home or school, but did improve parent–child interaction in the short term.

Family therapy

In four studies the impact of family therapy on adolescent conduct problems was evaluated (Alexander and Parsons, 1973; Gordon *et al.*, 1988; Parsons and Alexander, 1973; Stuart *et al.*, 1976). Stuart *et al.* (ibid.) compared behavioural family therapy with an attention placebo condition. Within the family therapy condition parents established contingency contracts with their adolescents in which specified privileges that could be earned by meeting specific responsibilities and sanctions for lapses in contract compliance were specified. Home–school report cards were also used so parents and teachers could co-operate in implementing the contingency contracts. The programme involved 36 hours of contact over nine months. Effect sizes based on parent and teacher ratings following treatment were 0.6 and 0.7 respectively. Thus the average treated case fared better than 73–76 per cent of cases in the control group.

Three studies specifically evaluated the effects of functional family therapy (Alexander and Parsons, 1973; Gordon *et al.*, 1988; Parsons and Alexander, 1973). Cases in the first two studies were from middle-class Mormon backgrounds and in the third study (Gordon *et al.*, ibid.) cases were from predominantly low socio-economic groups and were repeat offenders. All three studies included a treatment group in which cases received between eight and sixteen sessions of functional family therapy and one or more control groups in which no treatment, an alternative treatment or an attention placebo procedure occurred.

Alexander and Parsons (1973) found that eighteen months following treatment the recidivism rate for the treated group was only 26 per cent compared with 50 per cent of controls. Gordon *et al.* (ibid.) found that 2.5

years following treatment the recidivism rates for the treatment and control groups were 11 per cent and 67 per cent respectively. Effect sizes based on researcher ratings of healthy family communication in Parsons and Alexander's (1973) and Alexander and Parsons's (1973) study were 0.9 and 1.1 respectively. Thus the average treated case fared better than 82 per cent and 86 per cent of untreated controls in these studies in terms of healthy family communication.

The results from two additional reports which build on Alexander and Parson's (1973) study deserve mention (although they are not included in Tables 6.1–6.4). Klein *et al.* (1977) showed that 2.5 to 3.5 years following treatment recidivism rates for siblings of cases who received functional family therapy in the 1973 study were 20 per cent compared with 40 per cent for untreated controls and 63 per cent for cases who received humanistic counselling. In a process analysis of data from the 1973 study, Alexander *et al.* (1976) found that, together, relationship and structuring skills accounted for 60 per cent of the variance in outcome. Relationship skills accounted for 45 per cent of the outcome variance and structuring skills for only 15 per cent. Relationship skills included affect-behaviour integration, warmth and humour. Structuring skills included directiveness and self-confidence.

From the four studies reviewed in this section it may be concluded that eight to 36 hours of behavioural or functional family therapy was effective in improving family communication, reducing conduct problems and reducing recidivism rates in delinquent adolescents with severe conduct problems from a range of socio-economic backgrounds. Short-term improvements were maintained eighteen months to 3.5 years after treatment, with recidivism rates in treated cases being half that for cases receiving routine probation. Furthermore, the effects of treatment of the target adolescent generalized to siblings and reduced their recidivism rates in one study. While structuring directive skills were important for effective therapy, the capacity of therapists to make and maintain warm collaborative relationships with family members was a particularly important determinant of positive outcome.

Multisystemic therapy

In six studies the effects of multisystemic therapy on adolescent conduct problems was evaluated (Henggeler *et al.*, 1986, 1992, 1993; Mann *et al.*, 1990; Scherer *et al.*, 1994; Borduin *et al.*, 1995a, 1995b). In all six studies the effectiveness of multisystemic therapy in the treatment of repeat adolescent offenders from lower socio-economic groups referred by the courts was compared with that of routine probation or community services. Individualized multisystemic treatment plans were developed for each case based on the principles of multisystemic therapy outlined above and treatment intensity ranged from a total of fourteen sessions to twenty hours per month over 47 months.

Following treatment, effect sizes based on parent-reported improvement in conduct problems on standardized behaviour checklists ranged from 0.3 to 1.5 with a mean effect size across the studies being 0.8. Thus, in terms of parent-reported improvement in home-based conduct problems, the average treated case fared better than 79 per cent of controls. Effect sizes following treatment based on self-reported improvement in conduct problems on standardized behaviour checklists ranged from 0.6 to 1.7 with the mean effect size across studies being 1.2. Thus, in terms of self-reported improvement in home-based conduct problems, the average treated case fared better than 88 per cent of controls.

Following treatment, effect sizes based on adolescent or parent reports or researcher ratings of improvements in family functioning ranged from 0.3 to 1.8 with the mean effect size across studies being 0.7. Thus, in terms of improvement in the functioning of the family system, the average treated case fared better than 76 per cent of controls.

Recidivism rates between two and four years following treatment were given in three studies. The average effect size based on the recidivism rates of these three studies was 1.2. Thus, two to four years following treatment, the average treated case fared better in terms of recidivism than 88 per cent of controls. The mean recidivism rate for treated cases in these studies two to four years after treatment was 36 per cent compared with 75 per cent for controls. Thus multisystemic treatment halved the recidivism rate in these three studies.

A number of specific findings from the six studies reviewed here deserve mention because they highlight the broad-ranging effects of multisystemic therapy and suggest possible mechanisms of change. First, Henggeler *et al.* (1992, 1993) found that multisystemic therapy not only reduced recidivism rates but also markedly reduced re-incarceration rates. Second, Borduin *et al.* (1995a) showed that multisystemic therapy was particularly effective in reducing sexual reoffending among adolescents convicted of sexual offences. This suggests that the effectiveness of multisystemic therapy is not confined to non-sexual conduct problems. Third, multisystemic therapy led to improvements, not only in adolescent functioning, but also in parental psychological symptomatology (Mann *et al.*, 1990; Scherer *et al.*, 1994). Fourth, Mann *et al.* (ibid.) found that improvements in the psychological symptomatology of both adolescents and their fathers was associated with improvements in the quality of the mother–father relationship brought about by multisystemic therapy. These last two findings underline the impact that multisystemic therapy has on family members as individuals and on the parental subsystem and suggests that improved functioning of the parental subsystem may be linked to improvements in adolescents' mental health.

From the six studies reviewed in this section it may be concluded that for repeat adolescent offenders from low socio-economic groups with severe conduct problems, intensive multisystemic therapy was effective in reducing family-based conduct problems and halving community-based recidivism rates. Multisystemic therapy also improved family functioning.

Treatment fostercare studies

In three studies the effects of treatment fostercare were evaluated (Chamberlain, 1990; Chamberlain and Reid, 1991; Kirgin *et al.*, 1982). Kirgin *et al.* (1982) compared the effects of the Achievement Place treatment fostercare programme with routine fostercare. The programme was staffed by married couples who received year-long training in behavioural principles and were familiarized with manualized treatment procedures. The treatment programme incorporated skills teaching, self-government, motivation, relationship development and youth advocacy procedures applied by a married couple in a structured family setting. In both of Chamberlain's studies (Chamberlain, 1990; Chamberlain and Reid, 1991) the effects of the Oregon Social Learning Centre Treatment Foster Care Program (Chamberlain, 1994) were compared with routine residential or fostercare. In the treatment fostercare programme foster families were carefully selected, intensively trained in behaviour management principles, and intensively supervised. One child was placed in each home to minimize association with deviant peers. Children received weekly individual therapy sessions using a social learning treatment model and the children's schoolteachers were also involved in liaison meetings with fosterparents to arrange home–school contingency contracts.

Recidivism rates following treatment and at one to two years' follow-up were given in two of the three treatment fostercare studies (Chamberlain, 1990; Kirgin *et al.*, 1982). The average effect size based on the recidivism rates of these studies was 0.9 after treatment and at follow-up. Thus, following treatment and one to two years later, the average treated case fared better in terms of recidivism than 82 per cent of controls. The mean recidivism rate for treated cases in these studies after treatment was 39 per cent compared with 76 per cent for controls. At one to two years' follow-up, the mean recidivism rate for treated cases in these studies after treatment was 46 per cent compared with 77 per cent for controls, so there was little change in gains made during treatment.

Kirgin *et al.* (1982) found effect sizes of 3.8 and 0.8 for self-reported and teacher-reported improvements in conduct problems after treatment respectively, indicating that the average treated case fared better than 79 per cent of untreated cases from teachers' perspectives and 99 per cent of cases from adolescents' perspectives following treatment. Chamberlain and Reid (1991) found an effect size of 1.4 for parent-reported improvement in conduct problems at follow-up. Thus from parents' perspectives the average treated case fared better than 92 per cent of controls.

From these three studies it may be concluded that treatment fostercare was effective in reducing conduct problems and recidivism rates in the short- and long-term with repeat offenders and adolescents hospitalized for severe conduct problems.

Conclusions

From this review of fifteen studies of four distinct yet related approaches to family intervention for adolescent conduct problems the following conclusions may be drawn. First, behavioural parent training, functional family therapy, multisystemic therapy and treatment fostercare are each effective treatments for adolescent conduct problems in a proportion of cases. Second, intensive behavioural parent training with frequent telephone contact amounting to 45 hours over a one-year period may reduce recidivism during active treatment and reduce incarceration following treatment but less intensive parent training is of little long-term value even with non-offending conduct-disordered adolescents. Third, up to 36 hours of functional family therapy may in both the short and long term improve family communication and reduce conduct problems and recidivism rates in delinquent adolescents with severe conduct problems from a range of socio-economic backgrounds. Functional family therapy may also reduce arrest rates in siblings of treated cases. Fourth, for repeat adolescent offenders from low socio-economic groups with severe conduct problems, intensive multisystemic therapy involving up to twenty hours per month over two to 47 months may be effective in improving family functioning and reducing family-based conduct problems and halving recidivism rates. Fifth, treatment fostercare is effective in reducing conduct problems and recidivism rates in the short and long term with repeat offenders and adolescents hospitalized for severe conduct problems.

With respect to service development, it may be most efficient to offer services for adolescent conduct disorder on a continuum of care (Chamberlain and Rosicky, 1995). Less severe cases may be offered parent training or functional family therapy. Moderately severe cases and those who do not respond to circumscribed family interventions may be offered multisystemic therapy. Extremely severe cases and those who are unresponsive to intensive multisystemic therapy may be offered treatment fostercare. Such a continuum of care service may be developed and managed within a clinical psychology department with referrals coming from multiple sources including the courts and probation departments.

With respect to research, there is a need to evaluate the effectiveness of the four approaches to family intervention addressed in this chapter with cases that are homogeneous for severity and co-morbidity with other disorders, if we are eventually to be able to match interventions to case types in a reliable way. There is also a need for further research on treatment processes, such as that conduced by Alexander's group which linked relationship and structuring skills to therapy outcome. Similar work is required to identify process factors which lead to positive outcomes in multisystemic therapy and treatment fostercare.

ASSESSMENT

Achenbach, T. (1991). *Integrative Guide for the 1991 CBCL/4-18, YSR and TRF profiles*. Burlington, VT: University of Vermont Department of Psychiatry.

Eyberg, S. (1980). Eyberg Child Behaviour Inventory. *Journal of Clinical Child Psychology*, 9, 29.

Quay, H. and Peterson, D. (1987). *Manual for the Revised Behaviour Problem Checklist*. Coral Gables, FL: University of Miami, Department of Psychology.

TREATMENT MANUALS AND RESOURCES

Alexander, J. and Parsons, B. (1982). *Functional Family Therapy*. Montereny, CA: Brooks Cole.

Chamberlain, P. (1994). *Family Connections: A Treatment Foster Care Model For Adolescents With Delinquency*. Eugene, OR: Castalia Press.

Dishion, T. and Kavanagh, K. (1989) *The Adolescents Transition Programme* (Manuals and accompanying video vignettes) Eugene, OR: Independent Video Services.

Dishion, T., Kavanagh, K. and Soberman, L. (in press). *The Adolescents Transition Programme. Assessment and Interventions Sourcebook*. New York: Guilford.

Dowling, E. and Osborne, E. (1994). *The Family and The School. A Joint Systems Approach to Problems with Children* (Second Edition). London: Routledge.

Forgatch, M. and Patterson, G. (1989). *Parents and Adolescents Living Together: Part 2. Family Problem Solving*. Eugene, OR: Castalia Press.

Henggeler, S. and Borduin, C. (1990). *Family Therapy and Beyond: A Multisystemic Approach to Treating the Behaviour Problems of Children and Adolescents*. Pacific Grove, CA: Brooks Cole.

Patterson, G. and Forgatch, M. (1987). *Parents and Adolescents Living Together. Part 1. The Basics*. Eugene, OR: Castalia Press.

FURTHER READING FOR PARENTS

Herbert, M. (1987b). *Living with Teenagers*. Oxford: Basil Blackwell.

7　Drug abuse

Coleen Cormack and Alan Carr

Within both ICD 10 (WHO, 1992) and DSM IV (APA, 1994) a distinction is made between drug abuse which refers to drug taking that leads to personal harm and drug dependence which refers to those situations where there is a compulsive pattern of use that may involve physiological changes that accompany the phenomena of tolerance and withdrawal. Definitions of abuse and dependence are given in Figure 7.1.

Drug abuse (or substance abuse as it is sometimes termed) in adolescence is of particular concern because it may have a negative long-term effect on youngsters who abuse drugs and a negative intergenerational effect on their children. For adolescents, habitual drug abuse may negatively affect mental and physical health; criminal status; educational status; the establishment of autonomy from the family of origin; and the development of long-term intimate relationships (Newcomb and Bentler, 1988). The children of habitual teenage drug abusers may suffer from drug-related problems such as fetal alcohol syndrome, intrauterine addiction or HIV infection (Pagliaro and Pagliaro, 1996).

A number of behavioural, physiological, affective, perceptual, cognitive and interpersonal features of drug abuse may be identified (Bailey, 1989; Buckstein, 1995; Farrell and Taylor, 1994; Pagliaro and Pagliaro, 1996; Schinke *et al.*, 1991). Drug abuse is associated with a wide variety of behaviour patterns. These patterns may be described in terms of the age of onset; the duration of drug abuse; the frequency of use; the range of substances used; and the amount used. Thus useful distinctions may be made between adolescents who began abusing drugs early or later in their development; between those who have recently begun experimenting with drugs and those who have a chronic history of drug abuse; between daily users, weekend users and occasional users; between those who confine their drug abuse to a limited range of substances such as alcohol and THC and those who use a wide range of substances; and between those who use a little and those who use a great deal of drugs. Chronic and extensive daily polydrug abuse with an early onset is associated with more difficulties than experimental, occasional use of a limited number of drugs with a recent onset. The former usually entails a constricted drug-focused lifestyle and multiple

DSM IV	ICD 10
Substance abuse	**Harmful use**
A. A maladaptive pattern of substance use leading to clinically significant impairment or distress as manifested by one or more of the following occurring within a 12-month period: 1. Recurrent substance abuse resulting in a failure to fulfil major obligations at work, school or home 2. Recurrent substance abuse in situations in which it is physically hazardous 3. Recurrent substance-related legal problems 4. Continued substance use despite having persistent or recurrent social or interpersonal problems caused by or exacerbated by the effects of the substance B. The symptoms have never met the criteria for substance dependence for this type of substance.	A pattern of psychoactive substance abuse that is causing harm to health. The damage may be physical (as in cases of hepatitis from the self-administration of injected drugs) or mental (e.g. episodes of depressive disorder secondary to heavy consumption of alcohol). The fact that pattern of use of a particular substance is disapproved of by a culture or may have led to socially negative consequences such as arrest or marital arguments is not in itself evidence of harmful use.
Substance dependence	**Dependence syndrome**
A maladaptive pattern of substance abuse, leading to clinically significant impairment or distress, as manifested by 3 or more of the following occurring at any time in the same 12-month period: 1. Tolerance defined by either: (a) A need for markedly increased amounts of the substance to achieve intoxication (b) Markedly diminished effect with continued use of the same amount of the substance 2. Withdrawal as manifested by either of the following: (a) The characteristic withdrawal syndrome for the substance (b) The same substance is taken to relieve or avoid withdrawal symptoms 3. The substance is taken in larger amounts over a longer period than was intended 4. There is a persistent desire or unsuccessful efforts to cut down or control substance use 5. A great deal of time is spent in activities necessary to obtain the substance, use the substance or recover from its effects 6. Important social, occupational or recreational activities are given up or reduced because of substance use 7. The substance use is continued despite knowledge of having persistent or recurrent physical or psychological problems that are likely to have been caused or exacerbated by the substance. Specify with or without physiological dependence.	A cluster of physiological, behavioural and cognitive phenomena in which the use of a substance or a class of substances takes on a much higher priority than other behaviours that once had greater value. Three or more of the following in a 12-month period: (a) A strong desire or sense of compulsion to take the substance (b) Difficulty in controlling substance-taking behaviour in terms of onset, termination or levels of use (c) A physiological withdrawal state when substance use has ceased or been reduced as evidenced by: the characteristic withdrawal syndrome for the substance; use of the substance to avoid withdrawal symptoms (c) Evidence of tolerance such as increased doses of the substance are required in order to achieve the effects originally produced by lower doses (e) Progressive neglect of alternative pleasures or interests because of psychoactive substance use, increased amount of time necessary to obtain or take the substance or to recover from its effects (f) Persisting with substance use despite clear evidence of overtly harmful consequences such as harm to the liver through excessive drinking, depressive mood states consequent to periods of heavy substance abuse, or drug-related impairment of cognitive functioning.

Figure 7.1 DSM IV and ICD 10 diagnostic criteria for drug abuse and dependence.

Source Adapted from DSM IV (APA, 1994) and ICD 10 (WHO, 1992, 1996).

associated physical and psychosocial problems, whereas the latter does not. A consistent finding is that only a minority of youngsters progress from experimental to habitual drug abuse and from the use of a single legal drug to multiple illegal drugs.

Behavioural patterns of drug abuse evolve within specific contexts and drug-using behaviour often comes to be associated with particular locations, times, modes of administering the drug, physiological states, affective states, control beliefs and social situations. With recreational experimental drug use, weekly oral drug taking at peer group gatherings while in a positive mood state may occur and youngsters may have strong beliefs that they are in control of their drug-taking behaviour. With habitual drug abuse, solitary daily injections to prevent withdrawal and alleviate negative mood may occur. This type of drug abuse may be accompanied by strong feelings of being unable to control the frequency of drug abuse or to cut down on the amount taken.

Physiological features of drug abuse may be grouped into those associated with intoxication; those that follow intoxication; those associated with withdrawal following the development of dependence; and medical complications which arise from drug abuse.

A central reason for many forms of drug abuse is to pharmacologically induce a pleasant affective state. It is therefore not surprising that for many drugs, including alcohol, stimulants, hallucinogens and opioids, elation is a central feature of initial intoxication. With sedatives, in contrast, intoxication leads to apathy. Many polydrug abusers refer to drugs by their primary mood-altering characteristics. Thus a distinction is made between *uppers* and *downers*, and particular cocktails of drugs or sequences of drugs are used to regulate mood in particular ways. Negative mood states typically follow intoxication for most classes of drugs. This is particularly true for drugs such as opioids or cocaine that lead to tolerance and dependence. The intense negative mood states which characterize withdrawal syndromes associated with such addictive drugs motivate habitual drug abuse. The health problems, financial difficulties and psychosocial adjustment problems that evolve as part of habitual drug abuse may also contribute to frequent and intense negative mood states and paradoxically motivate drug abusers to use more drugs to improve their mood state. Negative mood states typically include some combination of depression, anxiety and anger.

At a perceptual level, some types of drugs, but particularly hallucinogens, lead to pronounced abnormalities during intoxication and withdrawal. In the 1990s widely used hallucinogens included LSD (known as *acid*) or MDMA (known as *E*). The hallucinations and perceptual distortions that occur during intoxication are not always experienced as pleasant. In some situations they lead to great distress. Brief flashbacks or enduring psychotic states which involve hallucinations and perceptual distortions may occur following intoxication and these are invariably experienced as distressing.

With respect to cognition, most street drugs lead to impaired concentration, reasoning and judgement during intoxication and withdrawal. Long-term regular drug abuse in many instances leads to impaired cognitive functioning. The nature, extent and reversibility of this impairment varies depending upon the pattern of drug abuse. With teenagers the impaired cognitive functioning associated with regular drug abuse may lead to a decline in academic performance.

Drug abuse may have an impact on interpersonal adjustment. Within the family, drug abuse often leads to conflict or estrangement between adolescents and their parents. At school, drug abuse may lead to conflict between the adolescent and teachers both because of declining academic performance and because of antisocial behaviour such as theft or aggression associated with drug abuse. Youngsters who abuse drugs within a peer group situation may become deeply involved in a drug-oriented subculture and break ties with peers who do not abuse drugs. Some youngsters develop a solitary drug-using pattern and become more and more socially isolated as their drug using progresses. Within the wider community, drug-related antisocial behaviour such as aggression, theft and selling drugs may bring youngsters into contact with the juvenile justice system. Drug-related health problems and drug dependency may bring them into contact with the health service. Conflict between drug abusers and health care professionals may arise in situations where youngsters expect to be offered prescribed drugs (such as methadone) as a substitute for street drugs (such as heroin) and this does not occur.

Drug abuse often occurs with other co-morbid psychological problems including conduct disorder, ADHD, specific learning difficulties, mood disorders, anxiety disorders, schizophrenia and bulimia. The relationship between these co-morbid psychological problems and drug abuse is complex. Any or all of them may precede drug abuse and contribute in some way to the development of drug-using behaviour. In addition, drug abuse may precipitate or maintain these other psychological problems. For example, the use of hallucinogens may precipitate the onset of schizophrenia. Chronic polydrug abuse may lead to learning difficulties and chronic alcohol use can lead to amnesic syndrome. Amphetamine usage may lead to anxiety problems. Drug dependence may lead to chronic conduct problems such as assault and theft. Negative drug-related experiences such as losses and drug-related accidents may lead to mood disorder which in turn may lead to further drug use. Drug abuse is also an important risk factor for suicide in teenagers.

Epidemiology

Experimentation with drugs in adolescence is common (Farrell and Taylor, 1994; Liddle and Dakof, 1995; Schinke *et al.*, 1991). Major US and UK surveys have shown that by nineteen years of age approximately 90 per cent of teenagers have drunk alcohol; 60 per cent have tried cigarettes; 50 per cent have used cannabis; and 20 per cent have tried other street drugs such as solvents, stimulants, hallucinogens or opiates. The prevalence of drug abuse and dependence is harder to gauge and varies with the population studied and the definitions used. A conservative estimate based on a review of available surveys is that between 5 and 10 per cent of teenagers under age nineteen have drug problems serious enough to require clinical intervention. These epidemiological results show that fewer than half of those youngsters who experiment with street drugs go on to develop serious drug-abuse problems.

Previous reviews

The bulk of treatment outcome research in the field of adolescent drug abuse has been grounded in predominantly individual rather than family-based treatment modalities (Catalano *et al.*, 1991). Such treatments have included individual or group-based interventions conducted within the context of outpatient settings, inpatient hospital settings or residential therapeutic communities. Interventions have included pharmacological therapy, counselling, psychotherapy, educational programmes, recreational programmes and milieu therapy. One consistent finding from authoritative reviews of this literature on individually based treatment programmes is the association between parental involvement and positive outcome. That is, where programmes involve parents in individually based treatment programmes for adolescent drug abusers, the youngsters are more likely to reduce their drug abuse or become abstinent (Catalano *et al.*, ibid.). This finding along with research which highlights the significance of family factors in the development and maintenance of some types of adolescent drug abuse suggests that family-based approaches to the treatment of adolescent drug abuse deserve special consideration as potentially effective interventions (Liddle and Dakof, 1995).

A second important set of findings from reviews of the individually based treatment outcome literature is the association between educational attainment and involvement in pro-social peer groups on the one hand and positive treatment outcome on the other. Youngsters with better attainment and integration into their school systems and youngsters who have access to pro-social peer groups are more likely to show a reduction in drug abuse in individually based programmes (Catalano *et al.*, 1991). In view of this set of findings, a strong case may be made for reviewing the effectiveness of multisystemic ecologically based therapy programmes for adolescent drug abuse which address not only family factors, but also school- and peer group-based factors in the treatment of drug-related difficulties (Henggeler and Borduin, 1990).

In light of these considerations, this chapter will focus exclusively on family-based and multisystemic approaches to the treatment of adolescent drug abuse. Family systems theories of drug abuse implicate family disorganization in the etiology and maintenance of adolescent drug-taking behaviour and there is considerable empirical support for family disorganization as an etiological factor for many types of adolescent drug abuse (Hawkins *et al.*, 1992; Stanton and Heath, 1995; Szapocznik and Kurtines, 1989). Family systems theorists argue that drug abuse evolves as part of a broader pattern of family disorganization which includes parental psychological problems; interparental conflict; poor parenting skills; poor problem-solving skills; parent–child conflict; lack of clear communication, hierarchies, boundaries, rules, roles and routines; extreme enmeshment or disengagement; difficulty negotiating a life cycle transition such as a family member leaving home; and a family perception of the drug abuser as a problem independent of the pattern of interaction around him or her. These patterns may include criticism, overprotection, excessive nurturance, excessive attention, or denial of all other problems. Family-based interventions aim to reduce drug abuse by engaging families in treatment and helping family members change these patterns of family functioning in which the drug abuse is embedded. Family therapy helps family members clarify communication, rules, roles, routine hierarchies and boundaries; resolve conflicts; optimize emotional cohesion; develop parenting and problem-solving skills; and manage life cycle transitions. Family-based treatment programmes for adolescent drug abuse involve the following processes which while overlapping, may be conceptualized as stages of therapy: engagement, problem definition and contracting; becoming drug free; facing denial and creating a context for a drug-free lifestyle; family reorganization; disengagement and planning for relapse prevention (Stanton and Heath, ibid.).

Multisystemic ecological treatment approaches to adolescent drug abuse are based on the theory that problematic processes, not only within the family but also within the child as an individual and within the wider social system including the school and the peer group may contribute to the etiology and maintenance of drug abuse (Henggeler and Borduin, 1990). This conceptualization of drug abuse is supported by considerable empirical evidence (Hawkins *et al.*, 1992; Henggeler *et al.*, 1991a). At a personal level, adolescent drug abusers have been shown to have social skills deficits, depression, behaviour problems, and favourable attitudes and expectations about drug abuse. Their families are characterized by disorganization as has previously been outlined and in some instances by parental drug abuse. Many adolescent drug abusers have experienced rejection by pro-social peers in early childhood and have become members of a deviant peer group in adolescence. Within a school context they show a higher level of academic failure and a lower commitment to school and academic achievement compared to their drug-free counterparts. Multisystemic ecological intervention programmes for adolescent drug abusers have evolved out of the family therapy tradition (Henggeler and Borduin, 1990). In each case treated with multisystemic therapy, around a central family therapy intervention programme, an additional set of individual, school-based and peer group-based interventions are offered which target specific risk factors identified in that case. Such interventions may include self-management skills training for the adolescent, school-based consultations or peer group-based interventions. Self-management skills training may include coaching in social skills, social problem-solving and communication skills, anger control skills, and mood regulation skills. School-based interventions aim to support the youngster's continuation in school, to monitor and reinforce academic achievement and pro-social behaviour in school, and to facilitate home–school liaison in the management of academic and behavioural problems. Peer group interventions include creating opportunities for pro-social peer group membership and assertiveness training to empower youngsters to resist deviant peer group pressure to abuse drugs.

Three important reviews of the literature on family and multisystemic therapy have been published in the last few years (Liddle and Dakof, 1995; Stanton and Shadish, 1997; Waldron, 1996). Liddle and Dakof (ibid.) and Waldron (ibid.) concluded that in controlled clinical trials, family-based therapy has been found to be more effective than other treatments in engaging and retaining adolescents in treatment and also in the reduction of drug use. Reviews by Liddle and Dakof (ibid.) and Waldron (ibid.) were further supported by a meta-analysis conducted in 1997 by Stanton and Shadish. They concluded that family-based therapy was more effective in reducing drug abuse than individual counselling or therapy; peer group therapy; and family psychoeducation. Furthermore, family-based therapy led to fewer drop-outs from treatment compared with other therapeutic approaches. Their final conclusion was that while family-based therapy was effective as a stand-alone treatment modality, it could also be effectively combined with other individually based approaches and lead to positive synergistic outcomes. Thus, family therapy could empower family members to help adolescents engage in treatment; remain committed to the treatment process; and develop family rules, roles, routines, relationships, and belief systems which supported a drug-free lifestyle. In addition, family therapy could provide a context within which youngsters could benefit from individual, peer group or school-based interventions.

A central aim in the present chapter was to segregate available well-designed family-based intervention studies for adolescent drug abusers into those which evaluated systemic engagement procedures; family therapy treatment programmes; and multisystemic therapy programmes, and to review the outcome of these three groups of studies in a rigorous manner.

Method

A computer-based literature search of the PsychLit database was conducted. Terms which define illicit drug taking such as *drug abuse, substance abuse, addiction, alcohol addiction, drug experimentation, alcohol, marijuana, LSD, amphetamines, cocaine, MDMA, heroin, opiates,* and *polydrug abuse* were combined with terms that define family-based psychological intervention such as *family treatment, family therapy, family engagement, family psychotherapy, family intervention, family-based behaviour therapy, relapse prevention, parent training, multisystemic therapy, multidimensional family therapy* and *ecobehavioural therapy.* The search was limited to adolescents and confined to English language journals, covering the period from 1977 to 1997 inclusively. A manual search through bibliographies of all recent review papers on family-based interventions for drug abuse was also conducted. Treatment outcome studies were selected for inclusion in this review if they contained a family-based treatment group and a control or comparison group; if at least five cases were included in the active treatment group; and if reliable and valid pre- and post-treatment measures were included in the design of the study. Single-case designs were not included in the review. Using these inclusion and exclusion criteria, from a pool of over a hundred papers located, thirteen studies were selected for inclusion in the present review.

Characteristics of the studies

The characteristics of the thirteen studies are set out in Table 7.1. Of the thirteen studies, two evaluated a systemic approach to engaging families in therapy, seven evaluated family therapy, and four evaluated multisystemic family therapy. All of the studies were conducted in the USA and in all instances the adolescents were polydrug abusers. The studies were reported or published between 1979 and 1995. The studies contained a total of 1097 cases with 269 in the family therapy engagement studies; 480 in the family therapy studies and 348 in the multisystemic therapy studies. Participant adolescents' ages ranged from twelve to 21 years. Seventy-one per cent of cases were male and 29 per cent were female. In five of the studies participants were predominantly Hispanic and in a further five, participants were of mixed ethnic background. In three studies, families were from mixed socio-economic groups and in three studies, they were from low or low to middle socio-economic groups. In four studies, cases were referred from multiple sources including the courts, schools, physicians and social service agencies. In two studies they were referred predominantly from the courts and in two studies cases were largely self-referred. In all studies treatment was offered on an outpatient basis. In eight instances treatment was offered in community-based clinics and in two studies treatment was conducted in university settings. For the two family therapy studies concerned with engagement, engagement efforts spanned three to eight weeks. In the remaining seven family therapy studies and the four multisystemic family therapy studies treatment ranged from eight to 36 sessions over four to six months.

Table 7.1 Characteristics of family therapy studies for adolescent drug abusers

Study no.	Study type	Authors	Year	N per gp	Age	Gender	Family characteristics	Referral	Treatment setting	Treatment duration
1	FT-Engagement	Szapocznik et al.	1988	SE = 56 EAU = 52	12–21 y	m 67% f 33%	Mixed SES H.spanic 100%	Self-referral	Community OP	3 w
2	FT-Engagement	Santisteban et al.	1996	SE + FT = 52 EAU + FT = 67 EAU + GT = 42	16 y 12–18 y	m 70% f 30%	Mixed SES H.spanic 100%	Self-referral	Community OP	8 w
3	FT-Treatment	Azrin et al.	1994	FT = 15 SUP = 11	16 y 13–18 y	m 77% f 23%	Mixed ethnic groups	Multiple sources	University OP	15 sess over 6 m
4	FT-Treatment	Joanning et al.	1992	FT = 40 PT = 42 SST = 52	15 y		Low to middle SES		University OP	FT & GT: 12 sess FE: 6 sess
5	FT-Treatment	Lewis et al.	1990	FT = 44 PT = 40	16 y 12–22 y	m 84% f 16%	Mixed SES, Divorced parents 46%	Multiple sources	Community OP	2 sess
6	FT-Treatment	Friedman	1989	FT = 85 PT = 50	18 y 14–21 y	m 60% f 40%	Anglo-American 90% African-American 10%		Community OP	24 sess
7	FT-Treatment	Szapocznik et al.	1983	FT = 18 OPFT = 19	17 y	m 78% f 22%	Hispanic 100%	Multiple sources	Community OP	8 sess
8	FT-Treatment	Szapocznik et al.	1986	FT = 17 OPFT = 18	17 y		Low to middle SES Hispanic 100%	Multiple sources	Community OP	13 sess
9	FT-Treatment	Krinsley	1991	FT + SI = 12 SI = 17	14 y 12–15 y	m 66% f 34%	Anglo-American 82% African-American 18%			8 sess
10	MFT-Treatment	Henggeler et al.	1991b	MFT = 28 SUP = 19	15 y	m 72% f 28%	African-American 78% Low SES 77%	Court	Community OP	36 h over 4 m
11	MFT-Treatment	Henggeler et al.	1991a	MFT = 92 SUP = 84	14 y	m 67% f 33%	Low SES; SPF 46% IF 54%	Court	Community OP	26 h
12	MFT-Treatment	Liddle et al.	1995	MFT = 32 PT = 32 GT = 31	16 y	m 80% f 20%	Mixed ethnic groups		OP	12 sess over 4 m
13	MFT-Treatment	Scopetta et al.	1979	MFT = 15 FT = 15	17 y	m 64% f 36%	Hispanic 100%		OP	12 sess

Key SE = Systemic engagement. EAU = Engagement as usual. FT = Family therapy. GT = Group therapy. IC = Individual counselling. FE = Family education. PT = Parent training. OPFT = One-person family therapy. SI = School intervention. MFT = Multisystemic family therapy. SES = Socio-economic status. SPF = Single parent family. IF = Intact family. OP = Outpatient. h = hours. w = weeks. m = months. y = years. sess = sessions.

Methodological features

The methodological features for all thirteen studies are given in Table 7.2. All studies were of diagnostically homogenous groups where participants were randomly assigned to treatment and control or comparison conditions. With the exception of the two engagement studies, pre-treatment assessments were conducted in all studies and either post-treatment or follow-up assessments were conducted in all studies. In six studies follow-up data for a period of six months or longer were available. In two studies, six month follow-up data were available (Szapocznik *et al.*, 1983, 1986). In two studies, nine-month follow-up data were reported (Friedman, 1989; Krinsley, 1991). One-year follow-up data were available for Liddle *et al.*'s (1995) study and four-year re-arrest data were reported by Henggeler *et al.* (1991b). Data on demographic similarity were given in 92 per cent of studies but information about co-morbidity was not included in any of the papers. The adolescents' symptoms were assessed in all studies. In the engagement studies, the symptom was taken to be degree of engagement in treatment, whereas in the other studies indices of drug abuse were the principal symptomatic assessments. Aspects of the adolescent's social system such as family relationships were assessed in 38 per cent of studies. Ratings of the symptom or the adolescent's social system were provided by researchers in 85 per cent of studies; by the adolescents themselves in 76 per cent of studies and by parents in 62 per cent of studies. In none of the studies were ratings by teachers and therapists reported. Drop-out rates were reported in 62 per cent of studies, but deterioration was reported in only 8 per cent of studies. In the two engagement studies, it was clear that cases engaged in further treatment after the engagement intervention but information about involvement in further treatment was not reported in any of the other studies. In all studies the statistical significance of gains made by the treatment group were reported but in only 62 per cent of studies was information on the clinical significance of treatment gains reported. Manualized treatments with regular supervision occurred in 70 per cent of studies, with experienced therapists being used in 92 per cent of studies. However, the integrity of treatment was assessed and reported in only 28 per cent of studies. Treatments were equally valued in 46 per cent of the studies and in the remainder, the treatment offered to the comparison group was a treatment-as-usual control group. Overall, from a methodological perspective, this was a fairly robust group of studies and so conclusions may be drawn from this body of literature with considerable confidence.

Substantive findings

A summary of effect sizes and outcome rates from the nine studies included in this review are set out in Table 7.3 and a narrative account of the main conclusions is given if Table 7.4. Below, a detailed account of the main

Table 7.2 Methodological features of family therapy studies of drug abuse

Feature	Study number												
	S1	S2	S3	S4	S5	S6	S7	S8	S9	S10	S11	S12	S13
Control group	1	1	1	1	1	1	1	1	1	1	1	1	1
Random assignment	1	1	1	1	1	1	1	1	1	1	1	1	1
Diagnostic homogeneity	0	1	1	1	1	1	1	1	1	1	1	1	1
Comparable for co-morbidity	0	0	0	0	0	0	0	0	0	0	0	0	0
Demographic similarity	1	1	1	1	1	1	1	1	1	1	1	1	1
Pre-treatment assessment	0	0	1	1	1	1	1	1	1	1	1	1	1
Post-treatment assessment	1	1	1	1	1	1	1	1	1	1	1	1	1
Follow-up assessment	0	0	0	0	0	0	1	1	1	0	0	1	0
Children's self-report	0	0	0	1	1	1	1	0	1	1	0	1	1
Parent's ratings	1	1	1	1	1	1	1	1	1	1	0	0	0
Teacher's ratings	0	0	0	0	0	0	0	0	0	0	0	0	0
Therapist's ratings	0	0	0	0	0	0	0	0	0	0	0	0	0
Researcher's ratings	1	1	1	1	1	1	1	1	0	0	1	1	1
Child's symptom assessed	1	1	1	1	1	1	1	1	1	1	1	1	1
System assessed	0	0	1	1	0	0	0	1	1	0	0	0	0
Deterioration assessed	0	0	0	0	1	0	0	0	0	0	0	0	0
Drop-out assessed	1	1	1	1	1	0	1	0	0	0	1	1	0
Clinical significance of change assessed	1	1	1	1	1	1	1	1	1	0	0	1	1
Experienced therapists used	1	1	1	1	0	1	1	1	1	1	1	1	1
Treatments were equally valued	0	0	0	0	1	1	1	1	0	0	0	1	1
Treatments were manualized	0	1	0	1	1	1	1	1	1	1	1	0	0
Therapy supervision was provided	1	1	1	1	1	0	0	1	0	1	1	0	0
Treatment integrity checked	1	0	0	0	1	1	0	0	0	0	0	0	0
Data on concurrent treatment given	0	0	1	0	0	0	0	0	0	0	0	0	0
Data on subsequent treatment given	0	0	0	0	0	0	0	0	0	0	0	0	0
Total	14	13	16	16	17	14	17	16	13	11	12	14	12

Key S = study. 1 = design feature was present. 0 = design feature was absent.

Table 7.3 Summary of treatment effects and outcome rates from family therapy studies for adolescent drug abusers

Variable	Study 1	Study 2	Study 3	Study 4		Study 5	Study 6	Study 7	Study 8	Study 9	Study 10	Study 11	Study 12		Study 13
	SE > EAU	SE > EAU	FT > SUP	FT > PT	FT > SST	FT > PT	FT > PT	FT > OPFT	FT > OPFT	FT + SI > SI	MFT > SUP	MFT > SUP	MFT > PT	MFT > GT	MFT > FT
Symptomatic improvement after treatment															
Children's self-report	–	–	0.8	0.63	1.0	0.6	–	–	0.0	0.1	0.5	–	0.8	0.8	0
Parent's ratings	–	–	–	–	–	–	–	–	–	–	–	–	–	–	–
Teacher's ratings	–	–	–	–	–	–	–	–	–	–	–	–	–	–	–
Therapist's ratings	–	–	–	–	–	–	–	–	–	–	–	–	–	–	–
Researcher's ratings or urinalysis	0.0	–	0.9	–	–	–	–	−0.1	–	–	–	–	–	–	–
Symptomatic improvement at follow-up															
Children's self-report	–	–	–	–	–	–	0.0	–	–	0.3	–	–	0.9	0.4	–
Parent's ratings	–	–	–	–	–	–	0.0	–	–	–	–	–	–	–	–
Teacher's ratings	–	–	–	–	–	–	–	–	–	–	–	–	–	–	–
Therapist's ratings	–	–	–	–	–	–	–	–	–	–	–	–	–	–	–
Researcher's ratings	–	–	–	–	–	–	–	−0.2	–	–	–	0.9	–	–	–
Systemic improvement after treatment															
Children's self-report	–	–	0.7	0.0	0.0	–	–	−0.8	0.0	0.0	–	–	–	–	–
Parent's ratings	–	–	0.8	–	–	–	–	−0.3	0.0	0.0	–	–	–	–	–
Teacher's ratings	–	–	–	–	–	–	–	–	–	–	–	–	–	–	–
Therapist's ratings	–	–	–	–	–	–	–	–	–	–	–	–	–	–	–
Researcher's ratings	–	–	–	–	–	–	–	−0.2	–	–	–	–	–	–	–

Systemic improvement at follow-up

Measure	Reported values
Children's self-report	—
Parent's ratings	—
Teacher's ratings	—
Therapist's ratings	−0.3 / −0.3 / 0.0 / 0.0
Researcher's ratings	−0.3

Positive clinical outcomes

% Engaged in treatment	93% > 42% · 80%; 81% > 60%; 93% > 67%; 93%; 57%
% Drug free after treatment	73% > 9%; 54% > 28%; 54% > 16%; 30%; 57% > 57%
% Improved after treatment	55% > 38%; 56% > 52%; 91%
% improved at follow-up	97%

Negative clinical outcomes

Measure	Reported values
% Deterioration	32% > 35%
% Drop-out	17% > 41%; 31% > 33%; 10%; 13%; 18%; 40%; 20%; 28% > 48%; 0

Key SE = Systemic engagement. EAU = Engagement as usual. FT = Family therapy. GT = Group therapy. IC = Individual counselling. FE = Family education. PT = Parent training. OPFT = One-person family therapy. SI = School intervention. MFT = Multisystemic family therapy.

Table 7.4 Key findings from family therapy studies for adolescent drug abusers

Study no.	Study type	Authors	Year	N per gp	Treatment duration or number of sessions	Group differences	Key findings
1	FT-Engagement	Szapocznik et al.	1988	1. SE = 56 2. EAU = 52	3 w	1 > 2	• Systemic engagement led to an increased engagement rate and a lower drop-out rate than engagement as usual. • Systemic engagement and engagement as usual did not lead to differential reductions in drug usage.
2	FT-Engagement	Santisteban et al.	1996	1. SE + FT = 52 2. EAU + FT = 67 3. EAU + GT = 42	8 w	1 > 2 > 3	• Systemic engagement led to an increased engagement rate compared with routine engagement procedures.
3	FT-Treatment	Azrin et al.	1994	1. FT = 15 2. SUP = 11	15	1 > 2	• Compared with adolescents who received individual supportive counselling, adolescents who received behavioural family therapy showed greater abstinence from drug abuse, greater improvements in behaviour at home and school and greater improvements in mood during the 6-month period in which treatment occurred.
4	FT-Treatment	Joanning et al.	1992	1. FT = 40 2. PT = 42 3. SST = 52	12 6 12	1 > 2 > 3	• Family therapy was twice as effective as parent training and three times as effective as social skills training in helping adolescents become drug free in the short term. • All three treatments led to improvements in parent–adolescent communication.
5	FT-Treatment	Lewis et al.	1990	1. FT = 44 2. PT = 40	12	1 > 2	• Family therapy was more effective than parent training in reducing adolescents' drug usage.
6	FT-Treatment	Friedman	1989	1. FT = 85 2. PT = 50	24	1 = 2	• Family therapy led to a greater rate of engagement than parent training. • Adolescents in both the family therapy and the parent training treatment programmes 9 months after treatment showed similar reductions in drug usage, similar improvements in home-based behaviour and family relationships and similar improvements in psychological symptomatology.

7	FT-Treatment	Szapocznik et al.	1983	1. FT = 18 2. OPFT = 19	8	2 > 1	Adolescents in both the family therapy and the one-person family therapy programmes after treatment and at 6 months' follow-up showed similar reductions in drug usage, similar improvements in home-based behaviour and family relationships and similar improvements in psychological symptomatology.
8	FT-Treatment	Szapocznik et al.	1986	1. FT = 17 2. OPFT = 18	13	2 > 1	Adolescents in both the family therapy and the one-person family therapy programmes after treatment and at 6 months' follow-up showed similar reductions in drug usage, similar improvements in home-based behaviour and family relationships, and similar improvements in psychological symptomatology.
9	FT-Treatment	Krinsley	1991	1. FT + SI = 12 2. SI = 17	8	1 > 2	After treatment and at 9 months' follow-up adolescents in the family therapy group showed lower levels of drug use and better school-based adjustment than those who received the school intervention only.
10	MFT-Treatment	Henggeler et al.	1991a	1. MFT = 28 2. SUP = 19	36	1 > 2	Following treatment adolescents in the multisystemic family therapy group reported less drug abuse than those who received routine individual supportive counselling services.
11	MFT-Treatment	Henggeler et al.	1991b	1. MFT = 92 2. SUP = 84	26	1 > 2	Four years after treatment adolescents in the multisystemic family therapy group had fewer drug-related arrests than those who received routine individual supportive counselling services.
12	MFT-Treatment	Liddle et al.	1995	1. MFT = 32 2. PT = 32 3. GT = 31	12	1 > 2 = 3	Following treatment adolescents in the multidimensional family therapy group showed less drug usage and their parents showed greater improvements in parenting practices compared with cases in the parent training and group therapy programmes. These gains were maintained at 1-year follow-up.
13	MFT-Treatment	Scopetta et al.	1979	1. MFT = 15 2. FT = 15	12	1 = 2	Cases in both family therapy and multisystemic family therapy showed similar reductions in drug usage and similar improvements in personal and family functioning following treatment.

Key: SE = Systemic engagement. EAU = Engagement as usual. FT = Family therapy. GT = Group therapy. IC = Individual counselling. FE = Family education. PT = Parent training. OPFT = One-person family therapy. SI = School intervention. MFT = Multisystemic family therapy. w = weeks.

results summarized in these two tables will be given according to the following plan. First, the two studies on the impact of systemic engagement will be considered (Santisteban *et al.*, 1996; Szapocznik *et al.*, 1988). Next the seven studies on the effects of family therapy will be reviewed (Azrin *et al.*, 1994; Friedman, 1989; Joanning *et al.*, 1992; Krinsley, 1991; Lewis *et al.*, 1990; Szapocznik *et al.*, 1983, 1986). Finally the four studies which deal with multisystemic family therapy will be addressed (Henggeler *et al.*, 1991a, 1991b; Liddle *et al.*, 1995; Scopetta *et al.*, 1979).

Systemic approaches to engagement

Two studies examined the impact of a systemic approach to engaging adolescent drug abusers and their families in therapy on subsequent attendance for treatment (Santisteban *et al.*, 1995; Szapocznik *et al.*, 1988). In both studies the effect of systemic engagement was compared with routine engagement practices. Cases who were engaged in therapy in the usual manner received routine enquiries in a preliminary phone call about the presenting problem and family membership and were offered a straightforward invitation for all family members to participate in therapy. The systemic engagement process, in contrast, involved the use of two traditional structural family therapy techniques – joining and restructuring – in both referral phone calls and in preliminary meetings with one or more family members. With systemic engagement, wherever possible, the therapist joined with the family in a way that did not challenge the family structure and only resorted to restructuring those interactions that prevented the family from attending treatment. Phone-based joining interventions used with concerned family members included enquiring about the presenting drug problems; expressing concern; enquiring about the availability of family members for therapy; enquiring about family members' personal interests and concerns; enquiring about family interactions; and offering an invitation to all family members to participate in therapy. Coaching the concerned family member to involve other family members in therapy was the main phone- or office-based restructuring intervention used in systemic engagement. Out-of-office restructuring interventions included visiting family members, joining with them using the techniques listed earlier and reframing the invitation to treatment-resistant family members to participate in therapy so as to highlight the benefits of attending therapy in terms of the resistant family members' expressed concerns and wishes.

In Szapocznik *et al.*'s (1988) study 93 per cent of cases in the systemic engagement group attended treatment sessions compared with only 42 per cent of cases who were engaged in treatment in the usual manner. In Santisteban *et al.*'s (1996) study 81 per cent of cases in the systemic engagement group attended treatment sessions compared with only 42 per cent of cases in which routine engagement procedures were used. Drop-out rates for the two groups in this study were just over 30 per cent. However, in

Szapocznik *et al.*'s (ibid.) study only 17 per cent of cases in the systemic engagement group dropped out of treatment compared with 41 per cent of cases in the routine engagement group. No significant differences were found between the two groups in terms of reduction in drug abuse after completing the family therapy treatment programme.

From these two studies it may be concluded that a systemic approach to engagement led to a higher level of engagement in treatment and to lower drop-out rates but not to better overall treatment outcome in terms of reduction in drug abuse.

Family therapy for drug abuse

Seven studies evaluated the effects of family therapy as a treatment for drug abuse (Azrin *et al.*, 1994; Friedman, 1989; Joanning *et al.*, 1992; Krinsley, 1991; Lewis *et al.*, 1990; Szapocznik *et al.*, 1983, 1986). Azrin *et al.* (ibid.) examined the effects of a behaviourally oriented family therapy programme for drug abuse by comparing the outcome for cases who received this treatment with the outcome for cases who received routine individual supportive counselling. Within the behaviourally oriented family treatment programme adolescents and their parents learned to use stimulus control, urge control, contracting and problem-solving skills to reduce the adolescent's drug intake. Stimulus control involved planning to reduce time spent in risky situations and increase time spent in safe situations where drug abuse was less likely. Developing routines to disrupt internal stimuli that precipitated drug abuse was the main feature of the urge control treatment component. With contracting, parents and adolescents were helped to negotiate about the scheduling of safe rather than risky activities. Problem-solving skills training involved defining problems in solvable terms and then developing, implementing and evaluating feasible solutions to these. A typical behaviour therapy format was used which included therapist modelling, rehearsal, written assignments and weekly review. In the routine individual counselling the main emphasis was on providing support and facilitating insight into drug-related difficulties. In this routine treatment condition, sessions were conducted weekly with one hour devoted to individual counselling and two hours to group work, and parents attended one session per month. In contrast in the behavioural family therapy condition, whole family sessions occurred twice weekly.

After treatment 73 per cent of cases in the behavioural family therapy programme were drug free compared with 9 per cent of cases in the routine individual treatment group and the drop-out rate from both programmes was only 10 per cent. Effect sizes for regular urinalysis and self-reported drug abuse over the six months of treatment were 0.9 and 0.8 respectively. Thus, in terms of drug abuse, the average case treated with behavioural family therapy fared better than 79–82 per cent of cases in the routine treatment condition. Effect sizes for improvement in family relationships as assessed by adolescent and parent satisfaction ratings were 0.7 and 0.8 following treatment, indicating that the average case in the behavioural family therapy programme experienced greater improvements in family relationships than 76–79 per cent of cases who received routine individual treatment.

In three studies the effects of family therapy were compared with those of parent training (Friedman, ibid.; Joanning *et al.*, ibid.; Lewis *et al.*, ibid.). In Joanning *et al.*'s study (ibid.) family therapy consisted of twelve 90-minute weekly sessions conducted by a three-member family therapy team and the therapy protocol was based on an integration of structural, strategic and systemic family therapy (Quinn *et al.*, 1988, 1989). The parent training programme involved six biweekly sessions of 2.5 hours each and three or four families attended these drug information meetings. A social skills training group condition involving twelve weekly sessions was also included in this study.

Family therapy was more effective than parent training or social skills training. Following treatment, 54 per cent of cases in the family therapy group were drug free compared with 28 per cent of cases in the parent training group and 16 per cent of cases in the social skills training group. These outcome figures are based upon combined data from multiple sources including urinalysis, self-reported drug use, videotaped family assessment interviews, therapist evaluations, school records, and legal involvement. Only 13 per cent of cases dropped out of treatment. The three groups did not differ following treatment on a variety of self-reported indices of family system functioning.

Lewis *et al.* (1990) compared the effects of the Purdue brief family therapy programme with a parent training programme. The twelve-session family therapy programme integrated some of the most effective elements of structural, strategic, functional and behavioural family therapies (Lewis *et al.*, 1989). The programme aimed to reduce adolescent drug abuse by reducing family resistance to drug treatment, redefining drug use as a family problem, re-establishing parental influence, interrupting dysfunctional family interaction and providing assertiveness training for both the adolescent and siblings to resist peer pressure to engage in drug abuse. The parent training programme included twelve sessions on drug education.

Following treatment, 55 per cent of cases in the family therapy group were clinically improved in comparison with 38 per cent of cases in the parent training group. Deterioration rates for the family therapy and parent training groups were 32 per cent and 35 per cent respectively and the overall drop-out rate from the study was 18 per cent.

Friedman (1989) compared the effects of functional family therapy and parent training in the treatment of adolescent drug abuse. Functional family therapy involved joining with all family members, reframing drug abuse as a family problem, using behavioural strategies to disrupt drug-abuse maintaining interaction patterns, and improving family communication (Alexander and Parsons, 1982). The parent training programme focused on drug education and teaching parents communication and conflict resolution skills. It included elements from the Parent Effectiveness Training method (Gordon, 1977); the Parent Communication Project of the Canadian Addiction Research Foundation (Shain *et al.*, 1980); and the Parent Assertiveness Training programme (Silberman and Wheelan, 1980). Both programmes spanned a six-month period and included 24 sessions.

The single domain in which cases in the family therapy programme fared better than the parent training group was that of engagement. Ninety-three per cent of cases in the family therapy programme engaged in treatment in comparison with only 67 per cent of cases in the parent training programme. The outcomes for the family therapy group and the parent education groups on indices of drug abuse were similar. Following treatment 56 per cent of adolescents in the family therapy group and 54 per cent in the parent training group reported that they had found treatment helpful in reducing drug abuse. There was a 50 per cent reduction in drug use in both groups; a reduction in psychological symptoms; and an improvement in home-based behaviour problems.

Across these three studies that compared a brief family therapy programme with a parent education programme, global improvement rates for drug abuse were very similar and ranged from 54–56 per cent, but effect sizes ranged from 0.0 to 0.6. It is noteworthy that in the first two studies that yielded the larger effect sizes of 0.6, the parent training programmes focused largely on drug education. In the third study, the parent training programme covered communication and conflict resolution skills which are also a focus for attention in family therapy. It may be that parents in Freedman's parent training group developed similar skills in this area to those that attended the family therapy programme.

Szapocznik *et al.* (1983, 1986) in two studies, compared the effects of conjoint family therapy with one-person family therapy. Conjoint family therapy in this study was similar to the other family therapy programmes described in this section and involved joining with the family, redefining the adolescent's drug problem in interactional terms, disrupting drug abuse, maintaining interactional patterns, using family restructuring tasks, and facilitating parental joint problem-solving and clear family communication (Szapocznik and Kurtines, 1989). One-person family therapy aimed to produce changes in dysfunctional family structures and drug-abuse maintaining interaction patterns by working primarily with one family member. One-person family therapy is based on the notion that if one family member understands the patterns of family interaction that maintain drug abuse and changes his or her behaviour so as to disrupt these patterns, then other members of the family will also have to change their behaviour. In this way the family factors that maintain drug abuse can be altered (Szapocznik and Kurtines, ibid.).

In both studies, the differences between outcomes for the two forms of family therapy were negligible. Significant reductions in drug abuse, parent-reported behaviour problems and psychological difficulties occurred for participants in both programmes. In the first study, in the one-person family therapy programme following treatment adolescents reported greater family cohesion on the Family Environment Scale (Moos, 1974). The effect size here was −0.8. All other effect sizes were negligible (less than an absolute value of 0.3).

Krinsley (1991) compared the effects of family therapy combined with a supportive school-based intervention with those of a school-based intervention alone in the treatment of drug abuse. The family therapy programme focused on family problem-solving and communications training and the parental use of contingency management to provide incentives to youngsters to reduce drug abuse. The school intervention involved providing adolescents with teacher-sponsors who offered support throughout the school year, encouraged continued school attendance and discouraged dropping out of school. The programmes spanned eight sessions. Following treatment, intergroup differences, while statistically significant, showing the family therapy group to be faring better than the school intervention group were clinically negligible (d = 0.3).

In summary, the seven studies reviewed in this section showed that family therapy was more effective than individual supportive therapy and social skills training in the treatment of adolescent drug abuse. Family therapy was also more effective than parent training which focused exclusively on drug education. Family therapy was as effective as one-person family therapy, parent training which included a communication and conflict resolution skills training component and a school-based supportive sponsor programme in helping adolescents overcome drug abuse.

Multisystemic family therapy of drug abuse

Four studies addressed the effects of multisystemic ecological family-based therapy on adolescent drug abuse (Henggeler *et al.*, 1991a, 1991b; Liddle *et al.*, 1995; Scopetta *et al.*, 1979). Henggeler *et al.* (ibid.) in both the Family and Neighbourhood Services Project in South Carolina and the Missouri Delinquency Project compared the effects of multisystemic family therapy with those of supportive individual counselling provided through a probation service for adolescent delinquents with drug problems. In both studies the multisystemic family therapy programme was that described earlier in this chapter (Henggeler and Borduin, 1990) and the two programmes ranged in duration from 26 to 36 hours.

In the Family and Neighbourhood Services Project the drug use subscales of the National Youth Survey Delinquency Scale were used to assess self-reported drug abuse in the preceding three months (Elliott *et al.*, 1985). Following treatment cases in the multisystemic family treatment programme reported significantly less drug abuse than their control group counterparts. The effect size was 0.5 indicating that the average case in the multisystemic family treatment programme fared better than 69 per cent of cases in the control group.

In the Missouri Delinquency Project the principal measure used was the frequency of arrests for substance-related offences during the four-year period following treatment. Four years after treatment only 4 per cent of cases in the multisystemic family therapy programme had been arrested for substance-related offences compared with 16 per cent of cases in the control group. These rates yield an effect size of 0.9.

Liddle *et al.* (1995) compared the effects of multidimensional family therapy with those of parent training and supportive group therapy. Multidimensional family therapy is similar to Henggeler and Borduin's (1990) multisystemic family therapy and includes, in addition to a core family therapy intervention, individual sessions for abusers and their parents and school-based and peer group-based interventions. The parent training programme offered information on drug abuse to parents and provided a forum for parental support. The group therapy programme was predominately supportive. Following treatment, effect sizes for drug abuse based on a combination of self-report and urinalysis data were 0.8 for comparisons of the multidimensional family therapy programme with both of the other conditions. This indicates that the average case treated in the multidimensional family therapy programme fared better than 79 per cent of those in the parent training and supportive group therapy programmes. These gains were maintained at one-year follow-up.

Scopetta *et al.* (1979) compared the effects of multisystemic family therapy and routine family therapy. The multisystemic and routine family therapy programmes were similar to those described earlier in the chapter (Henggeler and Borduin, 1990; Szapocznik and Kurtines, 1989). Outcomes for both programmes were similar. In both programmes following treatment 57 per cent of cases reported being drug free.

The four studies reviewed in this section showed that multisystemic family therapy is more effective in the short term than individual or group-based supportive counselling and parent education in treating adolescent drug abuse. However, it was no more effective than family therapy.

Conclusions

From this review, clear conclusions may be drawn about the use of systemic engagement procedures for families reluctant to enter treatment and about the effectiveness of both family therapy and multisystemic family therapy in the treatment of adolescent drug abusers. A systemic approach to engagement leads to a higher level of engagement in treatment and to lower dropout rates than routine engagement procedures. However, a systemic approach to engagement probably does not lead to a greater reduction in drug abuse following treatment. Systemic engagement procedures should span three to eight weeks and may involve numerous phone calls and pre-therapy meetings with various members of the adolescent's family. These meetings should focus on building good working relationships with all family members and reducing their resistance to participating in family-based treatment.

Family therapy spanning six to 24 sessions is more effective than traditional individually based interventions for drug abuse such as supportive therapy or social skills training. However, where families cannot be engaged in treatment, an individually based variant of family therapy – one-person family therapy – is an effective alternative to routine conjoint family therapy for the treatment of adolescent drug abuse.

Family therapy is more effective than drug education for parents, but not more effective than parent training that includes both drug education and a communication and conflict resolution skills training component.

Multisystemic family therapy spanning twelve to 36 sessions is more effective in the short term than individual or group-based supportive counselling. It is also more effective than parent education in treating adolescent drug abuse. However, it is probably no more effective than family therapy in the short term. There are good reasons to believe that in the long term, multisystemic family therapy may lead to greater maintenance of treatment gains, since multisystemic family therapy aims to alter drug-abuse maintaining factors, not only within the family but also within the individual, the school and the peer group. However, data on the long-term effects of family therapy and multisystemic family therapy are not yet available.

The results of this review have important implications for treatment provision. For cases of adolescent polydrug abuse six to 24 sessions of family therapy should be offered routinely as a treatment of choice. Where engagement problems occur, systemic engagement procedures should be used. Where there is clear evidence that factors within the individual or the wider system are maintaining the youngster's drug abuse, a multisystemic approach should be taken. If youngsters have problem-solving, social skills, or self-regulation skills deficits, training in these should be provided. Where school-based factors are contributing to the maintenance of drug abuse, school-based interventions should be offered. Where deviant peer group membership is maintaining drug abuse, alternative peer group activities should be arranged. In cases where systemic engagement procedures are ineffective in recruiting all family members into therapy, alternatives to family therapy may be offered to the adolescent. Where parents resist entry into treatment, one-person family therapy may be offered. Where adolescents resist entry into treatment, parent training which involves both drug education and training in communication skills and conflict resolution may be offered.

With respect to service development, the broad approach to treatment outlined above may be offered from community-based outpatient primary care centres. However, in those instances where adolescents have developed physiological dependence, facilities for detoxification on either an inpatient or an outpatient basis should be provided.

The results of the handful of studies reviewed in this chapter, while promising in their findings, highlight the need for further research in a number of areas. First, more studies on the long-term effects of family therapy, multisystemic therapy, one-person family therapy and comprehensive parent training in the treatment of adolescent drug abuse are required. Second, treatment process and outcome studies which examine in detail the relative contributions of the various components of multisystemic therapy to outcome and their mechanisms of action are required. Third, the effects of court-mandated family-based treatment compared with voluntary treatment deserve evaluation, since no studies on this policy-related issue have yet been conducted. Fourth, for adolescents physiologically dependent on specific drugs such as heroin, studies that evaluate treatment programmes which include family-based therapy and pharmacological interventions such as methadone maintenance are required. No such studies have yet been conducted with adolescents. In future studies, there is an urgent need for researchers around the world to agree on a scalar measure of polydrug abuse, so that the severity of drug problems of cases in studies may be more easily inferred from published reports.

ASSESSMENT

Kaiminer, Y., Wagner, E., Plummer, E. and Seifer, R. (1993). Validation of the Teen Addiction Severity Index (T-ASI): Preliminary Findings. *The American Journal of Addictions*, 3, 250–4.

Mayer, J. and Filstead, W. (1979). The adolescent alcohol involvement scale: An instrument for measuring adolescent use and misuse of alcohol. *Journal of Studies in Alcohol*, 40, 291–300.

Skinner, H. (1982). The drug abuse screening test. *Addictive Behaviour*, 7, 363–71.

Tarter, R. (1990). Evaluation and treatment of adolescent substance abuse: A decision tree method. *American Journal of Drug and Alcohol Abuse*, 16, 1–46.

Winters, K. (1989). *Personal Experience Screening Questionnaire*. Los Angeles, CA: Western Psychological Services.

Winters, K. and Henly, G. (1989). *Personal Experience Inventory*. Los Angeles, CA: Western Psychological Services. Phone +1-310-478-2061.

TREATMENT MANUALS AND RESOURCES

Henggeler, S. and Borduin, C. (1990). *Family Therapy and Beyond: A Multisystemic Approach to Treating the Behaviour Problems of Children and Adolescents*. Pacific Grove, CA: Brooks Cole.

Stanton, M. and Todd, T. (1982). *The Family Therapy of Drug Abuse and Addiction*. New York: Guilford.

Szapocznik, J. and Kurtines, W. (1989). *Breakthroughs In Family Therapy With Drug Abusing Problem Youth*. New York: Springer.

8 Anxiety disorders

Maggie Moore and Alan Carr

Definitions

Fear and anxiety

Fear occurs in response to threat and includes cognitive, affective, physiological, behavioural and relational aspects (Barrios and Hartman, 1997; Herbert, 1994; Silverman and Kurtines, 1996). At a cognitive level, an anxiety provoking situation is construed as threatening or dangerous. At an affective level, there are feelings of apprehension and tension. At a physiological level, autonomic arousal occurs so as to prepare the person for confronting or escaping from the threatening situation. With respect to behaviour, the individual may either confront the danger or avoid it. The interpretation of situations as threatening and the patterning of approach or avoidant behaviour are determined by the social context within which they occur and the way the child's response affects members of his or her social network. For children this social network usually includes parents, siblings, schoolteachers and peers.

Throughout childhood and adolescence the types of stimuli which elicit fear change and these changes parallel developments in cognitive and social competencies and concerns (Klein, 1994; Morris and Kratochwill, 1991; Ollendick *et al.*, 1994a). Stimuli which elicit fear at different stages of development are listed in Figure 8.1. In the first six months extreme stimulation such as loud sounds or loss of support elicit fear. However, with the development of object-constancy and cause-and-effect schemas during the latter half of the first year, separation anxiety appears and the child fears strangers and separation from caretakers. In early childhood, during the pre-operational period, as the skills required for make-believe and imagination develop, but those for distinguishing fantasy from reality are not yet acquired, the child comes to fear imaginary or supernatural creatures. At this time children's mobility also increases and they come to fear animals and potential burglars. In middle childhood as their awareness of the natural world and of the world portrayed on the media develops, they come to fear natural disasters such as floods or thunder and lightening and media-based

Age	Psychological and social competencies and concerns relevant to development of fears, phobias and anxiety	Principal sources of fear	Principal anxiety disorders
Early infancy 0–6 months	• Sensory abilities dominate infants' adaptation	• Intense sensory stimuli • Loss of support • Loud noises	
Late infancy 6–12 months	• Sensori-motor schemas • Cause and effect • Object-constancy	• Strangers • Separation	
Toddler years 2–4 years	• Pre-operational thinking • Capacity to imagine but inability to distinguish fantasy from reality	• Imaginary creatures • Potential burglars • The dark	• Separation anxiety*
Early childhood 5–7 years	• Concrete operational thinking • Capacity to think in concrete logical terms	• Natural disasters (fire, flood, thunder) • Injury • Animals • Media-based fears	• Animal phobia • Blood phobia
Middle childhood 8–11 years	• Esteem centres on academic and athletic performance in school • Rigid orderly routines and rituals of early childhood are supplanted by orderly hobbies such as collecting	• Poor academic and athletic performance	• Test anxiety • School phobia • OCD
Adolescence 12–18 years	• Formal operational thought • Capacity to anticipate future dangers • Esteem is derived from peer relationships	• Peer rejection	• Social phobias • Agoraphobia • Panic disorder

Figure 8.1 Fears at different ages.

Source Adapted from Morris and Kratchowill (1991); Ollendick *et al.* (1994a); Schroder and Gordon (1991).

* Separation anxiety appears in early childhood but peaks in late childhood.

fears such as epidemics of diseases. In late childhood, failure in academic and athletic performance at school becomes a source of fear. With the onset of adolescence the period of formal operational thinking, the capacity for abstract thought emerges. The youngster can project what will happen in the future and anticipate with considerable sophistication potential hazards, threats and dangers in many domains, particularly that of social relationships. Fears about peer rejection emerge at this stage.

Anxiety disorders

Normal adaptive fears which are based on a realistic appraisal of the potential threat posed by a stimulus may be distinguished from anxiety which is based on an unrealistic appraisal of the threat posed to one's well-being by a particular situation (Ollendick *et al.*, 1994a). From Figure 8.1 it may be seen that the emergence of anxiety disorders, which will be defined in more detail below, follows a developmental course which parallels that of normal fears (Klein, 1994; Silverman and Rabian, 1994). Separation anxiety may present as a clinically significant problem at the transition to school although it is noteworthy that separation anxiety disorder is most prevalent among children in late childhood. The onset of animal phobias is most prevalent in early childhood. The onset of test anxiety and other types of performance anxiety peaks in later childhood. Social anxiety, panic disorder, and agoraphobia which often occurs secondary to panic disorder, tend to first appear in adolescence along with generalized anxiety. Obsessive compulsive disorder is distinct from the normal rituals of childhood which are prominent in the preschool years and wane by the age of eight or nine years, when hobbies involving collecting and ordering selected objects, toys and trinkets probably take their place. It is often at this time that obsessive compulsive disorder emerges. From a clinical perspective, typically children are referred for treatment of an anxiety problem, when it prevents them from completing developmentally appropriate tasks such as going to school or socializing with friends. Within DSM IV (APA, 1994) and ICD 10 (WHO, 1992) distinctions are made between a variety of different anxiety disorders based on the developmental timing of their emergence, the classes of stimuli that elicit the anxiety, the pervasiveness and the topography of the anxiety response, and the role of clearly identifiable factors in the etiology of the anxiety.

Separation anxiety

With separation anxiety, inappropriate fear is aroused by separation from an attachment figure. Although not the only cause of school refusal, it is one of the most common causes of this complaint. Separation anxiety with chronic school refusal is a serious condition since it has such a poor prognosis if left untreated. As many as a third of youngsters with this condition go on to develop panic disorder and agoraphobia (Tonge, 1994).

Phobias

Phobic anxiety is the intense fear which occurs when faced with an object, event or situation from a clearly definable class of stimuli which is out of proportion to the danger posed by the stimulus, and leads to persistent avoidance. In DSM IV specific phobias are distinguished from social phobias and agoraphobia. Specific phobias are subdivided in DSM IV into those associated with animals, injury (including injections), features of the natural environment (such as heights or thunder), and particular situations (such as elevators or flying). With social phobias the principal fear is of being evaluated by other unfamiliar people and behaving in an embarrassing way while under their scrutiny. Social phobia leads to a constriction of social life. In earlier versions of the DSM the term *avoidant disorder* has been used to designate this condition.

Generalized anxiety disorder

When youngsters experience generalized anxiety, they have an ongoing apprehension that misfortunes of various sorts will occur. Their anxiety is not focused on one particular object or situation. In earlier versions of the DSM the term *overanxious disorder* has been used to designate this condition.

Panic disorder

With panic disorder there are recurrent unexpected panic attacks. These attacks are experienced as acute episodes of intense anxiety and are extremely distressing. Youngsters come to perceive normal fluctuations in autonomic arousal as anxiety provoking, since they may reflect the onset of a panic attack. Commonly secondary agoraphobia develops. The youngster fears leaving the safety of the home in case a panic attack occurs in a public setting.

Post-traumatic stress disorder

Post-traumatic stress disorder (PTSD) occurs in many children following a catastrophic trauma which the child perceived to be potentially life-threatening for themselves or others. In PTSD children have recurrent intrusive memories of the trauma that leads to intense anxiety. They try to avoid this by suppressing the memories and avoiding situations that remind them of the trauma.

Obsessive compulsive disorder

Obsessive compulsive disorder (OCD) is a condition typically characterized by distressing obsessional thoughts or impulses on the one hand and compulsive rituals which reduce the anxiety associated with the obsessions on the other.

The clinical features of the six types of anxiety disorders described above are presented in Figure 8.2. Clinical features in the domains of perception,

	Separation anxiety	Phobias	Generalized anxiety disorder	Panic disorder	PTSD	Obsessive compulsive disorder
Perception	• Separation is perceived as threatening	• Specific objects, events or situations are perceived as threatening	• The whole environment is perceived as threatening • The child is hypervigilant, scanning the environment for threats to well-being	• The recurrence of a panic attack is seen as threatening • Attention is directed inward and benign somatic sensations are perceived but misinterpreted as threatening	• Cues that remind the person of the trauma are perceived as threatening • Hallucinations or illusions may occur where aspects of the trauma are reperceived	• Specific situations, such as those involving dirt, are perceived as threatening and elicit obsessional thoughts
Cognition	• The child believes that harm to the parent or the self will occur following separation	• The child believes that contact with the phobic object or entry into the phobic situation will lead to catastrophe	• The child catastrophizes about many minor daily events	• The youth believes that the panic attacks may lead to death or serious injury	• Recurrent memories of the trauma occur • The child tries to distract him or herself from recalling these traumatic memories	• Obsessional thoughts, images or impulses intrude into consciousness and may involve themes of contamination, sex or aggression • The child tries to exclude these thoughts from consciousness
Affect	• Intense fear or anger occurs when separation is anticipated, during separation or following separation	• Intense fear or anger is experienced if contact with the feared object or situation is anticipated or occurs	• A continual moderately high level of fear is experienced, often called free floating anxiety	• During panic attacks intense fear occurs and between attacks a moderate level of fear of recurrence is experienced	• Against a background of hyperarousal, periodic intrusive episodes of intense fear, horror or anger like those that occurred during the trauma are experienced • The child feels emotionally blunted and cannot experience tender emotions • Depression may occur	• The obsessions cause anxiety
Arousal	• Episodes of hyperarousal • Sleep problems	• Episodes of hyperarousal • Sleep problems	• Continual hyperarousal • Sleep problems	• Episodes of extreme hyperarousal against a background of moderate hyperarousal • Sleep problems	• Episodes of extreme hyperarousal against a background of moderate hyperarousal • Sleep problems	• Ongoing moderate hyperarousal occurs • Hyperarousal occurs when compulsions are resisted
Behaviour	• Separation is avoided or resisted • The child refuses to go to school • The child refuses to sleep alone	• The phobic object or situation is avoided	• As worrying intensifies social activities become restricted	• The youth may avoid public places in case the panic attacks occur away from the safety of home. This is secondary agoraphobia	• Young children may cling to parents and refuse to sleep alone • Teenagers may use drugs or alcohol to block the intrusive thoughts and emotions • Suicidal attempts may occur	• Motivated by their obsessional beliefs, children engage in compulsive rituals which they believe will prevent a catastrophe from occurring or undo some potentially threatening event which has occurred • These rituals are usually unrealistic
Interpersonal adjustment	• Peer relationships may deteriorate • Academic performance may deteriorate	• With simple phobias interpersonal problems are confined to phobic situations • Agoraphobia may lead to social isolation	• Peer relationships may deteriorate • Academic performance may deteriorate	• If agoraphobia develops secondary to the panic attacks social isolation may result	• Complete social isolation may occur if the trauma was solitary • Where the trauma was shared, the child may confine interactions to the group who shared the trauma	• Members of the child's family or social network may become involved in helping the child perform compulsive rituals and inadvertently reinforce them

Figure 8.2 Clinical features of anxiety disorders

cognition, affect, arousal, behaviour and interpersonal adjustment are given. With respect to perception, the five disorders differ in the classes of stimuli which elicit anxiety. With separation anxiety, the stimulus is separation from the caregiver. For phobias it is specific creatures (e.g. animals), events (e.g. injury), or situations (e.g. meeting new people) that elicit anxiety. With generalized anxiety disorder, the person interprets many aspects of their environment as potentially threatening. In panic disorder, somatic sensations of arousal such as tachycardia are perceived as threatening since they are expected to lead to a full-blown panic attack. With PTSD, internal and external cues that remind the person of the trauma that led to the disorder elicit anxiety. With OCD, stimuli that evoke obsessional thoughts elicit anxiety. For example, potentially dirty situations may evoke obsessional ideas about cleanliness and anxiety about contamination.

Cognitions in all six anxiety disorders have the detection and/or avoidance of danger as the central organizing theme. In separation anxiety, children believe that they or their parents will be harmed if separation occurs. With phobias, the child believes that contact with the feared object or creature, or entry into the feared situation will result in harm such as being bitten by a dog in the case of dog phobia or being negatively judged by strangers in the case of social phobia. With generalized anxiety, children catastrophize about many features of their environment. For example, they may fear that the house will burn down, their parents' car will crash, they will be punished for soiling their clothes, their friends will leave them and so forth. In panic disorder, the child believes that further panic attacks may be fatal and often secondary beliefs evolve that lead to agoraphobia. That is, youngsters believe that, provided they stay in the safety of the home, the panic attacks are less likely to occur. With PTSD, there is a belief that provided the memories of the trauma are excluded from consciousness, the danger of re-experiencing the intense fear and danger associated with the trauma that led to PTSD can be avoided. With OCD, the most common obsessions are with dirt and contamination; catastrophes such as fires, illness or death; symmetry, order and exactness; religious scrupulosity; disgust with bodily wastes or secretions such as urine, stools or saliva; unlucky or lucky numbers; and forbidden sexual thoughts. There is also the belief that engaging in specific rituals will neutralize the threat posed by specific obsession-related stimuli.

In all six of the anxiety disorders listed in Figure 8.2 the beliefs about threat and danger are accompanied by an affective state, characterized by feelings of tension, restlessness and uneasiness. If the child is compelled to approach the feared stimuli, or in the case of OCD prevented from executing a compulsive ritual, outbursts of anger may occur. For example, children with separation anxiety may have aggressive tantrums if forced to remain at school while their mothers leave. A similar display of anger may occur if children with water phobia are carried into a swimming pool by well-intentioned parents trying to teach them to swim. In PTSD, in addition to the affective experiences of uneasiness and tension, an affective experience of emotional blunting, arising from the child's attempt to exclude all affective material from consciousness may develop.

The patterning of arousal varies depending upon the frequency with which the youngster comes into contact with feared stimuli. With separation anxiety hyperarousal occurs only when separation is threatened and with specific phobias it occurs only in the presence of the feared object. With generalized anxiety disorder, there is a pattern of ongoing continual hyperarousal. With panic disorder and PTSD there is a moderate level of chronic hyperarousal punctuated by brief episodes of extreme hyperarousal. These occur in panic disorder during panic attacks and in PTSD when memories of the traumatic event intrude into consciousness. With OCD, specific obsession-related cues evoke acute and intense episodes of arousal.

Avoidance behaviours characterize all anxiety disorders. With specific phobias, these may lead to only a moderate constriction in lifestyle. For example, a child may refuse to engage in sports or athletics or to ride a bicycle because of an injury phobia. However, with separation anxiety, generalized anxiety disorder, panic disorder and PTSD, the avoidance behaviour may lead the youngster to become housebound. With PTSD, alcohol or drug abuse may occur. Alcohol and drugs are used to reduce negative affect and suppress traumatic memories. With OCD the child engages in compulsive rituals to reduce anxiety associated with obsessional thoughts. Common compulsions include washing; repeating an action; checking; removing contaminants; touching; ordering; and collecting.

Interpersonal relationships are affected by different anxiety disorders in different ways. With simple phobias there may be minimal disruption although conflict with parents, teachers or peers may occur where the youngster refuses to conform or co-operate with routine activities so as to avoid the feared stimuli. For example, parent–child conflict may occur if a child refuses to get into an elevator at a shopping mall because of claustrophobia. With separation anxiety, panic disorder, generalized anxiety and PTSD complete social isolation may occur and the youngster's peer relationships and school attendance may cease. With OCD parents may attempt to reduce the child's anxiety by participating in compulsive rituals or in other instances they may increase the child's anxiety by punishing the child for their compulsive behaviour.

Epidemiology

In a review of major epidemiological studies Anderson (1994) concluded that the overall prevalence of anxiety disorders in children and adolescents is approximately 2–9 per cent. The prevalence of separation anxiety is 2–5 per cent; of simple phobias 2–9 per cent; of social phobias 1 per cent; of generalized anxiety disorders 3–6 per cent; and of OCD 1–2 per cent. Many children met criteria for two or more anxiety disorders, so the prevalence rates for individual disorders sum to more than 9 per cent. Epidemiological data on the prevalence of panic disorder and post-traumatic stress disorder (PTSD) for children are unavailable. Evidence from studies of adults indicates that the lifetime prevalence of panic disorder is 1.5–3.5 per cent and the lifetime prevalence of PTSD is 1–14 per cent (APA, 1994). There are clear gender differences in the prevalence of anxiety disorders. More girls than boys have separation anxiety, phobias, generalized anxiety disorder and panic attacks although the precise gender ratios vary from study to study and from one disorder to another (Anderson, 1994). With respect to age trends, it has already been noted that simple phobias and separation anxiety are more common among preadolescents and generalized anxiety disorder, panic disorder, social phobia and OCD are more common among adolescents (Klein, 1994). Comorbidity among anxiety disorders is quite high. In clinical samples 50 per cent of cases with one anxiety disorder also meet the diagnostic criteria for another anxiety disorder. In community samples, up to 39 per cent of cases meet the criteria for two or more anxiety disorders (Anderson, 1994). For anxiety disorders, comorbidity with conduct disorders is 14.8 per cent, with attention deficit hyperactivity disorder it is 11.8 per cent and with major depression it is 16.2 per cent (McConaughy and Achenbach, 1994).

Previous reviews

Kendall (1993) summarized findings from studies evaluating treatment methods for anxiety disorders in children and adolescents. For phobias, interventions involving exposure to the feared stimulus, either gradual or intensive, coupled with training in coping skills and support have been shown to be effective. These treatments include systematic desensitization and flooding. The most effective treatment for generalized anxiety disorder is cognitive behaviour therapy which involves training children to monitor and challenge catastrophic thoughts. Typically cognitive behavioural programmes also include exposure to feared situations and training in a range of coping strategies including relaxation skills. March (1995) has reviewed the effectiveness of cognitive and behavioural methods in the treatment of OCD and concluded that there is tentative support for the effectiveness of parent-assisted exposure and response prevention, in which the child is encouraged to confront cues that elicit obsessional thoughts, but resists engaging in anxiety reducing compulsive rituals. Estrada and Pinsof (1995) reviewed evidence for the effectiveness of family-based approaches in the treatment of childhood fears and anxieties. Their findings suggest tentative support for the effectiveness of approaches that involve parents in the treatment of their children's fears and anxieties, particularly in relation to night fears, school phobia and generalized anxiety disorder. Target and Fonagy (1996) reviewed available evidence on the effectiveness of psychodynamic treatment of anxiety disorders and tentatively concluded that intensive psychodynamic psychotherapy may be effective with generalized anxiety disorder, particularly severe cases where there is considerable comorbidity. There is little evidence for the effectiveness of pharmacological interventions for most anxiety disorders in children and adolescents (Klein, 1994). However clomipramine has been shown to be effective in the treatment of OCD (March, 1995). In these reviews of psychological interventions for anxiety disorders in children a methodologically heterogeneous group of studies were included ranging from uncontrolled single-case studies to controlled trials. It is therefore difficult to assess the degree of confidence that can be placed in the conclusions summarized here.

Method

One aim of this chapter was to review well-designed studies of the effects of psychological interventions for children and adolescents with anxiety disorders. A computer-based literature search of the PsychLit database was conducted. Terms that define the anxiety disorders were combined with terms that define psychological intervention and the search was limited to children or adolescents. A variety of terms were used to define anxiety disorders including *anxiety, fears, phobias, obsessive compulsive disorder, post-traumatic stress disorder, generalized anxiety disorder* and *overanxious disorder*. Terms that defined interventions included *treatment, therapy, intervention, behaviour therapy, cognitive behaviour therapy, family therapy, desensitization, flooding,* and *exposure and response prevention*. The search, which was confined to English language journals, covered the period 1975 to 1997 inclusively. A manual search through bibliographies of all recent review papers on psychological interventions for anxiety disorders was also conducted. Treatment outcome studies were selected for inclusion in this review if they contained a psychological treatment group and a control or comparison group; if at least five cases were included in the active treatment group; and if reliable and valid pre- and post-treatment measures were included in the design of the study. Single-case designs and studies reported in dissertations or convention papers were not included in the review. Using these inclusion and exclusion criteria only five studies were initially selected for review. One uncontrolled trial of cognitive behaviour therapy for OCD was added to this group, since no controlled comparative studies could be located. No studies of panic disorder or PTSD were included in the review because none could be located.

Characteristics of the studies

Characteristics of the six studies are set out in Table 8.1. All of the studies were conducted between 1975 and 1996. Four were conducted in the USA, one in Australia and one in the UK. Two studies contained participants with a heterogeneous group of severe anxiety disorders including generalized

Table 8.1 Characteristics of treatment outcome studies for anxiety disorders

Study No	Authors	Year	Country	N per gp	Mean age & range	Gender	Primary diagnosis	Co-morbid diagnosis	Family characteristics	Referral	Treatment setting	Treatment duration
1	Graziano and Mooney	1980	USA	RT + SIT + PT = 17 C = 16	9 y 6–13 y	m 55% f 45%	Darkness phobia			Media Self	University	3 sess over 3 w
2	Kanfer et al.	1975	USA	SIT-CON = 15 SIT-RI = 15 C = 15	5–6 y	m 67% f 33%	Darkness phobia		Middle class Urban	School	School	3 sess over 2 h
3	Blagg and Yule	1984	UK	FBT = 30 MIT = 16 HT = 20	13 y 11–16 y	m 50% f 50%	School phobia				Community OP	FBT 6 sess MIT & HT 1 y
4	Kendall	1994	USA	CBT = 27 C = 20	9–13 y	m 60% f 40%	OAD 64% SAD 17% AD 19% DSM III R	Phobias 60% Depression 32% ADHD 15% ODD 13% CD 2%		Multiple sources	University	17 sess over 4 m
5	Barrett et al.	1996	Australia	CBT = 28 CBT + FAM = 25 C = 26	9 y 7–14 y	m 56% f 44%	OAD 38% SAD 28% SP 24% DSM III R	Phobias 22% Depression 6% ODD 3%		Multiple sources	University	24 sess over 3 m Child 12 sess Parents 12 sess
6	March et al.	1994	USA	CBT + PT + CT = 15	14 y 8–18 y	m 33% f 66%	CCD DSM III R	Depression 93%		Multiple sources	University	16 sess over 4 m

Key RT = Relaxation training. SIT = Self-instructional training. PT = Parent training. SIT-CON = Self-instructional training focusing on personal control. SIT-RI = Self-instructional training focusing on reinterpretation of feared stimulus. BFT = Behavioural family therapy. MIT = Multimodal inpatient therapy. HT = Home tutor. CBT = Cognitive behaviour therapy. FAM = Family anxiety management. CT = Clomipramine therapy. C = Control group. DSM III R = *Diagnostic and Statistical Manual of Mental Disorders* (Third edition, revised). OAD = Overanxious disorder. SAD = Separation anxiety disorder. AD = Avoidant disorder. SP = Social phobia. ADHD = Attention deficit hyperactivity disorder. ODD = Oppositional defiant disorder. CD = Conduct disorder. OP = Outpatient. d = day. w = week. m = month. y = year. sess = sessions.

anxiety disorder (or overanxious disorder as it used to be designated); separation anxiety disorder; and social phobia (or avoidant disorder as it used to be termed). These two studies were randomized controlled trials of cognitive behavioural therapy (Barrett *et al.*, 1996; Kendall, 1994). Another two studies in this review, concerned with darkness phobia, were brief randomized controlled interventions, but not on the scale typical of randomized controlled clinical trials (Graziano and Mooney, 1980; Kanfer *et al.*, 1975). One study was a comparative treatment outcome investigation of school phobia (Blagg and Yule, 1984) and the final paper reported on a single group outcome study of cognitive behavioural intervention for OCD (March *et al.*, 1994). Two hundred and eighty-five children participated in these studies and of these, 208 were in active treatment groups and 77 were in control groups. Participants' ages ranged from five to eighteen years. With respect to gender, 54 per cent of cases were male and 46 per cent were female. Co-morbidity data were reported in only three studies and for these in order of decreasing frequency depression, specific phobias, ADHD, oppositional defiant disorder and conduct disorder were the reported co-morbid conditions. In three studies cases were referred from multiple sources including physicians, schools and health professionals. In one study all referrals came from schools. In one study participants were self-referred or solicited through the media and in one study no information on referral was given. In four studies treatment was conducted in a university-based outpatient clinic and in one study treatment was offered in a school setting. In the comparative treatment outcome study of school phobia, the family-based behavioural treatment was conducted at a community-based outpatient clinic, the multimodal inpatient programme was offered in a hospital setting and home tuition occurred in the youngster's home. The number of sessions of treatment ranged from three to seventeen sessions over one to sixteen weeks except for the multimodal inpatient and home tuition programme each of which spanned about a year.

Methodological features

Methodological features of the six studies included in this review are presented in Table 8.2. Five of the studies included in this review contained control or comparison groups. Four of the studies contained diagnostically homogeneous groups which were assessed before and after treatment on reliable and valid measures. Follow-up data were collected a year after treatment or later in five of the six studies. To assess children before and after treatment researcher ratings were used in five studies; parent ratings in three studies; self-report ratings in two studies and teacher ratings in one study. While symptomatic improvements were evaluated in all studies, improvements in relationships within the child's family system and social network were conducted in only one study. In four studies cases were randomly assigned to conditions and in four studies groups were demographically

Table 8.2 Methodological features of studies of anxiety disorders

Feature	Study number					
	S1	S2	S3	S4	S5	S6
Control or comparison group	1	1	1	1	1	0
Random assignment	1	1	0	1	1	0
Diagnostic homogeneity	1	1	1	0	0	1
Comparable for co-morbidity	0	0	0	0	0	0
Demographic similarity	1	1	0	1	1	0
Pre-treatment assessment	1	1	1	1	1	1
Post-treatment assessment	1	1	1	1	1	1
One-year follow-up assessment	1	0	1	1	1	1
Children's self-report	0	0	0	1	1	0
Parent's ratings	1	0	0	1	1	0
Teacher's ratings	0	0	0	1	0	0
Therapist's ratings	0	0	0	0	0	0
Researcher's ratings	0	1	1	1	1	1
Child's symptom assessed	1	1	1	1	1	1
System assessed	0	0	1	0	1	0
Deterioration assessed	1	0	0	0	0	0
Drop-out assessed	1	1	0	1	1	0
Clinical significance of change assessed	1	1	1	1	1	1
Experienced therapists used	0	0	1	0	1	1
Treatments were equally valued	0	0	1	0	0	0
Treatments were manualized	0	0	0	1	1	1
Therapy supervision was provided	0	0	0	0	0	1
Treatment integrity checked	0	1	0	1	1	0
Data on concurrent treatment given	0	0	0	0	0	1
Data on subsequent treatment given	0	0	0	0	0	0
Total	12	11	11	15	16	11

Key: S = study. 1 = design feature was present. 0 = design feature was absent.

similar. However, in none of the studies were cases matched for co-morbidity. In one study deterioration was assessed and in four studies drop-out rates were reported. In no studies was information on engagement in further or subsequent treatment given and in only one study was information on concurrent treatment given. In all studies information on both statistical and clinical significance of treatment gains was reported. Experienced therapists were used in three studies and in two of the three studies where two or more treatments were compared, information given in the reports suggested that treatments were equally valued by the research team. In three studies treatments were manualized but in only one study was information on supervision given. In three studies treatment integrity was checked. Overall, this was a fairly methodologically robust group of studies, so reliable conclusions may be drawn from them with considerable confidence.

Substantive findings

A summary of the main findings of the six studies is given in Tables 8.3 and 8.4. The six studies will be reviewed below under the following headings: darkness phobia (Graziano and Mooney, 1980; Kanfer *et al.*, 1975); school phobia (Blagg and Yule, 1984); severe anxiety disorders including generalized anxiety disorder, separation anxiety disorder; and social phobia (Kendall, 1994; Barrett *et al.*, 1996); and OCD (March *et al.*, 1994).

Darkness phobia

The two studies of the treatment of darkness phobia involved relatively brief interventions with children who suffered from severe and highly disruptive night-time fears of more than two years' duration or fears of remaining in the dark for more than 27 seconds (Graziano and Mooney, 1980; Kanfer *et al.*, 1975). In Graziano and Mooney's (ibid.) study children were trained in relaxation skills and the use of self-instructions to reduce fear and anxiety over a three-week period. Concurrent parent training involved coaching parents in using social learning principles of prompting and reinforcement to modify their children's fearful behaviours and build up courageous alternatives. An effect size of 1.3 occurred for the treatment group based on the proportion of days when the child went to bed fearlessly, which indicates that the average treated case fared better than 90 per cent of untreated cases in the control group immediately following treatment. Using fearless night-time behaviour for ten consecutive nights as the criterion for clinically significant improvement, following treatment 82 per cent of cases had improved and this figure increased to 88 per cent a year later.

Kanfer *et al.* (ibid.) examined the effects of two different types of self-instructional training conditions and a control condition or willingness to tolerate darkness in children with darkness phobia. Children in the self-instructional training group that focused on competence were coached in using self-instructions that emphasized the child's active control or competence in managing their anxiety about the dark, for example, I can take care of myself in the dark. Children in the self-instructional training group that focused on reinterpretation of darkness as a non-threatening situation were coached in using self-instructions that emphasized positive features of the dark, for example, the dark is a fun place to be. Children in the control group were asked to use neutral sentences when trying to cope with the darkness, for example, Mary had a little lamb. Following training, children were asked to remain in the dark until their fear became so intense that they needed to increase the illumination or in another condition to reduce the intensity of the light using a control dial to the lowest tolerable level. The duration of darkness tolerance and the lowest level of illumination were the principal measures used to assess the effectiveness of the treatments. For both of these indices, the self-instructional training that focused on control and competence was more effective than that which focused on reinterpretation and both treatments were more effective than the neutral statements used by children in the control group. An effect size of 1.7 for the self-instructional training that focused on control and 1.0 for the training which focused on reinterpretation showed that the average treated case in these groups was functioning better than between 96 per cent and 84 per cent of children in the control group.

From these two studies it may be concluded that effective treatment programmes for darkness phobias should include self-instructional training focusing on control and competence in managing the dark; relaxation training; and parent training on how to prompt and reinforce courageous behaviour while extinguishing anxious behaviour.

School phobia

Blagg and Yule (1984) compared the effectiveness of family-based behaviour therapy; a hospital-based multimodal inpatient programme; and a home tuition and psychotherapy programme for the treatment of school phobia. All cases in the study met the following diagnostic criteria for school phobia: extreme difficulty in attending school for at least three days; accompanying marked emotional upset; the child remains at home with parent's permission; and absence of antisocial problems (Berg *et al.*, 1969). The family-based behaviour therapy programme included detailed clarification of the child's problem; discussion of the principal concerns of the child, parents and teacher; development of contingency plans to ensure maintenance of gains once the child returned to school; *in vivo* flooding where the child was returned to school as soon as possible; and follow-up appointments with parents and teachers until the child had been attending school without problems for at least six weeks. The hospital-based multimodal inpatient programme involved hospitalization; daily hospital-based group and milieu therapy; daily educational and occupational therapy; pharmacological

Table 8.3 Summary of treatment effects and outcome rates in studies of anxiety disorders

Variable	Study number and treatment condition							
	Study 1	*Study 2*		*Study 3*	*Study 4*	*Study 5*		*Study 6*
	RT + SIT + PT	SIT-CON	SIT-RI	FBT > MIT	CBT	CBT	CBT + FAM	CBT + PT + CT
Symptomatic improvement after treatment								
Children's self-report	1.3	–	–	–	0.8	0.4	0.8	–
Parent's ratings	–	–	–	–	1.4	0.9	1.1	–
Teacher's ratings	–	–	–	–	0.4	–	–	–
Therapist's ratings	–	1.7	–	–	–	–	–	–
Researcher's ratings	–	–	1.0	–	–	–	–	–
Symptomatic improvement at follow-up								
Children's self-report	–	–	–	–	–	–	–	–
Parent's ratings	–	–	–	–	–	–	–	–
Teacher's ratings	–	–	–	–	–	–	–	–
Therapist's ratings	–	–	–	–	–	–	–	–
Researcher's ratings	–	–	–	2.6	–	–	–	–

Systemic improvement after treatment						
Children's self-report	–	–	–	–	–	–
Parent's ratings	–	–	–	–	–	–
Teacher's ratings	–	–	–	–	–	–
Therapist's ratings	–	–	–	–	–	–
Researcher's ratings	–	–	–	–	–	–
Systemic improvement at follow-up						
Children's self-report	–	–	–	–	–	–
Parent's ratings	–	–	–	–	–	–
Teacher's ratings	–	–	–	–	–	–
Therapist's ratings	–	–	–	–	–	–
Researcher's ratings	–	2.2	–	–	–	–
Positive clinical outcomes						
% improved after treatment	82%	–	64%	57%	84%	80%
% improved at follow-up	88%	93%	–	70%	96%	80%
Negative clinical outcomes						
% Deterioration	0%	–	0%	–	–	–
% Drop-out	0%	0%	–	22%	10%	8%
% Engaged in further treatment	–	–	–	–	–	–

Key RT = Relaxation training. SIT = Self-instructional training. SIT-CON = Self-instructional training focusing on personal control. SIT-RI = Self-instructional training focusing on reinterpretation of feared stimulus. BFT = Behavioural family therapy. MIT = Multimodal inpatient therapy. CBT = Cognitive behaviour therapy. FAM = Family anxiety management. PT = Parent training. CT = Clomipramine therapy.

Table 8.4 Key findings from treatment studies of children and adolescents with anxiety disorders

Study no.	Authors	Year	Primary diagnosis	N per gp	No of sessions	Group differences	Key findings
1	Graziano and Mooney	1980	Darkness phobia	1. RT + SIT + PT = 17 2. C = 16	3	1 > 2	• For children with darkness phobia, relaxation training and self-instructional training combined with parent training led to a rapid reduction in night-time fears and these improvements were maintained at one-year follow-up.
2	Kanfer et al.	1975	Darkness phobia	1. SIT-CON = 15 2. SIT-RI = 15 3. C = 15	3	1 > 2 > 3	• For children with darkness phobia, self-instructional training focusing on personal control in the feared situation was more effective than self-instructional training focusing on reinterpretation of the feared stimulus and both were more effective than a neutral control treatment in reducing fear of the dark.
3	Blagg et al.	1984	School phobia and separation anxiety	1. FBT = 30 2. MIT = 16 3. HT = 20	6	1 > 2 > 3	• Family-based behaviour therapy led to a far more rapid resolution of school attendance problems associated with school phobia and separation anxiety compared with a multimodal inpatient treatment programme and a home tuition programme. • The gains in school attendance and separation anxiety for children in the behaviour therapy programme were maintained at one-year follow-up, while little progress was made by the other two groups. • The home tuition programme was the least effective in reducing separation anxiety.

	Author	Year	Diagnosis	Treatment	Sessions	Results	Findings
4	Kendall	1994	OAD 64% SAD 17% AD 19% DSM III R	1. CBT = 27 2. C = 20	17	1 > 2	• Immediately following cognitive behaviour therapy and a year later children with overanxious disorder, separation anxiety disorder and avoidant disorder showed clinically significant reductions in anxiety compared with a control group.
5	Barrett et al.	1996	OAD 38% SAD 28% SP 24% DSM III R	1. CBT = 28 2. CBT + FAM = 25 3. C = 26	24	2 > 1 > 3	• Immediately following cognitive behaviour therapy or cognitive behaviour therapy combined with a family anxiety management programme children with overanxious disorder, separation anxiety disorder and social phobia showed clinically significant reductions in anxiety compared with a control group. • Treatment gains made by both groups were sustained at one-year follow-up but the group receiving the combined treatment fared better in the long term. • Younger female children responded best to the combined treatment programme.
6	March et al.	1994	OCD DSM III R	CBT + PT + CT = 15 T1 = pre treat T2 = post treat T3 = 18m	16	T3 > T2 = T1	• Cognitive behaviour therapy and parent training combined with clomipramine significantly reduced OCD symptomatology and these gains were maintained at 18 months' follow-up.

Key RT = Relaxation training. SIT = Self-instructional training. PT = Parent training. SIT-CON = Self-instructional training focusing on personal control. SIT-RI = Self-instructional training focusing on reinterpretation of feared stimulus. BFT = Behavioural family therapy. MIT = Multimodal inpatient therapy. HT = Home tutor. CBT = Cognitive behaviour therapy. FAM = Family anxiety management. CT = Clomipramine therapy. C = Control group. DSM III R = *Diagnostic and Statistical Manual of Mental Disorders* (Third edition, revised). OAD = Overanxious disorder. SAD = Separation anxiety disorder. AD = Avoidant disorder. SP = Social phobia. The number of sessions for Blagg *et al.*'s study is an estimate of the duration of the FBT programme.

treatment of anxiety symptoms; regular liaison with parents and school-teachers; and planned discharge. The home tuition and psychotherapy programme involved daily tuition in the tutor's home or the child's own home, fortnightly individual psychotherapy, and fortnightly concurrent parent counselling.

The average duration of treatment for the family-based behaviour therapy was three weeks and involved about six sessions whereas for the multimodal inpatient programme and the home tuition and psychotherapy programme, the average duration of treatment was approximately a year. A year after treatment, 93 per cent of children who received family-based behaviour therapy were judged to have been successful in returning to school compared with 38 per cent of children in the multimodal inpatient programme and 10 per cent of those from the home tuition and psychotherapy programme. The three programmes also had different effects on family functioning as assessed by the presence or absence of separation anxiety. A year after treatment, 100 per cent of children who received family-based behaviour therapy showed no clinically significant separation anxiety compared with 93 per cent of children in the multimodal inpatient programme and 33 per cent of those from the home tuition and psychotherapy programme.

From this single study, it may be concluded that for the treatment of school phobia, family-based behaviour therapy is probably more effective than multimodal inpatient care or a combined programme of home tuition and psychotherapy.

Generalized anxiety disorder, separation anxiety and social phobia

Both Kendall (1994) and Barrett *et al.* (1996) examined the effectiveness of cognitive behaviour therapy in the treatment of severe anxiety disorders including generalized anxiety disorder, separation anxiety disorder and social phobia. Cases were excluded from both studies if there was a main diagnosis of specific phobia, an IQ below 80, a disabling physical condition, psychotic symptoms or if children were taking anti-anxiety medications.

Diagnoses in both studies were based on information from the Anxiety Disorder Interview Schedule (Silverman and Nelles, 1988) and conformed to DSM III R criteria.

The cognitive behavioural treatment package offered in both studies was based on Kendall *et al.*'s (1990) detailed treatment manual. In addition, in Kendall's (1994) study, children worked through the *Coping Cat Workbook* (Kendall, 1992) and in Barrett *et al.*'s (1996) study an Australian adaptation of the same workbook the *Coping Koala Workbook* (Barrett *et al.*, 1991) was used. Children were trained to monitor and challenge anxiety-provoking cognitions about potentially threatening situations and to use coping self-instruction and relaxation skills to reduce anxiety. They were also coached in self-reinforcement for coping with anxiety-provoking situations. During the initial skills development part of the programme, modelling, role playing, shaping and social reinforcement were used. During the latter part of therapy, children were exposed to both visualized and actual feared stimuli and practised coping skills in these situations. In the final sessions of the programme children created a personalized advertisement, poem or song which was videotaped or audiotaped and which focused on communicating to other children how to manage anxiety.

In Barrett *et al.*'s (1996) study, in addition to the group that received the individually based treatment programme like that just described, a second treatment group was included which received both the individual programme and a family anxiety management treatment module (Sanders and Dadds, 1993). Parents and children attended all sessions of this family-based intervention. The module involved training parents in contingency management, personal anxiety management, and problem-solving and communications skills. With contingency management parents were coached in how to reinforce their children's courageous behaviour and extinguish anxiety-related behaviours using token systems, verbal reinforcers and planned ignoring. In the personal anxiety management sessions parents were taught similar skills to those of their children including challenging catastrophic thoughts and using relaxation and coping skills in anxiety-provoking situations. In the problem-solving and communications skills training sessions, coaching in speaking and listening skills occurred. Families were also coached in ways to manage conflict and solve family problems systematically.

Following treatment, 64 per cent of cases in Kendall's (1994) individual programme and 57 per cent of cases in Barrett *et al.*'s (1996) individual programme showed clinically significant recovery and this figure rose to 70 per cent a year after treatment for cases in Barrett *et al.*'s (ibid.) study. In these analyses cases were defined as showing clinically significant recovery if they no longer met the diagnostic criteria for anxiety disorders in the DSM III R and the Anxiety Disorder Interview Schedule (Silverman and Nelles, 1988; Silverman and Albano, 1996). In contrast to these results for individual treatment, in Barrett *et al.*'s (ibid.) combined individual and family-based intervention programme 84 per cent of cases showed clinically significant recovery following treatment and this figure rose to 96 per cent a year later.

For the individual programmes following treatment, effect sizes based on children's self-reported anxiety on the Revised Children's Manifest Anxiety Scale (Reynolds and Richmond, 1978) ranged from 0.4 to 0.8 and those based on parent reports as indexed by the internalizing behaviour problem scale of the Child Behaviour Checklist (Achenbach, 1991) ranged from 0.9–1.4. Thus from children's perspectives the average treated case fared better than 66–79 per cent of untreated cases in the control group. From parents' perspectives the average treated case fared better than 82–92 per cent of untreated cases. For Barrett *et al.*'s (1996) combined individual and family-based programme effect sizes were 0.8 and 1.1 for child- and parent-reported improvements respectively. Thus, from children's perspectives, the average treated case fared better than 79 per cent of untreated cases and from parent perspectives the average treated case fared better than 86 per cent of untreated cases in the control group.

From the results of these two studies it may be concluded that an individual cognitive behavioural treatment programme combined with a family-based treatment programme is highly effective in alleviating severe anxiety problems including generalized anxiety disorder, separation anxiety and social phobia. A combined individual and family-based programme is more effective and so preferable to a programme that is exclusively individually based.

Obsessive compulsive disorder

March *et al.* (1994) examined the effectiveness of combined pharmacological treatment and cognitive behavioural treatment for children and adolescents with OCD in a single group outcome study. Participants were included if they obtained a score above 10 on the Yale Brown Obsessive Compulsive Scale (Goodman *et al.*, 1986) and met the DSM III R criteria for OCD. Fourteen of the fifteen participants received clomipramine throughout the study. The cognitive behavioural treatment programme, *How I ran OCD off my Land* (March and Mulle, 1994, 1996), included psychoeducation, symptom mapping and monitoring, anxiety management training, exposure and response prevention and parent training. In the psychoeducational component the child and parents were helped to view OCD as a medical illness separate from the youngster's core identity. Children were encouraged to externalize the disorder by giving it a nasty nickname and to make a commitment to driving this nasty creature out of their lives. In the mapping component of the programme a graded hierarchy of stimulus situations that elicit obsessions and lead to compulsions of varying strengths were mapped out, and those situations in which the child successfully controlled OCD symptoms were noted. These situations were referred to as the transition zone and were subsequently monitored on a weekly basis, since they defined children's success in managing OCD. In the anxiety management training sessions children were coached in coping with anxiety by using self-instruction and relaxation skills. In the exposure and response prevention component of the programme children were invited to enter increasingly anxiety-provoking situations and to use anxiety management skills to help them avoid engaging in compulsive rituals. Parent training included coaching parents to support their children through the exposure and response prevention process, to avoid punishing children for OCD-related symptoms and to reinforce them for successful attempts at response prevention when exposed to anxiety-provoking situations. Eighty per cent of children in the programme showed substantial clinical improvement following treatment and this was sustained eighteen months later. Forty per cent of patients were asymptomatic at post-treatment; 56 per cent were asymptomatic at follow-up; and 40 per cent were able to stop taking clomipramine without experiencing a relapse.

From this study it may tentatively be concluded that clomipramine combined with a comprehensive cognitive behavioural treatment programme involving both individual and parent training components is effective in reducing the symptoms of OCD. However, caution is warranted because of the absence of a control group in this study. It is noteworthy that the outcome rate for this study (56 per cent improvement at eighteen-month follow-up) is higher than that of 37 per cent for a multicentre clomipramine trial (DeVeaugh-Geiss *et al.*, 1992).

Conclusions

From this review a number of conclusions may be drawn about effective treatments for anxiety disorders in children. For darkness phobia, effective treatment programmes should include an individual component which entails self-instructional training focusing on control and competence in managing the dark and relaxation training on the one hand and a parent training component on the other which coaches parents in how to prompt and reinforce their children's courageous behaviour while not reinforcing anxious behaviour. Effective treatment may usually be completed within three sessions.

For school phobia a six-session family-based behaviour therapy programme is the treatment of choice. Such programmes should include a detailed clarification of the child's problem; discussion of the principal concerns of the child, parents and teacher; development of contingency plans to ensure maintenance of gains once the child returned to school; *in vivo* flooding where the child is returned to school as soon as possible; and follow-up appointments with parents and teachers until the child had been attending without problems for at least six weeks.

For severe anxiety problems including generalized anxiety disorder, separation anxiety and social phobia a combined 24-session programme of individual and family-based cognitive behaviour therapy is the treatment of choice. The individual component of the programme should coach children in how to monitor and challenge anxiety-provoking cognitions about potentially threatening situations; how to use coping self-instructions and relaxation skills to reduce anxiety; and how to use self-reinforcement for consolidating successful coping responses. The family-based treatment component should focus on contingency management, personal anxiety management for parents, and problem-solving and communications skills training for all family members.

For OCD a combined treatment approach that includes clomipramine and a comprehensive sixteen-session cognitive behavioural therapy package is currently the treatment of choice. The cognitive behavioural treatment programme should include psychoeducation, symptom mapping and monitoring, anxiety management training, exposure and response prevention and parent training.

In developing services for children with anxiety disorders account should be taken of their prevalence (2–9 per cent) and the fact that brief outpatient rather than extended inpatient treatment is preferable. The majority of anxiety disorders can be effectively treated in programmes ranging from three to 24 sessions which include both individual therapy for the child and family intervention. Protocols for phobias, generalized anxiety disorder, separation anxiety disorder and OCD have been developed and should be flexibly applied in clinical settings. Currently there are no well-conducted treatment evaluation studies for panic disorder or post-traumatic stress disorder although accounts of clinical work with children (Ollendick *et al.*, 1994a; Yule, 1994) and reviews of carefully conducted evaluation studies with adults (Barlow *et al.*, 1998; Keane, 1998) suggest that programmes like those used in Barrett *et al.*'s (1996) study, with minor modifications, are probably an appropriate basis for treatment. For panic disorder, because bodily sensations associated with normal levels of arousal are typically misinterpreted as catastrophic signs of imminent personal danger, psycho-education about this process and exposure to internal arousal cues should be incorporated into the treatment of panic disorder. For PTSD, psycho-education about the condition and exposure to internal and external cues that elicit anxiety should be incorporated into treatment protocols for PTSD.

With respect to research priorities, the most outstanding feature of the material reviewed in this chapter is the paucity of controlled trials for all anxiety disorders in children and adolescents, and the complete absence of studies in some important areas such as panic disorder and PTSD. Controlled trials of the type conducted by Kendall (1994) and Barrett *et al.* (1996) need to be conducted for all anxiety disorders in children, and there is an urgent need for trials evaluating the treatment of PTSD and panic disorder, building on accounts of clinical practice and the results of controlled treatment trials with adults (Barlow *et al.*, 1998; Keane, 1998; Ollendick *et al.*, 1994a; Yule, 1994). Experimental treatments for PTSD, notably eye movement desensitization, also deserve controlled evaluation with child and adolescent populations.

ASSESSMENT

Beidel, S., Turner, S. and Fink, C. (1996). Assessment of Childhood Social Phobia: Construct, convergent and discriminative validity of the Social Phobia Anxiety Inventory for Children (SPAI-C). *Psychological Assessment*, 8, 235–40.

Chambless, D., Caputo, C., Bright, P. and Gallagher, R. (1984). Assessment of fear of fear in agoraphobics: the Body Sensations Questionnaire and the Agoraphobia Cognitions Questionnaire. *Journal of Consulting and Clinical Psychology*, 62, 1090–7.

Clark, D. and Donovan, J. (1994). Reliability and validity of the Hamilton Anxiety Rating Scale in an Adolescent Sample. *Journal of the American Academy of Child and Adolescent Psychiatry*, 33, 354–60.

Clum, G., Broyles, S., Borden, J. and Watkins, P. (1990). Validity and reliability of the Panic Attack Symptoms and Cognitions Questionnaire. *Journal of Psychopathology and Behavioural Assessment*, 12, 233–45.

Fredrick, C. and Pynooss, R. (1988). *The Child Post-Traumatic Stress Disorder Reaction Index*. Los Angeles: University of California.

Glennon, B. and Weisz, J. (1978). An observational approach to the assessment of anxiety in young children. *Journal of Consulting and Clinical Psychology*, 46, 1246–57.

Goodman, W., Price, L., Rasmusen, S., Mazure, C., Rappoport, J., Heringes, G. and Charney, D. (1986). The Children's Yale Brown Obsessive-Compulsive Scale. Reprinted in Francis, G. and Gragg, R. (1996). *Obsessive Compulsive Disorder*. Thousand Oaks, CA: Sage.

Gullone, E. and King, N. (1992). Psychometric evaluation of a revised fear survey schedule for children and adolescents. *Journal of Child Psychology and Psychiatry*, 33, 987–8.

Horowitz, M., Wilner, N. and Alverez, W. (1979). Impact of events scale. A measure of subjective stress. *Psychosomatic Medicine*, 41, 209–18.

Kearney, C. and Silverman, W. (1993). Measuring the function of school refusal behaviour: The school refusal assessment scale (SRAS). *Journal of Clinical Child Psychology*, 22, 85–96.

Ost, L. (1990). The Agoraphobia Scale: An evaluation of its reliability and validity. *Behaviour Research and Therapy*, 28, 697–708.

Reynolds, C. and Richmond, B. (1978). What I think and feel: A revised measure of children's manifest anxiety. *Journal of Abnormal Child Psychology*, 6, 271–80.

Saigh, P. (1989). The development and validation of the Children's Post Traumatic Stress Disorder Inventory. *International Journal of Special Education*, 4, 75–84.

Silverman, W. and Albano, A. (1996). *The Anxiety Disorder Interview Schedule for Children-IV-Child and Parent Version*. Albany, NY: Greywind Publications.

Silverman, W., Fleisig, W., Rabian, B. and Peterson, R. (1991). Childhood anxiety sensitivity index. *Journal of Clinical Child Psychology*, 20, 162–8.

Spielberger, C. (1973). *Preliminary Manual of State-Trait Anxiety Inventory For Children*. Palo Alto, CA: Consulting Psychologists Press.

TREATMENT MANUALS AND RESOURCES

Bernstein, A. and Borkovec, T. (1993). *Progressive Relaxation Training*. Champaign, Ill: Research Press.

Dwivedi, K. and Varma, V. (1997). *A Handbook of Childhood Anxiety Management*. Aldershot: Arena.

Kendall, P., Kane, M., Howard, B. and Siqueland, L. (1990). *Cognitive-behavioural Therapy for Anxious Children. Treatment Manual*. Admore, PA: Workbook Publishing.

Kendall, P., Chansky, T., Kane, M., Kim, R., Kortlander, E., Ronan, K., Sessa, F. and Siqueland, L. (1992). *Anxiety Disorder in Youth: Cognitive Behavioural Interventions*. Needham Heights, USA: Allyn and Bacon.

March, J. and Mulle, K. (1994). *How I Ran OCD Off My Land: A Cognitive-Behavioural Program for the Treatment Of Obsessive-Compulsive Disorder in Children And Adolescents* (Revision 1.8). (Unpublished Manuscript. Department of Psychiatry, Duke University Medical Centre, Box 3527, Durham, NC 27710.)

Ollendick, T., King, N. and Yule, W. (1994). *International Handbook of Phobic and Anxiety Disorders in Children and Adolescents*. New York: Plenum.

Rapoport, J. (1989). *Obsessive Compulsive Disorder in Children and Adolescents*. New York: American Psychiatric Press.

Sanders, M. and Dadds, M. (1993). *Behavioural Family Intervention*. New York: Pergamon Press.

Silverman, W. and Kurtines, W. (1996). *Anxiety and Phobic Disorders: A Pragmatic Approach*. New York: Plenum.

FURTHER READING FOR CLIENTS

Barrett, P., Dadds, M. and Rappee, R. (1991). *Coping Koala Workbook*. (Unpublished manuscript, School of Applied Psychology, Griffith University, Nathan, Australia.)

Davis, M., Robbins-Eshelman, E. and McKay, M. (1988). *The Relaxation and Stress Reduction Workbook* (Third Edition). Oakland, CA: New Harbinger Publications.

Kendall, P. (1992). *Coping Cat Workbook*. Admore, PA: Workbook Publishing.

9 Depression and grief

Maggie Moore and Alan Carr

Definitions

The psychological treatment of depression and grief following the death of a parent are the principal issues addressed in this chapter.

Depression

Diagnostic criteria for episodes of major depression from the DSM IV (APA, 1994) and ICD 10 (ICD, 1992) classification systems are presented in Figure 9.1. Major depression is a recurrent condition involving low mood; selective attention to negative features of the environment; a pessimistic cognitive style; self-defeating behaviour patterns; a disturbance of sleep and appetite; and a disruption of interpersonal relationships (Harrington, 1993; Kovacs, 1997; Reynolds and Johnson, 1994). Loss is often the core theme linking these clinical features: loss of an important relationship, loss of some valued attribute such as athletic ability or health, or loss of status. With respect to perception, having suffered a loss, depressed children tend to perceive the world as if further losses were probable. Depressed children selectively attend to negative features of the environment and this in turn leads them to engage in depressive cognitions and unrewarding behaviour patterns which further entrench their depressed mood. In severe cases of adolescent depression, youngsters may report mood congruent auditory hallucinations. With respect to cognition, depressed children describe themselves, the world and the future in negative terms. They evaluate themselves as worthless and are critical of their academic, athletic, musical and social accomplishments. Often this negative self-evaluation is expressed as guilt for not living up to certain standards or letting others down. They see their world, including family, friends and school as unrewarding, critical and hostile or apathetic. They describe the future in bleak terms and report little if any hope that things will improve. Where they report extreme hopelessness and this is coupled with excessive guilt for which they believe they should be punished, suicidal ideas or intentions may be reported. Extremely negative thoughts about the self, the world and the future may be woven

DSM IV Criteria for a major depressive episode	ICD 10 Depressive episode
A. Five or more of the following symptoms have been present during the same two-week period nearly every day and represent a change from previous functioning; at least one of the symptoms is ether (1) depressed mood or (2) loss of interest or pleasure. Symptoms may be reported or observed.	In a typical depressive episode the individual usually suffers from depressed mood, loss of interest and enjoyment and reduced energy leading to increased fatigability and diminished activity. Marked tiredness after only slight effort is common. Other common symptoms are:
1. Depressed mood. In children and adolescents can be irritable mood.	a. reduced concentration and attention b. reduced self-esteem and confidence c. ideas of guilt and unworthiness d. bleak and pessimistic views of the future e. ideas or acts of self-harm or suicide f. disturbed sleep
2. Markedly diminished interest or pleasure in almost all daily activities.	g. diminished appetite.
3. Significant weight loss or gain (of 5% per month) or decrease or increase in appetite. In children consider failure to make expected weight gains.	The lowered mood varies little from day to day and is often unresponsive to circumstances and may show a characteristic diurnal variation as the day goes on.
4. Insomnia or hypersomnia.	Some of the above symptoms may be marked and develop characteristic features that are widely regarded as having special significance; for example, the *somatic symptoms* which are: loss of interest or pleasure in activities that are normally enjoyable; lack of emotional reactivity to normally pleasurable surroundings; waking in the morning two hours or more before the usual time; depression worse in the mornings; psychomotor retardation or agitation; marked loss of appetite or weight; marked loss of libido. Usually the somatic syndrome is not regarded as present unless at least four of these symptoms are present.
5. Psychomotor agitation or retardation.	
6. Fatigue or loss of energy.	
7. Feelings of worthlessness, excessive guilt.	
8. Poor concentration and indecisiveness.	
9. Recurrent thoughts of death, suicidal ideation or suicide attempt.	
B. Symptoms do not meet criteria for mixed episode of mania and depression.	
C. Symptoms cause clinically significant distress or impairment in social, occupational, educational or other important areas of functioning.	*Atypical presentations* are particularly common in adolescence. In some cases anxiety, distress and motor agitation may be more prominent at times than depression and mood changes may be masked by such features as irritability, excessive consumption of alcohol, histrionic behaviour and exacerbation of pre-existing phobic or obsessional symptoms or by hypochondriacal preoccupations.
D. Symptoms are not due to the direct effects of a drug or a general medical conditions such as hypothyroidism.	
E. The symptoms are not better accounted for by uncomplicated bereavement.	A duration of two weeks is required for a diagnosis.

Figure 9.1 Definitions of depression.
Source Adapted from DSM IV (APA, 1994) and ICD 10 (WHO, 1992).

together in severe cases into depressive delusional systems. In addition to the content of the depressed youngster's thought being bleak, they also display logical errors in their thinking and concentration problems. Errors in reasoning are marked by a tendency to maximize the significance and implications of negative events and minimize the significance of positive events. Concentration and attention difficulties lead to difficulties managing school work or leisure activities demanding sustained attention. With respect to affect, low mood is a core feature of depression.

Depressed mood is usually reported as a feeling of sadness, loneliness or despair and an inability to experience pleasure. Alternatively irritability, anxiety and aggression my be the main features with sadness and inability to experience pleasure being less prominent. This is not surprising since normal grief is characterized by sadness at the absence of the lost object, anger at the lost person for abandoning the grieving person and anxiety that further losses may occur. These grief processes are discussed in detail below. Depressed children and adolescents may show some cocktail of all three emotional processes, i.e. depressed mood, irritability and anxiety. At a behavioural level, depressed youngsters may show either reduced and slowed activity levels (psychomotor retardation) or increased but ineffective activity (psychomotor agitation). They may show a failure to engage in activities that would bring them a sense of achievement or connectedness to family or friends and much of their behaviour may be self-defeating. Somatic or vegetative features such as loss of energy, disturbances of sleep and appetite; weight loss or failure to make age-appropriate weight gain; abdominal pains or headaches; and diurnal variation in mood are all associated with more severe conditions. Teenagers may also report losing interest in sex. These features of depression are consistent with findings that dysregulation of neurophysiological, endocrine and immune functions are associated with depression and that sleep architecture is also affected. At an interpersonal level, depressed children report a deterioration in their relationships with family, friends, teachers and other significant figures in their lives. They describe themselves as lonely and yet unable or unworthy of taking steps to make contact with others.

The outcome for depression in childhood and adolescence is not favourable. While the majority of youngsters recover from a depressive episode within a year, they do not *grow out of* their mood disorder (Harrington, 1993; Kovacs, 1997; Reynolds and Johnson, 1994). Depressed youngsters are more likely than their non-depressed counterparts to develop episodes of depression as adults although they are no more likely to develop other types of psychological problems. Double depression, that is an ongoing persistent mood disorder (dysthymia) and an episodic major depressive condition; severe depressive symptoms; maternal depression; and the absence of co-morbid conduct problems have all been shown in longitudinal studies to be predictive of worse outcome. While depressed youngsters with conduct difficulties have been found to be less at-risk for recurrent episodes of depression they are at greater risk for the development of relationship problems in adulthood.

Major depression, the condition of central concern in this chapter, is one of a number of mood disorders classified in both DSM IV and ICD 10. Both systems make distinctions between unipolar and bipolar mood disorders; between severe episodic disorders and the milder but more persistent conditions of dysthymia and cyclothymia; and between primary depression and depression which occurs secondary to some other medical condition. The distinctions between primary and secondary mood problems; between unipolar and bipolar conditions; and between recurrent and persistent disorders have replaced distinctions used in earlier classifications systems. These include the distinctions made between neurotic and psychotic mood disorders; endogenous and reactive conditions; and overt and masked depression. Reviews of the classification of mood disorders identify the following reasons for abandoning these earlier distinctions (Farmer and McGuffin, 1989; Harrington, 1993; Kendell, 1976). The neurotic and psychotic distinction, based originally on inferred psychodynamic etiological factors and differences in observable symptoms has been discarded because evidence for inferred psychodynamic etiological differences has not been supported by empirical evidence. The endogenous–reactive distinction has been abandoned because evidence from stressful life event research shows that almost all episodes of depression, regardless of quality or severity, are preceded by stressful life events and in that sense are reactive. The recognition that youngsters with depression may show co-morbid conduct disorders has rendered the concept of masked depression unnecessary, since the term was often used in child and adolescent psychology to classify depressed youngsters who *masked* their low mood with angry outbursts of aggressive or destructive behaviour.

Grief-related adjustment problems

For children, following bereavement there is considerable variability in grief processes, response patterns and related adjustment difficulties (Silverman and Worden, 1993; Wortman and Silver, 1989). Some children manage the death of significant members of their network with considerable courage and resilience. Others do not. Following bereavement, children may be referred for psychological consultation because they display one or more highly salient adjustment difficulties. These include internalizing or externalizing behaviour problems; somatic complaints such as stomach aches; school problems; and relationship difficulties within the family or peer group. All of these types of problems typically reflect the child's involvement in one or more of the following grief processes: shock; denial or disbelief; yearning and searching; anger; despair, hopelessness and depression; guilt, anxiety and bargaining; and acceptance. There is not a clearcut progression through these processes from one to the next (Black, 1994; Papadatou and Papadatou,

1991; Stroebe *et al.*, 1993; Walsh and McGoldrick, 1991; Webb, 1993). Rather, at different points in time, one or other process predominates and there may be movement back and forth between processes.

Shock is the most common initial reaction; it can take the form of physical pain numbness, apathy or withdrawal. The child may appear to be stunned and unable to think clearly. This may be accompanied by denial, disbelief or avoidance of the reality of the bereavement, a process can last minutes, days, or even months. During denial children may behave as if the dead person is still living, albeit elsewhere. Thus, the child may speak about future plans that involve the deceased. A yearning to be with the deceased, coupled with disbelief about their death, may lead the child to engage in frantic searches for the dead person, wandering or running away from the home in a quest for the person who has died. The child may phone relatives or friends trying to trace the person who has died. During this process children who have lost family members or very close friends may report seeing them or being visited by them. Some children carry on full conversations with what presumably are hallucinations of the deceased person. Mistaking other people for the deceased is also a common experience during the denial process. When denial gives way to a realization of the irreversibility of the death of the lost person, anger at the deceased for abandoning the child may occur on the one hand and also despair, hopelessness and depression associated with a profound sense of loss on the other. The experience of despair may be accompanied by other symptoms of clinical depression including low energy, sleep disruption, a disturbance of appetite, tearfulness, an inability to concentrate and a retreat from social interaction. Young children experiencing the despair process may regress and develop problems such as enuresis.

Complementing the despair process, there is also an anger process. Temper tantrums, misbehaviour, defiance, delinquency, drug and alcohol abuse, refusal to go to school or to complete school work are some of the common ways that grief-related anger finds expression in children and teenagers. The expression of such anger may often be followed by remorse or fear of retribution. Young children may fear that the deceased person will punish them for their anger and so it is not surprising that they may want to leave the light on at night and may be afraid to go to bed alone. In older children and adolescents, anxiety is attached to reality-based threats. So, children who have lost a friend or family member through illness or an accident may worry that they too will die from similar causes. This can lead to a belief that one is seriously ill and to a variety of somatic complains such as stomach aches and headaches. It may also lead to a refusal to leave home lest a fatal accident occur. The guilt process is marked by self-blame for causing or not preventing the death of the deceased. There may also be thoughts that if the surviving child died this might magically bring back the deceased. Thus the guilt process may underpin suicidal ideation or self-injury.

The final grief process is acceptance. The child reconstructs his or her view of the world so that the deceased person is construed as no longer living in this world. In the case of death of a parent a benign and accessible representation of the deceased is constructed which is consistent with the family's belief system. For the bereaved child, new lifestyle routines are evolved as part of the process of accepting the death and the child's family system and broader social network is reorganized to take account of the absence of the deceased person. If children have been well supported during the early stages of grief, they may show increased maturity and psychological strength once they take steps towards acceptance. Children who lose friends or siblings through death may become more compassionate and understanding. Those who lose a parent may become more responsible and helpful in the management of the household. A summary of the grief processes and related adjustment problems that may lead to referral is presented in Figure 9.2.

Children's adjustment to bereavement is in part dependent upon their understanding of the concept of death. Much of the work on the development of the concept of death has been guided by Piagetian theory which argues that the child's concept of death is constrained by the availability of certain cognitive skills (Spence and Brent, 1984; Stambrook and Parker, 1987). According to Piagetian theory, the pre-operational child (under 7 years) should not be able to understand the irreversibility of death and may confuse it with sleep. Also pre-operational children's inability to distinguish thought and action may lead them to hold beliefs such as their anger towards someone caused them to die. Once children reach the concrete operational stage, according to Piagetian theory, they understand the irreversibility of death but they may have difficulty accepting its universality and so may not be able to conceptualize death as something that will happen to them. Rather they may view it as being confined to the old, the frail and those in apparent danger. With the onset of the formal operational period in early adolescence, the universality of death comes to be fully appreciated. That is, according to Piaget, young teenagers realize that they will die.

Empirical studies reviewed by Spence and Brent (1984) show that the evolution of the concept of death follows the broad pattern suggested by Piaget but there are many exceptions and this is because children's concept of death evolves not only as cognitive maturation occurs but also as experience of death broadens. The key features of death may be appreciated by children during the pre-operational stage, provided they have been exposed to particular death-related experiences, such as having a terminal illness or having experienced multiple bereavements. These key features include the irreversibility of death which entails the view that the dead cannot return to life; the universality of death which entails the view that all creatures die; and the functionality of death which entails the view that all functions cease at death. While most adolescents recognize the inevitability of their

Grief process	Underlying theme	Behavioural expressions of grief processes
Shock	• I am stunned by the loss of this person	• Complete lack of affect and difficulty engaging emotionally with others • Poor concentration and poor school work
Denial	• The person is not dead	• Reporting seeing or hearing the deceased • Carrying on conversations with the deceased
Yearning and searching	• I must find the deceased	• Wandering or running away • Phoning relatives
Sadness	• I am sad, hopeless and lonely because I have lost someone on whom I depended	• Persistent low mood, tearfulness, low energy and lack of activity • Appetite and sleep disruption • Poor concentration and poor school work
Anger	• I am angry because the person I needed has abandoned me	• Aggression, tantrums, defiance, delinquency • Conflict with parents, siblings, teachers and peers • Drug or alcohol abuse • Poor concentration and poor school work
Anxiety	• I am frightened that the deceased will punish me for causing their death or being angry at them. I am afraid that I too may die of an illness or fatal accident	• Separation anxiety, school refusal, regressed behaviour, bedwetting • Somatic complaints, hypochondriasis and agoraphobia associated with a fear of accidents • Poor concentration and poor school work
Guilt and bargaining	• It is my fault that the person died so I should die	• Suicidal behaviour
Acceptance	• I loved and lost the person who died and now I must carry on without them while cherishing their memory	• Return to normal behavioural routines

Figure 9.2 Behavioural expressions of themes underlying children's grief processes following bereavement.

own death at a cognitive level, the full emotional significance of this is not apprehended until adulthood, unless multiple bereavements or other traumatic events occur.

Reviews of empirical studies of bereavement and loss allow a number of conclusions to be drawn about children's grief reactions following death of a parent (Black, 1994; Shackleton, 1983; Silverman and Worden, 1993; Stroebe, 1993; Wortman and Silver, 1989). Failure to show emotional distress initially does not necessarily mean that later adjustment problems are inevitable. It appears that there is considerable variablity in coping strategies used by children to cope with loss. Some use distraction or avoidance, while others use confrontation with the grief experience and working through. Those who effectively use the former coping strategy may not show emotional distress. Extreme distress following bereavement commonly occurs in those who show protracted grief reactions. Detachment from the deceased does not occur as part of children's grief processes. Rather, an internal representation of the deceased is constructed and the child continues to have a relationship with the deceased. Grief may have a marked effect on physical functioning. Infections and other illnesses are more common among bereaved children and this is probably due to the effect of loss-related stress on the functioning of the immune system. Loss of a parent leaves children vulnerable to depression in adult life. Adults bereaved as children have double the risk of developing depression when faced with a loss experience in adult life compared with their non-bereaved counterparts. Bereaved children most at-risk for depression in adulthood are girls who were young when their parents died a violent or sudden death and who subsequently received inadequate care associated with the surviving parent experiencing a prolonged grief reaction.

Epidemiology

Depression

Depression is not a rare condition and is more prevalent among adolescents than children (Harrington, 1993). In community samples prevalence rates of depression in preadolescence range from 0.5–2.5 per cent and in adolescents from 2–8 per cent. Depression is very common among clinic referrals. In clinic studies about 25 per cent of referrals have major depression. Sex differences in the distribution of depression have consistently been found. Depression is equally common in preadolescent boys and girls but more common in adolescent girls than boys (Cohen *et al.*, 1993). This greater preponderance of depression among teenage girls compared to boys is similar to the sex distribution of depression among adults. The relative contribution of biological factors and psychosocial factors to this sex difference in prevalence is currently unclear. Hypotheses about differential impact of hormonal changes in puberty on boys and girls and differing role demands on male and female adolescents deserve exploration. Depression quite commonly occurs in conjunction with other disorders particularly in children referred for treatment. In community studies of childhood depression co-morbidity rates of 10–17 per cent have been found for conduct disorder, anxiety disorders, and attention deficit disorder (McConaughy and Achenbach, 1994).

Premature parental death

Between 3 and 5 per cent of children under eighteen lose a parent by death (Garmezy and Masten, 1994). The principal causes of premature parental death are cancer, heart disease and road traffic accidents. Silverman and Worden (1993) in a major US study of parental bereavement found that a year after the parent's death 19 per cent of children continued to show clinically significant adjustment problems on the Child Behaviour Checklist (Achenbach, 1991).

Previous reviews

Harrington (1993) and Target and Fonagy (1996) in a review of the literature on the treatment of depression in children and adolescents identified five types of psychological interventions that are widely used to treat mood disorders with individuals under eighteen years of age. These were cognitive behavioural therapy, social skills training, family therapy, interpersonal therapy, and individual psychodynamic psychotherapy.

Cognitive behavioural interventions empower children to monitor and challenge depressive cognitions, to increase activity levels, to increase the number of positive events and interactions in their daily routines, to develop relaxation skills to cope with stress, and to use self-reinforcement to consolidate adaptive coping skills. Thus they aim to improve mood by modifying depressive cognitions and behaviour patterns. Both reviewers concluded that there is some support for the effectiveness of cognitive behavioural interventions in the treatment of childhood depression. Such intervention programmes are based on treatment models originally developed with adult populations, notably Beck's (1976) cognitive therapy and Lewinsohn's behavioural approach to the treatment of depression (Lewinsohn *et al.*, 1990; Lewinsohn and Gotlib, 1995). Currently, for adults, a substantial body or research supports the effectiveness of cognitive behaviour therapy, particularly when combined with antidepressant medication, in the treatment of depression and the prevention of relapse (Craighead *et al.*, 1998).

Social skills interventions aim to alleviate depression by equipping youngsters with the interpersonal skills required to increase positive social interactions and decrease self-defeating behaviour patterns (Matson, 1989). Harrington (1993) and Target and Fonagy (1996) conclude that there is currently some evidence to suggest that social skills training can alleviate childhood depression.

Modifying patterns of family interaction and family belief systems that maintain depression is one goal of family therapy with depressed youngsters. Family therapy may also empower family members to help the depressed youngster to develop and use mood regulating skills such as monitoring and challenging depressive cognitions and engaging in positive interactions with family members (Schwartz *et al.*, 1998). Harrington (1993) in his review states that there is currently insufficient evidence available to confidently draw conclusions about the efficacy of family therapy in the treatment of childhood depression. However, the positive results of controlled trials of marital therapy for the treatment of depression in adults suggest that further research on family therapy for childhood depression is warranted (Baucom *et al.*, 1998).

Interpersonal psychotherapy aims to alleviate depression by helping patients develop insight into the interpersonal processes that precipitate and maintain depression (Mufson *et al.*, 1993). Grief, interpersonal role disputes, role transitions, interpersonal deficits and living in a single parent family are the core themes and processes addressed in interpersonal therapy, with due account being taken of developmental issues particularly individuation from parents, developing intimate relationships, and managing peer pressure. Harrington (1993) and Target and Fonagy (1996) concluded that there is currently some limited evidence to suggest that interpersonal psychotherapy can alleviate adolescent depression, and argue that the positive results from controlled trials of this type of therapy with depressed adults are grounds for further evaluation of its efficacy with adolescents (Craighead *et al.*, 1998).

Psychodynamic psychotherapy for depression aims to help adolescents to gain insight into the defences they use in dealing with critical current and past relationship issues and work through ambivalent feelings associated with these. Unlike the other approaches to intervention described above, psychodynamic psychotherapy is not a brief intervention. Target and Fonagy (1996) concluded that there is some preliminary evidence that psychodynamic psychotherapy may be effective in treating juvenile depression.

With adults, a range of antidepressant medications have been shown to alleviate depressive symptoms. Indeed the current treatment of choice for depressed adults is antidepressant medication to alleviated depressive symptoms and brief structured psychological interventions such as cognitive behaviour therapy or interpersonal therapy to prevent relapse (Craighead *et al.*, 1998; Nemeroff and Schatzberg, 1998). Unfortunately, the results of a handful of controlled trials have failed to consistently demonstrate the effectiveness of tricyclic antidepressants in the treatment of juvenile depression, but preliminary results suggest that serotonin re-uptake inhibitors may be effective in alleviating depressive symptomatology in adolescents (Kutcher, 1997).

Smith and Pennell (1996) in a review of intervention for bereaved children concluded that individual, group-based and family-based interventions all have a place in the management of grief-related adjustment problems. However, such conclusions were based largely on clinical observations rather than empirical studies.

A problem with the reviews summarized in this section is that the studies they covered varied considerably in methodological rigour and so it is difficult to assess the confidence that may be placed in the conclusions drawn from them.

Method

One aim of this chapter was to review well-designed studies of the effects of psychological therapies for depressed children and adolescents and youngsters who had suffered bereavement arising from parental death. A computer-based literature search of the PsychLit database was conducted. The terms *depression, bereavement* and *parental death* were combined with terms that define psychological intervention such as *treatment, therapy, psychotherapy, intervention, behaviour therapy, cognitive behaviour therapy, family therapy, social skills training* and *interpersonal therapy* and the search was limited to children or adolescents. The search, which was confined to English language journals, covered the period 1977 to 1997 inclusively. A manual search through bibliographies of all recent review papers on psychological interventions for depression was also conducted. Treatment outcome studies were selected for inclusion in this review if they contained a psychological treatment group and a control or comparison group; if at least five cases were included in the active treatment group; and if reliable and valid pre- and post-treatment measures were included in the design of the study. Single-case designs and studies reported in dissertations or convention papers were not included in the review. Using these inclusion and exclusion criteria, from a pool of over a hundred papers located, nine studies were selected for review.

Characteristics of the studies

Characteristics of the nine studies are set out in Table 9.1. All of the studies were conducted between 1980 and 1997. Four were conducted in the USA, three in the UK and two in Canada. All of the studies were conducted between 1975 and 1996. All of the studies included nine or more cases in the treatment groups. Across the nine studies there were 349 cases. Two hundred and forty-five of these participated in treatment and the remaining 104 were allocated to control groups. The principal treatments investigated were cognitive behaviour therapy; relaxation training; social skills training; self-instructional training; problem-solving skills training; parent training; and family therapy. In eight of the studies participants had a diagnosis of depression and in the remaining study children had adjustment difficulties associated with bereavement through death of a parent. In four of the

Table 9.1 Characteristics of treatment outcome studies for depression

Study no.	Authors	Year	Country	N per gp	Mean age & range	Gender	Primary diagnosis	Co-morbid diagnosis	Family characteristics	Referral	Treatment setting	Treatment duration
1	Wood et al.	1996	UK	CBT = 24 RT = 24	14 y 9–17 y	m 31% f 69%	Depression DSM III R	CD 23% OAD 56%		Physicians	Community OP	6 sess over 3 m
2	Kroll et al.	1996	UK	CBT = 17 C = 12	14 y 9–17 y	m 41% f 59%	Depression DSM III R	CD 10% OAD 52%		Physicians	Community OP	7 sess over 6 m
3	Reynolds and Coats	1986	USA	CBT = 9 RT = 11 C = 10	16 y 14–18 y	m 34% f 66%	Depression BID > 20			School screening	School	10 sess over 1 m
4	Kahn et al.	1990	USA	CBT = 17 RT = 17 MODT = 17 C = 17	10–14 y	m 49% f 51%	Depression BID > 20	CD 6%		School screening	School	12 sess over 2 m
5	Lewinsohn et al.	1990	USA	CBT = 19 CBT + PT = 21 C = 19	16 y 14–18 y	m 39% m 91%	Depression DSM III R		IF 41% SPF 52% Alone 7%	Multiple sources	School	21 sess over 2 m Adol. 14 sess Parents 7 sess
6	Butler et al.	1980	Canada	CBT = 14 SST = 14 SUP = 13 C = 13	11–12 y	m 62% f 38%	Depression CDI			School screening	University	10 sess over 3 m
7	Fine et al.	1991	Canada	SST = 30 SUP = 36	15 y 13–17 y	m 18% f 82%	Depression DSM III R		IF 50% SPF 42% FCF 8%	Physicians	Community OP	6 sess over 3 m
8	Stark et al.	1987	USA	SIT = 9 PSST = 10 C = 9	11 y 9–12 y	m 57% f 43 %	Depression CDI > 13		IF 61% SPF 18% RF 21%	School screening	University	12 sess for 5 w
9	Black and Urbanowicz	1987	UK	FT = 21 C = 24	0–16 y	m 67% f 33%	Parental bereavement			Hospital	Home	6 sess over 5 m

Key CBT = Cognitive behaviour therapy. RT = Relaxation training. PT = Parent training. MODT = Self-modelling therapy. SST = Social skills training. SUP = Supportive therapy. SIT = Self-instructional training. PSST = Problem-solving skills training. FT = Family therapy. C = Control group. IF = Intact family. SPF = Single parent family. RF = Reconstituted family. DSM III R = *Diagnostic and Statistical Manual of Mental Disorders* (Third edition, revised). BID = Bellevue Index of Depression. CDI = Childhood Depression Inventory. OAD = Overanxious disorder. CD = Conduct disorder. OP = Outpatient. d = day. w = week. m = month. y = year. sess = sessions.

depression studies the DSM III (APA, 1980) or DSM III R (APA, 1987) diagnostic criteria for major depression were used as inclusion criteria. In the other four depression studies clinical cut-off scores on the Childhood Depression Inventory (Kovacs and Beck, 1977) or the Bellevue Index of Depression (Petti, 1978) were used. Participants' ages ranged from five to eighteen years. With respect to gender, 44 per cent of cases were male and 56 per cent were female. Co-morbidity data were reported in only three studies and for these overanxious disorder and conduct disorder were the main co-morbid conditions. In three studies data on family composition were given, and these showed that across the three studies the proportion of cases coming from intact families ranged from 41–61 per cent with remaining cases coming from single parent families or foster families. In five studies cases were referred from physicians, hospital sources or multiple sources for the treatment of clinical depression. In four studies cases with low mood at-risk for clinical depression were screened from school classes with psychometric instruments. In three studies cases were treated in community-based outpatient clinics. In two studies treatment occurred in university-based outpatient clinics and in one study treatment was conducted in clients' homes. The number of sessions of treatment ranged from six to 21 sessions over four to 24 weeks.

Methodological features

Methodological features of the nine studies included in this review are presented in Table 9.2. All of the studies included demographically and diagnostically homogeneous cases and control or comparison groups, but in only three studies was there evidence that groups were similar in terms of co-morbidity. In seven studies cases were randomly allocated to groups. In all studies cases were assessed before and after treatment on reliable and valid measures. In four studies follow-up data were collected after six months or later. Shorter term follow-up data were available in three studies, but methodologically are of little consequence to the robustness of the studies. To assess children before and after treatment researcher ratings were used in eight studies; self-report ratings in seven studies; parent ratings in four studies; and teacher ratings were not used in any of the nine studies. While symptomatic improvement was evaluated in all studies, improvements in relationships within the child's family system and social network were evaluated in only one study. In one study deterioration was assessed and in seven studies drop-out rates were reported. In no study was information on engagement in subsequent treatment given and in only one study was information on concurrent treatment provided. In all studies information on statistical significance of treatment gains was reported and in eight studies information on the clinical significance of improvement was given. Experienced therapists were used in five studies and in four of the five studies where two or more active treatments were compared, information

Table 9.2 Methodological features of studies of depressive disorders

Feature	Study number								
	S1	*S2*	*S3*	*S4*	*S5*	*S6*	*S7*	*S8*	*S9*
Control or comparison group	1	1	1	1	1	1	1	1	1
Random assignment	1	0	1	1	1	0	1	1	1
Diagnostic homogeneity	1	1	1	1	1	1	0	1	1
Comparable for co-morbidity	1	1	0	1	0	0	0	0	0
Demographic similarity	1	0	0	1	1	1	1	1	1
Pre-treatment assessment	1	1	1	1	1	1	1	1	1
Post-treatment assessment	1	1	1	1	1	1	1	1	0
Six months' follow-up assessment	1	1	0	0	1	0	0	1	1
Children's self-report	1	0	1	1	1	1	0	0	0
Parent's ratings	1	0	0	0	1	0	0	1	1
Teacher's ratings	0	0	0	0	0	0	1	0	0
Therapist's ratings	1	0	0	0	0	0	0	0	0
Researcher's ratings	1	1	1	1	0	1	1	1	1
Child's symptom assessed	1	1	0	1	1	1	1	1	1
System assessed	0	0	0	0	0	0	0	0	0
Deterioration assessed	0	1	0	0	0	0	0	0	0
Drop-out assessed	1	1	1	0	1	1	0	1	1
Clinical significance of change assessed	1	1	1	1	1	0	0	1	0
Experienced therapists used	1	1	0	0	0	0	1	1	1
Treatments were equally valued	0	0	1	1	1	1	1	0	0
Treatments were manualized	1	1	1	1	1	0	1	1	0
Therapy supervision was provided	1	1	1	1	1	0	1	0	1
Treatment integrity checked	1	1	1	1	1	0	0	1	0
Data on concurrent treatment given	1	0	0	0	0	0	0	0	0
Data on subsequent treatment given	0	0	0	0	0	0	0	0	0
Total	20	15	14	15	16	9	14	16	13

Key S = study. 1 = design feature was present. 0 = design feature was absent.

given in the reports suggested that treatments were equally valued by the research team. In seven studies treatments were manualized and supervision was regularly provided to therapists. In six studies treatment integrity was checked. Overall, this was a fairly methodologically robust group of studies, so reliable conclusions may be drawn from them with considerable confidence.

Substantive findings

A summary of effect sizes and outcome rates from the nine studies included in this review are set out in Table 9.3 and a narrative account of the main conclusions is given if Table 9.4.

Below, a detailed account of the main results summarized in these two tables will be given. First, two studies on the effects of individually based cognitive behaviour therapy with clinically depressed youngsters will be reviewed (Kroll *et al.*, 1996; Wood *et al.*, 1996). Second, two studies of group-based cognitive behaviour therapy with schoolchildren and adolescents screened for low mood will be considered (Kahn *et al.*, 1990; Reynolds and Coats, 1986). Third, a review will be given of a study comparing a combined group-based cognitive behaviour therapy and parent training programme and a routine group-based cognitive behaviour therapy programme (Lewinsohn *et al.*, 1990). Fourth, two studies of social skills training will be described. One targets schoolchildren screened for low mood and the other is concerned with children referred for treatment of clinical depression. (Butler *et al.*, 1980; Fine *et al.*, 1991). Fifth, a study evaluating the effects of self-instructional training and problem-solving skills training will be reviewed (Stark *et al.*, 1987). The final study reviewed below examines the effects of family therapy in cases of parental death (Black and Urbanowicz, 1987).

Individually based cognitive behaviour therapy for referred cases of depression

Harrington's group at the Royal Manchester Children's Hospital conducted two studies on the use of cognitive therapy in the treatment of depression (Wood *et al.*, 1996) and the prevention of relapse following remission of depressive symptomatology (Kroll *et al.*, 1996). Wood *et al.* (ibid.) examined the effect of individually based cognitive behavioural therapy on DSM III R major depression in youngsters between nine and seventeen years old referred by physicians for treatment. Relaxation training was included in this study as a control condition (Bernstein and Borkovec, 1973). Diagnoses were made using the Kiddie Schedule for Affective Disorders and Schizophrenia (Puig-Antich and Chambers, 1978). Cases with psychotic features, learning disabilities, serious physical illness and epilepsy and those requiring hospitalization or medication were excluded from the study. The six-session individually based cognitive behavioural therapy programme was

Table 9.3 Summary of treatment effects and outcome rates in studies for depression in children and adolescents

Variable	Study number														
	Study 1	Study 2	Study 3		Study 4			Study 5		Study 6		Study 7	Study 8		Study 9
	CBT > RT	CBT	CBT	RT	CBT	RT	MODT	CBT	CBT + PT	CBT	SST	SST > SUP	SIT	PSST	FT
Symptomatic improvement after treatment															
Children's self-report	1.0	–	1.2	1.8	1.3	0.9	0.9	1.0	1.4	1.0	1.1	-0.5	1.1	1.0	–
Parent's ratings	0.4	–	–	–	–	–	–	0.2	1.1	–	–	–	0.0	0.4	0.5
Teacher's ratings	–	–	–	–	–	–	–	–	–	–	–	–	–	–	–
Therapist's ratings	–	–	–	–	–	–	–	–	–	–	–	–	–	–	–
Researcher's ratings	0.8	1.5	2.5	2.2	0.8	0.6	0.7	–	–	–	–	-0.6	0.8	0.6	–
Symptomatic improvement at follow-up															
Children's self-report	0.2	–	–	–	–	–	–	–	–	–	–	–	–	–	–
Parent's ratings	0.1	–	–	–	–	–	–	–	–	–	–	0.1	–	–	0.5
Teacher's ratings	–	–	–	–	–	–	–	–	–	–	–	–	–	–	–
Therapist's ratings	–	–	–	–	–	–	–	–	–	–	–	–	–	–	–
Researcher's ratings	0.4	0.9	–	–	–	–	–	–	–	–	–	-0.2	–	–	–
Systemic improvement after treatment															
Children's self-report	–	–	–	–	–	–	–	–	–	–	–	–	–	–	–
Parent's ratings	–	–	–	–	–	–	–	–	–	–	–	–	–	–	0.6
Teacher's ratings	–	–	–	–	–	–	–	–	–	–	–	–	–	–	–
Therapist's ratings	–	–	–	–	–	–	–	–	–	–	–	–	–	–	–
Researcher's ratings	–	–	–	–	–	–	–	–	–	–	–	–	–	–	–

Systemic improvement at follow-up

Children's self-report	–	–	–	–	–	–	–	–	–	–	–	–	–	–	1.4
Parent's ratings	–	–	–	–	–	–	–	–	–	–	–	–	–	–	–
Teacher's ratings	–	–	–	–	–	–	–	–	–	–	–	–	–	–	–
Therapist's ratings	–	–	–	–	–	–	–	–	–	–	–	–	–	–	–
Researcher's ratings	–	–	–	–	–	–	–	–	–	–	–	–	–	–	–

Positive clinical outcomes

% improved after treatment	54% >21%	94%	83%	75%	88%	76%	59%	43%	48%	–	64%	40% >50%	78%	60%	–
% improved at follow-up	54% >38%	82%	–	–	–	–	88%	88%	–	–	–	63% >71%	–	–	–

Negative clinical outcomes

% Deterioration	–	6%	–	–	–	–	–	–	–	–	–	–	–	–	–
% Drop-out	4% >11%	6%	0%	0%	–	–	14%	10%	0%	0%	–	–	3%	3%	33%
% Engaged in further treatment	–	–	–	–	–	–	–	–	–	–	–	–	–	–	–

Key CBT = Cognitive behaviour. RT = Relaxation training. PT = Parent training. MODT = Self-modelling therapy. SST = Social skills training. SUP = Supportive therapy. SIT = Self-instructional training. PSST = Problem-solving skills training. FT = Family therapy. Follow-up data for studies has been included where the follow-up period exceeded six months. One to two-month follow-up data from studies 3,4 and 8 have been omitted.

Table 9.4 Key findings from treatment studies of children and adolescents with depressive disorders

Study no.	Authors	Year	Primary diagnosis	N per gp	No of sessions	Group differences	Key findings
1	Wood et al.	1996	Depression DSM III R	1. CBT = 24 2. RT = 24	6	Post treatment 1 > 2 Follow-up 1 = 2	• Immediately following individual treatment adolescents in the cognitive behaviour therapy programme showed greater improvement than those in the relaxation training programme. • These differences disappeared at three months' follow-up due to the continued improvement of cases receiving relaxation treatment and relapses in the other group.
2	Kroll et al.	1996	Depression DSM III R	1. CBT = 17 2. C = 12	7	1 > 2	• Adolescents who continued to have individual cognitive behaviour therapy after remission had fewer relapses than those in the control group who ceased cognitive behaviour therapy once their symptoms abated.
3	Reynolds and Coats	1986	Depression BID > 20	1. CBT = 9 2. RT = 11 3. C = 10	10	1 = 2 > 3	• Following group treatment and five weeks later depressed adolescents in both the cognitive behaviour therapy group and the relaxation training group made clinically significant gains compared with the control group. There was little difference between the outcomes of the two treatment groups.
4	Kahn et al.	1990	Depression BID > 20	1. CBT = 17 2. RT = 17 3. MODT = 17 4. C = 17	12	1 = 2 = 3 > 4	• Following group treatment and a month later depressed adolescents in the cognitive behaviour therapy group, the relaxation training group and the self-modelling therapy group made clinically significant gains compared with the control group. There was little difference between the outcomes of the three treatment groups.
5	Lewinsohn et al.	1990	Depression DSM III	1. CBT = 19 2. CBT + PT = 21 3. C = 19	21	1 = 2 > 3	• Following group treatment and at two years' follow-up depressed adolescents in both the cognitive behaviour therapy group and the combined cognitive behaviour therapy and parent training group made clinically significant gains compared with the control group. There was little difference between the outcomes of the two treatment groups.

6	Butler et al.	1980	Depression CDI	1. CBT = 14 2. SST = 14 3. SUP = 13 4. C = 13	10	2 > 1 > 3 = 4	• Following group treatment and a month later depressed adolescents in the cognitive behaviour therapy group and the social skills training group made clinically significant gains compared with the attention-placebo support group and the waiting list control group. Gains made by the social skills training group were better than those made by the cognitive behaviour therapy group.
7	Fine et al.	1991	Depression DSM III R	1. SST = 30 2. SUP = 36	6	Post treatment 2 > 1 Follow-up 1 = 2	• Immediately following individual treatment adolescents in the supportive therapy programme showed greater improvement than those in the social skills training programme. • These differences disappeared at nine months' follow-up due to the continued improvement of cases receiving social skills training.
8	Stark et al.	1987	Depression CDI > 13	1. SIT = 9 2. PSST = 10 3. C = 9	12	1 = 2 > 3	• Following group treatment and two months later depressed adolescents in both the self-instructional training programme and the problem-solving skills training group made clinically significant gains compared with the control group. There was little difference between the outcomes of the two treatment groups.
9	Black and Urbanowicz	1987	Parental bereavement	1. FT = 21 2. C = 24	6	1 > 2	• Following treatment and at one and two years' follow-up children who received family therapy for grief following the death of a parent showed gains in health and psychological adjustment compared to the control group.

Key CBT = Cognitive behaviour therapy. RT = Relaxation training. PT = Parent training. MODT = Self-modelling therapy. SST = Social skills training. SUP = Supportive therapy. SIT = Self-instructional training. PSST = Problem-solving skills training. FT = Family therapy. C = Control group. IF = Intact family. SPF = Single parent family. FCF = Fostercare family. RF = Reconstituted family. DSM III R = *Diagnostic and Statistical Manual of Mental Disorders* (Third edition, revised). BID = Bellevue Index of Depression. CDI = Childhood Depression Inventory.

conducted over three months and included a cognitive therapy component, a social problem-solving component; and a psychoeducational component. Within the cognitive therapy component youngsters learned to monitor and challenge depressive cognitions and cognitive distortions (Beck, 1976). Within the social problem-solving component, the focus was on learning to define interpersonal difficulties in solvable terms, to generate solutions to these problems, implement them and evaluate their impact (Stark, 1990). The psychoeducational component offered information on depressive symptomatology, sleep hygiene and activity scheduling (Vostanis and Harrington, 1994).

Following treatment on the self-report version of the Mood and Feelings Questionnaire (Angold *et al.*, 1987) an effect size of 1.0 occurred indicating that the average case treated with cognitive behaviour therapy fared better than 84 per cent of cases in the relaxation training control condition immediately after treatment. However, six months later this effect size reduced to 0.2 indicating that intergroup differences at this point were negligible. A similar pattern occurred for effect sizes based on the parent-report version of the Mood and Feelings Questionnaire (Angold *et al.*, ibid.) and research ratings of global improvement (Shaffer *et al.*, 1983). Effect sizes for parent ratings reduced from 0.4 to 0.2 and those for researcher ratings reduced from 0.8 to 0.4. Following the same pattern, the proportion of cases classified as clinically remitted on the Kiddie Schedule for Affective Disorders and Schizophrenia (an index of clinically significant improvement) in each group converged from post-treatment to six-month follow-up. Following treatment, 54 per cent of cases in the cognitive behaviour therapy group and 21 per cent in the relaxation training control group were classified as clinically remitted. Six months later the number of remitted cases in the cognitive behaviour therapy group remained stable at 54 per cent but the number of remitted cases in the relaxation training control group had increased to 38 per cent. However, it should be noted that almost half of the cases in the cognitive behaviour therapy group that remitted following treatment relapsed before the six-month follow-up assessment, so the apparently stable figure of 54 per cent reflects both continued improvement on the part of some cases and relapse on the part of others.

In the second study from the Manchester Group, Kroll *et al.* (1996) examined the effect of continued cognitive behaviour therapy following remission of symptoms on relapse rates in youngsters aged nine to seventeen years with a previous diagnosis of DSM III R major depression. Similar assessment, screening and treatment procedures were used in this study as were used in the first study by Wood *et al.* (1996). The cumulative risk of relapse for cases having the cognitive behaviour therapy was lower than for the historical control group at three- and six-month follow-up. At six-month follow-up only three of seventeen treated cases had relapsed compared to six of twelve untreated cases. Effect sizes based on relapse rates were 1.5 and 0.9 at three- and six-month follow-up indicating that the average treated case fared better in terms of relapse than 93 per cent of untreated cases at three-month follow-up and better than 82 per cent of untreated cases at six-month follow-up.

It may be concluded from these two studies that cognitive behaviour therapy may be useful in both the treatment of depression and the prevention of relapse in cases following remission. In the first study cognitive behaviour therapy led to rapid remission in over 50 per cent of cases and was significantly more effective in leading to rapid remission than relaxation training, but in the long term both groups of cases had similar outcomes due to continued improvement in the relaxation training group and a mixed pattern of recovery and relapse in the cognitive behaviour therapy group. The results of the second study show that following recovery individually based cognitive behaviour therapy effectively reduced relapse rates for youngsters whose depression was in remission.

Group-based cognitive behaviour therapy and relaxation training for screened cases of mild depression

Reynolds and Coats (1986) and Kahn *et al.* (1990) examined the effects of group-based cognitive behavioural therapy and relaxation training on children and adolescents who had been screened for depression. Cases were identified using cut-off scores of 12 on the Beck Depression Inventory (Beck *et al.*, 1961) or 15 on the Childhood Depression Inventory (Kovacs and Beck, 1977) and 72 on the Reynolds (1987) Adolescent Depression Scale. Those who scored in the clinical range on these self-report measures were included in the treatment study if they obtained a score greater than 20 on the Bellevue Index of Depression (Petti, 1978) which is an interview-based assessment instrument for depression. Cases were excluded from the study if they were already receiving treatment for depression or other psychological disorders. In Reynolds and Coats' (1986) study cases were fourteen to sixteen years old while in Kahn *et al.*'s (1990) study they were ten to fourteen years of age. Following screening, cases were randomly allocated to cognitive behaviour therapy, relaxation training or waiting list control groups in both studies and in Kahn *et al.*'s (1990) study there was an additional self-modelling treatment group. The cognitive behaviour therapy and relaxation training programmes were similar to those described above for Wood *et al.*'s (1996) study. However, they were offered on a group basis with four or five cases per group and the programme included ten to twelve sessions over one to two months. In the self-modelling treatment, youngsters were given carefully edited videotaped feedback of themselves engaging in non-depressive social interactions.

Following treatment for self-reported depression effect sizes for the cognitive behaviour therapy programmes ranged from 1.2 to 1.3 indicating that the average treated case fared better than 88–90 per cent of untreated cases in the control group. Following treatment for self-reported depression effect sizes for the relaxation training programmes ranged from 0.9 to 1.8, indicating that the average treated case fared better than 82–96 per cent of untreated cases in the control group. In line with these results based on self-reports, effect sizes on the researcher-rated Bellevue Index of Depression (Petti, 1978) for the cognitive behaviour therapy groups ranged from 0.8 to 2.5 (mean = 1.7) and for the relaxation training programmes they ranged from 0.6 to 2.2 (mean = 1.4) across the two studies. Thus the average case treated with either cognitive behaviour therapy or relaxation training fared better than more than 90 per cent of untreated cases. These gains were maintained at a follow-up assessment conducted four to five weeks after treatment. Using clinical cut-off scores on the Beck Depression Inventory (Beck *et al.*, 1961) or the Childhood Depression Inventory (Kovacs and Beck, 1977) to classify cases as showing clinically significant improvement, 83–88 per cent of cases who received cognitive behaviour therapy and 75–76 per cent of cases who participated in relaxation training were clinically improved following treatment. For the self-modelling treatment, only 59 per cent showed clinically significant improvement.

From these two studies it may be concluded that for schoolchildren and adolescents screened for low mood, brief group-based cognitive behaviour therapy and relaxation training programmes were effective in alleviating mild to moderate depressive symptomatology in the short term.

Comparison of group-based cognitive behaviour therapy and group-based cognitive behaviour therapy combined with parent-based training

Lewinsohn *et al.* (1990) examined the effects of group-based cognitive behaviour therapy combined with parent training by comparing the outcome of cases receiving this treatment package with those of cases receiving routine cognitive behaviour therapy and a control group. Adolescents aged fourteen to eighteen with DSM III major depression and their parents participated in this study. Diagnoses were made using the Kiddie Schedule for Affective Disorders and Schizophrenia (Puig-Antich and Chambers, 1978). Cases were excluded from the study if they had learning difficulties; organic, psychotic, anxiety, or substance use disorders; suicidal intent; or an immediate need for hospitalization. The combined cognitive behavioural therapy and parent training programme included a fourteen-session programme for adolescents and a seven-session programme for parents. The entire programme was run over seven weeks. The adolescents' cognitive behaviour therapy programme (Clarke and Lewinsohn, 1984) was similar to that described above for Wood *et al.*'s (1996) study. The parent training programme included a psychoeducation component, a contingency management component and a communication and problem-solving skills training component (Lewinsohn and Clarke, 1986). The psychoeducation component offered information on depression and cognitive behavioural strategies for managing depressed mood, so parents would share a similar view of depression to that gained by their youngsters in the cognitive behavioural programme for adolescents. The contingency management component of the programme provided parents with guidance on prompting their adolescents to use coping strategies, increase activity levels and engage in positive interactions and reinforcing such behaviour. The problem-solving and communications skills training component provided guidelines for resolving parent–adolescent conflict with a minimum of negative interactions.

Immediately following treatment, effect sizes for self-reported depression on the Beck Depression Inventory (Beck *et al.*, 1961) were 1.4 for the combined cognitive behavioural therapy and parent training programme and 1.0 for the routine cognitive behaviour therapy programme, indicating that the average case in the combined treatment programme fared better than 92 per cent of untreated cases and the average case following routine treatment fared better than 84 per cent of untreated cases in the waiting list control group. For parent-reported improvement on the depression scale of the Child Behaviour Checklist (Achenbach and Edelbrock, 1983) following treatment effect sizes were 1.1 and 0.2. Thus while there were negligible differences between parent-rated improvements in the routine treatment programme and the control group, the average case in the combined treatment condition fared better than 86 per cent of cases in the control group on parent-rated improvement. Judgements about clinically significant improvement were based on researcher ratings of remission of DSM III depression on the Kiddie Schedule for Affective Disorders and Schizophrenia. Following treatment 48 per cent of cases in the combined cognitive behaviour therapy and parent training programme and 44 per cent of cases in the routine cognitive behaviour therapy programme were in remission compared with 5 per cent of cases in the waiting list control group. Two years after treatment 88 per cent of cases in both treatment groups were in remission.

From this study it may be concluded that in the long term both the combined group-based cognitive behavioural therapy and parent training programme and the routine group-based cognitive behaviour therapy programme were equally effective in alleviating depression in adolescents. In the short term the combined programme led to greater improvements in parent-rated depression but to equivalent levels of improvement as rated by the researcher and reported by the adolescents themselves.

Group-based social skills training for screened cases of depression

Butler *et al.* (1980) compared the effects of group-based cognitive behaviour therapy with those of social skills training for eleven- and twelve-year-old schoolchildren screened for low mood. Cases were screened for inclusion in the study from a school population using a cut-off score of 1.5 standard deviations above the mean on a battery of self-report instruments which contained the Childhood Depression Inventory (Kovacs and Beck, 1977) and other instruments. The cognitive behaviour therapy programme was similar to that used in Wood *et al.* (1996). In the social skills training programme, role playing was used to coach children in managing inter-personal problems and initiating positive social interactions. An attention placebo support group and a waiting list control group were also included in this study. Following treatment, effect sizes based on the Childhood Depression Inventory (Kovacs and Beck, 1977) scores were 1.1 for the social skills training group and 1.0 for the cognitive behaviour therapy group. Thus the average treated case in the social skills training group fared better than 86 per cent of controls and the average case treated with cognitive behaviour therapy fared better than 84 per cent of untreated cases. Differences in outcome for the two treatment groups were negligible.

Fine *et al.* (1991) examined the effect of group-based social skills training on adolescent depression in cases referred for treatment. Cases included in the study were screened for DSM III R major depression with the Kiddie Schedule for Affective Disorders and Schizophrenia (Chambers *et al.*, 1985). Those who met the criteria for depression but also had neurological damage or learning difficulties were excluded. Cases were assigned to either the social skills training group or an attention placebo support group. The social skills training programme included assertiveness training, communication skills training and social problem-solving skills training. In the social skills programme, only 40 per cent were in remission following treatment on the Kiddie Schedule for Affective Disorders and Schizophrenia compared with 50 per cent of cases in the support control group. Nine months later 63 per cent of cases from the socials skills programme were in remission compared with 71 per cent of cases in the support group. Effect sizes based on the Children's Depression Inventory (Kovacs and Beck, 1977) following treatment and at follow-up were −0.5 and 0.1. Thus, the average treated case fared worse after treatment than 69 per cent of cases in the support group, but at nine months' follow-up intergroup differences were negligible.

Taken together, the results of these two studies suggest that social skills training was as effective as cognitive behaviour therapy in alleviating mild or moderate depressive symptoms in schoolchildren screened for depressed mood. However, with clinically depressed youngsters referred for treatment, social skills training was not particularly effective in the short term and in the long term led to no greater gains than those arising from support group membership.

Self-instructional training and problem-solving skills training

Stark *et al.* (1987) examined the effects of group-based self-instructional training and problem-solving skills training on nine- to eleven-year-old schoolchildren screened for low mood. Cases with scores above 13 on the Children's Depression Inventory (Kovacs and Beck, 1977) were admitted to the study and assigned to a self-instructional training group, a problem-solving skills training group or a waiting list control group. The self-instructional training programme was based on Rehm's (1977) self-control model of depression which assumes that depression is maintained by select-ive self-monitoring of negative events and short-term rather than long-term consequences of behaviour; setting unrealistically high personal standards; using a depressive attributional style when accounting for personal successes and failures; engaging in excessive self-punishment; and engaging in little self-reinforcement. In the self-instructional training programme children learned accurate self-monitoring of situations, cognitions and mood and were then coached in using self-instructions to make more adaptive attribu-tions for success and failure; to set more realistic standards for themselves; and to reinforce themselves for mood enhancing behaviour. The problem-solving skills training programme was based on Lewinsohn and Gotlib's (1995) theory. This states that depression is maintained by a low rate of response-contingent positive reinforcement. Mood may be enhanced by using problem-solving skills to increase the rate of such reinforcement through planning a daily schedule of pleasant events. Within the problem-solving programme youngsters were coached in systematic problem-solving skills including defining problems in solvable terms, generating alternative solutions, selecting and implementing the most feasible of these, planning and carrying out the solution, and evaluating its impact. The focus was on solving problems that would increase positive social interactions, pleasant events and activity levels. In addition, training in self-monitoring was given to participants in the problem-solving skills training programme.

Following treatment, effect sizes based on the Children's Depression Inventory (Kovacs and Beck, 1977) for the self-instructional training group and the problem-solving skills training group were 1.1 and 1.0 respectively. The average treated case in the treatment programmes fared better than 84–6 per cent of untreated cases in the waiting list control group. Effect sizes based on researcher ratings made on the Revised Children's Depres-sion Rating Scale (Pozanski *et al.*, 1984) were 0.8 and 0.6 for the self-instructional training group and the problem-solving skills training group respectively. So from the researcher's perspective the average treated case fared better than 73–9 per cent of untreated cases. For parent-reported improvement on the depression scale of the Child Behaviour Checklist (Achenbach and Edelbrock, 1983) negligible effect sizes of 0.0 and 0.4 were obtained for the self-instructional training group and the problem-solving skills training group respectively. When cases were classified as showing clinically significant improvement using the clinical cut-off score on the Children's Depression Inventory 78 per cent of cases in the self-instructional training group and 60 per cent of cases in the problem-solving skills training group were clinically improved following treatment. These gains were main-tained when a follow-up assessment was conducted two months later.

From this study it may be concluded that for schoolchildren screened for low mood, twelve-session group-based self-instructional training and problem-solving skills training programmes were both effective in alleviating mild to moderate depressive symptoms.

Family therapy for children following parental death

Black and Urbanowicz (1987) examined the effects of family therapy on children who had suffered a bereavement through loss of a parent. In all cases the parental death occurred two months prior to the study and cases were randomly assigned to a family therapy condition or a non-treatment control condition. The family therapy programme involved six sessions spaced over five months conducted in the families' homes by a bereavement counsellor. Therapy involved helping family members review events leading up to the death of the parent; looking at momentoes and photographs of the deceased; and encouraging the children and surviving parent to talk about the deceased and their feelings of loss.

For parent-rating of children's behaviour problems using the Rutter A scale (Rutter *et al.*, 1970) an effect size of 0.5 was obtained one and two years following treatment, indicating that the average treated child fared better than 69 per cent of cases in the control group in the short and long term. For ratings of parental health problems (Parkes, 1975), an index of family system functioning, effect sizes of 0.6 and 1.4 occurred indicating that the average treated case fared better than 73 per cent of controls a year after treatment and better than 92 per cent of controls two years after treatment.

These results suggest that family therapy alleviated child and family adjustment difficulties which follow bereavement through parental death.

Conclusions

From the review of these nine studies the following conclusions may be drawn. First, with children and adolescents referred for the treatment of clinical depression individually based cognitive behaviour therapy may be effective in alleviating depression and preventing relapse following remission of depressive symptoms. Furthermore, response to cognitive behaviour therapy is more rapid than response to a simple stress management intervention such as relaxation training. However, continued cognitive behavioural treatment following remission for up to a total of twelve sessions is probably important in preventing relapse. Second, for clinical depression, a fourteen-session programme of group-based cognitive behaviour therapy is effective in both the short and long term in alleviating depression in adolescents. Third, there is little long-term advantage to be gained from adding group-based parent training to a programme of group-based cognitive behaviour therapy for clinically depressed adolescents. However, in the short term a combined programme has the benefit of either improving youngsters' home-based adjustment or positively influencing parents' perceptions of their depressed adolescents or both. Fourth, for schoolchildren and adolescents screened for low mood a number of brief ten- to twelve-session group-based programmes conducted over two to three months are effective in modifying depressive symptomatology. These programmes include cognitive behaviour therapy, relaxation training, social skills training, self-instructional training and problem-solving skills training. Fifth, for clinically depressed youngsters referred for treatment, social skills training is no more effective than support group membership. Sixth, for children bereaved through the death of a parent, a six-session programme of family therapy which focuses on family-based grief work may improve both child and parental adjustment in the short and long term.

With respect to service development, the results of this review suggest that it would be valuable to develop community-based psychological intervention services for schoolchildren and adolescents at-risk for depression and also for those with clinical depression referred for treatment. In a small minority of cases, inpatient services for suicidal, psychotic, complex and treatment-resistant cases are essential. Children at-risk for depression may be identified through school screening programmes using self-report instruments such as the Childhood Depression Inventory (Kovacs and Beck, 1977) and also through public health records of untimely parental deaths. For children at-risk for depression identified through school-based screening, brief twelve-session structured group-based intervention programmes in cognitive behaviour therapy, relaxation training, social skills training, self-instructional training or problem-solving skills training may be offered. For those identified as at-risk for depression or other adjustment problems following parental death, brief home-based family therapy may be offered. For cases of clinical depression referred for treatment, either individual or group-based cognitive behaviour therapy programmes of twelve to fourteen sessions may be offered either alone or in conjunction with concurrent parent training.

With respect to research there is an urgent need for more well-designed controlled clinical trials of manualized individual and family treatments with clinically depressed children and teenagers referred for treatment. Few such studies have been conducted. There is also an urgent need for trials of similar psychological treatments alone and in combination with newer antidepressant medications such as serotonin re-uptake inhibitors with severely depressed children and adolescents. No such studies have been conducted.

ASSESSMENT

Battle, J. (1992). *Culture-Free Self-Esteem Inventories*. Examiner's Manual. Austin, TX: Pro-ed.

Beck, A. and Steer, R. (1991) *Beck Scale for Suicide Ideation*. New York: The Psychological Corporation.

Birleson, P. (1981). The validity of depressive disorder in childhood and the development of a self-rating scale: A research report. *Journal of Child Psychology and Psychiatry*, 22, 73–88.

Birleson, P., Hudson, I., Buchanan, D. and Wolff, S. (1987). Clinical evaluation of a self-rating scale for depressive disorder in childhood (Depression Self-Rating Scale). *Journal of Child Psychology and Psychiatry*, 28, 43–60.

Chambers, W., Puig-Antich, J., Hirsch, M. *et al.* (1985). The assessment of affective disorders in children and adolescents by semi-structured interview. *Archives of General Psychiatry*, 42, 696–703. (K-SADS.)

Faschingbauer, T. (1981). *Texas Revised Inventory of Grief (TRIG)*. Houston, TX: Honeycomb.

Kazdin, A. (1983). Hopelessness, depression and suicidal intent among psychiatrically disturbed inpatient children. *Journal of Consulting and Clinical Psychology*, 51, 504–10.

Kazdin, A., Colbus, D. and Rogers, A. (1986). Assessment of depression and diagnosis of depressive disorder among psychiatrically disturbed children. *Journal of Abnormal Child Psychology*, 14, 499–515.

Kovacs, M. and Beck, A. (1977). An empirical clinical approach towards definition of childhood depression. In J. Schulterbrandt and A. Raskin. (eds) *Depression in Children* (pp. 1–25). New York: Raven.

Leitenberg, H., Yost, L. and Carroll-Wilson, M. (1986). Negative cognitive errors in children: Questionnaire development, normative data, and comparisons between children with and without self-reported symptoms of depression, low self-esteem and evaluation anxiety. *Journal of Consulting and Clinical Psychology*, 54, 528–36.

Petti, T. (1978). Depression in hospitalized child psychiatry patients: approaches to measuring depression. *Journal of the American Academy of Child Psychiatry*, 17, 49–59. (Bellevue Index of Depression.)

Pozanski, E., Grossman, J., Buchsman, Y., Banegras, M., Freeman, L. and Gibbons, R. (1984). Preliminary studies of the reliability and validity of the Children's Depression Rating Scale. *Journal of the American Academy of Child and Adolescent Psychiatry*, 23, 191–7.

Radloff, L. (1977). The CES-D: A self-report depression scale for research in the general population. *Applied Psychological Measurement*, 1, 358–401.

Reynolds, W. (1987). *Reynolds Adolescent Depression Scale*. Odessa, FL: Psychological Assessment Resources, Inc.

Reynolds, W. (1991). Development of a semistructured clinical interview for suicidal behaviour in adolescents. *Psychological Assessment: A Journal of Consulting and Clinical Psychology*, 2, 382–90.

Sanders, C., Maugher, P. and Strong, P. (1985). *Grief Experiences Inventory*. Palo Alto, CA: Consulting Psychologists' Press.

Seligman, M., Peterson, C., Kaslow, N., Tanenbaum, R., Alloy, L. and Abramson, L. (1984). Attributional style and depressive symptoms among children. *Journal of Abnormal Psychology*, 93, 235–8.

TREATMENT MANUALS AND RESOURCES

Berman, A. and Jobes, D. (1993) *Adolescent Suicide: Assessment and Intervention*. Washington DC: APA.

Clarke, G. and Lewinsohn, P. (1984). *The Coping with Depression course –
Adolescent Version: A psychoeducational intervention for unipolar depression in
high school students*. Eugene, OR: Peter Lewinsohn.

Corr, C. and Balk, D. (1996). *Handbook of Adolescent Death and Bereavement*.
New York: Springer.

Harrington, R. (1993). *Depressive Disorder in Childhood and Adolescence*.
Chichester: Wiley.

Herbert, M. (1996d). *Supporting Bereaved and Dying Children and Their Parents*.
Leicester: British Psychological Society.

Kübler-Ross, E. (1983). *On Children and Death*. New York: Macmillan.

Lewinsohn, P. and Clarke, G. (1986). *The Coping with Depression Course –
Adolescent Version: Parent Manual*. Eugene, OR: Peter Lewinsohn.

Matson, J. (1989). *Treating Depression in Children and Adolescents*. New York:
Pergamon.

Mufson, L., Moreau, D., Weissman, M. and Kerman, G. (1993). *Interpersonal
Psychotherapy for Depressed Adolescents*. New York: Guilford.

Oster, G. and Caro, J. (1990). *Understanding And Treating Depressed Adolescents
And Their Families*. New York: Wiley.

Reynolds, H. and Johnson, F. (1994). *Handbook of Depression in Children and
Adolescents*. New York: Plenum Press.

Schwartz, J., Kaslow, N., Racusin, G. and Carton, E. (1998). Interpersonal family
therapy for depression. In V. VanHasslet and M. Hersen (eds), *Handbook of
Psychological Treatment Protocols for Children and Adolescents* (pp. 109–51).
Mahwah, NJ: Lawrence Erlbaum.

Smith, S. and Pennell, M. (1996). *Interventions With Bereaved Children*. London:
Kingsley.

Stark, K. (1990). *Childhood Depression: School-based Intervention*. New York:
Guilford.

Stark, K. and Kendall, P. (1996). *Treating Depressed Children: Therapists Manual
for ACTION*. Ardmore, PA: Workbook Publishing.

Stroebe, M., Stroebe, W. and Hansson, R. (1993). *Handbook of Bereavement:
Theory, Research, and Intervention*. New York: Cambridge University Press.

Walsh, F. and McGoldrick, M. (1991). *Living Beyond Loss: Death in the Family*.
New York: Norton.

Webb, N. (1993). *Helping Bereaved Children: A Handbook for Practitioners*. New
York: Guilford.

Worden, J. (1997). *Children and Grief: When A Parent Dies*. New York: Guilford.

FURTHER READING FOR CLIENTS

Dyregrov, A. (1992). *Grief in Children: A Handbook for Adults*. London: Kingsley.

James, J. and Cherry, F. (1988). *The Grief Recovery Handbook: A Step-by-Step
Programme For Moving Beyond Loss*. New York: Harper Row.

Krementz, J. (1981). *How it Feels When a Parent Dies*. New York: Knopf.

Lukas, C. and Seiden, H. (1987). *Silent Grief: Living in the Wake of Suicide*. New
York: Scribners.

Rainbow Collection Catalogue gives up-to-date lists of literature and audio-visual aids to help children, families and schools deal with grief-related problems. Available from 447 Hannah Branch Road, Burnsville, NC 28714, USA.

Rando, T. (1991). *How to go on Living When Someone You Love Dies.* New York: Bantam.

Stark, K., Kendall, P., McCarthy, M., Stafford, M., Barron, R. and Thomeer, M. (1996). *A Workbook for Overcoming Depression.* Ardmore, PA: Workbook Publishing.

Ward, B. (1993). *Good Grief: Exploring Feelings of Loss and Death.* (Volume 1: With under elevens. Volume 2: with over elevens and adults.) London: Kingsley.

10 Anorexia and bulimia

Kathleen Mitchell and Alan Carr

Definitions

An excessive concern with the control of body weight and shape along with an inadequate and unhealthy pattern of eating are the central features of eating problems in children and adolescents (Bryant-Waugh and Lask, 1995a). In both DSM IV (APA, 1994) and ICD 10 (WHO, 1992) a distinction has been made between anorexia nervosa and bulimia nervosa with the former being characterized primarily by weight loss and the latter by a cyclical pattern of bingeing and purging. Diagnostic criteria for these disorders from DSM IV and ICD 10 are set out in Figures 10.1 and 10.2. The distinction made between anorexia nervosa and bulimia nervosa, while descriptively useful, does not take full account of variations in eating problems seen in clinical practice. Many anorexic patients present with bulimic symptoms and many bulimic patients develop anorexia. For this reason, in DSM IV, a distinction is made between two subtypes of anorexia: the restricting type and the binge–purge type.

Clinical features of eating disorders are present in the domains of perception, cognition, affect, behaviour, relationships and physiological functioning (Hsu, 1990; Lask and Bryant-Waugh, 1993; Szmukler *et al.*, 1995). With respect to perception, in most clinical cases of eating disorder there is a distortion of body image. The patient perceives the body or parts of the body such as the stomach, buttocks, thighs and so forth to be larger than they are.

With respect to cognition, there is a preoccupation with food. In cases where bingeing is occurring, there is a belief that the bingeing behaviour is out of control. There may also be conflict concerning dependence and maturity. On the one hand there may be a wish to remain a dependent child and a fear of maturity and independence. On the other there may be a wish to escape from parental control and the lack of autonomy and privacy that this entails. Low self-esteem, low self-efficacy and perfectionism are also common. Thus, many youngsters with eating disorders view themselves as worthless because they construe themselves as failing to meet high perfectionistic standards and in addition, they believe themselves to be powerless to ever achieve these standards.

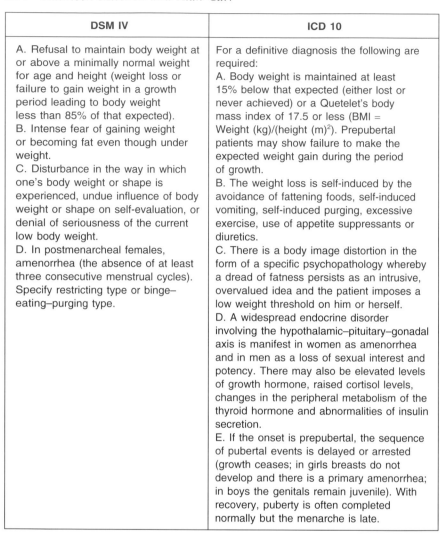

DSM IV	ICD 10
A. Refusal to maintain body weight at or above a minimally normal weight for age and height (weight loss or failure to gain weight in a growth period leading to body weight less than 85% of that expected). B. Intense fear of gaining weight or becoming fat even though under weight. C. Disturbance in the way in which one's body weight or shape is experienced, undue influence of body weight or shape on self-evaluation, or denial of seriousness of the current low body weight. D. In postmenarcheal females, amenorrhea (the absence of at least three consecutive menstrual cycles). Specify restricting type or binge–eating–purging type.	For a definitive diagnosis the following are required: A. Body weight is maintained at least 15% below that expected (either lost or never achieved) or a Quetelet's body mass index of 17.5 or less (BMI = Weight (kg)/(height (m)^2). Prepubertal patients may show failure to make the expected weight gain during the period of growth. B. The weight loss is self-induced by the avoidance of fattening foods, self-induced vomiting, self-induced purging, excessive exercise, use of appetite suppressants or diuretics. C. There is a body image distortion in the form of a specific psychopathology whereby a dread of fatness persists as an intrusive, overvalued idea and the patient imposes a low weight threshold on him or herself. D. A widespread endocrine disorder involving the hypothalamic–pituitary–gonadal axis is manifest in women as amenorrhea and in men as a loss of sexual interest and potency. There may also be elevated levels of growth hormone, raised cortisol levels, changes in the peripheral metabolism of the thyroid hormone and abnormalities of insulin secretion. E. If the onset is prepubertal, the sequence of pubertal events is delayed or arrested (growth ceases; in girls breasts do not develop and there is a primary amenorrhea; in boys the genitals remain juvenile). With recovery, puberty is often completed normally but the menarche is late.

Figure 10.1 Diagnostic criteria for anorexia nervosa.
Source Adapted from DSM IV (APA, 1994) and ICD 10 (WHO, 1992).

With respect to emotional status, there is an intense fear of fatness and in some instances a depressive mood. The fear of fatness in conjunction with the distorted perception of the body as larger than it actually is and perfectionistic strivings to achieve thinness may underpin a sense of failure and associated depressive affect.

At a behavioural level, restrictive eating is typical of anorexia. A cycle of restrictive eating, bingeing and compensatory behaviours is typical of

DSM IV	ICD 10
A. Recurrent episodes of binge eating. An episode of binge eating is characterized by both of the following: 1. Eating, in a discrete period of time (e.g. within a two-hour period), an amount of food that is definitely larger than most people would eat during a similar period of time and under similar circumstances. 2. A sense of lack of control over eating during the episode (e.g. a feeling that one cannot stop eating or control what or how much one is eating). B. Recurrent inappropriate compensatory behaviour in order to prevent weight gain, such as self-induced vomiting; misuse of laxatives; diuretics, enemas or other medications; fasting or excessive exercise. C. The binge eating and inappropriate compensatory behaviours both occur, on average, at least twice a week for three months. D. Self-evaluation is unduly influenced by body shape and weight. E. The disturbance does not occur exclusively during episodes of anorexia nervosa. Specify purging or non-purging type.	For a definitive diagnosis all of the following are required: A. There is a persistent preoccupation with eating and an irresistible craving for food; the patient succumbs to episodes of overeating in which large amounts of food are consumed in short periods of time. B. The patient attempts to counteract the fattening effects of food by one or more of the following: self-induced vomiting; purgative abuse; alternating periods of starvation; use of drugs such as appetite suppressants, thyroid preparations or diuretics. When bulimia occurs in diabetic patients they may choose to neglect their insulin treatment. C. The psychopathology consists of a morbid dread of fatness and the patient sets herself or himself a sharply defined weight threshold, well below the premorbid weight that constitutes the optimum of healthy weight in the opinion of the physician. There is often but not always a history of an earlier episode of anorexia nervosa, the interval between the two disorders ranging from a few months to several years. This earlier episode may have been fully expressed or may have assumed minor cryptic form with a moderate loss of weight and/or a transient phase of amenorrhea.

Figure 10.2 Diagnostic criteria for bulimia nervosa.
Source Adopted from DSM IV (APA, 1994) and ICD 10 (WHO, 1992).

bulimia. These compensatory behaviours may include vomiting, using diuretics and laxatives or excessive exercising. Usually particular classes of situations that are interpreted as threatening or stressful lead to a negative mood state and it is these that precipitate a bout of bingeing. Such situations include interpersonal conflicts, isolation, and small violations of a strict diet such as eating a square of chocolate. While bingeing brings immediate relief, it also leads to physical discomfort and to guilt for not adhering to a strict diet. Purging relieves both guilt and physical discomfort but may also induce shame and fear of negative consequences of the binge–purge cycle. In addition to abnormal eating patterns, youngsters with eating disorders may display a variety of self-destructive behaviours including self-injurious behaviour, suicide attempts and drug abuse. These self-destructive behaviours are often construed as self-punishments for not living up to perfectionistic standards or attempts to escape from conflicts associated with self-worth and individuation.

With respect to interpersonal adjustment, poor school performance, withdrawal from peer relationships and deterioration in family relationships may all occur during the development of eating problems. Many youngsters who develop eating disorders are described by their parents as model children prior to the onset of the eating problems. This good premorbid adjustment is often, although not always, in stark contrast to the family- and school-based relationship difficulties that arise once eating disorders become entrenched.

A wide variety of physical complications may also occur when children or adolescents develop eating disorders. These include an endocrine disorder affecting the hypothalamic–pituitary–gonadal axis manifested by amenorrhea or delayed onset of puberty; starvation symptomatology such as reduced metabolic rate, bradycardia, hypotension, hypothermia and anaemia; lanugo hair on the back; delayed gastric emptying; electrolyte abnormalities; renal dysfunction and zinc deficiency. In bulimia, erosion of dental enamel may occur due to vomiting and lesions on the back of the dominant hand may develop if the hand is used to initiate vomiting. With both anorexia and bulimia a particularly serious concern is that the youngster may develop electrolyte abnormalities which may lead to a fatal arrhythmia.

Epidemiology

Anorexia nervosa and bulimia nervosa are most common among female adolescents (APA, 1993; Bryant-Waugh and Lask, 1995a, 1995b; Szmukler and Patton, 1995; West, 1994). About 3–4 per cent of the adolescent female population suffer from eating disorders. The prevalence of anorexia nervosa among teenage girls is about 1 per cent. The prevalence of bulimia nervosa is between 1 and 3 per cent. The female:male ratio for anorexia and bulimia is about 9:1 in adolescents and 4:1 in preadolescents. Community studies show that, contrary to earlier data from clinical studies, there is not a significant relationship between eating disorders and social class. Over the past 30 years there has been an increase in the incidence of both anorexia and bulimia and eating disorders are more common in Western industrialized countries. In clinical rather than community populations, co-morbid mood disorders and obsessive compulsive disorders are common in cases of anorexia and for bulimia co-morbid drug abuse and borderline personality disorder are relatively common.

The outcome for eating disorders is a cause for considerable concern (APA, 1993; Szmukler *et al.*, 1995). For anorexia nervosa about half of all cases have a good outcome, a quarter have moderate outcome and a quarter have a poor outcome. At twenty-year follow-up, the mortality rate is about 20 per cent. Poor prognosis is associated with lower weight, a more chronic condition, bulimic symptoms and problematic family relationships. For bulimia nervosa about a quarter of cases have a good outcome, a third have a poor outcome and the remainder (about two-fifths) have a moderate outcome.

Previous reviews

Key findings from previous reviews of the effectiveness of psychological treatments for anorexia nervosa and bulimia are summarized in this section. The theoretical rationales which underpin the principal approaches to the treatment of eating disorders are also outlined.

Anorexia nervosa

Wilson and Fairburn (1998) in an extensive literature review concluded that both individual and family therapy and combinations of these modalities with and without initial hospital-based feeding programmes are effective in treating anorexia nervosa. They also concluded that inpatient refeeding programmes must be supplemented with outpatient follow-up care involving either individual or family-based psychotherapy if weight gains made while in hospital are to be maintained following discharge. A third conclusion was that antidepressants, antipsychotics, anxiolytics, gut motility stimulants and other medications convey no added benefit to the effectiveness of routine inpatient feeding programmes in restoring body weight. The rationales for behaviourally based refeeding programmes and both individual and family psychotherapy deserve some elaboration.

Behavioural approaches

Slade (1982) has presented a sophisticated behavioural explanation for the development of anorexia nervosa which also provides a rationale for its treatment using operant methods. According to Slade (ibid.) particular setting events and personal characteristics combine with particular triggering events to predispose youngsters to find restrictive eating reinforcing. Important setting events include family-based difficulties in establishing autonomy, social anxiety in peer relationships, and stressful events such as academic failure or rejection by peers. When these setting events occur and the youngster has perfectionistic strivings to be in control and achieve a high level of success, critical comments from peers or family members may lead to pronounced dieting behaviour. Weight loss, a sign of success and control, within this context is positively reinforcing. Also, the avoidance of fatness and criticism for being overweight is negatively reinforcing. These contingencies maintain the dieting behaviour and eventually weight loss is such that physiological changes, notably those in the endocrine system, occur and these may render food avoidance particularly reinforcing. Slade's model is supported by evidence for perfectionistic strivings, interpersonal difficulties and precipitating stressful life events among youngsters with eating disorders (Lask and Bryant-Waugh, 1993). Inpatient behavioural programmes aim to alter the contingencies associated with the youngsters' eating routine. With inpatient operant weight gain programmes, privileges are withdrawn from patients when they are admitted to hospital and confined to bed. As target weight increments are achieved or specific eating routines are followed, specific desired privileges are returned to the patient to reinforce weight gain and appropriate eating routines. There is some evidence that both strict and lenient applications of such programmes are effective (e.g. Touyz *et al.*, 1984).

Psychodynamic approaches

Individual psychodynamic psychotherapy for anorexia was pioneered by Hilda Bruch (1973) who argued that the mothers of anorexic girls adopt a parenting style in which parental needs for control and compliance take primacy over the child's needs for self-expression and autonomy. The child has difficulty learning how to interpret need-related internal physiological states and in developing a coherent sense of self separate from caregivers. In adolescence the fear of fatness, obsession with food, and guilt for eating are part of an attempt to manage a central conflict related to the attainment of autonomy and a coherent sense of self. The youngster experiences a fear of separation from parents and a fear of being overly controlled by the parents; a fear of maturation, sexuality, intimacy and independence; and a fear of having little control over the self or body size (as a symbol of self). This conflict about autonomy is characterized by low self-esteem coupled with perfectionistic strivings to improve the self. There is ample evidence for distorted body image, maturity fears, perfectionistic strivings, low self-esteem and low self-efficacy among teenagers with eating disorders (Lask and Bryant-Waugh, 1992). Evidence pointing to the centrality of a dysfunctional parent–child relationship is lacking (Eisler, 1995). However, early stressful life events such as loss of a parent through bereavement and child sexual abuse are more common among children and teenagers with eating disorders, particularly bulimia (Eisler, ibid.). Psychoanalytic psychotherapy aims to help the patient gain insight into the way in which the psychodynamics of past relationships with parents underpin the transference–countertransference patient–therapist relationship and the relationships that the patient has with other significant people in her life. In addition, the therapist facilitates the patient's search for less destructive ways to assert autonomy from the parents and develop a strong sense of personal identity.

Family systems approaches

Family systems formulations of anorexia, pioneered by Minuchin *et al.* (1978) and Selvini Palazzoli (1978), point to a number of organizational features of families that may predispose youngsters to developing anorexia or maintain the condition once it emerges. For example, Minuchin *et al.* (ibid.) characterized the families of teenagers with anorexia as enmeshed, rigid and overprotective. He also argued that there was a lack of conflict resolution and an involvement of children in parental conflicts, through triangulation. Selvini Palazzoli (1978) pinpointed the following features as typical of the anorexic family: an ethic of self-sacrifice, the rejection of personal leadership by the parents, blame-shifting, unclear communication and secret alliances between parents and the child which go hand in hand with covert marital dissatisfaction. Weber and Stierlin (1981) suggest that a process occurs where individuation in adolescence is complicated by the child's fantasy that the parents will have nothing left in common when the child matures and gains autonomy. The youngster copes by playing the role of a model child but eventually the parents become interested in another child or pursuit. The child retaliates by doggedly pursuing autonomy through self-starvation which achieves the twin gains of providing a type of pseudo-autonomy centring on control of the shape of the body and eliciting parental attention which has been lost. Available empirical evidence clearly shows that there is not a single dysfunctional family constellation that causes anorexia and bulimia (Eisler, 1995; Vandereycken *et al.*, 1989). Rather there are a variety of different patterns of family organization that may be associated with eating disorders. For example, Vandereycken *et al.* (ibid.) found that a range of family types could be identified with differing levels of enmeshment, rigidity and conflict avoidance. These patterns of organization probably reflect extreme forms of relational styles that preceded the onset of eating disorders and are attempts by parents and siblings to cope with these perplexing difficulties. Unfortunately they inadvertently maintain the youngsters' dysfunctional eating habits. Family therapy aims to help family members understand these patterns of family interaction and to develop more functional organizational structures and clearer patterns of communication.

Bulimia nervosa

Hartmann *et al.* (1992) in a review of eighteen trials of various psychological intervention with older adolescents and adults with bulimia nervosa found a mean effect size of just over 1 across all types of treatments, indicating that the average treated case fared better than 84 per cent of untreated cases. Effect sizes were based on the frequency of bulimic episodes. Hartmann *et al.* also found that briefer treatments with thirteen or fewer sessions were less effective than longer treatments with fifteen or more sessions. Most of the studies used cognitive behavioural approaches to treatment. Wilson and Fairburn (1998), in an extensive review of controlled studies of bulimia in adolescents and young adults, concluded that manualized cognitive behavioural interventions for bulimia nervosa are the treatment of choice. He estimated that more than 50 per cent of cases show remission of bingeing and purging following behavioural treatment and these gains are maintained a year after treatment. While antidepressants have a short-term positive impact on bulimia, they add little to the effectiveness of cognitive behavioural treatment. However, they may usefully be used in older teenagers and young adults to treat co-morbid depression. Interpersonal psychotherapy is the only other therapy showing benefits similar to those of cognitive behaviour therapy, although less evidence is available on its effectiveness. Because of the importance of the cognitive behavioural approach to the treatment of bulimia nervosa, an outline of the formulation model which underpins this approach to treatment is warranted.

Cognitive behavioural model of bulimia

With bulimia, cognitive behavioural models focus primarily on the binge–purge cycle (Fairburn *et al.*, 1990). Extreme personal value is attached to a thin body shape and low body weight. This leads to restricted food intake, which in turn renders youngsters vulnerable to loss of control over eating, a factor that accounts for bingeing. Episodes of bingeing are maintained by negative reinforcement since they temporarily reduce negative affect. Purging and other extreme forms of weight control compensate for the effects on weight of bingeing behaviour. Purging may also maintain binge eating because it reduces anxiety about weight gain resulting from bingeing. It also disrupts the learned satiety that regulates the intake of food. Episodes of binge eating and purging are followed by distorted cognitions about the significance of the bingeing and the negative implications of bingeing both for body shape and self-evaluative beliefs. Thus, bulimic episodes create setting conditions that lead to further dietary restraint and subsequent binge eating. Cognitive behaviour therapy helps patients to map out the binge–purge cycle, to monitor eating patterns and related cognitions and contingencies and use cognitive and behavioural strategies to disrupt the cycle and manage relapses. These strategies include avoiding trigger situations or habituating to them through exposure and response prevention routines. A second set of strategies involves using cognitive therapy to help patients interpret potential trigger situations in ways that do not lead to negative affect and bingeing. A third strategy involves helping patients avoid persisting with bingeing once it starts by coaching them in countering self-deprecatory cognitions and related negative mood states that occur once bingeing starts. Cognitive behaviour therapy programmes typically conclude with relapse prevention training.

Method

The aim in this chapter was to review well-designed studies of the effects of psychological interventions for adolescents with eating disorders. A computer-based literature search of the PsychLit data base was conducted. Terms that defined eating disorders, such as *anorexia nervosa, bulimia nervosa* and *eating disorder* were combined with terms that defined interventions such as *treatment, therapy, intervention, behaviour therapy, cognitive behaviour therapy* and *family therapy*. The search, which was confined to English language journals, covered the period 1977 to 1997 inclusively. A manual search through bibliographies of well-designed studies and recent review papers on psychological interventions for eating disorders was also conducted. A manual review of the contents of selected journals that frequently included studies on eating disorders (such as *International Journal of Eating Disorders*) was also undertaken. Treatment outcome studies were selected for inclusion in this review if the design contained a psychological treatment group and a control or comparison group; if at least nine cases were included in the active treatment group; and if reliable and valid pre- and post-treatment measures were included in the design of the study. We had great difficulty identifying studies in which all cases were under twenty years of age and so included studies that contained some young adults but in which a reasonable proportion of participants were adolescents. Single-case designs and studies reported in dissertations or convention papers were not included in the review. Using these inclusion and exclusion criteria, from a pool of over a hundred papers, seven studies were selected for inclusion in the review.

Characteristics of the studies

A summary of the main characteristics of the studies is given in Table 10.1. Five of the studies were conducted in the UK and two in the USA and all were published between 1985 and 1997 in six of the seven studies DSM III-R (APA, 1987) diagnostic criteria were used to select cases for inclusion. In four studies, cases had a primary diagnosis of anorexia nervosa. In two studies, bulimia nervosa was the main diagnosis. One study contained subgroups of anorexic and bulimic cases. Family therapy was evaluated in five studies; individual psychotherapy in three; combined family therapy and individual therapy in two; and cognitive behavioural therapy in two. Multimodal inpatient therapy; concurrent group therapy for cases and parents; concurrent counselling for youngsters and parents; and behaviour therapy were evaluated in one study each. In all, there were 328 cases in the seven studies. Ninety-seven per cent of cases were female and they ranged in age, across the seven studies, from twelve to 30 years, although a large proportion of cases studied were under twenty years of age. Cases were predominantly from middle-class backgrounds and were referred by

Table 10.1 Characteristics of treatment outcome studies for cases of anorexia and bulimia nervosa

Study no.	Authors	Year	Country	N per gp	Mean age & range	Gender	Primary diagnosis	Previous treatment	Family characteristics	Referral	Treatment duration
1	Crisp et al.	1991	UK	MIT + FT + IPT = 20 FT + IPT = 30 PGT + GT = 20 C = 20	22 y	f 100%	100% AN DSM-III-R			Physicians	MIT: 7 m & 12 sess FT: 12 sess over 12 w GT: 20 sess over 10 w
2	Hall and Crisp	1987	UK	FT + IPT = 15 C = 15	20 y 13–27 y	f 100%	100% AN	60%	83% SES 1 & 2	Physicians	12 sess over 18 w
3	Robin et al.	1995	USA	FT = 11 IPT = 11	14 y 12–19 y	f 100%	100% AN DSM-III-R			Physicians School Psychologists	36 sess over 16 m
4	Le Grange et al.	1992	UK	FT = 9 PC + IPT = 9	15 y 12–17 y	m 11% f 89%	100% AN DSM-III-R			Psychologists Physicians	9 sess over 6 m
5	Russell et al. Eisler et al.	1987 1997	UK	FT – EOSH = 10 IST – EOSH = 11 FT – EOLH = 10 IST – EOLH = 9 FT – LO = 7 IST – LO = 7 FT – BN = 9 IST – BN = 10	EOSH: 17 y EOLH: 21 y LO: 28 y BN: 24 y	m 4% f 96%	71% AN 29% BN DSM-III-R	61%	78% IF 63% SES 1 & 2	Inpatient refeeding programme	18 sess over 12 m
6	Ordman and Kirschenbaum	1985	USA	CBT = 10 C = 10	20 y 18–30 y	f 100%	100% BN DSM-III	30%	90% students	Media Self	15 sess over 15 w
7	Fairburn et al.	1991 1993	UK	CBT = 25 IPT = 25 BT = 25	24 y 17–29 y	f 100%	100% BN DSM-III-R	76%	25% married 36% students	Physicians	19 sess over 18 w

Key: MIT = Multimodal inpatient therapy. FT = Family therapy. IST = Individual supportive therapy. IPT = Individual psychodynamic psychotherapy. GT = Group therapy for patients with eating disorders. PGT = Group therapy for parents. PC = Parent counselling. CBT = Cognitive behaviour therapy. C = Control group. EOSH = Early onset short history (< 3 years) of anorexia nervosa. EOLH = Early onset long history (> 3 years) of anorexia nervosa. LO = Late onset of anorexia nervosa. BN = Bulimia nervosa. SES = Socio-economic-status. sess = session. y = year. m = month.

physicians or a hospital unit for treatment in six of the seven studies. In only one study were cases media-solicited. Treatment ranged in intensity and duration from nine sessions over six months to several months of inpatient care with outpatient follow-up. From this overview it can be concluded that these studies assessed the outcome of both individually focused and family-based interventions in inpatient and outpatient treatment centres for older teenage girls with anorexia and bulimia nervosa living in the US and the UK.

Methodological features

A summary of the methodological features of the seven studies is given in Table 10.2. All studies contained diagnostically homogeneous treatment and comparison or control groups. Random assignment was used to allocate cases to groups in all studies. In all studies groups were demographically similar and in 71 per cent of studies groups were comparable for co-morbidity. Pre-treatment assessments and either post-treatment or follow-up assessments using multiple reliable and valid assessment instruments occurred in all studies. Post-treatment assessments were conducted in four studies and follow-up assessments in six studies. Of these, four were conducted a year after treatment (Crisp et al., 1991; Fairburn et al., 1991, 1993; Hall and Crisp, 1987; Robin et al., 1995); one was conducted five years after treatment (Eisler et al., 1997; Russell et al., 1987); and one was conducted eight months after treatment (Le Grange et al., 1992). In all studies, objective researcher ratings of symptomatology or systemic functioning were employed. For example, weight gain was used as a variable in all studies and the Morgan-Russell Rating Scales were used in four of the five studies of anorexia (Morgan and Hayward, 1988). Self-report scales were used in 57 per cent of studies and parent-report scales in only 28 per cent of studies. Teacher or therapist ratings were not used in any study. Symptoms were assessed routinely in all seven studies but features of the adolescent's family or social system were assessed in only 42 per cent of studies. Deterioration rates were not reported in any study but drop-out rates were reported in 85 per cent of studies. Engagement in further treatment was assessed in only 28 per cent of studies. The clinical significance of change was assessed in 71 per cent of studies. Experienced therapists participated in 85 per cent of studies and in those where comparative treatments were offered they were equally valued. In only 28 per cent of studies were treatments manualized. Supervision was regularly provided for therapists in 57 per cent of studies. Treatment integrity was checked in only 28 per cent of studies. Data on concurrent treatment were not given in any of the studies and information on engagement in subsequent treatment was given in only 28 per cent of studies. Overall this was a sufficiently methodologically robust group of studies to permit reliable and valid conclusions to be drawn about effective treatments for adolescents with anorexia and bulimia nervosa.

Table 10.2 Methodological features for studies of anorexia and bulimia nervosa

Feature	Study number						
	S1	*S2*	*S3*	*S4*	*S5*	*S6*	*S7*
Control or comparison group	1	1	1	1	1	1	1
Random assignment	1	1	1	1	1	1	1
Diagnostic homogeneity	1	1	1	1	1	1	1
Comparable for co-morbidity	0	0	1	1	1	1	1
Demographic similarity	1	1	1	1	1	1	1
Pre-treatment assessment	1	1	1	1	1	1	1
Post-treatment assessment	0	0	1	0	1	1	1
Follow-up assessment at six months or later	1	1	1	1	1	0	1
Children's self-report	0	0	1	1	0	1	0
Parent's ratings	0	0	1	1	0	0	0
Teacher's ratings	0	0	0	0	0	0	0
Therapist's ratings	0	0	0	0	0	0	0
Researcher's ratings	1	1	1	1	1	1	1
Child's symptom assessed	1	1	1	1	1	1	1
System assessed	0	0	1	1	0	1	1
Deterioration assessed	0	0	0	0	0	0	0
Drop-out assessed	1	1	1	1	1	0	1
Clinical significance of change assessed	0	1	1	1	1	0	1
Experienced therapists used	1	1	1	1	1	0	1
Treatments were equally valued	1	1	1	1	1	0	1
Treatments were manualized	0	0	1	0	0	0	1
Therapy supervision was provided	0	0	0	1	1	1	1
Treatment integrity checked	0	0	1	0	0	0	1
Data on concurrent treatment given	0	0	0	0	0	0	0
Data on subsequent treatment given	0	1	0	0	1	0	0
Total	11	13	19	17	16	12	18

Key S = study. 1 = design feature was present. 0 = design feature was absent.

Substantive findings

A summary of the effect sizes and outcome rates for the seven studies is presented in Table 10.3 and a narrative account of the main findings of the studies is presented in Table 10.4. In setting out the categories of Table 10.3, account has been taken of the types of variables typically assessed in the studies reviewed. Weight gain assessed as either percentage weight gain or increase in body-mass index (Beumont *et al.*, 1988) is probably the most valid index of symptomatic change in studies of anorexia nervosa and was used in all studies. The frequency of bingeing and vomiting is a central variable to assess in studies of bulimia, hence its inclusion in the table. Self-reported eating attitudes and beliefs have been included because of their importance as an index of outcome for eating disorders, particularly bulimia. The subscale and global outcome categories for the Morgan-Russell Scale (Morgan and Hayward, 1988) have been listed since this scale was used in four of the seven studies reviewed. The subscale categories are menstruation, nutrition, psychological functioning, social functioning and sexual functioning.

In the following two sections, the seven studies have been grouped into those that deal with anorexia nervosa and those that deal with bulimia. The first five studies evaluated the impact of psychological interventions on anorexia nervosa (Crisp *et al.*, 1991; Eisler *et al.*, 1997; Hall and Crisp, 1987; Le Grange *et al.*, 1992; Robin *et al.*, 1995; Russell *et al.*, 1987). The remaining two studies were concerned with bulimia nervosa (Fairburn *et al.*, 1991, 1993; Ordman and Kirschenbaum, 1985). Below, studies of anorexia will be reviewed first and then the results of the bulimia studies will be considered.

Anorexia nervosa

Crisp *et al.* (1991), at St George's Hospital in London, compared the effects of three treatment programmes for anorexia nervosa. A complex multimodal inpatient treatment programme followed by a course of outpatient individual and family therapy was compared with the effects of an outpatient programme of combined individual and family therapy and an outpatient programme of concurrent group therapy for patients and their parents. A control group was also included in the study design and patients in this group, following assessment, were referred back to their family doctors for routine care. The multimodal inpatient treatment programme was intensive, involving much greater patient contact than the other treatments and comprised weight restoration, individual therapy, family therapy, group therapy, dietary counselling and occupational therapy. It was followed by a twelve-session outpatient programme of combined individual and family therapy similar to that offered to the second treatment group. The combined individual and family therapy outpatient programme focused on dietary advice; food- and weight-related issues; personal issues, particularly increasing

Table 10.3 Summary of effect sizes from treatment outcome studies for anorexia and bulimia nervosa

Variable	Study number and treatment components										
	Study 1			Study 2	Study 3	Study 4	Study 5		Study 6	Study 7	
	MIT+FT+IPT > C	FT+IPT > C	GT+PGT > C	FT+IPT > IST	FT > IPT	FT > PC+IST	EOSH FT > IST	EOLH FT > IST	CBT > C	CBT > BT	IPT > BT
Symptomatic improvement after treatment											
Self-reported eating attitudes and beliefs	–	–	–	–	–	–	–	–	1.6	0.4	–0.3
Frequency of binging and purging	–	–	–	–	–	–	–	–	1.1	2.6	–1.8
Weight gain	–	–	–	–	0.0	–	0.7	0.0	–	0.1	–0.1
Menstruation	–	–	–	–	0.7	–	1.9	0.0	–	–	–
Nutrition	–	–	–	–	–	–	1.5	0.0	–	–	–
Psychological adjustment	–	–	–	–	–	–	0.2	0.0	1.1	0.3	0.1
Sexual adjustment	–	–	–	–	–	–	1.3	0.0	–	–	–
Social adjustment	–	–	–	–	–	–	0.7	0.0	–	0.2	–
Global improvement on Morgan-Russell scales	–	–	–	–	–	–	2.0	0.2	–	–	0.0
Symptomatic improvement at follow-up											
Self-reported eating attitudes and beliefs	–	–	–	–	–	–0.1	–	–	–	–	–
Frequency of binging and purging	–	–	–	–	–	–0.7	–	–	–	–	–
Weight gain	0.8	0.8	0.8	0.0	1.1	–	0.5	–0.8	–	–	–
Menstruation	0.0	0.1	0.2	0.3	0.0	–	1.0	–0.2	–	–	–
Nutrition	0.8	0.3	0.6	–	–	–	0.3	0.1	–	–	–

	1	2	3	4	5	6	7	8	9	10
Psychological adjustment	0.0	0.1	−0.2	–	–	–	0.4	−0.2	–	–
Sexual adjustment	0.1	−0.2	0.2	1.0	–	–	0.6	0.1	–	–
Social adjustment	0.0	0.7	0.0	1.0	–	–	0.6	0.3	–	–
Global improvement on Morgan-Russell scales	0.2	0.2	0.0	0.0	–	−0.4	1.0	−0.3	–	–
Systemic improvement after treatment										
Self-report	–	–	–	–	0.0	–	–	0.0	–	–
Parent's ratings	–	–	–	–	0.0	–	–	–	–	–
Researcher's ratings	–	–	–	–	0.8	–	–	–	–	–
Systemic improvement at follow-up										
Self-report	–	–	–	–	0.0	0.1	–	–	–	–
Parent's ratings	–	–	–	–	0.0	−0.1	–	–	–	–
Researcher's ratings	–	–	–	–	–	4.0	–	–	–	–
Positive clinical outcomes										
% improved after treatment	–	–	–	–	55% > 46%	–	90% > 18%	40% > 33%	44% > 36%	44% > 28%
% improved at follow-up	–	–	–	80%	82% > 50%	67% > 67%	90% > 54%	40% > 55%	36% > 44%	36% > 44%; 20% > 20%; 20%
Negative clinical outcomes										
% Drop-out	40%	10%	15%	6%	0%	0%	10% > 18%	18% > 10%	16% > 12%	–
% Engaged in further treatment	–	–	–	73%	–	–	10% > 37%	57% > 62%	25% > 25%	–

Key MIT = Multimodal inpatient therapy. FT = Family therapy. IST = Individual supportive therapy. IPT = Individual psychodynamic psychotherapy. GT = Group therapy for patients with eating disorders. PGT = Group therapy for parents. PC = Parent counselling. CBT = Cognitive behaviour therapy. C = Control group. EOSH = Early onset short history (< 3 years) of anorexia nervosa. EOLH = Early onset long history (> 3 years) of anorexia nervosa.

Table 10.4 Key findings from treatment studies of adolescents and young adults with anorexia and bulimia nervosa

Study No	Authors	Year	Primary diagnosis	N per gp	No of sessions	Group differences	Key Findings
1	Crisp et al.	1991	AN	1. MIT + FT + IPT = 20 2. FT + IPT = 30 3. PGT + GT= 20 4. C = 20	1 = 7 m inpatient 2 = 12 3 = 20	For weight gain 1 = 2 = 3 > 4 For menstruation, social and sexual adjustment 1 = 2 = 3 = 4	• A year after treatment improvement in weight gain was greater in the three treatment groups than in the control group who received routine community-based treatment. • A year after treatment the four groups did not differ on improvements in menstruation, social and sexual adjustment.
2	Hall and Crisp	1987	AN	1. FT + IPT = 15 2. IST = 15	12	For weight gain & menstruation 1 = 2 For social & sexual adjustment 1 > 2	• A year after treatment improvements in weight gain and menstruation were the same for both groups. • The group that received combined individual and family psychotherapy showed better social and psychosexual adjustment than the group that received individual supportive therapy and dietary advice.
3	Robin et al.	1995	AN	1. FT = 11 2. IPT = 11	36	For weight gain 1 > 2 For menstruation 1 = 2 For family relationships 1 > 2	• Both groups showed similar levels of improvement immediately after treatment for weight gain but a year later more cases in the family therapy group maintained these gains compared with those in the individual psychotherapy group. • At one-year follow-up all girls in both groups were menstruating. • In both groups significant improvement in communication after treatment and at one-year follow-up, but mothers in the family therapy group showed less negative and more positive communication than mothers in the individual psychotherapy group immediately after therapy.
4	Le Grange et al.	1992	AN	1. FT = 9 2. PC + IST = 9	9	For weight gain, menstruation and family relationships 1 = 2	• Eight months after the start of treatment both groups had made similar gains in weight, menstruation and family adjustment. • Poor outcome on the Morgan-Russell scales overall score was associated with poorer family adjustment at intake.

	Authors	Year	Disorder	Treatment groups (n)	No.	Outcome	Results
5	Russell et al. Eisler et al.	1987 1997	AN BN	1. FT – EOSH = 10 2. IST – EOSH = 11 1. FT – EOLH = 10 2. IST – EOLH = 9 1. FT – LO = 7 2. IST – LO = 7 1. FT – BN = 9 2. IST – BN = 10	18	For EOSH 1 > 2 For EOLH 1 = 2 For LO 2 > 1 For BN 1 = 2	• On the Morgan-Russell scales, the anorexic patients with an early onset and short history who received family therapy fared better at one and five years following treatment than those who received individual supportive therapy. • For the late onset group, those who received individual therapy fared better one and five years after treatment than those who received family therapy. • For patients with an early onset and long history of anorexia and for patients with bulimia, neither treatment was particularly effective.
6	Ordman and Kirschenbaum	1985	BN	1. CBT = 10 2. C = 10	15	For binge-purge cycle and psychological adjustment 1 > 2	• After treatment, cases that received a comprehensive cognitive behaviour therapy programme showed greater improvement than a minimal treatment control group.
7	Fairburn et al.	1991 1993	BN	1. CBT = 25 2. IPT = 25 3. BT = 25	19	For binge-purge cycle, beliefs about weight and shape, and psychological adjustment 1 = 2 > 3	• After treatment, cognitive behaviour therapy was more effective than interpersonal psychotherapy in modifying extreme attitudes to weight and body shape, dieting and vomiting, but a year after treatment these differences were gone and cases in both groups showed substantial levels of recovery, suggesting that different mechanisms of recovery are associated with these two treatments. • Immediately after treatment only the cognitive behaviour therapy group had a better outcome than the behaviour therapy group, but a year later both the interpersonal psychotherapy and the cognitive behaviour therapy group fared better than the behaviour therapy group.

Key MIT = Multimodal inpatient therapy. FT = Family therapy. IST = Individual supportive therapy. IPT = Individual psychodynamic psychotherapy. GT = Group therapy for patients with eating disorders. PGT = Group therapy for parents. PC = parent counselling. CBT = Cognitive behaviour therapy. C = Control group. EOSH = Early onset short history (< 3 years) of anorexia nervosa. EOLH = Early onset long history (> 3 years) of anorexia nervosa. LO = Late onset of anorexia nervosa. AN = Anorexia nervosa. BN = Bulimia nervosa. m = Month.

self-esteem; and wider family issues. The concurrent group therapy for patients and their parents comprised ten sessions for the anorexic patients and ten sessions for their parents at monthly intervals and covered similar issues to those addressed in the concurrent individual and family therapy programme.

In this study, the highest drop-out rate of 40 per cent occurred for the multimodal inpatient programme. In the two outpatient programmes far lower dropout rates of 10 per cent and 15 per cent occurred. Clearly, the demands of the inpatient programme made it difficult for patients to remain engaged with treatment. A year following treatment, for weight gain, effect sizes of 0.8 occurred in each of the three treatment groups, indicating that for all three programmes the average treated case fared better than 79 per cent of cases in the control group. On the global improvement rating of the Morgan-Russell scale, differences between three treatment groups and the control group were negligible after treatment. When effect sizes for these individual subscales of the Morgan-Russell scale were calculated, two noteworthy results emerged. First, for nutritional status a very large effect size of 0.8 occurred in the group that received the multimodal inpatient programme (compared with smaller effect sizes of 0.3 and 0.6 in the other two treatment groups). This indicates that the average case who received inpatient care fared better than 79 per cent of the untreated cases control group. For social adjustment the largest effect size, of 0.7, occurred in the group that received the combined individual and family therapy psychotherapy outpatient programme. This effect size indicates that the average case treated in this programme fared better than 79 per cent of cases in the control group. Overall, this study points to the effectiveness and economy of a relatively brief combined individual and family therapy twelve-session outpatient programme. While briefer and less time and labour intensive than the other programmes, the combined individual and family therapy programme was equally effective. Also it may lead to greater improvement in social adjustment than the other approaches.

This tentative finding is further supported by the results of Hall and Crisp's (1987) earlier study in which they compared the effects of their combined individual and family therapy psychotherapy outpatient programme with a control group that received dietary advice only. A year after treatment, both groups had made similar improvement in weight gain, but on the social and sexual adjustment subscales of the Morgan-Russell scale, effect sizes of 1.0 occurred in the treatment group. Thus, the average treated case fared better than 84 per cent of cases in the control group in terms of social and sexual adjustment. Eighty per cent of cases in the treatment group were judged to have made clinically significant improvements, although it is noteworthy that 73 per cent of cases expressed a wish to extend treatment beyond the twelve-session limit of the treatment trial. Attrition from this study was extremely low with a drop-out rate of 6 per cent.

Robin *et al.* (1995), in the US, compared the effects of a family therapy programme and an individual psychodynamic psychotherapy programme.

Each programme, which was manualized, contained approximately 36 sessions and was conducted over about sixteen months. The family therapy programme aimed to empower the parents to use contingency management procedures to help their child gain weight. Once this had begun to occur, control over body weight was returned to the child and therapy focused on helping the youngster develop age-appropriate autonomy. Techniques from structural family therapy such as reducing enmeshment, reducing triangulation and clarifying the family hierarchy were used (Minuchin *et al.*, 1978). Techniques from social learning theory such as problem-solving and communications skills training were also employed (Robin and Foster, 1989). The individual therapy programme aimed to improve the youngster's ego strength, coping strategies, and individuation from the family of origin and provide insight into the links between eating patterns and interpersonal and intrapsychic issues. Support and interpretation and an accepting stance were the principal techniques used (Goodsitt, 1985). In the individual therapy programme, parents met bimonthly with the therapist for psychoeducation and support. All patients underwent a common medical and dietary programme with a paediatrician and dietician. Five patients in the family therapy programme and three patients in the individual therapy programme who were considered to be in acute medical danger were hospitalized at the beginning of the study and were discharged when they reached 80 per cent of their weight.

Immediately after treatment the individual and family therapy groups both showed substantial weight gain and differences between the two groups were negligible. However, a year later, in the family therapy group an effect size of 1.1 occurred indicating that the average case receiving family therapy fared better than 86 per cent of cases that received individual therapy. At one-year follow-up 82 per cent of cases receiving family therapy were judged to be clinically improved in terms of weight gain and menstruation compared with 50 per cent in the individual therapy group. The family therapy group also showed greater improvement in family relationships immediately after therapy compared with cases that received individual therapy. For researcher ratings of the quality of mothers' communication within conflictual family discussions, an effect size of 0.7 occurred in the family therapy group, indicating that the average case treated with family therapy fared better on this variable than 76 per cent of cases that received individual therapy. This study lent support to the argument that family therapy is more effective than individual therapy in promoting sustained weight gains and in improving family functioning.

Le Grange and colleagues at the Maudsley Hospital in London (1992) in an attempt to determine if conjoint family meetings were essential to the effectiveness of family therapy compared the impact of routine family therapy with a family counselling treatment in which the parents on the one hand and the youngster on the other received separate concurrent counselling. Family therapy involved all household members, including on occasion children who had left home and a separated or divorced parent. It was active and directive, and was influenced by the work of Selvini Palazzoli (1978) and Minuchin *et al*. (1978). The therapy was structured in three phases and progressed from the parents assuming responsibility for their child's eating through a middle phase where responsibility for continued weight gain was shifted towards the youngster to a final stage where the focus moved to the issue of adolescent individuation and other non-food-related concerns. Similar issues were addressed in the family counselling programme, but conjoint parent–child sessions were not held. Eight months after the beginning of therapy, there were no significant differences between the groups on the Morgan-Russell scale, the Eating Attitudes Test (Garner *et al*., 1982) and family functioning as assessed by the researcher-rated expressed emotion scales (Vaughn and Leff, 1976) and the self-report Family Adaptability and Cohesion Scales-111 (Olson *et al*., 1985). However, 67 per cent of cases in both groups made clinically significant improvements. Interestingly, poorer outcome on the Morgan-Russell scale was associated with poorer family adjustment scores at the start of treatment. The central conclusion from this study is that family involvement in treatment rather than conjoint family sessions is probably the important feature of family-based therapy.

Russell and colleagues at the Maudsley Hospital in London (1987; Eisler *et al*., 1997) examined the effectiveness of family therapy with eating disorder patients with different prognostic profiles. On discharge from an inpatient refeeding programme the patients were subdivided into four prognostically homogeneous groups according to age of onset of their eating disorder, duration of illness and the presence of bulimic symptoms. The first group included patients with an early onset and short history whose illness began before the age of eighteen and had persisted for less than three years. The second group included patients with an early onset and long history whose illness began before the age of eighteen and had persisted for more than three years. The eating disorders of those in the third group had a late onset, beginning after the age of eighteen. Patients with bulimic symptoms were included in the fourth group. Approximately equal numbers of patients in each of these four subgroups were randomly assigned to either family therapy or individual supportive therapy. Family therapy followed the same format as that outlined for Le Grange *et al*.'s (1992) study. The individual supportive therapy was primarily symptom focused, supportive and educational. It differed from family therapy in that other family members were never included in the sessions.

Since our central concern in this review is with the treatment of adolescents rather than adults, only the results for the two early onset groups from Russell *et al*.'s (1987) study have been tabulated in Table 10.4. The overall clinical improvement rate for the early onset group with a short history of anorexia that received family therapy was 90 per cent following treatment and this was sustained at five years' follow-up. In contrast only

18 per cent of the early onset group with a short history of anorexia who received individual therapy were judged to be clinically improved after treatment and this figure rose to only 54 per cent at five years' follow-up. On the global improvement rating of the Morgan-Russell scale an effect size of 2.0 after treatment and an effect size of 1.0 five years later occurred for the early onset group with a short history of anorexia that received family therapy. This indicates that the average treated case in this group fared better after treatment than 98 per cent of similar cases that received individual therapy and 84 per cent of cases in this group five years later. For the early onset group with a long history of anorexia, improvement rates were poor and differences between cases that received individual and family therapy were negligible. These results from this study showed that for adolescents family therapy was particularly effective where the history of anorexia was less than three years. A detailed account of the findings for the older groups will not be given here since they are irrelevant to this review. However, it will suffice to note that, for late onset anorexia the individual treatment led to better outcomes than family therapy.

From these five studies it may be concluded that outpatient family therapy or family-based treatment programmes of nine to 36 sessions led to sustained weight gain and improvement in psychosocial adjustment from one to five years after treatment and that outcome was best for cases where the history of anorexia was less than three years. Multimodal inpatient therapy and outpatient individual therapy were either less effective or more labour intensive than family therapy.

Bulimia nervosa

Ordman and Kirschenbaum (1985) compared the effects of a fifteen-session manualized comprehensive cognitive behaviour therapy programme with a brief three-session psychoeducational control condition. The comprehensive programme included psychoeducation, self-monitoring, stimulus control, cognitive restructuring and relapse prevention. After treatment for the frequency of bulimic episodes, an effect size of 1.1 occurred in the treatment group indicating that the average treated case fared better than 86 per cent of cases in the control group. For the Eating Attitudes Test (Garner and Garfinkel, 1979) the effect size was 1.6 and for the Symptom Checklist 90 (Derogatis *et al.*, 1973) the effect size was 1.1. Thus the average treated case fared better than 86 per cent or more of cases in the control group on these measures of eating attitudes and psychological adjustment. It may be concluded from this study that a comprehensive programme of cognitive behaviour therapy was effective in reducing the symptoms of bulimia, in altering eating attitudes and in improving psychological adjustment in the short term.

Fairburn *et al.* (1991, 1993) examined the efficacy of cognitive therapy compared with two other types of treatment and also explored persistence of treatment gains. They compared the effects of cognitive behaviour therapy, interpersonal therapy and behaviour therapy for bulimia nervosa and followed up cases a year after treatment. Cognitive behaviour therapy followed the rationale and format outlined earlier in the chapter. Interpersonal psychotherapy helped clients to explore the links between interpersonal and relationship issues and their eating problems (Klerman *et al.*, 1984). Behaviour therapy focused exclusively on self-monitoring the normalization of eating habits. Following treatment, 44 per cent of cases in the cognitive therapy group were improved compared with 36 per cent in the behaviour therapy group and 28 per cent in the interpersonal therapy group. However, at follow-up the interpersonal therapy group fared best with 44 per cent showing clinically significant improvement, compared with 36 per cent in the cognitive behaviour therapy group and 20 per cent in the behaviour therapy group. Fairburn *et al.* (1993) concluded that cognitive behaviour therapy and interpersonal therapy are both effective treatments for bulimia but that the temporal patterning of improvement is different for the two therapies and so probably different mechanisms of change are associated with these two different treatments.

Conclusions

From this review it may be concluded that outpatient family therapy or family-based treatment programmes involving concurrent therapy for parents and adolescents lead to sustained weight gain and improvement in psychosocial adjustment particularly in cases where the history of anorexia is less than three years. Such programmes should span nine to 36 sessions over six to eighteen months. Where an adolescent's weight falls below 75 per cent of ideal weight, outpatient care should be preceded by an inpatient weight restoration programme. Effective family therapy should include psychoeducation to inform parents and adolescents about the risks associated with eating disorders and other relevant information. It should empower the parents to implement a home-based refeeding programme in which they take charge of the adolescent's weight restoration. Once this has occurred, effective family therapy programmes shift the responsibility for maintaining body weight back to the adolescent. This is followed by therapy which focuses on helping the family develop a pattern of organization that promotes age-appropriate individuation for the adolescent. In this penultimate phase of therapy the emphasis moves away from feeding and on to the negotiation of issues such as the levels of privacy, freedom and responsibility appropriate for the adolescent. The final phase of treatment is concerned with the discussion of relapse prevention and disengagement. Multimodal inpatient therapy and outpatient individual therapy are either less effective or more labour intensive than family therapy and so are not the treatment of choice.

For bulimia nervosa, either cognitive behaviour therapy or interpersonal psychotherapy lead to sustained improvement in bulimic symptoms and psychological adjustment. With cognitive behaviour therapy, improvement is rapid and sustained. With interpersonal therapy, improvement occurs gradually over about a year. Effective cognitive behaviour therapy begins with psychoeducation. Patients are helped to map out the binge–purge cycle, to monitor eating patterns and related cognitions and contingencies and use cognitive and behavioural strategies to disrupt the cycle and manage relapses. These strategies include stimulus control techniques which entail avoiding trigger situations or habituating to them through exposure and response prevention routines. A second set of strategies involves using cognitive therapy to help patients interpret potential trigger situations in ways that do not lead to negative affect and bingeing. A third strategy involves helping patients to avoid persisting with bingeing once it starts by coaching them in countering self-deprecatory cognitions and related negative mood states that occur once bingeing starts. Cognitive behaviour therapy programmes conclude with relapse prevention training. Interpersonal therapy in contrast begins by helping patients understand the interpersonal context within which the eating problem occurs. Treatment then focuses on resolving interpersonal difficulties rather than altering eating behaviours or eating-related cognitions. The later phase of interpersonal therapy focuses on managing the interpersonal process of disengagement from the therapy situation.

In terms of service development, agencies providing treatment for eating disorders require versatile staff trained in both family therapy and cognitive behaviour therapy who have access routinely to outpatient facilities but who can have access to inpatient facilities where cases are at medical risk and require hospital-based weight restoration. Referral routes to eating disorder clinics should facilitate early referral since cases with short histories show a better response to therapy.

In terms of research there is a clear need for controlled trials of family therapy, interpersonal therapy and cognitive behaviour therapy with younger patients, particularly younger patients with histories of eating disorders that exceed three years.

ASSESSMENT

Beumont, P., Al-Alami, M. and Touyz, S. (1988). Relevance of a standard measurement of undernutrition to the diagnosis of anorexia nervosa: Use of Quetelet's body mass index (BMI). *International Journal of Eating Disorders*, 7, 399–405.

Cooper, Z. and Fairburn, C. (1987). The Eating Disorder Examination: A semi-structured interview for the assessment of the specific psychopathology of eating disorders. *International Journal of Eating Disorders*, 6, 1–8.

Cooper, P., Osborn, M., Gath, D. and Feggetter, G. (1982). Evaluation of a modified self-report measure of social adjustment. *British Journal of Psychiatry*, 141, 68–75.

Cooper, P., Taylor, M., Cooper, Z. and Fairburn, C. (1987). The development and validation of the Body Shape Questionnaire. *International Journal of Eating Disorders*, 6, 485–94.

Fichter, M., Elton, M., Engel, K. *et al.* (1990). The structured interview for anorexia and bulimia nervosa (SIAB): Development and characteristics of a (semi-) standardized instrument. In M. Fichter (ed.), *Bulimia nervosa: Basic Research Diagnosis and Therapy* (pp. 57–70). Chichester: Wiley.

Garner, D. (1991). *Eating Disorder Inventory-2 (EDI-2)*. Psychological Assessment Resources, PO Box 998, Odessa, Florida 33556.

Garner, D., Olmsted, M., Bohr, Y. and Garfinkel, P. (1982). The Eating Attitudes Test, psychometric features and clinical correlates. *Psychological Medicine*, 12, 871–8.

Hawkins, R. and Clement, P. (1980). Development and construct validation of a self-report measure of binge eating tendencies. *Addictive Behaviours*, 5, 219–26.

Maloney, M., McGuire, J. and Daniels, S. (1988). Reliability testing of the Children's Version of the Eating Attitudes Test. *Journal of the American Academy of Child and Adolescent Psychiatry*, 27, 541–3.

Morgan, A. and Hayward, A. (1988). Clinical assessment of anorexia nervosa: the Morgan Russell outcome assessment schedule. *British Journal of Psychiatry*, 152, 367–71.

Palmer, R., Christie, M., Cordle, C. and Kendrick, J. (1987). The clinical eating disorder rating instrument (CEDRI): A preliminary description. *International Journal of Eating Disorders*, 6, 9–16.

Rolland-Cachera, M., Cole, T. *et al.* (1991). Body mass index variations: Centiles from birth to 87 years. *European Journal of Clinical Nutrition*, 45, 13–27.

Slade, P. and Dewey, M. (1986). Development and preliminary validation of SCANS: A screening instrument for identifying individuals at risk of developing anorexia and bulimia nervosa. *International Journal of Eating Disorders*, 5, 517–38.

Slade, P., Dewey, M., Kiemle, G. and Newton, T. (1990). Update on SCANS: A screening instrument for identifying individuals at risk of developing an eating disorder. *International Journal of Eating Disorders*, 9, 583–4.

TREATMENT MANUALS AND RESOURCES

American Psychiatric Association (1993). *Practice Guidelines for Eating Disorders*. Washington, DC: APA.

Brownell, K. and Fairburn, C. (1995). *Comprehensive Textbook of Eating Disorders and Obesity*. New York: Guilford.

Fairburn, C. and Wilson, G. (1993). *Binge Eating: Nature Assessment and Treatment*. New York: Guilford.

Garner, D. and Garfinkel, P. (1997). *Handbook of Treatment for Eating Disorders* (Second edition). New York: Guilford.

Lask, B. and Bryant-Waugh, R. (1993). *Childhood Onset Anorexia Nervosa and Related Disorders*. Hove: Lawrence Erlbaum.

Minuchin. S., Rosen, B. and Baker, L. (1978). *Psychosomatic Families*. Cambridge, MA: Harvard University Press.

Szmukler, G., Dare, C. and Treasure, J. (1995). *Handbook of Eating Disorders.* Chichester: Wiley.

Vandereycken, W., Kog, E. and Vanderlinden, J. (1989). *The Family Approach to Disorders: Assessment and Treatment of Anorexia Nervosa and Bulimia.* New York: PMA.

Woodside, B. and Shekter-Wolfson, L. (1991). *Family Approaches in Treatment of Eating Disorders.* Washington, DC: APA Press.

TREATMENT RESOURCES FOR CLIENTS

Cooper, P. (1995). *Bulimia Nervosa and Binge Eating: A Guide to Recovery.* London: Robinson Publishing.

Crisp, A., Joughin, N., Halek, C. and Bower, C. (1996). *Anorexia Nervosa: The Wish to Change. Self-help and Discovery, the Thirty Steps* (Second Edition). Hove: Psychology Press.

Crisp, A. (1980). *Anorexia Nervosa: Let Me Be.* London: Academic Press.

Fairburn, C. (1995). *Overcoming Binge Eating.* New York: Guilford.

Treasure, J. and Schmidt, U. (1993). *Getting Better Bit(e) By Bit(e): A Survival Kit For Sufferers Of Bulimia Nervosa And Binge Eating.* Hove: Lawrence Erlbaum.

Treasure, J. (1997). *Anorexia Nervosa. A Survival Guide For Families, Friends And Sufferers.* Hove: Psychology Press.

11 Paediatric pain problems

Eddie Murphy and Alan Carr

Definitions

Pain

Pain is an aversive and complex multidimensional phenomenon. In involves aversive sensations, negative affect, cognitions about the significance of the aversive experience, behavioural and interpersonal responses associated with the aversive experience often referred to as pain behaviour, and pain may also involve a physiological dimension such as tissue damage or muscle tension (McGrath *et al.*, 1985). The development of the child's concept of pain is affected by both cognitive maturation and the child's experience of pain (McGrath, 1995). Prior to eighteen months children can indicate that they are in pain by crying or simple verbalizations but are unable to conceptualize or verbalize different levels of pain intensity. Rating scales rather than self-report scales are probably the best way to assess changes in pain levels in children at this stage of development (McGrath *et al.*, 1985). Children of eighteen months can verbalize the fact that pain hurts. They can localize pain in their own bodies and they can identify pain in others. They can understand that their experience of pain may be alleviated by asking for medicine or receiving hugs and kisses from carers. They may also try to alleviate pain in others by offering to hug them. At about two years more elaborate descriptions of pain occur and children can more clearly attribute pain to external causes. By three or four years of age children can differentiate between differing intensities and qualities of pain and verbalize these. By three years children are also aware that specific strategies such as distraction may be used to cope with pain. So children at this age may be aware that playing when they have hurt themselves may make them feel better by distracting them from the pain. Between five and seven years children become more proficient at distinguishing between differing levels of pain intensity and may be able to use face scales to indicate fluctuations in pain experiences (Bieri *et al.*, 1990). On face scales, children indicate the intensity of their pain by selecting a face from an array of faces expressing a variety of levels of pain, which most closely reflects their own experience of pain. Between the ages of seven and ten years children can explain why pain hurts and once they reach adolescence they can explain the adaptive value of pain for protecting people from harm.

Somatization

Somatization refers to the expression of psychological distress through somatic symptoms (Campo and Fritsch, 1994; Garralda, 1992, 1996). When children somaticize psychological distress, their somatic symptoms are not fully explicable in terms of organic factors such as infection or tissue damage and it is assumed that psychological factors play a significant role in the etiology or maintenance of their complaints. Single-symptom or multisymptom somatization may occur although multisymptom presentations are the most common. Where multisymptom presentations occur, they typically cluster around a central complaint, the most common of which are headaches and abdominal pains.

Headaches

Where headaches are the chief complaint, they may occur in conjunction with chest pain, breathlessness, a pounding heart and dizziness. A distinction is made between tension headaches and migraine (Andrasik, 1986; Williamson, 1993). Tension headaches are very frequent, bilateral, accompanied by dizziness and are experienced as a tight band, a heavy weight or a fullness in the head. Tension headaches are usually associated with stressful anxiety-provoking situations at home or school. This leads to muscular tension in the muscles of the neck, shoulders and head which in turn leads to pain. Migraine is periodic, severe and unilateral accompanied by a visual aura, nausea, vomiting and photophobia. Migraine attacks usually follow a clear precipitant such as excitement, stress, eating certain foods such as chocolate or cheese, or exposure to stroboscopic effects. For research purposes, Vahlquist's (1955) criteria for childhood migraine are often used. These include having a one-year history of headaches, headache episodes separated by symptom-free intervals and have at least two of the following symptoms: visual or motor aura at the onset of the headaches, throbbing and pulsatile quality of the pain, nausea and/or vomiting. More recently similar criteria have been developed by the International Headache Societies (Abu-Arefeh and Russell, 1994).

Recurrent abdominal pain

In recurrent abdominal pain, repeated stomach aches are the central complaint (Apley, 1975; Bonner and Finney, 1996; Garralda, 1992; Lask and Fosson, 1989; Sanders *et al.*, 1994). For research purposes, Apley and Naish (1958) defined cases of recurrent abdominal pain as those showing three or more episodes severe enough to affect the child's activities, occurring over a period longer than three months in which no specific organic disease was found. Recurrent abdominal pain may occur as part of a wider constellation of somatic complaints including nausea, vomiting, headache, limb or joint pains. Episodes of abdominal pain may vary in length from a few minutes to a couple of hours and the frequency of such episodes may vary from more than one daily to a couple of times a month. Episodes of pain may occur at any time of the day but rarely at night. Sometimes episodes of pain occur in anticipation of separation from parents or going to school. In these instances, it is probable that separation anxiety is the central difficulty.

Distress associated with painful medical procedures

In a paediatric setting clinical psychologists may be asked to consult in cases where children are undergoing painful medical procedures. These include routine injections but also more complex painful procedures such as the management of burns, bone marrow aspirations, lumbar punctures, and surgery. In dental settings, fear of pain associated with drilling and extractions may lead to a referral to psychology (Ioannou, 1991; Lansdown and Sokel, 1993; Sarafino, 1994).

Epidemiology

Headaches

Reviews of epidemiological data concur that headaches are common among children and adolescents (Eminson *et al.*, 1996; Garralda, 1996). A conservative estimate based on community surveys is that occasional headaches occur in up to 70 per cent of children and adolescents and the frequency with which they occur increases with age. Headaches tend to be more common and more severe among girls compared with boys. Severe recurrent headaches may interfere with psychosocial and academic adjustment and so it is not surprising that headaches account for 1–2 per cent of paediatric consultations. A distinction may be made between tension or migraine headaches. Approximately 11 per cent of five to fifteen year olds in a UK community study met the International Headache Societies' diagnostic criteria for migraine (Abu-Arefeh and Russell, 1994). Approximately 30–40 per cent of children show spontaneous remission from headaches within one year.

Recurrent abdominal pain

Recurrent abdominal pain occurs in 10–20 per cent of school-aged children and accounts for 2–4 per cent of paediatric consultations (Apley, 1975;

Bonner and Finney, 1996; Garralda, 1992; Lask and Fosson, 1989; Sanders *et al.*, 1994). It is most common in the five- to twelve-year age group and is equally common among boys and girls.

Painful medical procedures

Bachanas and Roberts (1995) report that each year over 5,000,000 American children undergo aversive medical procedures for the diagnosis and treatment of illnesses. Kuttner *et al.* (1988) note that over time most children do not habituate to these repeated aversive medical procedures and may even become sensitized to such procedures. In addition to the short-term distress associated with aversive medical procedures, paediatric patients recall disturbing memories up to twelve years after treatment has ended (Kazak *et al.*, 1996).

Previous reviews

Kibby *et al.* (1998), in a broad meta-analysis which examined the effects of psychological intervention for children with a variety of chronic medical conditions, concluded that the average treated case fared better at the end of treatment than 86 per cent of untreated cases and these gains were maintained a year after the end of treatment. Children with a variety of painful conditions including headaches, juvenile arthritis, cystic fibrosis and cancer were included in this broad band of meta-analysis. Treatments evaluated in the studies included psychoeducation, relaxation training, contingency management, coping skills training, cognitive restructuring, biofeedback, hypnosis, social skills training and family therapy. In addition to Kibby's broad meta-analysis, a number of narrower focused reviews which specifically address the problems of headaches, recurrent abdominal pain and distress associated with painful medical procedures have also been conducted. These will now be considered.

Headache

Hermann *et al.*'s (1995) meta-analysis of behavioural and pharmacological interventions for paediatric migraine concluded that treatments combining biofeedback and progressive muscle relaxation were significantly more effective than other psychological interventions and pain medication.

Recurrent abdominal pain

In a review of somatoform disorders including recurrent abdominal pain, Fritz *et al.* (1997) concluded that family-based cognitive behavioural therapy was more effective than standard medical care in alleviating recurrent abdominal pain and that gains made during therapy were maintained a year after therapy. The core components of treatment included relaxation training and contingency management.

Painful medical procedures

Ellis *et al.* (1994) in their critical review of cognitive behavioural interventions for children's distress associated with bone marrow aspirations and lumbar punctures concluded that pain medication coupled with behavioural support was the optimal intervention. For less invasive painful medical procedures including injections and venipuncture, Lander and Fowler (1993) concluded that cognitive behavioural techniques were more effective than standard medical care. These techniques include preparatory psychoeducation and modelling; tension reduction through relaxation training, autohypnosis, visualization and desensitization; giving children a degree of control over the procedure and their responses to it by, for example, permitting the child to cry; distraction; cognitive coping through reframing or using self-instructions; contingency management; and parental involvement.

Previous reviews have combined methodologically robust and poorly designed studies in the same review and so there has been confusion about the confidence that may be placed in conclusions reached. In this chapter the aim was to review a selection of particularly well-designed studies so that conclusions about the efficacy of paediatric pain management procedures could be drawn with considerable confidence.

Method

In order to locate appropriate studies an extensive literature search covering the years 1977 to 1997 was undertaken. The major databases PsychLit, CINALH and MEDLINE were searched using combinations of the following terms: *pain, somatization, headache, migraine, recurrent abdominal pain, aversive medical procedures, procedural distress* combined with the terms *pain management, treatment, intervention, psychotherapy, biofeedback, relaxation, behaviour therapy* and other similar terms. This computer search was complemented by a manual search of relevant journals and the bibliographies of review papers in this research area. From over fifty studies identified in this search, eight which focused on the treatment of headaches and migraine; four which dealt with recurrent abdominal pain and nine which assessed the impact of psychological interventions with aversive medical procedures were selected. These studies were representative of the more methodologically robust investigations identified in the search.

Characteristics of the studies

The characteristics of the 21 studies selected for review are given in Table 11.1. Of these, fourteen were conducted in the USA, three in Canada, two in Australia, one in Sweden and one in the Netherlands. All of the studies were conducted between 1981 and 1997. All of the studies were comparative treatment outcome studies and included a control group or condition. Altogether across the 21 studies there were 1,459 children with 940 in psychological treatment groups and 519 children in control groups. Treatment and control group sizes ranged from four to 174. Participants' ages ranged from one to nineteen years and there were almost equal numbers of boys and girls across all 21 studies. With two exceptions, where participants were self-referred, in all studies cases were referred by physicians, usually paediatricians or paediatric specialists. Fifteen of the studies were conducted in outpatient hospital settings, four in inpatient paediatric settings, one in a school and one in a community clinic. Eight of the studies included a behaviour therapy treatment condition; six of the studies included an individual cognitive behavioural intervention; six included some form of distraction; three included biofeedback; one included a family-based cognitive behavioural intervention; one included transcutaneous electrical stimulation; one included hypnosis; and one included play therapy.

Methodological features

Methodological features of the studies included in this review are presented in Table 11.2. All studies included a control group or condition, although in only fourteen were cases randomly assigned to groups. In nineteen studies cases were diagnostically homogeneous and in all studies cases were comparable in terms of demographic characteristics and comorbidity. Pre- and post-treatment assessments were conducted in all studies and follow-up data were collected some months after treatment in eleven studies. In nineteen studies children's self-reports were the main source of data. In six studies parent ratings were obtained and in six research ratings were recorded. Therapist or teacher ratings were not used in any of the studies. In all studies the child's pain symptomatology or procedural distress were assessed but in no study were aspects of the child's social system assessed before and after treatment. Deterioration was assessed in three studies. Drop-out and engagement in further treatment were assessed in one study. In all studies the clinical significance of treatment gains was assessed and in all studies experienced therapists were used and comparative treatments were equally valued by clinicians using them. In only three studies were treatments manualized. In four, therapists received clinical supervision. In only one study was treatment integrity checked. Data on concurrent or subsequent treatment were not given in any of the studies. Taken together, this group of studies was fairly methodologically robust

Table 11.1 Characteristics of treatment outcome studies for headaches, recurrent abdominal pain and anxiety associated with painful medical procedures

Study no.	Authors	Year	Country	N per gp	Mean age & range	Gender	Primary diagnosis or problem	Severity & chronicity	Co-morbid diagnosis	Referral	Treatment setting	Treatment duration
1	Larson and Carlsson	1996	Sweden	RT = 13 C = 13	10–15 y	m 4% f 96%	Tension headache	> 3 per week		Self-referral	School	10 sess over 5 w
2	McGrath et al.	1988	Canada	RT = 32 P = 30 C = 37	13 y 9–7 y	m 30% f 69%	Migraine	> 1 per week for > 3 months	Excluded if IQ < 80	Physician	OP	6 sess over 6 w
3	Wisniewski et al.	1988	USA	RT = 5 C = 5	14 y 10–17 y	m 33% f 67%	Migraine & tension headache	> 1 per week for > 3 months	Excluded if IQ < 70	Physician	OP	8 sess
4	Engel et al.	1992	USA	ART = 5 PRT = 4 ART + PRT = 4 C = 4	17 y 11–21 y	m 35% f 65%	Migraine & tension headache	> 3 per month for > 6 months		Physician	Community	
5	Richter et al.	1986	Canada	CBT = 15 RT = 15 P = 12	13 y 9–18 y	m 33% f 67%	Migraine	> 2 per month	Excluded if IQ < 80	Physician	OP	6 sess over 6 w
6	Osterhaus et al.	1993	Netherlands	BF + RT + CBT = 32 C = 9	12–19 y	m 73% f 27%	Migraine			Self-referral	OP	8 sess, 4 group & 4 individual
7	Fentress et al.	1986	USA	BF + RT = 6 RT = 6 C = 6	10 y 8–12 y	m 39% f 61%	Migraine	> 2 per month		Physician	OP	9 sess over 11 w
8	Labbé and Williamson	1984	USA	BF + ART = 14 C = 14	11 y 7–6 y	m 50% f 50%	Migraine	> 2 per month		Physician	OP	10 sess over 7 w
9	Edwards et al.	1991	USA	RT = 11 DF = 11 Repeated measures design	9 y 6–12 y	m 36% f 74%	Recurrent abdominal pain	> 3 episodes over > 3 months (Apley's criteria)		Physician	OP	10 sess
10	Finney et al.	1989	USA	1. CBT + DF = 16 2. SMC = 16	11 y 6–13 y	m 38% f 62%	Recurrent abdominal pain	> 3 episodes over > 3 months (Apley's criteria)		Physician	OP	3 sess over 2 m
11	Sanders et al.	1989	Australia	CBT = 8 C = 8	9 y 6–12 y		Recurrent abdominal pain	> 3 episodes over > 3 months (Apley's criteria)	Excluded if IQ < 70, NMD or GID	Physician	OP	2 sess with 6 m follow-up

No	Author	Year	Country	Groups	Age	Gender	Condition	> 3 episodes over > 3 months (Apley's criteria)	Excluded if IQ < 70, NMD or GID		Setting	Sessions
12	Sanders et al.	1994	Australia	CBFI = 22 SMC = 22	9 y 7–14 y	m 36% f 64%	Recurrent abdominal pain	> 3 episodes over > 3 months (Apley's criteria)	Excluded if IQ < 70, NMD or GID	Physician	OP	6 sess over 8 w
13	Cohen et al.	1997	USA	NDIS = 32 PDIS = 31 C = 29	4 y 4–6 y	m 52% f 48%	Injection anxiety			Physician	OP	15 min sess
14	Malone	1996	USA	MUS = 20 C = 20	8 y 0–7 y	m 63% f 37%	Injection anxiety			Physician	IP	
15	Vessey et al.	1994	USA	DIS = 50 C = 50	7 y 3–13 y	m 62% f 38%	Venipuncture anxiety				OP	
16	Lander and Fowler	1993	Canada	TENS = 174 DIS = 172 C = 168	11 y 5–17 y	m 51% f 49%	Venipuncture anxiety			Physician	OP	12 min sess
17	Kuttner et al.	1988	USA	HY = 16 DIS = 16 C = 16	7 y 3–10 y	m 63% f 37%	Bone marrow aspiration anxiety			Physician	OP	5–20 min sess
18	Kazak et al.	1996	USA	MED + DIS = 47 MED = 45 C = 70	6 y 4–9 y	m 49% f 51%	Bone marrow aspiration & lumbar puncture anxiety			Physician	IP	3 sess over 2 w & 3 m follow-up
19	Jay et al.	1987	USA	CBT = 18 P = 18 MED = 18	7 y 3–13 y	m 64% f 36%	Bone marrow aspiration anxiety			Physician	OP	30 min sess
20	Rae et al.	1989	USA	TP = 10 DIS = 15 SUP = 10 C = 11	8 y 5–10 y	m 48% f 52%	Surgery anxiety			Physician	IP	2 sess of 30 mins
21	Peterson and Shigetomi	1981	USA	I = 16 CC = 17 M = 16 CC + M = 17	6 y 3–11 y	m 53% f 47%	Tonsillectomy anxiety			Physician	IP	45 min sess

Key RT = Relaxation training. ART = Autogenic relaxation training. PRT = Progressive muscle relaxation training. BF = Biofeedback. AF = Autogenic feedback. CC = Cognitive coping. CBT = Cognitive behaviour therapy. DF = Dietary fibre. FT = Family therapy. CBFI = Cognitive behavioural family intervention. MED = medication to relieve pain. MUS = Musical intervention. TENS = Transcutaneous electrical nerve stimulation. TP = Therapeutic play. SUP = Support. HYP = Hypnosis. DIS = Distraction. NDIS = Nurse led distraction. PDIS = Parent led distraction. I = Information. M = Modelling. SMC = Standard medical care. P = Placebo. C = Control. OP = Outpatient. IP = Inpatient. IF = Intact family. SPF = Single parent family. SES = Socio-economic-status. sess = session. min = minutes. d = day. m = month. y = year. NMD = History of neuromuscular disorder. GID = History of gastrointestinal disorder.

Table 11.2 Methodological features of treatment outcome studies for headaches, recurrent abdominal pain and anxiety associated with painful medical procedures

Feature	Study number																				
	S1	S2	S3	S4	S5	S6	S7	S8	S9	S10	S11	S12	S13	S14	S15	S16	S17	S18	S19	S20	S21
Control group	1	1	1	1	1	1	1	1	1	1	1	1	1	1	1	1	1	1	1	1	1
Random assignment	1	1	0	1	1	0	1	1	0	0	1	1	0	0	1	1	1	1	1	0	1
Diagnostic homogeneity	1	1	0	0	1	1	1	1	1	1	1	1	1	1	1	1	1	1	1	1	1
Comparable for co-morbidity	1	1	1	1	1	1	1	1	1	1	1	1	1	1	1	1	1	1	1	1	1
Demographic similarity	1	1	1	1	1	1	1	1	1	1	1	1	1	1	1	1	1	1	1	1	1
Pre-treatment assessment	1	1	1	1	1	1	1	1	1	1	1	1	1	1	1	1	1	1	1	1	1
Post-treatment assessment	1	1	1	1	1	1	1	1	1	1	1	1	1	1	1	1	1	1	1	1	1
Follow-up assessment	1	1	1	1	1	1	1	0	1	0	1	1	0	0	0	0	0	0	1	0	0
Children's self-report	1	1	1	1	1	1	1	1	0	1	1	1	1	0	1	1	1	1	1	1	1
Parent's ratings	0	0	0	0	0	0	0	0	1	0	1	0	0	0	0	0	0	0	0	1	0
Teacher's ratings	0	0	0	0	0	0	0	0	0	0	0	0	0	0	0	0	0	0	0	0	0
Therapist's ratings	0	0	0	0	0	0	0	0	0	0	0	0	0	0	0	0	0	0	0	0	1
Researcher's ratings	0	0	0	0	0	0	0	0	0	0	0	0	0	0	1	0	0	0	0	0	1
Child's symptom assessed	1	1	1	1	1	1	1	1	1	1	1	1	1	1	1	1	1	1	1	1	1
System assessed	0	0	0	0	0	0	0	0	0	0	0	0	0	0	0	0	0	0	0	0	0
Deterioration assessed	0	0	1	0	0	0	0	1	0	1	0	0	0	0	0	0	0	0	0	0	0
Drop-out assessed	0	0	0	0	0	0	0	0	0	1	0	0	0	0	0	0	0	0	0	0	0
Clinical significance of change assessed	1	1	1	1	1	1	1	1	1	1	1	1	1	1	1	1	1	1	1	1	1
Experienced therapists used	1	1	1	1	1	1	1	1	1	1	1	1	1	1	1	1	1	1	1	1	1
Treatments were equally valued	1	1	1	1	1	1	1	1	1	1	1	1	1	1	1	1	1	1	1	1	1
Treatments were manualized	0	0	1	1	1	0	0	0	0	0	0	1	0	0	0	0	0	0	0	0	0
Therapy supervision was provided	1	0	0	0	0	0	0	0	0	0	0	0	0	0	0	0	1	0	1	1	1
Treatment integrity checked	1	1	1	0	0	0	0	0	0	0	0	0	0	0	0	0	0	0	0	1	0
Data on concurrent treatment given	0	0	0	0	0	0	0	0	0	0	0	0	0	0	0	0	0	0	0	0	0
Data on subsequent treatment given	0	0	0	0	0	0	0	0	0	0	0	0	0	0	0	0	0	0	0	0	0
Total	15	14	15	13	14	12	13	14	13	13	15	14	11	11	13	12	14	12	15	13	14

Key S = study. 1 = design feature was present. 0 = design feature was absent.

and so reliable conclusions may confidently be drawn from a review of their findings.

Substantive findings

Table 11.3 and 11.4 contain summaries of the results of all 21 studies.

Headaches

Of the eight studies on the treatment of headaches, the first four compared the effectiveness of some form of relaxation training with some form of control group and across these four studies children received between six and ten sessions of treatment (Engel *et al.*, 1992; Larson and Carlsson, 1996; McGrath *et al.*, 1988; Wisniewski *et al.*, 1988). Larson and Carlsson (ibid.) compared the effects of group relaxation training with changes in a no-treatment control group. McGrath *et al.* (ibid.) compared pain ratings made by patients who received Cautela and Groden's (1978) relaxation training programme with those who attended a psychological placebo group and an own-best-effort control group. Wisniewski *et al.* (ibid.) compared the effects of Bernstein and Borkovec's (1973) relaxation training method to changes in pain ratings recorded by a waiting list control group. Engel *et al.* (ibid.), in a four-group study, compared the outcome for cases who received autogenic relaxation training; progressive muscle relaxation training; autogenic plus progressive muscle relaxation training with those of a waiting list control group. Cases in Larson and Carlsson's (ibid.) study had tension headaches. Those in McGrath *et al.*'s (ibid.) study had migraine, and cases of both tension headache and migraine were included in the other two studies (Engel *et al.*, 1992; Wisniewski *et al.*, 1988). In all four studies clinical change was assessed with pain diaries in which participants recorded the frequency and intensity of their headaches and their number of headache-free days. In all four studies cases receiving psychological interventions improved more than those in the control group. Effect sizes following treatment ranged from 0.2–1.8 for these four studies, with a mean effect size of 1.2 indicating that the average treated case fared better than 88 per cent of cases in the control groups. For these four studies, rates of clinically significant improvement ranged from 69–80 per cent following treatment. At follow-up three to six months after treatment, in two of the studies containing tension headache cases, rates of clinically significant improvement ranged from 73–92 per cent. However, in McGrath *et al.*'s (ibid.) study of children with migraine an effect size of 0 obtained at follow-up indicated that treated cases fared little better than control group cases in the long term.

The next four studies compared the effects of other forms of treatment – cognitive behaviour therapy packages, biofeedback and autogenic feedback – with either control conditions or relaxation training. These treatment programmes spanned six to ten sessions. In all four of these studies,

Table 11.3 Summary of results of treatment effects for headaches, recurrent abdominal pain and anxiety associated with painful medical procedures

Variable	Headaches										Recurrent abdominal pain							Anxiety associated with painful medical procedures							
Study	S1	S2	S3	S4	S5*	S5*	S6	S7	S7	S8	S9**	S10	S11	S12	S13	S13	S14	S15	S16	S17†	S17††	S18	S19	S20	S21
Treatment	RT	RT	RT	ART	RT	CBT	BF	RT	BF	BF	RT	RT	CBT	CBT	NDIS	PDIS	MUS	DIS	TENS	DIS	HY	DIS	CBT	TP	CC
Comparator	C	P	C	PRT	P	P	RT +CBT	C	C	ART +	C	SMC	C	SMC	C	C	C	C	C	C	C	MED	P	C	M
Relation	> C	> P	> C	> C	> P	> P	> C	> C	> C	> C	> C	> SMC	> C	> SMC	> C	> C	> C	> C	> C	> C	> C	> C	> P	> C	> M
Symptomatic improvement after treatment																									
Children's self-report	1.8	0.2	1.5	–	1.3	1.7	0.5	1.3	1.3	2.8	–	–	1.5	0.8	2.1	1.8	–	0.6	0.2	1.7	1.0	–	0.9	0.5	0.7
Parent's ratings	–	–	–	–	–	–	–	–	–	–	–	–	1.2	0.7	2.2	2.3	–	–	–	–	–	0.9	–	–	–
Teacher's ratings	–	–	–	–	–	–	–	–	–	–	–	–	–	–	–	–	–	–	–	–	–	–	–	–	–
Therapist's ratings	–	–	–	–	–	–	–	–	–	–	–	0.9	1.2	–	1.3	1.2	–	0.5	–	–	–	–	–	–	–
Researcher's ratings	–	–	–	–	–	–	–	–	–	–	–	–	–	–	–	–	1.0	–	–	1.0	0.7	–	1.0	–	0.7

Symptomatic improvement at follow-up

	1.3	0.0	–	1.6	0.9	1.0	0.5	1.3	1.3	–													1.3	0.8								
Children's self-report			–							–	–	–	–	–	–	–	–	–	–	–	–	–	1.3	0.8	–	–	–	–	–	–	–	–
Parent's ratings	–	–	–	–	–	–	–	–	–	–	–	–	–	–	–	–	–	–	–	–	–	–	–	0.0	–	–	–	–	–	–	–	–
Teacher's ratings	–	–	–	–	–	–	–	–	–	–	–	–	–	–	–	–	–	–	–	–	–	–	–	–	–	–	–	–	–	–	–	–
Therapist's ratings	–	–	–	–	–	–	–	–	–	–	–	–	–	–	–	–	–	–	–	–	–	–	–	–	–	–	–	–	–	–	–	–
Researcher's ratings	–	–	–	–	–	–	–	–	–	–	–	–	–	–	–	–	–	–	–	–	–	–	–	1.3	–	–	–	–	–	–	–	–

Positive clinical outcomes

% improved after treatment	69%	80%	–	–	–	–	45%	83%	83%	57%	81%	75%	71%										75%	55%								
	> 8%	> 0%					> 11%	> 33%	> 33%			> 25%	> 38%										> 25%	> 25%								
% improved at follow-up	73%	–	92%	–	–	–	54%	83%	83%	62%	81%	88%	82%										–	–								
	> 27%											> 38%	> 43%																			

Negative clinical outcomes

% Deterioration	–	20%	–	–	–	–	–	–	7%	–	19%	–	–										–	–								
% Drop-out	–	–	–	–	–	–	–	–	–	–	13%	–	–										–	–								
% Engaged in further treatment	–	35%	–	–	–	–	–	–	–	–	19%	38%	43%										–	–								

Key: RT = Relaxation training. ART = Autogenic relaxation training. PRT = Progressive muscle relaxation training. BF = Biofeedback. AF = Autogenic feedback. CC = Cognitive coping. CBT = Cognitive behaviour therapy. CBFI = Cognitive behavioural family intervention. MUS = Musical intervention. TENS = Transcutaneous electrical nerve stimulation. TP = Therapeutic Play. SUP = Support. HYP = Hypnosis. DIS = Distraction. NDIS = Nurse led distraction. PDIS = Parent led distraction. *Results for high severity cases only. **Results for non-constipated cases only. †Results for older children only. ‡Results for younger children in the first session only. ††Results for younger children in the first session only.

Table 11.4 Summary of key findings of treatment outcome studies for headaches, recurrent abdominal pain and anxiety associated with painful medical procedures

Study no.	Primary diagnosis or problem	Authors	Year	Country	N per gp	No of sessions	Group differences	Key findings
1	Tension headache	Larsson and Carlsson	1996	Sweden	1. RT = 13 2. C = 13	10	1 > 2	• Following treatment 69% of cases treated with relaxation showed clinically significant improvement as indexed by a 50% improvement in headache activity compared with 8% of controls. • At 6 months' follow-up 73% of treated cases were clinically improved compared with 27% of untreated controls.
2	Migraine	McGrath et al.	1988	Canada	1. RT = 32 2. P = 30 3. C = 37	6	1 = 2 = 3	• Following treatment and at one-year follow-up, cases who received relaxation training improved no more than those in an attention placebo discussion group and an own-best-effort control group.
3	Migraine and tension headache	Wisniewski et al.	1988	USA	1. RT = 5 2. C = 5	8	1 > 2	• Following treatment 80% of treated cases showed a 50% improvement in headache activity compared with 0% of controls. • At one-month follow-up 67% of cases maintained improvement.
4	Migraine and tension headache	Engel et al.	1992	USA	1. ART = 5 2. PRT = 4 3. ART + PRT = 4 4. C = 4		1 = 2 = 3 > 4	• Following treatment and at four-year follow-up 77% of treated cases reported reduced headache activity.
5	Migraine	Richter et al.	1986	Canada	1. CBT = 15 2. RT = 15 3. P = 12	6	For low severity headaches 1 = 2 = 3 For high severity headaches 1 = 2 > 3	• Following treatment and three months later, low severity cases who received cognitive behaviour therapy and relaxation training improved no more than cases in the attention placebo group. • Following treatment and four months later low severity case in both treatment groups showed more improvement than cases in the control group.
6	Migraine	Osterhaus et al.	1993	Netherlands	1. BF + RT + CBT = 32 2. C = 9	8	1 > 2	• Following treatment 45% of cases treated with biofeedback, relaxation training and cognitive training showed clinically significant improvement compared with 11% of controls.

No.	Condition	Authors	Year	Country	Groups	N	Result	Outcomes
7	Migraine	Fentress et al.	1986	USA	1. BF + RT = 6 2. RT = 6 3. C = 6	9	1 = 2 > 3	• At seven-month follow-up these gains were maintained. • Older girls with a shorter headache history who showed decreases in anxiety over treatment and increases in biofeedback finger temperature control showed the best treatment response.
8	Migraine	Labbé and Williamson	1984	USA	1. BF + ART = 14 2. C = 14	10	1 > 2	• Following treatment and a year later 83% of cases treated with biofeedback and relaxation training or relaxation training alone showed a 50% reduction in headache activity compared with 33% of untreated controls.
9	Recurrent abdominal pain	Edwards et al.	1991	USA	1. RT = 11 2. DF = 11 Repeated measures		For children with constipation 2 > 1 For children without constipation 1 > 2 1 > 2	• Following treatment 93% of treated cases showed a 50% reduction in headache activity compared with 7% of controls. • At six-month follow-up 62% of cases maintained improvement. • Following treatment with dietary fibre 100% of constipated children improved. • Following relaxation training 57% of cases without constipation showed some improvement.
10	Recurrent abdominal pain	Finney et al.	1989	USA	1. CBT + DF = 16 2. SMC = 16	3	1 > 2	• Following cognitive behaviour therapy and increased dietary fibre 81% of cases were symptom free and compared with controls reduced medical services usage.
11	Recurrent abdominal pain	Sanders et al.	1989	Australia	1. CBT = 8 2. C = 8	2	1 > 2	• Treated cases made more rapid improvement compared with untreated cases and three months after therapy 88% of treated cases were pain free compared with 38% of controls.
12	Recurrent abdominal pain	Sanders et al.	1994	Australia	1. CBFI = 22 2. SMC = 22	5	1 > 2	• Cases treated with a cognitive behavioural family intervention had a higher rate of complete elimination of pain after treatment and a lower relapse rate at six and twelve months' follow-up. • Predictors of treatment outcome were initial pain severity, parental acknowledgement of pain followed by distraction of child; parental ignoring pain complaints; and parental prompting independence in management of pain.

Table 11.4 (cont'd)

Study no.	Primary diagnosis or problem	Authors	Year	Country	N per gp	No of sessions	Group differences	Key findings
13	Injection anxiety	Cohen et al.	1997	USA	1. NDIS = 32 2. PDIS = 31 3. C = 29	1	1 = 2 > 3	• Both nurse and parent assisted distraction using a video of a cartoon were more effective than standard medical care in reducing injection anxiety and increasing coping behaviour in preadolescent children.
14	Injection anxiety	Malone	1996	USA	1. MUS = 20 2. C = 20	1	1 > 2	• Distraction through listening to live music was more effective than standard medical care in reducing injection anxiety in preadolescent children.
15	Venipuncture anxiety	Vessey et al.	1994	USA	1. DIS = 50 2. C = 50	1	1 > 2	• Distraction through viewing a kaleidoscope was more effective than standard medical care in reducing venipuncture anxiety in preadolescent children.
16	Venipuncture anxiety	Lander and Fowler	1993	Canada	1. TENS =174 2. DIS =172 3. C = 168	1	1 > 2 > 3	• Transcutaneous electrical nerve stimulation was more effective than distraction and standard medical care in reducing venipuncture anxiety in children and adolescents. • Adolescents showed a better response to treatment than children.
17	Bone marrow aspiration anxiety	Kuttner et al.	1988	USA	1. HYP = 16 2. DIS = 16 3. C = 16	2	For younger children 1 > 2 = 3 For older children 2 > 3 = 1	• Following a single session of hypnotic pain control treatment children under six showed less anxiety during bone marrow aspiration than children trained in distraction or those who received standard medical care. • Following a single session of training in distraction, children between seven and ten years showed less anxiety during bone marrow aspiration than children who received hypnotic treatment or standard medical care.

18	Bone marrow aspiration & lumbar puncture anxiety	Kazak et al.	1996	USA	1. MED + DIS = 47 2. MED = 45 3. C = 70	3	1 > 2 > 3	• Children treated with combined pain medication (midocaine, midazolam and morphine) and parent assisted distraction using various play materials showed lower anxiety during bone marrow aspirations or lumbar puncture than cases who receive pain medication only or standard medical care. • Younger children showed greater distress.
19	Bone marrow aspiration anxiety	Jay et al.	1987	USA	1. CBT = 18 2. P = 18 3. MED = 18 Repeated measures	1	1 > 2 = 3	• Children treated with cognitive behaviour therapy (video-modelling, rehearsal, breathing, distraction, and an incentive trophy) showed less anxiety and distress during bone marrow aspirations than cases treated with a placebo or medication (oral valium). • Younger children showed greater distress.
20	Surgery anxiety	Rae et al.	1989	USA	1. TP = 10 2. DIS = 15 3. SUP = 10 4. C = 11	2	1 > 2 = 3 = 4	• Children who were treated with play therapy prior to surgery showed less surgery anxiety than those who received distraction oriented play, verbal support or standard medical care.
21	Tonsillectomy anxiety	Peterson and Shigetomi	1981	USA	1. I = 16 2. CC = 17 3. M = 16 4. CC + M = 17	1	1 = 2 = 4 > 3	• Children undergoing tonsillectomy given information or treated with cognitive coping skills alone or with modelling training showed less distress than those who received modelling only.

Key RT = Relaxation training. ART = Autogenic relaxation training. PRT = Progressive muscle relaxation training. BF = Biofeedback. AF = Autogenic feedback. CC = Cognitive coping. CBT = Cognitive behaviour therapy. FT = Family therapy. CBFI = Cognitive behavioural family intervention. MED = medication to relieve pain. DF = Dietary fibre. MUS = Musical intervention. TENS = Transcutaneous electrical nerve stimulation. TP = Therapeutic play. SUP = Support. HYP = Hypnosis. DIS = Distraction. NDIS = Nurse led distraction. PDIS = Parent led distraction. I = Information. M = Modelling. SMC = Standard medical care. P = Placebo. C = Control.

participants met Vahlquist's (1955) criteria for childhood migraine having a one-year history of headaches, headache episodes separated by symptom-free intervals and have at least two of the following symptoms: visual or motor aura at the onset of the headaches, throbbing and pulsating quality of the pain, nausea and/or vomiting. Richter *et al.* (1986) compared the effects of a cognitive behavioural package with Cautela and Groden's (1978) relaxation programme and a placebo control group. The cognitive behavioural package included cognitive-restructuring, problem-solving training and stress-inoculation training (Bakal, 1982; Holroyd and Andrasiks, 1978). Osterhaus *et al.* (1993) compared the progress of a group of teenagers with migraine who received a cognitive behavioural therapy package that included cognitive coping skills training, relaxation training and temperature biofeedback with that of a waiting list control group. Fentress *et al.* (1986) compared a programme that entailed frontal EMG biofeedback and relaxation training with a progressive muscle relaxation training condition and a waiting list control group. Labbé and Williamson (1984) compared the effects of a package which included finger skin temperature biofeedback and autogenic relaxation training with gains made by a waiting list control group. Progress in all four of the studies described here was assessed with pain diaries in which participants recorded the frequency and intensity of their headaches and the frequency of their headache-free days.

Overall, cases who received psychological intervention fared better than those who did not. Following treatment, effect sizes for treatment conditions included in these four studies ranged from 0.5 to 2.8, indicating that the average treated case fared better than between 69 and 99 per cent of untreated controls. The largest effect size of 2.8 occurred in Labbé and Williamson's (ibid.) programme which included finger skin temperature biofeedback and autogenic relaxation training. Clinically significant improvement occurred in between 45 and 93 per cent of cases across conditions in these four studies and the best outcomes on this criterion were associated with Labbé and Williamson's programme also. At three to six months' follow-up effect sizes ranged from 0.5–1.3, indicating that at follow-up the average treated case fared batter than 69–90 per cent of untreated controls. Clinically significant improvement was noted in 54–83 per cent of cases. Relaxation training alone or with biofeedback had the best outcome six months after the end of treatment.

A number of variables were found to effect treatment response in these studies. Richter *et al.* (1986) found that only extremely severe cases showed a treatment response and Osterhaus *et al.* (1993) found that older females with a shorter headache history showed a better response to treatment.

Recurrent abdominal pain

Of the four studies concerned with recurrent abdominal pain, the first compared the effectiveness of relaxation training with that of a regime of increased dietary fibre (Edwards *et al.*, 1991) and the second compared the effects of a combination of relaxation training, increased dietary fibre and insistence on school attendance with those of standard medical care (Finney *et al.*, 1989). The other two studies evaluated the impact of a cognitive behavioural treatment package, one of which was exclusively individually based (Sanders *et al.*, 1989) and one of which was family based (Sanders *et al.*, 1994). The family-focused cognitive behavioural programme included psychoeducation, parentally administered contingency management, and pain management skills training covering relaxation and cognitive coping skills. In all studies cases met Apley and Naish's (1958) criteria for recurrent abdominal pain, namely: the pain being paroxysmal in nature, occurring greater than three times over a three-month period and severe enough to interfere with the child's activities of daily living, school attendance or relationships. Pain diaries were used in all four studies to assess the frequency and intensity of abdominal pains.

In all four studies, treatment groups showed statistically significant improvement compared with controls and in the three studies where follow-up data were available, these gains were maintained six to twelve months following treatment. For the multicomponent individually based programmes (Finney *et al.*, ibid.; Sanders *et al.*, 1989) following treatment clinically significant improvement occurred in 75–81 per cent of cases and at three- to six-month follow-up improvement continued to be shown by 81–8 per cent of cases. For the family-based cognitive behavioural programme at the end of treatment 71 per cent of cases were recovered compared with 38 per cent of controls. At one-year follow-up 82 per cent of treated cases were pain free compared with 43 per cent of controls.

A number of factors were found to affect treatment response. Edwards *et al.* (ibid.) found that constipated cases responded to increased dietary fibre alone whereas non-constipated cases responded to relaxation training. Sanders *et al.* (1994) found that response to treatment was associated with both the initial severity of the pain and parental approaches to child management during treatments. Less severe cases and cases in which parents prompted the use of child-coping strategies and did not reinforce pain behaviour responded better to treatment.

Painful medical procedures

Of the nine studies which assessed the effectiveness of psychological interventions in reducing distress associated with painful medical procedures, four included children who had anxiety associated with injections or venipucture procedures (Cohen *et al.*, 1997; Lander and Fowler, 1993; Malone, 1996; Vessey *et al.*, 1994); three included children with leukaemia whose distress was associated with bone marrow aspiration and/or lumbar puncture (Jay *et al.*, 1987; Kazak *et al.*, 1996; Kuttner *et al.*, 1988); and in two studies children were undergoing surgery (Peterson and Shigetomi, 1981; Rae *et al.*, 1989).

In the injection and venipuncture studies, three examined the effectiveness of distraction in reducing procedural distress (Cohen *et al.*, ibid.; Malone ibid.; Vessey *et al.*, ibid.) and one examined the impact of transcutaneous neural stimulation (Lander and Fowler, ibid.). In Cohen *et al.*'s study cartoons were used to distract children from procedural distress, and children were coached in distraction by either a nurse or their parents under the supervision of a nurse. Music was used to distract children in Malone's study and a kaleidoscope was employed in Vessey *et al.*'s study.

Distraction was very effective in reducing injection or venipuncture anxiety. On self-reported pain or distress rating scales and researcher ratings of pain behaviour, effect sizes for distraction ranged from 0.5 to 2.3, indicating that the average treated case experienced less procedural distress than between 69 per cent and 99 per cent of control group cases. The largest effect sizes occurred for parent (2.3) and nurse (2.2) assisted distraction using cartoons (Cohen *et al.*, ibid.). The effect size (0.2) for transcutaneous neural stimulation was far smaller and indicated that treated cases fared better than 58 per cent of cases in control and placebo conditions.

In the bone marrow aspiration studies the distress reducing effects of distraction, hypnosis and cognitive behaviour therapy were examined (Jay *et al.*, ibid.; Kazak *et al.*, ibid.; Kuttner *et al.*, ibid.). In the hypnotic intervention programme examined by Kuttner *et al.* children were helped to become imaginatively involved in a scenario unrelated to the medical procedure and so this was effectively a hypnotically enhanced distraction treatment. Children who participated in Jay *et al.*'s cognitive behavioural programme were shown a filmed model coping with the medical procedure and coached in breathing exercises and the use of imagery as a distraction technique. They were also given opportunities for behavioural rehearsal and positive incentives for coping with the procedures. In all three studies self-report instruments were used to assess pain and distress and in two of the studies parent and/or researcher ratings of pain-related behaviour were recorded (Jay *et al.*; Kuttner *et al.*).

Distraction, training in cognitive behavioural coping strategies and hypnosis were effective in reducing procedural distress for children undergoing bone marrow aspirations. In all three studies significant positive effects for the psychological intervention were observed with effect sizes ranging from 0.7–1.7 indicating that the average treated case fared better than between 76 and 96 per cent of untreated controls. Kuttner *et al.* found that children between three and seven years of age who received the hypnotic treatment showed significantly lower distress scores than those who received the distraction treatment or control group patients. Older children aged seven to ten years showed significant reductions in the distraction treatment condition compared with the control group. In Kazak *et al.*'s study, children in the combined psychological plus pharmacological intervention group were significantly less distressed during bone marrow aspirations than children who received pain medication only or control group cases. Jay *et al.* found that participants in the cognitive behavioural therapy intervention had significantly lower behavioural distress, lower pain ratings and lower pulse rates when compared to children in the control condition.

In the two surgery studies, the distress reducing effects of play therapy, distraction, support and a multicomponent cognitive behaviour therapy package were investigated (Peterson and Shigatomi, 1981; Rae *et al.*, 1989). Rae *et al.* (1989) in a study of children hospitalized for surgery compared the effects of play therapy, distraction and verbal support with the distress shown by a no-treatment control group. Peterson and Shigatomi (1981) in a study of children undergoing elective tonsillectomies, examined the effectiveness of cognitive coping skills training; observing a filmed model coping with surgery; a programme which combined both interventions; and a condition where children were given detailed information about their forthcoming operation. The coping skills training covered cue-controlled deep muscle relaxation (Russell and Sipich, 1974), using distracting mental imagery (Lazarus and Abramovitz, 1962) and engaging in comforting self-talk (Meichenbaum and Goodman, 1971). In both of these studies, specific psychological interventions improved surgery-related pain and distress. Rae *et al.* (ibid.) found that therapeutic play was more effective than distraction or support. Peterson and Shigatomi (ibid.) found that their combined treatment package which included observing a model and coping skills training, the coping skills training programme and the information condition were more effective than the modelling condition.

Conclusion

The evidence reviewed in this chapter supports the view that for children with persistent tension or migraine headaches, recurrent abdomen pain, or distress associated with painful medical procedures, psychological interventions were effective in reducing pain and distress.

For both tension and migraine headaches, relaxation training was a particularly effective treatment. For migraine, additional thermal biofeedback coupled with training in cognitive coping strategies enhanced the impact of relaxation training. Effective treatments spanned six to ten sessions.

For recurrent abdominal pain, both individual and family-based programmes were effective. Individual programmes included relaxation training and coping skills training. Family-based programmes combined these elements with psychoeducation and contingency management. Parents were trained to prompt children to use their pain control skills and to reinforce them for doing so. These programmes were offered over two to ten sessions spanning one to eight weeks.

For managing the pain and anxiety associated with aversive medical procedures such as injections, bone marrow aspirations or surgery, a variety of techniques was effective. Prior to undergoing painful procedures the following interventions were included in effective programmes: psychoeducation, observing a model coping with the procedure, relaxation skills training, cognitive coping skills training, behavioural rehearsal, play therapy and providing incentives to cope with the painful procedures. During painful procedures distraction with stimuli such as cartoons, music, a kaleidoscope or imagery were effective as was imagery-based distraction enhanced through hypnosis. These treatment programmes were offered over one to three sessions and sessions ranged from five to 45 minutes.

In terms of service development, the results of this review highlight the importance of clinical psychologists being attached to paediatric care teams to offer pain management programmes to children referred for headaches, recurrent abdominal pain and to those undergoing painful medical procedures.

Future research on treatment of children with pain problems should focus, among other things on the benefits of parental involvement in administering programmes and encouraging children to use pain management skills (Sanders *et al.*, 1994). The specific role of thermal biofeedback in migraine also deserves further investigation (Labbé and Williamson, 1984).

ASSESSMENT

Bieri, D., Reeve, R., Champion, G. and Addicoat, L. (1990). The faces pain scale for the self-assessment of the severity of pain experienced by children: Development, initial validation and preliminary investigation for ratio scale properties. *Pain*, 41, 139–50.

Blount, R., Cohen, L., Frank, N., Bachanas, P., Smith, A., Manimala, M. and Pate, J. (1997). The Child–Adult Medical Procedure Interaction Scale revised: An assessment of validity. *Journal of Paediatric Psychology*, 22, 73–88.

Elliott, C. and Jay, S. (1987). An observational scale for measuring children's distress during bone marrow aspirations and lumbar punctures: A critical review. *Journal of Pain and Symptom Management*, 9, 96–108.

Goodwin, D., Boggs, S. and Graham Poole, J. (1994). Development and validation of the Paediatric Oncology Quality Of Life Scale. *Psychological Assessment*, 6, 321–8.

Hester, N., Foster, R. and Kristensen, K. (1990). Measurement of pain in children: Generalizability and validity of the pain ladder and the poker chip tool. In D. Tyler and E. Krane (eds), *Paediatric Pain. Advances in Pain Research and Therapy* (Volume 15, pp. 79–84). New York: Raven.

Kazac, A., Penati, B., Waibel, M. and Blackall, G. (1996). The Perception of Procedures Questionnaire (PPQ). Psychometric properties of a brief parent report measure of procedural distress. *Journal of Pediatric Psychology*, 21, 195–207.

Labbé, E., Williamson, D. and Southard, D. (1985). Reliability and validity of children's reports of migraine headache symptoms. *Journal of Psychopathology and Behavioural Assessment*, 7, 375–83.

Le Baron, S. and Zeltzer, L. (1984). Assessment of acute pain and anxiety in children and adolescents by self-reports, observer reports and a behaviour checklist. *Journal of Consulting and Clinical Psychology*, 52, 729–38.

McGrath, P. (1987). The multidimensional assessment and management of recurrent pain syndromes in children. *Behaviour Research and Therapy*, 25, 251–62.

McGrath, P., Johnson, G., Goodman, J., Schillinger, J., Dunn, J. and Chapman, J. (1985). CHEOPS: A behavioural scale for rating post-operative pain in children. In H. Fields, R. Dubner and F. Cerveero (eds), *Advances in Pain Research and Therapy* (Volume 9, pp. 395–401). New York: Raven.

Mindell, J. and Andrasik, F. (1987). Headache classification and factor analysis with a paediatric population. *Headache*, 27, 96–101.

Varni, J., Thompson, K. and Hanson, V. (1987). The Varni-Thompson Paediatric pain Questionnaire: 1. Chronic-musculo-skeletal pain in juvenile rheumatoid arthritis. *Pain*, 28, 27–38.

TREATMENT MANUALS AND RESOURCES

Bernstein, D. and Borkovec, T. (1973). *Progressive Relaxation Training. A Manual for the Helping Professions.* Champaign, Ill: Research Press.

Blanchard, E. and Andrasik, F. (1985). *Management of Chronic Headache. A Psychological Approach.* New York: Pergamon Press.

Cautela, J. and Groden, J. (1978). *Relaxation: A Comprehension Manual for Adults, Children and Children with Special Needs.* Champaign, Ill: Research Press.

McGrath, P. (1990). *Pain In Children: Nature Assessment and Treatment.* New York: Guilford.

Olness, K. and Gardner, G. (1988). *Hypnosis and Hypnotherapy with Children.* Philadelphia, PA: Grune and Stratton.

READING FOR CLIENTS

Davis, M., Robbins-Eshelman, E. and McKay, M. (1988). *The Relaxation and Stress Reduction Workbook* (Third Edition). Oakland, CA: New Harbinger Publications.

McGrath, P., McGrath, P.J., Cunningham, S., Lascelles, M. and Humphries, P. (1990). *Help Yourself: A Treatment for Migraine Headaches.* Ottawa, Canada: University of Ottawa Press.

12 Adjustment to parental separation and divorce

Maria O'Halloran and Alan Carr

Epidemiology

Divorce is no longer considered to be an aberration in the normal family life cycle, but a normative transition for a substantial minority of families (Bray and Hetherington, 1993; Brody *et al.*, 1988). In the US and the UK between a quarter and a third of marriages end in divorce. About two-thirds of these involve children. Nine out of ten cases culminate in the child living with the mother. About three-quarters of divorced men and women remarry and 20–25 per cent of children whose parents have divorced develop long-term adjustment difficulties.

Socio-economic status, urban/rural geographical location, age at marriage, premarital pregnancy, psychological adjustment and parental divorce have all been associated with divorce (Raschke, 1987). Divorce is more common among those from lower socio-economic groups with psychological problems who live in urban areas and who have married before the age of twenty. It is also common where premarital pregnancy has occurred and where parental divorce has occurred. Divorce is less common among those from higher socio-economic groupings without psychological problems who live in rural areas and who have married after the age of 30. Where premarital pregnancy has not occurred and where the couple's parents are still in their first marriage divorce is also less common. The economic resources associated with high SES, the community integration associated with rural living, the psychological resources associated with maturity and the model of marital stability offered by non-divorced parents are the more common explanations given for the links between these factors associated with divorce. The relationship between these various factors and divorce, while consistent, are moderate to weak. That is, there are significant subgroups of people who show some or all of these risk factors but do not divorce.

Effects of divorce on parents

Divorce leads to multiple life changes which affect parental well-being and the impact of these changes on parental well-being is mediated by a range of personal and contextual factors (Bray and Hetherington, 1993; Raschke, 1987). Divorce leads custodial parents to experience major changes in their lives including a change in residential arrangements, economic disadvantage, loneliness associated with social network changes, and role strain associated with the task overload that results from having to care for children and work outside the home. Non-custodial parents experience all of these changes with the exception of role strain. Changes in divorced couples' residential arrangements, economic status, social networks and role demands lead to a deterioration in physical and mental health for the majority of individuals immediately following separation. Mood swings, depression, identity problems, vulnerability to common infections, and exacerbation of previous health problems are all common sequelae for adults who have separated or divorced. However, for most people these health problems abate within two years of the separation.

The stresses and strains of residential changes, economic hardship, role changes and consequent physical and psychological difficulties associated with the immediate aftermath of separation may compromise parents' capacity to cooperate in meeting their children's needs for safety, care, control, education and relationships with each parent (Amato, 1993). Authoritarian-punitive parenting, lax *laissez-faire* or neglectful parenting and chaotic parenting which involves oscillating between both of these extreme styles are not uncommon among both custodial and non-custodial parents who have divorced. Couples vary in the ways in which they coordinate their efforts to parent their children following divorce. Three distinct co-parenting styles have been identified in studies of divorced families (Bray and Hetherington, 1993). With *cooperative parenting* a unified and integrated set of rules and routines about managing the children in both the custodial and non-custodial households is developed. This is the optimal arrangement but occurs in only about one in five cases. With *parallel parenting* each parent has his or her own set of rules for the children and no attempt is made to integrate these. Most children show few adjustment problems when parallel parenting occurs and this is the most common pattern. When *conflictual parenting* occurs, the couple do not communicate directly with each other. All messages are passed through the child and this go-between role, forced upon the child, is highly stressful and entails sustained adjustment problems (Hetherington, 1989).

Effects of parental separation and divorce on children

Parental separation and divorce are major life stressors for all family members. For children, the experiences of separation and divorce may lead to short and longer term adjustment reactions (Amato, 1993; Amato and Keith, 1991a, 1991b, Wallerstein, 1991). During the two-year period immediately following divorce, most children show some adjustment problems. Boys tend to display conduct or externalizing behaviour problems and girls tend to experience emotional or internalizing behaviour problems. Both boys and girls may experience educational problems and relationship difficulties within the family, school and peer group. The mean level of maladjustment has consistently been found to be worse for children of divorce in comparison with those from intact families on a variety of measures of adjustment including conduct difficulties, emotional problems, academic performance, self-esteem and relationships with parents. This has led to the erroneous conclusion by some interpreters of the literature that divorce always has a negative effect on children. When the impact of divorce on children is expressed in terms of the percentages of maladjusted children, it is clear that divorce leads to maladjustment for only a minority of youngsters. A small proportion of individuals from families where divorce has occurred have difficulty making and maintaining stable marital relationships, have psychological adjustment difficulties and attain a lower socio-economic level in comparison with adults who have grown up in intact families.

Factors related to children's post-separation adjustment

Certain characteristics of children and certain features of their social contexts mediate the effects of parental divorce on their adjustment (Amato, 1993; Amato and Keith, 1991a; Hetherington, 1989; Raschke, 1987; Walker, 1993; Wallerstein, 1991). In terms of personal characteristics, males between the ages of three and eighteen are particularly at-risk for post-divorce adjustment problems, especially if they have biological or psychological vulnerabilities. Biological vulnerabilities may result from genetic factors, prenatal and perinatal difficulties, or a history of serious illness or injury. Psychological vulnerabilities may be entailed by low intelligence, a difficult temperament, low self-esteem, an external locus of control, or a history of previous psychological adjustment problems. Specific features of children's families and social networks may render them vulnerable to adjustment difficulties following parental separation or divorce. Children are more likely to develop post-separation difficulties if there have been serious difficulties with the parent–child relationship prior to the separation. Included here are insecure attachment, inconsistent discipline and authoritarian, permissive or neglectful parenting. Exposure to chronic family problems including parental adjustment problems, marital discord, domestic violence, family disorganization, and a history of previous separations and reunions also place children at-risk for post-separation adjustment problems. Early life stresses, such as abuse or bereavement, may also compromise children's capacity to deal with stresses entailed by parental separation. In contrast to these factors that predispose children to post-separation adjustment difficulties, better post-separation adjustment occurs where youngsters have a history of good physical and psychological adjustment and where their families have offered a stable parenting environment.

Following parental separation, adjustment difficulties may be maintained by a variety of psychological factors within the child and a range of psychosocial factors within the child's family and social network (Amato, ibid.; Amato and Keith, ibid.; Hetherington, ibid.; Raschke, ibid.; Walker, ibid.; Wallerstein, ibid.). At a personal level, adjustment problems may be maintained by rigid sets of negative beliefs related to parental separation. These beliefs may include the view that the child caused the separation and has the power to influence parental reunification, or a belief that abandonment by parents and rejection by peers is inevitable. Within the child's family and social network, adjustment problems following separation may be maintained by sustained parental conflict and routine involvement of the child in this ongoing parental acrimony. The use of non-optimal parenting styles, a lack of consistency in parental rules and routines across custodial and non-custodial households, a lack of clarity about new family roles and routines within each household, and confused family communication may all maintain children's post-separation adjustment problems. These parenting and co-parenting problems which maintain children's adjustment difficulties are in turn often a spin-off from parents' personal post-separation adjustment problems. The degree to which parental post-separation problems compromise their capacity to provide a co-parenting environment that minimizes rather than maintains their children's adjustment reactions is partially determined by the stresses parents face in the aftermath of separation. These include the loss of support, financial hardship and social disadvantage.

In contrast to these factors that maintain post-separation adjustment difficulties, better post-separation adjustment occurs in youngsters who have psychological strengths such as high self-esteem, an internal locus of control, realistic beliefs about their parents' separation and divorce, good problem-solving skills and good social skills. In terms of the child's family and social network, better adjustment occurs usually after a two-year period has elapsed, where parental conflict is minimal and not channelled through the child, and where an authoritative parenting style is employed. Where parents cope well with post-separation grief, have good personal psychological resources, and a high level of satisfaction within their new relationships, children show better post-separation adjustment. Parental commitment to resolving child-management difficulties and a track record of coping well with transitions in family life may be viewed as protective factors. The availability of social support for both parents and children from extended family and peers and the absence of financial hardship are also protective factors for post-separation adjustment. Where the school provides a concerned, student-centred, achievement-oriented ethos with a high level of student contact and supervision, children are more likely to show positive adjustment following separation.

The factors discussed in this section have a cumulative effect, with more predisposing and maintaining factors being associated with worse adjustment and more protective factors being associated with better adjustment.

Previous reviews

Lee *et al.* (1994) and Grych and Fincham (1992) in reviews of studies of the effectiveness of child- and parent-focused treatment programmes for children whose parents have divorced concluded that psychological interventions can lead to significant improvements in children's functioning across a range of domains. Child-focused treatment programmes for children whose parents have separated or divorced may aim to provide support; help children to develop realistic beliefs about their parents' separation; and help children to develop good problem-solving and social skills to deal with the practical and social problems entailed by parental separation. Child-focused programmes lead to significant improvements in divorce-related beliefs, self-esteem, and behaviour problems at home and at school. Parent-focused programmes in contrast may aim to provide parents with support and an opportunity to work through the emotional sequelae of separation, so that their intense post-separation experiences do not compromise their capacity to meet their children's needs. Parent-focused programmes may also offer parents training in the management of their children's post-separation emotional and behavioural adjustment problems and help them to maintain positive relationships with their children and improve cooperation with their ex-spouses about coordinating parenting roles. Parent-focused programmes significantly improve parental psychological adjustment and in some instances children's behavioural problems. Unfortunately a methodologically heterogeneous group of studies were covered in both of these reviews by Lee *et al.* (ibid.) and Grych and Fincham (ibid.), so only limited confidence may be placed in these conclusions.

Method

In this chapter the aim was to review methodologically sound treatment outcome studies for children whose parents had separated or divorced and draw reliable conclusions about the effectiveness of child- and parent-focused psychological interventions in helping children adjust to parental separation. A computer-based literature search of the PsychLit database was conducted. The terms *divorce* and *parental separation* were combined with terms that defined interventions such as *treatment, therapy, intervention, support group, behavioural parent training, problem-solving skills training*, and *social skills training*. The search, which was confined to English language journals, covered the period 1977 to 1997 inclusively. A manual search through bibliographies of recent review papers and treatment studies on psychological interventions for children whose parents had divorced or separated was also conducted. Treatment outcome studies were selected for inclusion in this review if they contained a psychological treatment group and a control group; if at least ten cases were included in the active treatment group; and if reliable and valid pre- and post-treatment measures were included in the design of the study. Single-case designs and studies reported in dissertations or convention papers were not included in the review. Using these inclusion and exclusion criteria nine studies were selected.

Characteristics of the studies

A summary of the main characteristics of the nine studies is set out in Table 12.1. The nine studies included in this review were published between 1985 and 1995 and all were conducted in the USA. Six studies evaluated child-focused interventions (Alpert-Gillis *et al.*, 1989; Bornstein *et al.*, 1988; Pedro-Carroll and Cohen, 1985; Pedro-Carroll *et al.*, 1992; Roseby and Deutsch, 1985; Skitka and Frazier, 1995). One study evaluated a parent-focused intervention (Wolchik *et al.*, 1993) and two evaluated combined child- and parent-focused interventions and compared them to single component programmes (Stolberg and Garrison, 1985; Stolberg and Mahler, 1994). Treatment programmes in all studies were based on psychoeducational and cognitive behavioural principles. In all, 709 cases participated in these studies and of these 432 received treatment and 277 were in control groups. Children between the ages of six and fifteen years participated in these nine studies. Approximately 53 per cent of children were female and 47 per cent were male. Ages of divorced mothers ranged from 27–50 years. Families in these studies were from middle- or lower-middle-class backgrounds. Across the nine studies there was some variability in the length of time since parental separation had occurred. This ranged from one year to more than four years. In those studies where information on custody arrangements was given, in the majority of instances mothers had custody of children. Cases in these studies were recruited rather than referred for treatment. However, this should not be taken to mean that the adjustment problems of children in these studies were not significant. For example, Stolberg and Mahler (1994) found that 42 per cent of cases in their study met DSM III criteria for a diagnosis, the most common of which was separation anxiety disorder. Families were recruited into studies from schools, courts, single parent groups, health professionals and through the media, notably school magazines and newsletters. Cases were treated in school settings in seven studies, and in two studies cases were treated in university-based outpatient clinics. All programmes were offered on a group basis and they ranged in duration from six to 24 sessions over six to sixteen weeks. From this overview it may be concluded that these studies focused largely on the impact of outpatient psychoeducational and cognitive behavioural group-based treatment on children residing in a middle-class North American environment following parental separation or divorce.

Table 12.1 Characteristics of treatment outcome studies for children's parental-separation adjustment problems

Study no.	Study type	Authors	Year	N per gp	Mean age & range	Gender	Family characteristics	Referral	Treatment setting	Treatment duration
1	CFI	Skitka and Frazier	1995	C-SUP = 67 C = 28	6–12 y	m 42% f 58%	From rural community	Schools	School	10 sess over 12 w
2	CFI	Roseby and Deutsch	1985	C-SST = 29 PC = 28	9–11 y		Middle class and low SES Separated > 3 y	Schools	School	10 sess over 10 w
3	CFI	Alpert-Gillis et al.	1989	C-SUP + C-PSST = 52 C = 52	7–8 y	m 53% f 47%	Middle class Separated 4 y	Teachers Media	School	16 sess over 16 w
4	CFI	Pedro-Carroll and Cowen	1985	C-SUP + C-PSST = 40 C = 32	8–12 y	m 56% f 44%	Middle class Separated 24 m Caucasian	Schools	School	10 sess over 10 w
5	CFI	Pedro-Carroll et al.	1992	C-SUP + C-PSST + C-SMT = 57 C = 38	9–12 y	m 59% f 41%	Middle class and low SES Separated 5 y	Schools Professionals Media	School	14 sess over 14 w
6	CFI	Bornstein et al.	1988	C-SUP + C-PSST + C-SMT = 15 C = 16	10 y	m 48% f 52%	Separated 1 y	Media Professionals	University OP	6 sess over 6 w
7	PFI	Wolchik et al.	1993	BPT + P-SMT = 34 C = 36	11 y 8–15 y	f 100%	Middle class Mother custodians 1–4 children Separated 2 y	Courts Schools Media	University OP	10 group and 2 individual 2 sess over 12 w
8	P & CI	Stolberg and Garrison	1985	C-SUP + C-PSST = 25 BPT + P-SMT = 11 C-SUP + C-PSST + BPT + P-SMT = 22 C = 24	11 y 7–13 y	m 52% f 48%	Mother custodians 2–3 children Separated < 3 y	Schools SPSG Media	School	24 sess over 12 w (Children 12 sess; Parents 12 sess)
9	P & CFI	Stolberg and Mahler	1994	C-SUP = 23 C-SUP + C-PSST = 28 PT + C-SUP + C-PSST = 29 C = 23	10 y 8–12 y	m 40% f 60%	Middle class 75% mother custodians Separated 2 y	Schools	School	14 group sess over 14 w

Key CFI = Child-focused intervention study. PFI = Parent-focused intervention study. P & CFI = Parent- and child-focused intervention study. C-SUP = Support and psychoeducation for children. C-SST = Social skills training for children. C-PSST = Problem-solving skills training for children. C-SMT = Stress management training for children. BPT = Behavioural parent training. PT = Parent training about children's responses to divorce. P-SMT = Stress management training for parents. C = Control group. OP = Outpatient. SPSG = Single parent support groups. d = day. w = week. m = month. y = year. sess = sessions. SES = Socio-economic status.

Methodological features

The methodological features of the studies are outlined in Table 12.2. All studies were of diagnostically homogeneous treatment and control groups which were evaluated before and after treatment with reliable and valid assessment instruments. In six studies cases or groups of cases from specific schools were randomly assigned to groups. In all but one study cases in treatment and control groups were demographically similar. Only one study published data on the comparability of treatment and control groups for co-morbid diagnosis. All studies included multiple measures of symptomatology completed by some combination of children, parents and teachers. Therapist and researcher ratings that could be used to calculate effect sizes across treatment and control groups were not included in any of the nine studies. Some aspect of the child's social system was evaluated in five studies. Drop-out from treatment was assessed in two studies and the clinical significance of improvements following treatment was evaluated in only one study. In all studies treatments were partially or fully manualized and in five there was evidence that supervision or training was provided. Time spent in training specifically for programme implementation ranged from two hours to three days. Highly experienced therapists delivered interventions in two of the nine studies and in the remainder less experienced therapists or graduate students conducted the treatment programmes. Treatment integrity was checked in one study only. None of the studies gave information on engagement in concurrent or further treatment. From a methodological viewpoint, it may be concluded that the studies reviewed here are basically well designed and so allow reasonably reliable conclusions to be drawn about the types of psychological treatment they evaluated.

Substantive findings

A summary of the effect sizes and improvement rates for the nine studies covered in this review is given in Table 12.3. A narrative account of the main conclusions drawn from each of the studies is presented in Table 12.4. Below, the substantive findings will be considered in two sections with the studies of child-focused interventions being covered first and those of interventions entailing parental involvement being addressed second.

Child-focused interventions

Six of the studies evaluated child-focused interventions only. The interventions ranged in complexity from a simple support group (Skitka and Frazier, 1995), through social skills training (Roseby and Deutsch, 1985), to support coupled with problem-solving skills training (Alpert-Gillis *et al.*, 1989; Pedro-Carroll and Cowen, 1985), and to elaborate programmes which entailed support, problem-solving skills training and stress management training (Bornstein *et al.*, 1988; Pedro-Carroll *et al.*, 1992).

Table 12.2 Methodological features of treatment outcome studies for children's parental-separation adjustment problems

Feature	Study number								
	S1	S2	S3	S4	S5	S6	S7	S8	S9
Control group	1	1	1	1	1	1	1	1	1
Random assignment	0	1	1	1	0	1	1	0	1
Diagnostic homogeneity	0	1	1	1	1	1	0	1	1
Comparable for co-morbidity	0	0	0	0	0	0	0	0	1
Demographic similarity	0	1	1	1	1	1	1	0	1
Pre-treatment assessment	1	1	1	1	1	1	1	1	1
Post-treatment assessment	1	1	1	1	1	1	1	1	1
Three months' follow-up assessment	0	0	0	0	0	0	1	1	1
Children's self-report	1	1	1	1	1	1	1	1	1
Parent's ratings	0	0	0	1	1	1	1	1	1
Teacher's ratings	1	1	1	1	1	1	1	0	1
Therapist's ratings	0	0	0	0	0	0	0	0	0
Researcher's ratings	0	0	0	0	0	0	0	0	0
Child's symptom assessed	1	1	1	1	1	1	1	1	1
System assessed	0	0	0	1	1	1	1	1	0
Deterioration assessed	0	0	0	0	0	0	0	0	0
Drop-out assessed	0	1	0	0	0	0	0	0	1
Clinical significance of change assessed	0	0	0	0	0	0	1	0	1
Experienced therapists used	0	0	0	0	0	0	1	1	0
Treatments were equally valued	0	0	1	0	0	0	0	1	1
Treatments were manualized	1	1	1	1	1	1	1	1	1
Therapy supervision was provided	0	1	1	1	0	0	0	0	1
Treatment integrity checked	0	0	0	0	0	0	0	0	0
Data on concurrent treatment given	0	0	0	0	0	0	0	0	0
Data on subsequent treatment given	0	0	0	0	0	0	0	0	0
Total	7	12	12	13	11	12	14	12	17

Key: S = study. 1 = design feature was present. 0 = design feature was absent.

Table 12.3 Summary of effect sizes from treatment outcome studies for children's parental-separation adjustment problems

Study number and treatment components

Variable	Study 1 C-SUP	Study 2 C-SST	Study 3 C-SUP + C-PSST	Study 4 C-SUP + C-PSST	Study 5 C-SUP + C-PSST + C-SMT	Study 6 C-SUP + C-PSST + C-SMT	Study 7 C-SUP + C-PSST	Study 7 BPT + P-SMT	Study 8 C-SUP + C-PSST	Study 8 BPT + P-SMT	Study 8 C-SUP + C-PSST + BPT + P-SMT	Study 9 C-SUP	Study 9 C-SUP + C-PSST	Study 9 C-SUP + C-PSST + PT
Symptomatic improvement after treatment														
Children's self-report	0.3	0.4	0.6	0.4	0.6	0.0	–	0.7	–	0.0	–	-0.4	-0.3	0.2
Parent's ratings	–	–	0.5	0.9	0.6	0.0	–	0.5	–	–	–	-0.1	0.6	0.3
Teacher's ratings	0.2	0.0	0.0	0.8	-0.3	1.4	–	–	–	–	–	-0.3	0.2	0.0
Therapist's ratings	–	–	–	–	–	–	–	–	–	–	–	–	–	–
Researcher's ratings	–	–	–	–	–	–	–	–	–	–	–	–	–	–
Symptomatic improvement at follow-up														
Children's self-report	–	–	–	–	–	–	–	–	–	–	–	-0.4	0.2	0.2
Parent's ratings	–	–	–	–	–	–	–	–	–	–	–	0.5	0.8	0.6
Teacher's ratings	–	–	–	–	–	–	–	–	–	–	–	-0.4	0.4	0.5
Therapist's ratings	–	–	–	–	–	–	–	–	–	–	–	–	–	–
Researcher's ratings	–	–	–	–	–	–	–	–	–	–	–	–	–	–
Systemic improvement after treatment														
Children's self-esteem	–	–	–	–	–	0.0	0.7	0.0	0.7	0.4	-0.1	–	–	–
Parent's ratings of divorce adjustment	–	–	–	–	–	–	0.0	0.6	0.0	0.3	-0.4	–	–	–
Teacher's ratings	–	–	0.3	–	-0.3	–	–	–	–	–	–	–	–	–
Therapist's ratings	–	–	–	–	–	–	–	–	–	–	–	–	–	–
Researcher's ratings	–	–	–	–	–	–	–	–	–	–	–	–	–	–

Table 12.3 (cont'd)

Variable	Study number and treatment components												
	Study 1	Study 2	Study 3	Study 4	Study 5	Study 6	Study 7	Study 8			Study 9		
	C-SUP	C-SST	C-SUP + C-PSST	C-SUP + C-PSST	C-SUP + C-PSST + C-SMT	C-SUP + C-PSST + C-SMT	BPT + P-SMT	C-SUP + C-PSST	BPT + P-SMT	C-SUP + C-PSST + BPT + P-SMT	C-SUP	C-SUP + C-PSST	C-SUP + C-PSST + PT
Systemic improvement at follow-up													
Children's self-report	–	–	–	–	–	–	–	–	–	–	–	–	–
Parent's ratings	–	–	–	–	–	–	–	–	–	–	–	–	–
Teacher's ratings	–	–	–	–	–	–	–	–	–	–	–	–	–
Therapist's ratings	–	–	–	–	–	–	–	–	–	–	–	–	–
Researcher's ratings	–	–	–	–	–	–	–	–	–	–	–	–	–
Positive clinical outcomes													
% improved after treatment	–	–	–	–	–	–	–	–	–	–	18%	38%	10%
% improved at follow-up	–	–	–	–	–	–	–	–	–	–	70%	36%	21%
Negative clinical outcomes													
% Deterioration	–	–	–	–	–	–	–	–	–	–	–	–	–
% Drop-out	–	19%	–	–	–	–	–	–	–	–	4%	4%	4%
% Engaged in further treatment	–	–	–	–	–	–	–	–	–	–	–	–	–

Key: C-SUP = Support and psychoeducation for children. C-SST = Social skills training for children. C-PSST = Problem-solving skills training for children. C-SMT = Stress management training for children. BPT = Behavioural parent training. PT = Parent training about children's responses to divorce. P-SMT = Stress management training for parents. Improvement rates in Study 9 are based on cases who showed significant psychopathology before treatment.

Table 12.4 Key findings from treatment studies for children's parental-separation adjustment problems

Study no.	Authors	Year	N per gp	Nɔ of sessions	Group differences	Key findings
1	Skitka and Frazier	1995	1. C-SUP = 67 2. C = 28	10	For children 1 = 2	• Children who completed the Rainbows programme fared no better than those in the control group.
2	Roseby and Deutsch	1985	1. C-SST = 29 2. PC = 28	10	For children 1 > 2	• Children in this social skills programme made improvements in school-based adjustment.
3	Alpert-Gillis et al.	1989	1. C-SSUP + C-PSST = 52 2. C = 52	16	For children 1 > 2	• Children in the programme made improvements in home- and school-based adjustment and divorce-related beliefs and coping strategies.
4	Pedro-Carroll and Cowen	1985	1. C-SUP + C-PSST = 40 2. C = 32	10	For children 1 > 2	• Children in the programme made improvements in home- and school-based adjustment and self-reported anxiety.
5	Pedro-Carroll et al.	1992	1. C-SUP + C-PSST + C-SMT = 57 2. C = 38	14	For children 1 > 2	• Children in the programme made improvements in home-based adjustment and divorce-related beliefs and coping strategies.
6	Bornstein et al.	1988	1. C-SUP + C-PSST + C-SMT = 15 2. C =16	6	For children 1 > 2	• Children in the programme made improvements in school-based adjustment.
7	Wolchik et al.	1993	1. BPT + P-SMT = 34 2. C = 36	12	For parents 1 > 2	• The group that received behavioural parent training involving disciplining and listening skills and anger management showed improvements in parent–child relationships, child behaviour problems and maternal mental health.

Table 12.4 (cont'd)

Study No	Authors	Year	N per gp	No of sessions	Group differences	Key findings
8	Stolberg and Garrison	1985	1. C-SUP + C-PSST = 25 2. BPT + P-SMT = 11 3. C-SUP + C-PSST + BPT + P-SMT = 22 4. C = 24	24	For children 1 > 2 > 3 > 4 For parents 2 > 1 > 4 = 3	• Children in the children's support group condition showed greater improvements in self-esteem than other groups after treatment and more improvements in social skills on the CBCL at five months' follow-up than other groups. • Parents in the single parents support group showed better post-divorce adjustment following treatment than other groups.
9	Stolberg and Mahler	1994	1. C-SUP = 23 2. C-SUP + C-PSST = 28 3. PT + C-SUP + C-PSST = 29 4. C = 23	14	For children's behaviour 2 > 3 = 1 = 4 For children's trait anxiety 3 > 2 = 1 = 4 For children poorly adjusted at pre-test 1 > 2 = 3 = 4	• For CBCL internalizing, externalizing and total scores, the skills and support group was better adjusted at post-testing and this group and the parent training, skills and support was better adjusted at follow-up. • For trait anxiety, the parent training skills and support was better adjusted at follow-up. • For children with significant clinical problems at pre-treatment, greatest gains were made by the support group. • At one-year follow-up all groups were as well adjusted as normal controls.

Skitka and Frazier (1995) evaluated The Rainbows for Children programme which is a well-structured supportive intervention and comes with workbooks, manuals and other materials. It is a highly popular programme and in 1995 over 100,000 children had been through the programme in the USA. The major assumption underlying the Rainbows programme is that for children whose parents have separated or divorced, adjustment problems, particularly low self-esteem and depression, will improve once problematic beliefs about separation and divorce are addressed through thematic discussion, expression of divorce-related beliefs and games that facilitate this process. Skitka and Frazier (1995) found that compared with the control group, negligible gains were made by the treatment group of six to twelve year olds on the Children's Beliefs About Parental Divorce Scale (Kurdek, 1987, d = 0.3) and the Behavioural Academic Self-Esteem Scale completed by children's teachers (Coopersmith and Gilbert, 1982, d = 0.2). There was no evidence that the Rainbows programme was effective in promoting better adjustment in children following parental separation or divorce.

Roseby and Deutsch (1985) evaluated a social skills training programme that included assertiveness and communications skills training along with role-playing scenarios involving divorce-related themes. The programme was based on Selman's (1980) Social-Role Taking theory. Compared with a discussion control group, Roseby and Deutsch (1985) found that the social skills training group of nine to eleven year olds showed statistically significant improvement on the Children's Attitude Toward Parental Separation Inventory (Berg and Kelly, 1979, d = 0.4), but not the Devereux Elementary School Behaviour Rating Scale (Spivack and Swift, 1967, d = 0).

Alpert-Gillis *et al.* (1989) evaluated the effects of the Children of Divorce Intervention Program with seven to eight year olds and Pedro-Carroll and Cowen (1985) evaluated the effects of a version of the same programme for older children aged eight to twelve years. This highly structured programme contained two core elements: a support component and a problem-solving skills training component. Within the support component the programme fostered group cohesion, facilitated the expression of divorce-related feelings and provided a forum for clarifying misconceptions about divorce and developing positive perception of the self and the family. Within the problem-solving component, children learned a systematic approach to solving divorce-related problems and other life difficulties. The approach involved problem clarification, distinguishing between controllable and uncontrollable problems, generation of alternative solutions, anticipating the consequences of these, selecting the most appropriate, implementing this solution and reviewing the outcome. Instruction, discussion, video-modelling, therapist-modelling, rehearsal, role-play and homework assignment and review were the principal training methods used.

In both of these studies, children in the treatment programme made statistically significant gains for parent-rated adjustment with effect sizes ranging from 0.5–0.9 indicating that the average treated case fared better than between 69 per cent and 82 per cent of untreated children in the control group. For teachers' ratings of reductions in problem behaviour and improvements in adjustment within the school system, effect sizes ranged from 0–0.8, with the largest effect sizes occurring in Pedro-Carroll and Cowen's (1985) study. In this study effect sizes for teacher-rated behaviour and competence ranged from 0.7 to 0.8 indicating that the average treated case fared better than between 76–79 per cent of untreated cases in the control group. For children's self-reported adjustment to divorce, effect sizes ranged from 0.4 to 0.6, with the largest effect size occurring in Alpert-Gillis *et al.*'s (1989) study in which the average treated case fared better than 73 per cent of untreated controls.

In the final two studies of child-focused interventions reviewed here, complex programmes were employed which contained not only support and problem-solving skills training components but also stress management training (Bornstein *et al.*, 1988; Pedro-Carroll *et al.*, 1992). The stress management component aimed to help children develop skills for coping with frustration and anger, two of the main negative mood states experienced by children following parental separation and divorce. Children were trained to identify specific features of the divorce process and their appraisals of these that underpinned their experiences of frustration and anger. They were then trained to control impulses to act out feelings of anger in socially inappropriate ways and coached in the skills required to express anger in socially acceptable ways (Novaco, 1975). Training covered identifying trigger situations, identifying and labelling angry feelings, using self-instructions to alter appraisals and control impulses, using relaxation exercises to reduce arousal, keeping a diary of angry feelings, foreseeing consequences of acting out angry feelings inappropriately, and using congruent and specific *statements* to express anger in appropriate situations.

Both of these studies found that programmes involving support, problem-solving skills training and stress management training had positive effects on children's adjustment. However, the positive effects occurred in different domains in each of the studies. In Pedro-Carroll *et al.*'s (1992) study improvements occurred on self-reported divorce-related distress and parent-reported behaviour problems. In both domains effect sizes of 0.6 were obtained indicating that the average treated case fared better than 73 per cent of untreated controls. However, for teacher-rated improvements significant gains were not made in this study. In contrast to this result, in Bornstein's *et al.*'s (1988) study an effect size of 1.4 for teacher-rated improvement occurred and this showed that the average treated case fared better than 92 per cent of untreated cases in the control group. However, significant gains were not made, in this study, on measures of self-reported or parent-reported adjustment.

Taken together, these six studies show that for children between six and twelve years of age, group-based child-focused intervention programmes of six to sixteen sessions which involve support, problem-solving training, social skills training and stress management training were effective in the short term in facilitating adjustment at home and school and in reducing divorce-related distress. However, supportive interventions without skills training were of little value. The patterning of results across the domains of child, parent and teacher reported improvements is difficult to explain and may be a function of the age of the children, the time lapse between parental separation and entry into the programme, the duration of the programme, the particular instruments used to assess adjustment or a range of contextual factors.

Interventions involving parents

Three studies evaluated interventions that involved parents. One study evaluated a parent-focused intervention (Wolchik *et al.*, 1993) and two evaluated combined child- and parent-focused interventions and compared them to single component programmes (Stolberg and Garrison, 1985; Stolberg and Mahler, 1994).

Wolchik *et al.* (ibid.) evaluated a programme that included both behavioural parent training and stress management training for parents. The behavioural parent training was based on the principles of social learning theory and drew on the programmes developed by Guerney (1977), Patterson (1975) and Forehand and McMahon (1981). Parents were trained to use listening skills to enhance the quality of their relationship with their children, to prompt and reinforce appropriate behaviour, and to use response cost and time-out methods to reduce the frequency of negative behaviour. The stress management programme was similar to that described in the previous section on child-focused interventions, but in this instance the techniques were taught to parents. Much of the programme focused on anger management techniques as outlined by Novaco (1975). The combined intervention was designed to affect mediating variables identified in studies of factors related to post-divorce adjustment problems. The variables were: the quality of the custodial parent–child relationship, contact with the non-custodial parent, interparental conflict, support from non-parental adults, and parental discipline strategies. Instruction, modelling, rehearsal, home practice assignments and review were the principal training methods used in this study.

Wolchik *et al.*'s programme led to significant improvements in child-reported aggression on an early version of the Youth Self-Report Form (Achenbach, 1991, $d = 0.7$); a reduction in behaviour problems on the Child Behaviour Checklist (Achenbach, ibid., $d = 0.5$); and improvements in the quality of parent–child relationships as assessed by the Open Family Communication subscale of the Parent–Adolescent Communication Scale (Barnes and Olson, 1982, $d = 0.6$). A mediational analysis showed that improvements in children's behaviour problems arising from the programme resulted largely from the impact that the programme had on enhancing the quality of the parent–child relationship.

Stolberg and Garrison (1985) compared the effects of three intervention programmes on the adjustment of seven- to thirteen-year-old children whose parents had separated or divorced. One programme was exclusively child-focused; the second was exclusively parent-focused and the third involved a combination of the parent- and child-focused interventions. The child-focused programme included support and problem-solving skills training components similar to those used by Alpert-Gillis *et al.* (1989) and Pedro-Carroll and Cowen (1985) which were described in the previous section. The parent-focused programme contained modules on behavioural parent training and stress management training similar to those contained in Wolchik *et al.*'s (1993) study. Each of these programmes was conducted over twelve sessions. For the combined intervention programme, parents attended twelve sessions and children attended twelve sessions.

Stolberg and Garrison (1995) found that the combined intervention programme was of little value and participants made negligible progress on a range of parent and child report measures of adjustment. However, the parent-focused and child-focused programmes each led to highly significant improvements, but in different domains. Parents in the parent-focused intervention group made significant gains in post-divorce adjustment (Fisher's (1976) Divorce Adjustment Scale, d = 0.4) with the average treated parent faring better than 66 per cent of untreated parents in the control group. Children in the child-focused programme made substantial gains in self-esteem (Piers-Harris (1969) Children's Self-Concept Scale, d = 0.7) and the average treated case fared better after treatment than 76 per cent of un-treated cases in the control group. At five-month follow-up, on the adaptive social skills dimension of the Child Behaviour Checklist (Achenbach, 1991), this group showed substantial improvements (d = 0.6). The average treated child was functioning better than 73 per cent of untreated children.

Stolberg and Mahler (1994) compared the effects of a child-focused support group; a child-focused support group combined with problem-solving skills training; and a child-focused support and problem-solving skills programme combined with parent training which aimed to help children transfer the skills they learned in the programme into their day-to-day lives. The support and problem-solving skills components of the programme were similar to those used by Alpert-Gillis *et al.* (1989) and Pedro-Carroll and Cowen (1985) which were described in the previous section. The precise procedures are documented in the *LeadersGuide* manual (Stolberg *et al.*, 1991). The parent training skills transfer component was conducted over four sessions and involved the use of parent and child workbooks. These workbooks contain guidelines for practising skills learned in the treatment session and outlined exercises that facilitated parent–child communication about divorce-related events.

Stolberg and Mahler (1994) found that after treatment, for parent-reported behaviour problems, on the main scale of the Child Behaviour Checklist (Achenbach, 1991), children in the support and problem-solving skills training programme had made the greatest improvements (d = 0.6). The average case in this programme fared better than 73 per cent of untreated cases in the control group. A year later children from this programme maintained their gains and cases in the combined child and parent treatment programme also showed major improvements in parent-reported behaviour problems (d = 0.6). This group also reported significant reductions in trait anxiety a year after treatment although the effect size was very small (Spielberger, 1973, d = 0.2).

Seventy per cent of children in the child-focused support programme, who had major clinical problems at pre-testing, were clinically improved at one-year follow-up. The support programme was far more effective than the other two programmes in promoting such improvement in children who had serious clinical problems when they entered treatment.

Conclusions

A number of conclusions may be drawn from the review of the nine studies considered in this chapter. First, psychological treatment programmes are effective in helping children and young teenagers deal with the sequelae of parental separation and divorce. Second, these programmes have a positive impact on negative mood states, divorce-related beliefs, self-esteem, home-based behaviour problems, school-based behaviour problems and relationships with family members and peers. Third, effective programmes span six to 24 sessions over six to sixteen weeks and may be conducted on a group basis in school or outpatient settings following a structured curriculum by trained and supervised therapists. Fourth, effective psychological intervention programmes include a number of key components, notably supportive psychoeducation, problem-solving skills training, social skills training and stress management training. The supportive psychoeducation component should both provide children with a safe forum within which to express divorce-related feelings and beliefs and also a reliable source of information about the experience of coming to terms with parental separation. The skills training components should equip children with the skills required to manage the psychological and social challenges they face as a result of their parents' separation. Fifth, instruction, discussion, video-modelling, therapist-modelling, rehearsal, role-play and homework assignment and review should be used in conducting skills training. Sixth, the effectiveness of such child-focused programmes may probably be enhanced by including a parallel parent training module. This should focus specifically on training parents in listening and discipline skills to enhance the quality of the parent–child relationship and should also enlist the aid of the parent in helping the child to transfer skills learned in treatment sessions into their day-to-day lives.

In terms of service development, these programmes are probably best conducted as school-based primary prevention programmes with child-focused and parent-focused modules running concurrently by a pair of psychologists or a psychologist and teacher.

A number of unanswered research questions are raised by this review, the most pressing of which is the way in which parent-focused work may be most effectively linked with child-focused work in providing comprehensive intervention programmes for children whose parents have separated or divorced. Of particular importance here is the exploration of ways in which non-custodial parents, especially fathers, may be effectively involved in treatments. There is considerable evidence that the involvement of fathers in family therapy and behavioural parent training enhances treatment effectiveness (Carr, 1997). It may be that the addition of a module for non-custodial fathers to treatment programmes for children with post-divorce adjustment problems would increase treatment effectiveness.

ASSESSMENT

Berg, B. (1979). *Children's Attitudes Toward Parental Separation Inventory.* Dayton, OH: University of Dayton Press.

Bricklin, B. (1990a). *Perception of Relationships Test.* Doylestown, PA: Village.

Bricklin, B. (1990b). *The Bricklin Perceptual Scales: Child Perception of Parent Series* (Revised edition). Doylestown, PA: Village.

Fisher, B. (1976). *Fisher Divorce Adjustment Scale. Manual, Scale and Computer Scoring Programme.* Available from Family Relations Learning Centre, 450 Ord Drive, Boulder, Colorado, 80303-4730.

Kurdek, L. (1987). Children's beliefs about parental divorce scale. Psychometric characteristics and concurrent validity. *Journal of Consulting and Clinical Psychology*, 55, 712–18.

Wolchik, S., Sandler, I., Braver, S. and Fogas, B. (1985). Events of parental divorce: Stressfulness ratings by children, parents and clinicians. *American Journal of Community Psychology*, 14, 59–74.

TREATMENT MANUALS AND RESOURCES

Bornstein, M., Bornstein, P. and Walters, H. (1985). Children of divorce: A group treatment manual for research and application. *Journal of Child and Adolescent Psychotherapy*, 2, 267–73.

Forehand, R. and McMahon, R. (1981). *Helping the Non-compliant Child: A Clinician's Guide to Parent Teaching.* New York: Guilford.

Guerney, B.G. (1977). *Relationships Enhancement: Skill-Training Programs For Therapy, Problem Prevention, and Enrichment.* San Francisco, CA: Jossey-Bass.

Herbert, M. (1996c). *Separation and Divorce: Helping Children Cope.* Leicester: British Psychological Society.

Hildebrand, J. (1988). *Surviving Marital Breakdown. Emotional and Behavioural Problems in Adolescents: A Multidisciplinary Approach to Identification and Management.* Windsor, Berks: NFER Nelson.

Hodges, W. (1986). *Intervention for Children of Divorce*. New York: Wiley.

Novaco, R.A. (1975). *Anger Control: The Development and Evaluation of an Experimental Treatment*. Lexington, MA: D.C. Heath.

Patterson, G. (1975). *Families: Applications of Social Learning to Family Life*. Champaign, Ill: Research Press.

Pedro-Carroll, J. (1989). Children of Divorce Intervention Programme (CODIP). Available from Dr Pedro-Carroll, Centre for Community Studies, University of Rochester, 575 Mt Hope Avenue, Rochester, New York 14620, USA.

Rice, J. and Rice, D. (1985). *Living Through Divorce: A Developmental Approach to Divorce Therapy*. New York: Guilford.

Stolberg, A., Zacharias, M. and Complair, C. (1991). *Children of Divorce: LeadsersGuide, KidsBook and ParentsBook*. Circle Pines, MN: American Guidance Service.

RESOURCES FOR CLIENTS

Althea (1980). *I Have Two Homes*. Cambridge: Dinosaur Publications.

Anderson, H. and Anderson, G. (1981). *Mom and Dad are Divorced But I'm Not. Parenting After Divorce*. Chicago: Nelson Hall.

Burgoyne, J. (1984). *Breaking Even: Divorce, Your Children and You*. Harmondsworth: Penguin.

Burrett, J. (1991). *To and Fro Children: A guide to successful parenting after divorce*. London: Thorsons.

Ives, S. and Fassler, D. (1985). *Changing Families: A Guide for Kids and Grownups*. Burlington, VT: Waterfront Books.

Ives, S. and Fassler, D. (1985). *The Divorce Workbook: A Guide for Kids and Families*. Burlington, VT: Waterfront Books.

LeShan, E. (1986). *What's Going to Happen to me: When Parents Separate or Divorce* (Revised edition). New York: Macmillan.

Magid, D. and Schriebman, W. (1980). *Divorce is. . . . A Kid's Colouring Book*. Gretna, LA: Pelican.

Rainbow Collection Catalogue gives up-to-date lists of literature and audio-visual aids to help children, families and schools deal with grief-related problems. Available from 447 Hannah Branch Road, Burnsville, NC 28714, USA.

Salk, L. (1978). *What Every Child would Like his Parents to know about Divorce*. New York: Harper and Row.

Shepard, M. and Soldma, G. (1979). *Divorced Dads. Their Kids, Ex-wives and New Lives*. New York: Berkeley.

Wallerstein, J. and Kelly, J. (1980). *Surviving the Break-up*. London: Grant McIntyre.

13 Conclusions

Alan Carr

The conclusions drawn in this chapter are based on the results of over 150 controlled studies containing more than 5,000 cases who received well-specified psychological interventions. For each of the eleven main problem areas listed below six or more studies containing more than 200 cases were reviewed. Each group of studies contained the most methodologically robust investigations that could be located through computer and manual literature search methods of English language journals for the period 1977 to 1997. The areas covered were:

- Child abuse and neglect
- Enuresis and encopresis
- Attention deficit hyperactivity disorder
- Oppositional defiant disorder
- Conduct problems in adolescence
- Drug abuse in adolescence
- Anorexia and bulimia
- Anxiety
- Depression
- Paediatric pain problems
- Adjustment to divorce

What works for child abuse and neglect?

The evidence reviewed in Chapter 2 showed that abused children and their families can benefit from psychological interventions which focus on the child, the parents or the social system within which the abuse occurs. For physical abuse and neglect, three child-focused interventions were particularly effective. These were residential treatment, therapeutic day care and resilient peer therapy. Residential treatment in which the child was placed at a special unit and visited daily by parents provided a protective, supportive and intellectually stimulating context within which positive parent–child interaction was fostered. Therapeutic day care where intellectual stimulation was provided within the context of supportive child–teacher relationships and high staffing levels promoted cognitive and social-emotional development. Resilient peer therapy, where at-risk children were given structured opportunities to be befriended by socially skilled peers enhanced social development.

For non-organic failure to thrive, which may occur as part of a pattern of neglect, multidisciplinary assessment and an intensive child-focused programme which aims to help the child develop regular and appropriate feeding patterns was effective in promoting children's growth.

Effective parent-focused interventions for physical abuse and neglect included behavioural parent training which equipped parents with child management skills and individual cognitive behaviour therapy which helped parents develop the skills required for regulating negative emotional states, notably anger, anxiety and depression.

Effective interventions for the family and wider system within which physical child abuse and neglect occurs entailed coordinated intervention with problematic subsystems based on a clear assessment of interaction patterns that may contribute to abuse or neglect. The aim of such multi-systemic intervention was to restructure relationships within the child's social system so that interaction patterns that contributed to abuse or neglect would not recur. Significant subsystems that required intervention included the child, the parents, the marital subsystem, the extended family, the school system and the wider professional network.

In developing services for families in which physical abuse, neglect or failure to thrive has occurred, programmes that begin with a comprehensive assessment and include parallel parent-focused and child-focused components with adjudicative family sessions should be prioritized. Parent-focused programmes should included training in both child management skills and negative mood regulation skills. They should also provide parents with ongoing social support, and so are probably best offered within a group treatment format. Where the core issue is failure to thrive, training in feeding practices is essential. Child-focused programmes, in contrast, should foster positive relationships between children and therapists and between the children themselves. There is a strong argument for including well-adjusted peers in such groups and pairing each of these with an abused or neglected child. Within such groups, the focus should be on training in self-regulation and social skills and promoting cognitive and linguistic development. Adjunctive family sessions should be used to help parents and children use their new skills to strengthen parent–child attachment and avoid negative patterns of interaction. Methods for preventing attrition should be built into such programmes. For example, the assistance of lay volunteers might be enlisted to transport parents and children to and from the treatment sessions, or sessions might be scheduled in local community centres within walking distance of clients' homes. To maximize the impact of such a programme, given our current state of knowledge, it would probably need to run over a six-month period with two half-day sessions per week during which parents would attend a parent training and support group and children would concurrently attend a therapeutic play group. For such programmes to be practically feasible, at least two therapeutically trained staff would be required, an equipped play room and a parent training room along with adequate administrative support and therapeutic supervision.

For children who have been sexually abused, individual or group therapy over twelve to 36 sessions was effective in promoting adjustment. Such therapy aimed to help youngsters deal with guilt and depression, abuse-related anger, victimization issues, sexuality issues and low self-esteem. It also provided a forum within which to develop assertiveness skills and learn relationship-building skills. In planning such a service it would be essential to precede entry to such a programme with comprehensive assessment and to couple the programme with adjunctive family sessions with the non-abusing parents. Where intrafamilial sexual abuse has occurred, it is essential that the offender live separately from the victim until they have completed a treatment programme and been assessed as being at low risk for reoffending.

What works for enuresis and encopresis?

From the evidence reviewed in Chapter 3, it may be concluded that urine alarm-based programmes were the most effective treatment for enuresis. Parents were centrally involved in the implementation of these programmes in which children learned bladder control by being awakened each time they bedwet by a urine-activated alarm system. Effective urine alarm programmes additionally included a psychoeducational component in which a rationale for treatment and treatment procedures were explained; a contingency management programme where children received rewards for avoiding bedwetting and were not inadvertently reinforced for wetting at night; and some procedure for ensuring that sufficient trials of waking when the bladder was full occurred to ensure that sufficient opportunities for learning occurred.

For encopresis, successful treatment approaches were family based and multimodal. They involved laxative use; increasing the intake of dietary fibre; shaping and maintaining toileting routines through contingency management where the child was rewarded for engaging in such routines; and anal sphincter biofeedback which facilitated learning sphincter control.

Effective programmes for elimination problems were typically offered on an acute care basis over a period of one to twelve one-hour sessions by multidisciplinary teams with input from paediatric medicine or nursing and clinical psychology.

What works for attention deficit hyperactivity disorder?

From the evidence reviewed in Chapter 4, it may be concluded that programmes which involved psychological interventions without pharmacological treatment were unequivocally ineffective. Multimodal programmes in which parent training or family therapy and training in self-regulation skills for children were used as adjuncts to pharmacological treatment of children with methylphenidate were the most effective interventions for youngsters with ADHD.

Parent training focused on helping parents develop the skills to monitor specific positive and negative behaviours; to identify their antecedents and consequences; and to modify targeted positive and negative behaviours by using stimulus control and contingency management techniques. Stimulus control techniques included prompting positive behaviours and preventing children from entering situations that elicit negative behaviours. Contingency management techniques included systematically reinforcing positive target behaviours and arranging for children to experience time-out from reinforcement following negative behaviours.

Family therapy focused on helping families to develop patterns of organization conducive to effective child management. Such patterns of organization included a high level of parental cooperation in problem-solving and child management; a clear intergenerational hierarchy between parents and children; warm supportive family relationships; clear communication; and clear moderately flexible rules, roles and routines.

Training in self-regulation focused largely on coaching children in some or all of the skills required for systematic problem solving. These skills include identifying a problem to be solved; breaking it into a number of solvable sub-problems; tackling these one at a time; listing possible solutions; examining the costs and benefits of these; selecting the most viable solution; implementing this; monitoring progress; evaluating the outcome; rewarding oneself for successful problem solving; modifying unsuccessful solutions; and monitoring the outcomes of these revised problem-solving plans.

In terms of service development, for short-term treatment gains multisystemic interventions involving multicomponent treatment packages combined with low dose stimulant therapy are the treatments of choice. Multicomponent treatment packages should include behavioural parent training, self-instructional training and school-based contingency management elements and span seventeen to 29 sessions over eight to twelve weeks. Low dose methylphenidate stimulant therapy should be based on 0.3 mg/kg body weight.

For effective long-term treatment, it is probable that a chronic care model of service delivery is required. Children with ADHD and their families, within such a model of service delivery, would be offered the option of infrequent but sustained contact with a psychological and paediatric service over the course of childhood and adolescence. It is likely that at transitional points within each yearly cycle (such as entering new school classes each autumn) and at transitional points within the life cycle (such as entering adolescence, changing school or moving house) increased service contact would be required. Intensive summer school day programmes may constitute part of a chronic care model of service delivery.

What works for oppositional defiant disorder?

From the evidence reviewed in Chapter 5 it may be concluded that behavioural parent training combined with child-focused problem-solving skills training, with or without video-modelling conducted over 40 sessions is a particularly effective intervention for children with oppositional defiant disorder. Such combined programmes are more effective than either behavioural parent training alone or child-focused problem-solving skills training alone. Group-based behavioural parent training programmes that include video-modelling are as effective and more cost-efficient than individually based behavioural parent training programmes. Group-based behavioural parent training programmes which do not incorporate video-modelling and programmes that involve video-modelling with minimal therapist contact are quite effective but less so than group-based behavioural parent training programmes that include video-modelling or individually based behavioural parent training programmes. Where a primary caretaker (typically a mother) is receiving little social support from her partner, then including a component to enhance the social support provided by the partner into a routine behavioural parent training programme may greatly enhance the programme's effectiveness. Child-focused problem-solving skills training over fifteen to twenty sessions is effective in the treatment of some cases of oppositional defiant disorder.

These conclusions have implications for service development. Services should be organized so that comprehensive child and family assessment is available for cases referred where preadolescent conduct problems are the central concern. Where it is clear that cases have circumscribed oppositional defiant disorder without other difficulties, group-based behavioural parent training with video-modelling may be offered to parents and child-focused problem-solving training may be offered to children. Each programme should involve ten to twenty sessions over a period of three to six months. Where there is evidence of marital discord both parents should be involved in treatment with the focus being on one parent supporting the other in implementing parenting skills in the home situation. Where parents are single and have poor social support networks, it may be advisable for them to include a potentially supportive member of their social network in the behavioural parenting programme. Where parents cannot engage in treatment, children may be offered child-focused problem-solving training on its own. Where service demands greatly outweigh available resources, cases on the waiting list may be offered video-modelling-based behavioural parent training with minimal therapist contact as a preliminary intervention. Following this intervention cases should be reassessed and if significant behavioural problems are still occurring they should be admitted to a combined

40-session programme of group-based behavioural parent training with video-modelling and child-focused problem-solving training.

What works for conduct problems in adolescence?

For conduct problems in adolescence, the evidence reviewed in Chapter 6 indicates that intensive behavioural parent training, family therapy, multisystemic therapy and treatment fostercare were all effective interventions.

Parent training aims to enhance the functioning of the parental system and in doing so to provide a parenting context which reduces rather than maintains adolescent conduct problems. Effective parent training interventions empower parents to use a set of contingency contracting strategies based on the principles of learning theory to help adolescents increase their prosocial behaviour and reduce their antisocial behaviour.

Family therapy aims to reduce the overall level of disorganization within the adolescent's family and thereby modify chaotic family routines and communication patterns which maintain his or her antisocial behaviour. Family therapy interventions effective with conduct disordered adolescents focus on facilitating high levels of parental cooperation in problem solving around the management of teenagers' problem behaviour; clear intergenerational hierarchies between parents and adolescents; warm supportive family relationships; clear communication; and clear family rules, roles and routines.

Effective multisystemic therapy offers individualized packages of interventions. These are designed to target conduct problem-maintaining factors within the multiple social systems of which the youngster is a member. These multiple systems include the self, the family, the school, the peer group and the community. Multisystemic interventions integrate family therapy with self-regulation skills training for adolescents; school-based educational and recreational interventions; and interagency liaison meetings to coordinate multiagency input.

In treatment fostercare, carefully selected and trained fosterparents in collaboration with a therapist offer adolescents a highly structured fostercare placement over a number of months in a foster family setting. Trained treatment fostercare parents use the principles of social learning theory to resocialize adolescents with extremely antisocial behaviour patterns. Contingency contracting involving reward systems and response cost systems is used. There is a gradual progression from a rigid authoritarian to a flexible authoritative approach in the design and implementation of these systems. This is coupled with parent training for the natural parents of the adolescents, ongoing family therapy for the adolescents and their natural parents, and regular liaison with the adolescents' schools and other involved agencies coordinated by a therapist within the treatment fostercare agency.

With respect to service development, it may be most efficient to offer services for adolescent conduct disorder on a continuum of care (Chamberlain and Rosicky, 1995). Less severe cases may be offered parent training or functional family therapy, up to 40 sessions over a one-year period. Moderately severe cases and those that do not respond to circumscribed family interventions may be offered multisystemic therapy up to twenty hours per month over a period of up to four years. Extremely severe cases and those who are unresponsive to intensive multisystemic therapy may be offered treatment fostercare for a period of up to a year and this may then be followed by ongoing multisystemic intervention. Such a continuum of care service may be developed and managed within a clinical psychology department with referrals coming from multiple sources including the courts and probation departments. It would be essential that such a service involve high levels of supervision and low case loads for front line clinicians because of the high stress load that these cases entail and the consequent risk of therapist burnout.

What works for drug abuse in adolescence?

From the evidence reviewed in Chapter 7 clear conclusions may be drawn about the use of systemic engagement procedures for families reluctant to enter treatment and about the effectiveness of both family therapy and multisystemic family therapy in the treatment of adolescent drug abusers. In the drug abuse treatment field, specialized engagement procedures have been developed because of the frequency with which members of families of drug abusers fail to engage in family therapy. A systemic approach to engagement leads to a higher level of engagement in treatment and to lower drop-out rates than routine engagement procedures. However, a systemic approach to engagement probably does not lead to a greater reduction in drug abuse following treatment. Systemic engagement procedures should span three to eight weeks and may involve numerous phone calls and pre-therapy meetings with various members of the adolescent's family. These meetings should focus on building good working relationships with all family members and reducing their resistance to participating in family-based treatment. Effective engagement procedures involve contacting all significant members of the adolescent's network directly or indirectly, identifying personal goals, and feared outcomes that they may have with respect to the resolution of the adolescent's drug problems and the family therapy associated with this, and then framing invitations for resistant family members to engage in therapy so as to indicate that their goals will be addressed and feared outcomes will be avoided.

Family therapy spanning six to 24 sessions is more effective than traditional individually based interventions for drug abuse such as supportive therapy or social skills training. Family therapy typically involves offering psychoeducation about drug abuse; helping the family to help the adolescent become drug free; offering a forum within which to deal with denial and the creation of a context for a drug-free lifestyle; facilitating family reorganization; and working towards disengagement and relapse prevention.

Multisystemic family therapy spanning twelve to 36 sessions is more effective in the short term than individual or group-based supportive counselling. It is also more effective than parent education in treating adolescent drug abuse. However, it is probably no more effective than family therapy in the short term. However, there are good reasons to believe that in the long term multisystemic family therapy may lead to greater maintenance of treatment gains, since multisystemic family therapy aims to alter drug abuse maintaining factors, not only within the family but also within the individual, the school and the peer group. Where there is clear evidence that factors within the individual or the wider system are maintaining the youngster's drug abuse, a multisystemic approach should be taken. If youngsters have problem-solving, social or self-regulation skills deficits, training in these should be provided. Where school-based factors are contributing to the maintenance of drug abuse, school-based interventions should be offered. Where deviant peer group membership is maintaining drug abuse, alternative peer group activities should be arranged.

In cases where systemic engagement procedures are ineffective in recruiting all family members into therapy alternatives to family therapy may be offered to the adolescent. Where parents resist entry into treatment, one-person family therapy may be offered. One-person family therapy was found in our review to be an effective alternative to routine conjoint family therapy for the treatment of adolescent drug abuse. Family therapy is more effective than drug education for parents, but not more effective than parent training that includes both drug education and a communication and conflict resolution skills training component. Thus where adolescents resist entry into treatment, parent training which involves both drug education and training in communication skills and conflict resolution may be offered.

With respect to service development, the broad approach to treatment outlined above may be offered from community-based outpatient primary care centres. However, in those instances where adolescents have developed physiological dependence, facilities for detoxification on either an inpatient or an outpatient basis should be provided.

What works for whom with anxiety disorders?

From the studies reviewed in Chapter 8 the following conclusions may be drawn about effective treatments for anxiety disorders in children. For darkness phobia, effective treatment programmes should include an individual component which entails self-instructional training focusing on control and competence in managing the dark and relaxation training on the one hand, and a parent training component on the other which coaches parents in how to prompt and reinforce their children's courageous behaviour while not reinforcing anxious behaviour. Effective treatment may usually be completed within three sessions.

For school phobia a six-session family-based behaviour therapy programme is the treatment of choice. Such programmes should include a detailed clarification of the child's problem; discussion of the principal concerns of the child, parents and teacher; development of contingency plans to ensure maintenance of gains once the child returned to school; *in vivo* flooding where the child is returned to school as soon as possible; and follow-up appointments with parents and teachers until the child had been attending without problems for at least six weeks.

For severe anxiety problems including generalized anxiety disorder, separation anxiety and social phobia a combined 24-session programme of individual and family-based cognitive behaviour therapy is the treatment of choice. The individual component of the programme should coach children in how to monitor and challenge anxiety-provoking cognitions about potentially threatening situations; how to use coping self-instructions and relaxation skills to reduce anxiety; and how to use self-reinforcement for consolidating successful coping responses. The family-based treatment component should focus on contingency management, personal anxiety management for parents, and problem-solving and communications skills training for all family members.

For OCD a combined treatment approach that includes clomipramine and a comprehensive sixteen-session cognitive behavioural therapy package is currently the treatment of choice. The cognitive behavioural treatment programme should include psychoeducation, symptom mapping and monitoring, anxiety management training, exposure and response prevention and parent training.

In developing services for children with anxiety disorders account should be taken of their prevalence (2–9 per cent) and the fact that brief outpatient rather than extended inpatient treatment is preferable. The majority of anxiety disorders can be effectively treated in programmes ranging from three to 24 sessions which include both individual therapy for the child and family intervention. Protocols for phobias, generalized anxiety disorder, separation anxiety disorder and OCD have been developed and should be flexibly applied in clinical settings. Currently there are no well-conducted treatment evaluation studies for panic disorder or post-traumatic stress disorder although accounts of clinical work with children (Ollendick *et al.*, 1994b; Yule, 1994) and reviews of carefully conducted evaluation studies with adults (Barlow *et al.*, 1998; Keane, 1998) suggest that programmes like those used in Barrett *et al.*'s (1996) study, with minor modifications, are probably an appropriate basis for treatment. For panic disorder, because bodily sensations associated with normal levels of arousal are typically misinterpreted as catastrophic signs of imminent personal danger, psychoeducation about this process and exposure to internal arousal cues should be incorporated into the treatment of panic disorder. For PTSD, psychoeducation about the condition and exposure to internal and external cues that elicit anxiety should be incorporated into treatment protocols for PTSD.

What works for whom with depression?

From the studies reviewed in Chapter 9 the following conclusions may be drawn. First, with children and adolescents referred for the treatment of clinical depression individually based cognitive behaviour therapy may be effective in alleviating depression and preventing relapse following remission of depressive symptoms. Furthermore, response to cognitive behaviour therapy is more rapid than response to a simple stress management intervention such as relaxation training. However, continued cognitive behavioural treatment following remission for up to a total of twelve sessions is probably important in preventing relapse. Second, for clinical depression, a fourteen-session programme of group-based cognitive behaviour therapy is effective in both the short and long term in alleviating depression in adolescents. Third, there is little long-term advantage to be gained from adding group-based parent training to a programme of group-based cognitive behaviour therapy for clinically depressed adolescents. However, in the short term a combined programme has the benefit of either improving youngsters' home-based adjustment or positively influencing parents' perceptions of their depressed adolescents or both. Fourth, for schoolchildren and adolescents screened for low mood a number of brief ten- to twelve-session group-based programmes conducted over two to three months are effective in modifying depressive symptomatology. These programmes include cognitive behaviour therapy, relaxation training, social skills training, self-instructional training and problem-solving skills training. Fifth, for clinically depressed youngsters referred for treatment, social skills training is no more effective than support group membership. Sixth, for children bereaved through the death of a parent, a six-session programme of family therapy which focuses on family-based grief work may improve both child and parental adjustment in the short and long term.

With respect to service development, the results of this review suggest that it would be valuable to develop community-based psychological intervention services for schoolchildren and adolescents at-risk for depression and also for those with clinical depression referred for treatment. In a small minority of cases, inpatient services for suicidal, psychotic, complex and treatment-resistant cases are essential. Children at-risk for depression may be identified through school screening programmes using self-report instruments such as the Childhood Depression Inventory (Kovacs and Beck, 1977) and also through public health records of untimely parental deaths. For children at-risk for depression identified through school-based screening, brief twelve-session structured group-based intervention programmes in cognitive behaviour therapy, relaxation training, social skills training, self-instructional training or problem-solving skills training may be offered. For those identified as at-risk for depression or other adjustment problems following parental death, brief home-based family therapy may be offered. For cases of clinical depression referred for treatment, either individual or group-based cognitive behaviour therapy programmes of twelve to fourteen sessions may be offered either alone or in conjunction with concurrent parent training.

What works for anorexia and bulimia nervosa?

From the evidence reviewed in Chapter 10 it may be concluded that for adolescents, particularly younger adolescents, with anorexia nervosa, the most effective treatments were family based and involved either family therapy or combined individual therapy or group therapy for adolescent and parent counselling. Key elements of treatment included engagement of the adolescent and parents in treatment; psychoeducation about the nature of anorexia and risks associated with starvation; weight restoration and monitoring; shifting the focus from the nutritional intake to normal psychosocial developmental tasks of adolescence; facilitating the adolescent's individuation and increasing autonomy within the family; and relapse prevention.

For older adolescents with bulimia nervosa, cognitive behaviour therapy was the most effective treatment. Cognitive behaviour therapy involved psychoeducation; self-monitoring; mapping the situational, cognitive, behavioural and affective antecedents and consequences of the binge–purge cycle; challenging the attitudes and beliefs that underpin the bingeing and purging cycle; using stimulus control techniques to regularize eating routines; and problem-solving training.

Effective treatment involved four to eighteen sessions over one to fifteen months and was offered on an outpatient basis. In some instances it was preceded by hospitalization for weight restoration. Hospitalization is essential where medical complications associated with weight loss or bingeing and purging place the youngster at risk.

What works for paediatric pain problems?

The evidence reviewed in Chapter 11 supports the view that for children with persistent tension or migraine headaches; recurrent abdominal pain; or distress associated with painful medical procedures, psychological interventions were effective in reducing pain and distress.

For both tension and migraine headaches, relaxation training was a particularly effective treatment. For migraine, additional thermal biofeedback coupled with training in cognitive coping strategies enhanced the impact of relaxation training. Effective treatments spanned six to ten sessions.

For recurrent abdominal pain, both individual and family-based programmes were effective. Individual programmes included relaxation training and coping skills training. Family-based programmes combined these elements with psychoeducation and contingency management. Parents were trained to prompt children to use their pain control skills and to reinforce them for doing so. These programmes were offered over two to ten sessions spanning one to eight weeks.

For managing the pain and anxiety associated with aversive medical procedures such as injections, bone marrow aspirations or surgery, a variety of techniques are effective. Prior to undergoing painful procedures the following interventions were included in effective programmes: psychoeducation, observing a model coping with the procedure, relaxation skills training, cognitive coping skills training, behavioural rehearsal, play therapy and providing incentives to cope with the painful procedures. During painful procedures distraction with stimuli such as cartoons, music, a kaleidoscope or imagery were effective as was imagery-based distraction enhanced through hypnosis. These treatment programmes were offered over one to three sessions and ranged from five to 45 minutes.

What works for post-divorce adjustment problems?

From the evidence reviewed in Chapter 12, it may be concluded that psychological treatment programmes are effective in helping children and young teenagers deal with the sequelae of parental separation and divorce. These programmes have a positive impact on negative mood states, divorce-related beliefs, self-esteem, home-based behaviour problems, school-based behaviour problems and relationships with family members and peers. Effective programmes span six to 24 sessions over six to sixteen weeks and may be conducted on a group basis in school or outpatient settings following a structured curriculum by trained and supervised therapists. They include a number of key components, notably supportive psychoeducation, problem-solving skills training, social skills training and stress management training. The supportive psychoeducation component should both provide children with a safe forum within which to express divorce-related feelings and beliefs and also a reliable source of information about the experience of coming to terms with parental separation. The skills training components should equip children with the skills required to manage the psychological and social challenges they face as a result of their parents' separation. A range of methods including instruction, discussion, video-modelling, therapist-modelling, rehearsal, role-play and homework assignment and review may be used in conducting skills training. The effectiveness of such child-focused programmes may be enhanced by including a parallel parent training module. This should focus specifically on training parents in listening and discipline skills to enhance the quality of the parent–child relationship and should also enlist the aid of the parent in helping the child to transfer skills learned in treatment sessions into their day-to-day lives.

In terms of service development, these programmes are probably best conducted as school-based primary prevention programmes with child-focused and parent-focused modules run concurrently by a pair of psychologists or a psychologist and teacher.

What does not work?

The evidence reviewed in this volume allows a number of conclusions to be drawn about ineffective approaches to the treatment of problems in childhood and adolescence. What follows are the main conclusions that may be drawn about *what does not work*.

1   **Talking supportively to children about their problems is not an effective treatment in and of itself.** For conversations with children to be therapeutic, they must have a clear theoretical rationale such as skills training or emotional processing and occur within the wider context of treatment programmes that address problem-maintaining interaction patterns in children's social systems including their families, schools, hospitals and involved agencies. This conclusion is particularly important because of the over-emphasis within clinical child psychology on one-to-one child psychotherapy treatment programmes. Such treatments are clearly inappropriate for such problems as wetting, soiling, anorexia, drug abuse and so forth. The evidence reviewed here suggests that all child-focused conversations should have a clear therapeutic rationale and occur as part of a multicomponent treatment package that aims to alter other important variables within the child's bio-psycho-social system. Such variables should be evaluated during multisystemic assessment and specified in a clear, logical multisystemic case formulation.

2   **Providing parents at-risk for child abuse or neglect with non-professional home help is not, alone, an effective method for reducing risk.** Lay therapy, involving home visiting by untrained staff in cases of child abuse and neglect was shown in Chapter 2 to have little impact on parents' anger control and potential for physical child abuse. Non-professional home-visiting programmes may have an adjunctive role to play in a complex multi-component treatment package involving professionally based psychological interventions for parents, children and the wider social network. Such programmes are described in Chapter 2. There is a danger that funding agencies may be attracted for economic reasons to offer non-professionally staffed home-visiting programmes involving home helpers and family support workers as a cheap alternative to professionally staffed child protection programmes. The data reviewed here suggest that this is not a viable way to reduce risk.

3   **An exclusive focus on family intervention to the exclusion of individual therapy is not effective in cases of physical child abuse or neglect.** In Chapter 2 it was shown that eco-behavioural interventions that focus broadly on family relationships and relationships within the wider network were

less effective than carefully structured individual programmes that targeted the child and the abusive parent, or selectively intervened in subsystems of the child's social system to disrupt interaction patterns that placed the child at-risk for further abuse.

4   **An exclusively individual approach to the treatment of adolescent problems, particularly anorexia nervosa and drug abuse, is ineffective.** This conclusion is being highlighted because of the tendency within adolescent clinical psychology to address the issue of individuation by insisting on an individual approach to treatment. For both drug abuse and anorexia nervosa, family-based approaches to intervention are the treatments of choice. Individually based treatments fail to address problem-maintaining patterns of interaction within the adolescent's family and wider social system. Thus, failure to recover or frequent relapses are virtually inevitable following individual treatments.

5   **Individually oriented group-based treatment programmes for adolescents with conduct problems may make them worse.** This is probably because they provide a forum within which adolescents learn skills associated with a deviant antisocial lifestyle. This conclusion is highly significant in view of the fact that there is a strong tradition for treating juvenile delinquents in outpatient group settings, community-based group homes, and group programmes in secure residential detention centres. For such adolescents, family-based therapies or treatment fostercare are the treatments of choice.

6   **In isolation psychological treatment or stimulant treatment for ADHD are ineffective.** An exclusively psychological approach to the treatment of ADHD without concurrent pharmacological treatment with a stimulant such as methylphenidate is extremely ineffective. Also, the pharmacological treatment of ADHD in isolation, without parent training or child-focused self-regulation skills training, is far less effective than the combination of both stimulant treatment and psychological treatment. This conclusion is particularly important because of the polarized position taken by factions that support the exclusive use of one or other type of treatment.

7   **For children and adolescents with all types of psychological problems, the best available treatment does not work for up to one-third of cases.** Up to a third of cases do not respond to the best available psychological treatments. Within this group of non-responders, there are those who remain in therapy but do not benefit from it. There are those who drop out of treatment. Finally there is a subgroup who deteriorate in response to psychological treatments. It is important to highlight this, especially since factors related to non-response, drop-out and deterioration are poorly understood. The research implications of this for process studies will be considered below.

Service development implications of outcome studies

The evidence reviewed in this volume has clear implications for the development of psychological services for children and adolescents. Effective psychological services for children and adolescents may be developed, offered and evaluated by clinical psychologists. Specific effective treatment programmes may be offered for specific problems. Assessment and formulation of presenting problems is therefore a prerequisite for selecting appropriate treatments. Clinical psychologists may take a variety of roles in service delivery. In some instances clinical psychologists may offer complete intervention programmes on a unidisciplinary basis (e.g. in parent training for childhood conduct problems). In others, treatment may be offered on a multidisciplinary basis with psychologists working in a shared care model alongside physicians (e.g. in stimulant treatment, parent training, and child-focused problem-solving training for ADHD). In still other situations, it may be more appropriate for psychologists to work in a managerial or consultative role (e.g. in organizing and delivering training of fosterparents for a treatment fostercare programme for adolescent delinquents).

Clinical psychology and multidisciplinary shared care. For particular problems, ideally clinical psychologists should share the care of clients with colleagues from other disciplines who have expertise unique to those problems. Colleagues from social work, because of their familiarity with legislation and child protection procedures may offer valuable input in the assessment of cases of child abuse and neglect, severe adolescent conduct problems and adjustment problems following divorce. Social work input is also essential where treatment fostercare programmes are being developed, since typically the recruitment and training of fosterparents is managed by social services departments. Colleagues from speech therapy may offer valuable input to the assessment and remediation of co-morbid language problems which are particularly prevalent in cases of ADHD and childhood conduct problems. Dieticians may advise on nutrition and dietary matters in cases of non-organic failure to thrive, recurrent abdominal pain, anorexia and bulimia nervosa. Colleagues from paediatric medicine may offer a medical perspective in cases of enuresis, encopresis, headaches, recurrent abdominal pain, pain and anxiety associated with aversive medical procedures, medical complications of drug abuse, medical complications where depressed children attempt suicide, and stimulant treatment of ADHD. Input from colleagues in child and adolescent psychiatry may also be particularly valuable in cases of ADHD where stimulant treatment is being offered; in cases of depression where adjunctive SSRI treatment is a possibility; in cases of drug abuse where detoxification is being considered; and in cases of anorexia nervosa where hospitalization is necessary. Of course, colleagues from all of the disciplines mentioned above may make valuable inputs to the management of all of the problems reviewed in this volume. However, what have been listed here are highly specific multidisciplinary inputs deserving special consideration.

Organizing services. Services which offer the treatments for the eleven types of problems reviewed in this book could be organized in many ways. One strategy would be to clump together services for cases that have similar broad characteristics, such as chronicity or complexity. Another would be to organize services along a continuum of care. A third strategy would be to organize specific services for specific problems. The approach which we favour takes all three principles into account in organizing services. We suggest that services be offered to the following groups:

- Acute focal childhood and adolescent problems
- Chronic focal childhood problems
- Chronic childhood problems that occur within the context of a multi-problem family
- Adolescent conduct problems (including drug abuse) services on a continuum of care
- Adolescent eating disorders on a continuum of care
- Child sexual abuse

With the exception of the first group of problems which are best dealt with in primary care settings, services in all of these categories are best offered at a secondary or tertiary level.

For acute focal problems, brief outpatient treatment of one to twenty sessions over one to six months could be offered within a primary care context. Such a service would be appropriate for such problem as:

- Enuresis and encopresis
- Headaches
- Recurrent abdominal pain
- Anxiety about pain associated with aversive medical procedures
- Anxiety and depression
- Conduct problems which occur in isolation and are not one aspect of a multiproblem family
- Divorce-related adjustment problems

For chronic problems such as ADHD, it would be useful for clinics to keep a register and offer multidisciplinary treatment within the context of a chronic care model. Intensive psychological treatment would be offered initially along with stimulant treatment and then regular review meetings at monthly or six-weekly intervals throughout childhood and adolescence to monitor medication and to provide booster sessions to parents and children on parenting and problem-solving skills usage.

For chronic childhood conduct problems which occur within the context of a multiproblem family and for multiproblem families in which physical child abuse or neglect have occurred, a comprehensive programme of concurrent treatment for parents and children would be the most efficient way to offer services. While parents attend an outpatient programme on parent training and parent stress management concurrently their children could attend a child-focused programme which addresses the development of self-regulation skills and social skills. Following an initial intensive period of treatment of up to twenty sessions over six months, monthly booster sessions could be provided.

For adolescent conduct problems, including drug abuse, services ideally should be organized on a continuum of care with up to fifty sessions of family therapy over a one-year period being offered to cases with conduct disorders characterized by low levels of severity and chronicity. In contrast severe chronic cases would be offered a one-year programme of treatment fostercare. Cases intermediate between these extremes would be offered multisystemic therapy.

For adolescent eating disorders, services should ideally be organized on a continuum of care with less severe cases of shorter duration receiving outpatient treatment of up to 25 sessions over a one-year period, while severe chronic cases would receive an initial inpatient weight restoration programme.

For adolescents who have been severely sexually abused, up to 50 sessions over a one-year period may be offered on an outpatient basis.

Implications for training, CPE and audit

The evidence reviewed in this volume indicates that specific intervention programmes are effective in the treatment of particular psychological problems in childhood and adolescence. It is essential that clinical psychology training programmes for new clinicians and continuing professional education (CPE) programmes for qualified clinicians offer training in how to implement some or all of these intervention programmes, particularly those appropriate for acute focal problems (Calhoun *et al.*, 1998). Clinical psychology training programmes and CPE programmes should also offer guidance on how to critically evaluate treatment outcome research so that clinicians may keep abreast of new effective treatment approaches. The effectiveness and quality of treatment offered by clinical psychologists should be regularly monitored through service audit to ensure that the outcomes and quality of treatments offered by practitioners in the field closely approximate those of treatments conducted as part of a research programme. The quality of treatment may be audited through the use of treatment integrity checklists, regular supervision and peer review. The effectiveness of treatment may be audited through the routine assessment of treatment outcome using appropriate psychometric instruments and standardized audit forms.

Implications for research on treatment outcome

The evidence reviewed in this volume highlights the need for more and better-designed treatment outcome studies for the problems of children and adolescents. There is a need for future outcome studies to be designed so as to meet the methodological criteria set out in the checklist presented in Chapter 1 and elsewhere (e.g. Kendall and Chambless, 1998). Studies should focus on diagnostically homogenous groups that have the same central problems and do not differ with respect to severity or chronicity of this condition; the presence of co-morbid diagnoses; family characteristics; and demographic characteristics. Cases should be randomly assigned to treatment and control groups and assessed using valid and reliable instruments before and after treatment and six months or a year after the end of treatment.

Instruments that assess the target problem and those that assess significant aspects of the child's social and intrapsychic systems should be used. Such instruments should measure those variables which the treatment aims to change so as to resolve the presenting problem. For example, with childhood conduct problems treated with parent training and child-centred problem-solving skills, it would be valuable to measure changes in both the parents' child management skills and the child's problem-solving skills, since these are the variables which, according to social learning theory, lead to changes in the frequency and intensity of the child's conduct problems.

Ideally parallel forms of assessment instruments should be completed by multiple informants including children, parents, teachers, therapists and researchers. Where this is not possible, instruments should be completed by the most appropriate informants. For example, in studies of depression or pain, the child is the most appropriate informant since the core problem is most salient to the child. In contrast with conduct problems, the most appropriate informants are parents and teachers since they are most likely to give truthful accounts of the child's conduct problems. In other instances, such as anorexia nervosa, therapists or researchers may be best placed to record the youngster's weight.

This review showed that a proportion of cases achieve clinically significant outcomes which may be interpreted in some instances as indicating that the treatment being evaluated was unsuccessful. These include deterioration in the main presenting problem, drop-out from treatment, or engagement in other types of treatment after the experimental treatment trial was over, so it is important that all outcome studies make provision for measuring these outcomes.

A distinction is made between statistical and clinical significance. Treatments which are shown to lead to statistically significant positive changes may not necessarily lead to changes that, from a clinical perspective, would be viewed as significant. For example, if the mean CBCL (Achenbach, 1991) externalizing problem scale T-scores of youngsters with conduct disorder dropped from 75 to 65 as a result of treatment, and the mean of the comparison group remained at 75, from a statistical viewpoint, significant change could be deemed to have occurred, if a t-test showed that the means of the two groups differed at $p < .05$. However, from a clinical perspective, both groups of cases would still have mean scores in the abnormal range (> 63). This example highlights the importance of assessing the clinical significance of change in treatment outcome studies. In addition to cut-off scores on well-standardized instruments, Reliable Change Indices may be used to assess whether or not clinically significant change has occurred (Hageman and Arrindell, 1993; Jacobson *et al.*, 1984). The frequency of cases showing clinically significant change in treatment and control groups should be compared using appropriate non-parametric statistics, such as chi-square or Fisher's exact probability test.

Future treatment outcome studies should take a number of steps to ensure that a *pure and potent* form of the treatment being evaluated is offered to clients. The purity or integrity of treatment may be enhanced by using clearly specified, manualized treatments; by routinely checking that therapists are adhering to the treatment manual; and by providing therapists with an adequate level of supervision so that they may reflect on ways to adhere to the treatment manual in specific cases. Treatment manuals should offer a theoretical framework within which to conceptualize the major components of the treatment process and the main therapeutic tasks; a set of step-by-step procedures for delivering the treatment; and clinical examples of how to manage typical treatment situations. The integrity of treatment may be checked by developing a checklist of therapist activities, which according to the manual, should be present during particular phases of treatment and assessing videotapes of therapy sessions using such checklists. Supervision should offer therapists a chance to review their attempts to adhere to the manual in the treatment of particular cases and to troubleshoot specific problems that are not explicitly covered in the manual. Supervision may also be used to help therapists develop flexible and sensitive ways for matching the procedures in the manual to the needs of particular clients and to avoid insensitive rigidity. These are all essentially quality control procedures.

While manuals, integrity checks and supervision ensure treatment purity, the potency of treatment is determined by the overall training and experience of the therapists; by the degree to which they are committed to the treatment procedures and programme; by the duration of treatment; and the appropriateness of the format used for treatment delivery. Ideally, experienced therapists with formal training or therapy qualifications in the particular therapy being evaluated and a commitment to the model of practice should deliver treatment. Where two treatments are being compared, this condition must be met for each of the conditions. In terms of duration, the length of individual sessions or treatment periods, the number of sessions and the spacing of sessions over time should conform to those required for optimal treatment. The format for treatment delivery should conform to the requirements of the manual and the constraints of the settings in which the treatment will ultimately be offered. So if a multimodal treatment package for children with ADHD is designed so that children receive weekly group-based self-control skills training; parents receive fortnightly group parent training sessions; and children also receive daily methylphenidate in an outpatient community-based setting, then all of these conditions should be met when conducting a controlled trial. If these conditions are not met, then it will not be possible to draw valid conclusions about the potency of the programme when offered in the way specified in the manual.

While there is no doubt that more controlled trials of treatments for all disorders are required, there are certain types of problems and certain treatment modalities that urgently require investigation. The disruptive behaviour disorders, including ODD, conduct disorders and ADHD have been relatively well researched. It is now timely to focus attention and effort on internalizing behaviour problems and the anxiety and mood disorders. Controlled trials of the type conducted by Kendall (1994) and Barrett *et al.* (1996) need to be conducted for all anxiety disorders in children, and there is an urgent need for trials evaluating the treatment of PTSD and panic disorder, building on accounts of clinical practice and the results of controlled treatment trials with adults (Barlow *et al.*, 1998; Keane, 1998; Ollendick *et al.*, 1994b; Yule, 1994). Experimental treatments for PTSD, notably eye movement desensitization, also deserve controlled evaluation with child and adolescent populations. For depression, the priority should be to conduct well-designed controlled clinical trials of manualized individual and family treatments with clinically depressed children and teenagers referred for treatment, rather than with analogue populations. Few such studies have been conducted. There is also an urgent need for trials of similar psychological treatments alone and in combination with newer antidepressant medications such as serotonin re-uptake inhibitors with severely depressed and suicidal children and adolescents. No such studies have been conducted.

Implications for research on treatment processes

While controlled treatment outcome studies are required to answer the question *What works for whom?*, other types of studies are required to throw light on how treatment works and important treatment processes. These studies should focus on factors that predict a positive response to treatment, or to put it another way, the characteristics of successful and unsuccessful cases. Such factors may include characteristics of problems (and the contexts within which they occur); clients (and their networks); therapists (and their networks); and intervention programmes (and their parameters). A framework of such factors is set out in Figure 13.1. Currently process studies of psychological interventions with children and adolescents are in their infancy and process research is sorely needed (Frielander *et al.*, 1994; Kazdin and Weisz, 1998; Shirk and Russell, 1996; Target and Fonagy, 1996).

With respect to variables centrally associated with presenting problems, systematic investigation into the impact of the following on treatment outcome is required: the nature, severity and chronicity of the core problem; the presence of other co-morbid difficulties; the level of the children's and parents' commitment to resolving the presenting problems; the children's and parents' capacity to engage in treatment; and history of previous treatment.

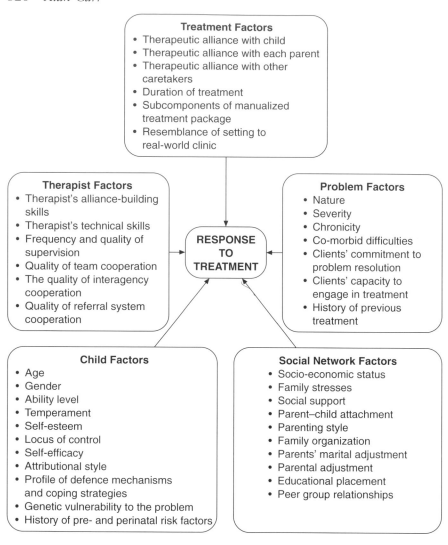

Figure 13.1 Factors associated with response to treatment deserving investigation.

With respect to therapy, the impact of a number of specific variables on therapy outcome require more detailed investigation. First, among these is the quality of the therapeutic alliance between the therapists and the children and that between the therapists and each of the parents or other significant caretakers in the child's network. A second variable in this category requiring investigation in duration of treatment: the so-called dose–effect relationship. For each specific intervention programme, the relative contribution of the various subcomponents of treatment needs to be determined. This will require a clear specification and manualization of treatment components and operational definitions of how specific treatment components are expected to lead to changes in specific variables that maintain presenting problems. For example, if mood problems are presumed, from a theoretical perspective, to be maintained by both family criticism and cognitive distortions, then it must be clearly outlined in the treatment manual how parent counselling targets the former and individual CBT targets the latter. A third variable, the impact of which requires exploration, is the degree to which the context within which clients are referred and treatment is offered resembles a routine real-world clinical setting rather than an experimental university-based context.

Systematic enquiry into the impact of a number of variables associated with the therapist and his or her professional system on treatment outcome is also needed. These include the therapist's skills, specifically those required to build and maintain therapeutic alliances on the one hand and those technical skills necessary to implement the intervention programme on the other. Also included here are the frequency and quality of supervision available to the therapists; the quality of cooperation among members of the team delivering the intervention programme; the quality of interagency cooperation where the programme is offered within a multi-agency context; and the quality of cooperation within the referral system which involves the clients, the referring agent, and the intervention team.

With respect to the broader characteristics of clients, the impact of the following factors on treatment outcome deserve investigation: age, gender, ability level, temperament, self-esteem, locus of control, self-efficacy, attributional style, profile of defence mechanisms and coping strategies, genetic vulnerability to the presenting problem and history of pre- and perinatal risk factors. Investigation into the impact of the following attributes of clients' social networks on treatment outcome is needed: socio-economic status, current and previous individual and family stresses, social support, parent–child attachment, parenting style, family organization, parents' marital adjustment, parental adjustment, educational placement and peer group relationships.

Systematic investigation of the impact of these variables would permit the profiling of treatment-resistant cases, non-responders, those who deteriorate following treatment, and treatment drop-outs. By developing a clearer picture of the attributes of problems, clients, therapists and treatments associated with treatment failure, a richer understanding of the processes central to effective therapy will be achieved.

Economic implications

A detailed consideration of the economic implications of the conclusions of this project is beyond the scope of this text and useful discussions of economic issues are given elsewhere (Knapp, 1997). However, a number of points may be made about factors that must be taken into account in costing services for children and adolescents. First, the prevalence of significant psychological problems among children and adolescents is about 20 per cent and economic estimates of service costs for populations should be based on this figure (Carr, 1993). Second, while some problems are self-limiting (such as enuresis and encopresis) many psychological problems if left untreated persist into adulthood and are associated with high costs for the state. For example, about 50 per cent of children with persistent conduct disorders have poor outcomes as adults and develop alcohol and drug problems and criminality (Kazdin, 1995). The mental health and criminal justice costs associated with these difficulties and the difficulties encountered by victims of such individuals are immense. Third, the vast majority of children and adolescents with psychological difficulties can be treated on an outpatient basis by clinical psychologists and with consultations as required from colleagues in other disciples, notably paediatric medicine and nursing, social work, speech and language therapy, and child and adolescent psychiatry. Fourth, a small proportion of cases require hospitalization or treatment fostercare. Fifth, in costing services it is reasonable to assume that a full-time clinical psychologist can offer a full course of effective treatment (involving 25 to 50 hours of contact with the child and members of the child's network and other professionals and case administration time) in an outpatient setting to 50 cases per year and for each of these cases up to five multidisciplinary consultations may be required involving colleagues in other disciplines, notably paediatric medicine and nursing, social work, speech and language therapy and child and adolescent psychiatry. In practice, for a clinical psychologist, this would amount to taking on one new case each week and at any one time carrying an active case load of about 25. Sixth, costing psychological services for cases requiring hospitalization and treatment fostercare is complex, since the role of the clinical psychologist is primarily that of training ward staff and fosterparents to implement psychological programmes and to offer supervision and support. Seventh, in order to provide effective treatment and avoid burnout, clinical psychologists and clinical psychologists in training require regular clinical supervision and a system for auditing their clinical work. In costing this, at least a day per month per psychologist should be factored in to cover this area. Eighth, costings of clinical psychology services should take into account costs of offices, utilities, equipment, travel, and administrative support. It would be helpful if future treatment outcome studies took account of these issues and offered estimates of unit costs of treatment or costs of treatment for particular populations.

References

Abidin, R. (1986). *Parenting Stress Index* (Second edn.). Charlottesville, VA: Pediatric Psychology Press.

Abikoff, H. (1991). Cognitive training in ADHD children: Less to it than meets the eye. *Journal of Learning Disabilities*, 24, 205–9.

Abikoff, H. and Gittleman, R. (1984). Does behaviour therapy normalise the classroom behaviour of hyperactive children? *Archives of General Psychiatry*, 41, 449–54.*

Abikoff, H. and Gittleman, R. (1985). Hyperactive children treated with stimulants: Is cognitive training a useful adjunct? *Archives of General Psychiatry*, 42, 953–61.*

Abu-Arefeh, I. and Russell, G. (1994). Prevalence of headache and migraine in schoolchildren. *British Medical Journal*, 309, 765–9.

Achenbach, T. (1991). *Integrative Guide for the 1991 CBCL/4-18, YSR and TRF Profiles*. Burlington, VT: University of Vermont, Department of Psychiatry.

Achenbach, T. and Edelbrock, C. (1983). *Manual for the Child Behaviour Checklist and Revised Child Behaviour Profile*. Burlington: University of Vermont, Department of Psychiatry.

Adams, J. (1990a). *You and Your Alarm*. Bristol: Enuresis Resource and Information Centre. (ERIC, 65 St Michael's Hill, Bristol BS2 8DZ. Phone 0117-9264920.)

Adams, J. (1990b). *Your Child's Alarm*. Bristol: Enuresis Resource and Information Centre. (ERIC, 65 St Michael's Hill, Bristol BS2 8DZ. Phone 0117-9264920.)

Alexander, J. (1973). Defensive and supportive communication in normal and deviant families. *Journal of Consulting and Clinical Psychology*, 40, 223–31.

Alexander, J. and Parsons, B. (1973). Short-term behavioural intervention with delinquent families: Impact on family process and recidivism. *Journal of Abnormal Psychology*, 81, 219–25.*

Alexander, J. and Parsons, B. (1982). *Functional Family Therapy*. Monterey, CA: Brooks Cole.

Alexander, J., Barton, C., Schiavo, R. and Parsons, B. (1976). Systems-behavioural intervention with families of delinquents: Therapist characteristics, family behaviour and outcome. *Journal of Consulting and Clinical Psychology*, 44, 656–64.

Alpert-Gillis, L., Pedro-Carroll, J. and Cowen, E. (1989). The Children of Divorce Intervention Program: Development, implementation and evaluation of a program for young children. *Journal of Consulting and Clinical Psychology*, 57, 583–9.*

Althea, A. (1980). *I Have Two Homes*. Cambridge: Dinosaur Publications.

Amato, P. (1993). Children's adjustment to divorce. Theories, hypotheses and empirical support. *Journal of Marriage and the Family*, 55, 23–38.

Amato, P. and Keith, B. (1991a). Parental divorce and the well-being of children: A meta-analysis. *Psychological Bulletin*, 110, 26–46.

Amato, P. and Keith, B. (1991b). Consequences of parental divorce for adult well-being: A meta-analysis. *Journal of Marriage and the Family*, 53, 43–58.

American Academy of Child and Adolescent Psychiatry (1991). Practice parameters for the assessment and treatment of ADHD. *Journal of the American Academy of Child and Adolescent Psychiatry*, 30, i–iii.

American Psychiatric Association (1980). *Diagnostic and Statistical Manual of the Mental Disorders (Third Edition, DSM-III)*. Washington, DC: APA.

American Psychiatric Association (1987). *Diagnostic and Statistical Manual of the Mental Disorders (Third Edition Revised, DSM III-R)*. Washington, DC: APA.

American Psychiatric Association (1993). *Practice Guidelines for Eating Disorders*. Washington, DC: APA.

American Psychiatric Association (1994). *Diagnostic and Statistical Manual of the Mental Disorders (Fourth Edition, DSM-IV)*. Washington, DC: APA.

Anastopoulos, A., Shelton, T., DuPaul, G. and Guevremont, D. (1993). Parent training for attention deficit hyperactivity disorder: Its impact on parent functioning. *Journal of Abnormal Child Psychology*, 21, 581–96.*

Anderson, H. and Anderson, G. (1981). *Mom and Dad are Divorced But I'm Not. Parenting After Divorce*. Chicago: Nelson Hall.

Anderson, J. (1994) Epidemiological issues. In T. Ollendick, N. King and W. Yule (eds), *International Handbook of Phobic and Anxiety Disorders in Children and Adolescents* (pp. 43–66). New York: Plenum.

Andrasik, F. (1986). Relaxation and biofeedback for chronic headaches. In A. Holzman and D. Turk (eds), *Pain Management: A Handbook of Psychological Treatment Approaches*. New York: Pergamon.

Angold, A., Costello, E., Pickles, A. and Winder, F. (1987). The development of a questionnaire for use in epidemiological studies of depression in children and adolescents. London: Medical Research Council Child Psychiatry Unit.

Apley, J. (1975). *The Child with Abdominal Pains*. London: Blackwell Scientific Publications.

Apley, J. and Naish, N. (1958). Recurrent abdominal pains: A field study of 1,000 school children. *Disease in Childhood*, 33, 165–70.

Aragona, J. and Eyberg, S. (1981). Neglected children: Mothers' report of child behaviour problems and observed verbal behaviour. *Child Development*, 52, 596–602.

Atkins, M., Pelham, W. and Licht, M. (1988). The development and validation of objective classroom measures for the assessment of conduct and attention deficit disorders. In R. Prinz (ed.), *Advances In Behavioural Assessment Of Children And Families* (Vol. 4, pp. 3–33). New York: Guilford.

Ayllon, T., Garber, S. and Pisor, K. (1975). The elimination of discipline problems through a combined school–home motivational system. *Behaviour Therapy*, 6, 616–26.

Azrin, N. and Besalel, V. (1979). *A Parent's Guide to Bedwetting Control*. New York: Simon and Schuster.

Azrin, N., Donohue, B., Besalel, V., Kogan, E. and Acierno, R. (1994). Youth drug abuse treatment: A controlled outcome study. *Journal of Child and Adolescent Substance Abuse*, 3, 1–16.*

Bachanas, P. and Roberts, M. (1995). Factors affecting children's attitudes to healthcare and response to reduced procedures. *Journal of Paediatric Psychology*, 20, 261–75.

Baer, R. and Nietzel, M. (1991). Cognitive and behaviour treatment of impulsivity in children: A meta-analytic review of the outcome literature. *Journal of Clinical Child Psychology*, 20, 400–12.

Bailey, G. (1989). Current perspectives on substance abuse in youth. *Journal of the American Academy of Child and Adolescent Psychiatry*, 28, 151–62.

Bakal, D. (1982). *The Psychobiology of Chronic Headache*. New York: Springer.

Bank, L., Marlowe, H., Reid, J., Patterson, G. and Weinrott, M. (1991). A comparative evaluation for parent-training interventions for families of chronic delinquents. *Journal of Abnormal Child Psychology*, 19, 1, 15–33.*

Barclay, D. and Houts, A. (1995). Childhood enuresis. In C. Schaefer (ed.), *Clinical Handbook of Sleep Disorders in Children* (pp. 223–52). Northvale, NJ: Jason Aronson.

Barkley, R. (1981). *Hyperactive Children: A Handbook for Diagnosis and Treatment*. New York. Guilford.

Barkley, R. (1987). *Defiant Children: A Clinician's Manual for Parent Training*. New York: Guilford.

Barkley, R. (1990). *Attention Deficit Hyperactivity Disorder: A Handbook for Diagnosis and Treatment* (Second edition). New York: Guilford.

Barkley, R. (1995a). ADHD: What do we know?; ADHD: What can we do?; ADHD in the classroom: Strategies for teachers. These videos are available from PAR Inc. PO Box 998, Odessa, Florida, USA. Phone +1–800–331–8378.

Barkley, R. (1995b). *Taking Charge of ADHD: The Complete Authoritative Guide for Parents*. New York: Guilford.

Barkley, R. and Edelbrock, C. (1987). Assessing situational variations in children's problem behaviours: The home and school situations questionnaires. In R.J. Prinz (ed.), *Advances In Behavioural Assessment of Children and Families* (Vol. 3, pp. 157–76). New York: JAI Press.

Barkley, R., Guevremont, D., Anastopoulos, A. and Fletcher, K. (1992). A comparison of three family therapy programs for treating family conflicts in adolescents with ADHD. *Journal of Consulting and Clinical Psychology*, 60, 450–62.*

Barlow, D., Esler, J. and Vitali, A. (1998). Psychosocial treatments for panic disorders, phobias, and generalized anxiety disorders. In P. Nathan and J. Gorman (eds), *A Guide to Treatments that Work* (pp. 288–318). New York: Oxford.

Barnes, H. and Olson, D.H. (1982). Parent–Adolescent Communication Scale. In D.H. Olson, H.I. McCubbin, H. Barnes, A. Larsen, M. Muxen and M. Wilson (eds), *Family Inventories, Inventories used in a National Survey of Family Life Cycle* (pp. 33–48). St Paul: Family Social Science, University of Minnesota.

Barrett, P., Dadds, M. and Rappee, R. (1991). *Coping Koala Workbook* (unpublished manuscript, School of Applied Psychology, Griffith University, Nathan, Australia).

Barrett, P., Dadds, M. and Rappee, R. (1996). Family treatment of childhood anxiety: A controlled trial. *Journal of Consulting and Clinical Psychology*, 64, 2, 333–42.*

Barrios, B. and Hartman, D. (1997). Fears and anxieties. In E. Mash and L. Terdal (eds), *Behavioural Assessment Of Childhood Disorders* (Third edition, pp. 230–327). New York: Guilford.

Battle, J. (1992). *Culture-Free Self-Esteem Inventories*. Examiner's Manual. Austin, TX: Pro-ed.

Baucom, D., Shoam, V., Mueser, K., Daiuto, A. and Stickle, T. (1998). Empirically supported couple and family interventions for marital distress and adult mental health problems. *Journal of Consulting and Clinical Psychology*, 66, 53–88.

Baumrind, D. (1971). Current patterns of parental authority. *Developmental Psychology Monographs*, 9, 239–76.

Bavolek, S. and Comstock, C. (1983). *Handbook For The Adult–Adolescent Parenting Inventory (AAPI)*. Eau Claire, WI: Family Development Associates.

Bayley, N. (1969). *Bayley Scales of Infant Development*. New York: The Psychological Corporation.

Beck, A. (1976). *Cognitive Therapy and the Emotional Disorders*. New York: International Universities Press.

Beck, A. and Steer, R. (1991). *Beck Scale for Suicide Ideation*. New York: The Psychological Corporation.

Beck, A., Ward, C., Mendelsohn, M., Mock, J. and Erbaugh, J. (1961). An inventory for measuring depression. *Archives of General Psychiatry*, 4, 561–71.

Becker, J., Alpert, J., Bigfoot, D. *et al.* (1995). Empirical research on child abuse treatment: Report by the Child Abuse and Neglect Treatment Working Group, American Psychological Association. *Journal of Clinical Child Psychology*, 24 (Suppl), 23–46.

Becker, W. (1960). The relationship of factors in parental ratings of self and each other to the behaviour of kindergarten children rated by mothers, fathers and teachers. *Journal of Consulting Psychology*, 24, 507–27.

Becker, W. (1971). *Parents are Teachers: A Child Management Programme*. Champaign, Ill: Research Press.

Behar, L. (1977). The Preschool Behaviour Questionnaire. *Journal of Abnormal Child Psychology*, 5, 265–75.

Behar, L. and Stringfield, S. (1974). *Manual for the Preschool Behaviour Questionnaire*. Chapel Hill: University of North Carolina.

Beidel, S., Turner, S. and Fink, C. (1996). Assessment of Childhood Social Phobia: Construct, convergent and discriminative validity of the Social Phobia Anxiety Inventory for Children (SPAI-C). *Psychological Assessment*, 8, 235–40.

Bennett, G., Walkden, V., Curtis, R., Burns, L., Rees, J., Gosling, J. and McQuire, N.L. (1985). Pad and buzzer training, dry bed training, and stop start training in the treatment of primary nocturnal enuresis. *Behavioural Psychotherapy*, 13, 309–19.*

Berg, B. (1979). *Children's Attitudes Toward Parental Separation Inventory*. Dayton, OH: University of Dayton Press.

Berg, B. and Kelly, R. (1979). The measured self-esteem of children from broken, rejected and accepted families. *Journal of Divorce*, 1, 183–7.

Berg, I., Nichols, K. and Pritchard, C. (1969). School Phobia: Its classification and relationship to dependence. *Journal of Child Psychology and Psychiatry*, 10, 23–41.

Bergin, A. and Garfield, S. (1994). *Handbook of Psychotherapy and Behavior Change* (Fourth edition). New York: Wiley.

Berliner, L. and Elliott, D. (1996). Sexual abuse of children. In J. Briere, L. Berliner, J. Bulkley, C. Jenny and T. Reid (eds), *The APSAC Handbook on Child Maltreatment* (pp. 51–71). Thousand Oaks, CA: Sage.

Berman, A. and Jobes, D. (1993). *Adolescent Suicide: Assessment and Intervention.* Washington, DC: APA.

Bernal, M., Klinnert, M. and Schultz, L. (1980). Outcome evaluation of behavioural parent training and client-centred parent counselling for children with conduct problems. *Journal of Applied Behavioural Analysis*, 13, 677–91.*

Bernstein, D. and Borkovec, T. (1973). *Progressive Relaxation Training. A Manual for the Helping Professions.* Champaign, Ill: Research Press.

Bernstein, A. and Borkovec, T. (1993). *Progressive Relaxation Training.* Champaign, Ill: Research Press.

Beumont, P., Al-Alami, M. and Touyz, S. (1988). Relevance of a standard measurement of undernutrition to the diagnosis of anorexia nervosa: Use of Quetelet's body mass index (BMI). *International Journal of Eating Disorders*, 7, 399–405.

Bieri, D., Reeve, R., Champion, G. and Addicoat, L. (1990). The faces pain scale for the self-assessment of the severity of pain experienced by children: Development, initial validation and preliminary investigation for ratio scale properties. *Pain*, 41, 139–50.

Birleson, P. (1981). The validity of depressive disorder in childhood and the development of a self-rating scale: A research report. *Journal of Child Psychology and Psychiatry*, 22, 73–88.

Birleson, P., Hudson, I., Buchanan, D. and Wolff, S. (1987). Clinical evaluation of a self-rating scale for depressive disorder in childhood (Depression Self-Rating Scale). *Journal of Child Psychology and Psychiatry*, 28, 43–60.

Bithoney, W., McJunkin, J., Michalek, J. and Sugden, I. (1991). The effect of a multidisciplinary team approach on weight gain in non-organic failure-to-thrive children. *Developmental and Behavioural Pediatrics*, 12 (4), 254–8.*

Black, D. (1994). Psychological reactions to life-threatening and terminal illness and bereavement. In M. Rutter, E. Taylor and L. Hersov (eds), *Child and Adolescent Psychiatry: Modern Approaches* (Third edition, pp. 677–793). London: Blackwell.

Black, D. and Urbanowicz, M. (1987). Family intervention with bereaved children. *Journal of Child Psychology and Psychiatry*, 28 (3), 467–76.*

Blagg, N. and Yule, W. (1984). The behavioural treatment of school refusal: a comparative study. *Behaviour Research and Therapy*, 2, 119–27.*

Blanchard, E. and Andrasik, F. (1985). *Management of Chronic Headache. A Psychological Approach.* New York: Pergamon Press.

Bloomquist, M., August, G. and Ostrander, R. (1991). Effects of a school-based cognitive-behavioural intervention for ADHD children. *Journal of Abnormal Child Psychology*, 19, 591–605.*

Blount, R., Cohen, L., Frank, N., Bachanas, P., Smith, A., Marimala, M. and Late, J. (1997). The Child–Adult Medical Procedure Interaction Scale revised: An assessment of validity. *Journal of Paediatric Psychology*, 22, 73–88.

Bonner, M. and Finney, J. (1996). A psychosocial model of children's health status. In T. Ollendick and R. Prinz (eds), *Advances in Clinical Child Psychology* (Vol. 18, pp. 331–8). New York: Plenum Press.

Borduin, C., Henggeler, S., Blaske, D. and Stein, R. (1995a). Multisystemic treatment of adolescent sexual offenders. *International Journal of Offender Therapy and Comparative Criminology*, 39, 105–13.*

Borduin, C., Mann, B., Cone, L. and Henggeler, S. (1995b). Multisystemic treatment of serious juvenile offenders: Long-term prevention of criminality and violence. *Journal of Consulting and Clinical Psychology*, 63, 569–78.*

Bornstein, M., Bornstein, P. and Walters, H. (1985). Children of divorce: A group treatment manual for research and application. *Journal of Child and Adolescent Psychotherapy*, 2, 267–73.

Bornstein, M., Bornstein, P. and Walters, H. (1988). Children of divorce: Evaluation of a group treatment program. *Journal Of Clinical Child Psychology*, 17, 248–54.*

Bradley, C. (1937). The behaviour of children receiving benzedrine. *American Journal of Psychiatry*, 94, 577–85.

Braswell, L. and Bloomquist, M. (1991). *Cognitive Behavioural Therapy for ADHD Children: Child, Family and School Interventions*. New York: Guilford.

Bray, J. and Hetherington, M. (1993). Special section: Families in transition. *Journal of Family Psychology*, 7, 3–103.

Bricker, D. (1982). *Intervention with At Risk and Handicapped Infants*. Baltimore, MD: University Park Press.

Bricklin, B. (1990a). *Perception of Relationships Test*. Doylestown, PA: Village.

Bricklin, B. (1990b). *The Bricklin Perceptual Scales: Child Perception of Parent Series* (Revised edition). Doylestown, PA: Village.

Briere, J., Berliner, L., Bulkley, J., Jenny, C. and Reid, T. (1996). *The APSAC Handbook on Child Maltreatment*. Thousand Oaks, CA: Sage.

Brigance, A. (1978). *Brigance Diagnostic Inventory of Early Development*. North Billerica, MA: Curriculum.

Brody, G., Neubaum, E. and Forehand, R. (1988). Serial marriage: A heuristic analysis of an emerging family form. *Psychological Bulletin*, 103, 211–22.

Brown, R., Wynne, M. and Medenis, R. (1985). Methylphenidate and cognitive therapy: A comparison of treatment approaches with hyperactive boys. *Journal of Abnormal Child Psychology*, 13, 69–87.*

Brown, R., Borden, K., Wynne, M., Schleser, R. and Clingerman, S. (1986). Methylphenidate and cognitive therapy with ADD children: A methodological reconsideration. *Journal of Abnormal Child Psychology*, 14, 481–97.*

Brown, R., Wynne, M., Borden, K., Clingerman, S., Geniesse, R. and Spunt, A. (1986). Methylphenidate and cognitive therapy in children with attention deficit disorder: A double blind trial. *Journal of Developmental and Behavioural Paediatrics*, 7, 163–70.*

Browne, K. (1995). Child abuse: Defining, understanding and intervening. In K. Wilson and A. James (eds), *The Child Protection Handbook* (pp. 43–65). London: Baillière Tindall.

Browne, A. and Finklehor, D. (1986). The impact of child sexual abuse: A review of the research. *Psychological Bulletin*, 99, 66–77.

Brownell, K. and Fairburn, C. (1995). *Comprehensive Textbook of Eating Disorders and Obesity*. New York: Guilford.

Bruch, H. (1973). *Eating Disorders*. New York: Basic Books.

Brunk, M., Henggeler, S. and Whelan, J. (1987). Comparison of multisystemic therapy and parent training in the brief treatment of child abuse and neglect. *Journal of Consulting and Clinical Psychology*, 55, 171–8.*

Bryant-Waugh, R. and Lask, B. (1995a). Annotation: Eating disorder in children. *Journal of Child Psychology and Psychiatry*, 36, 191–202.

Bryant-Waugh, R. and Lask, B. (1995b). Eating disorders: An overview. *Journal of Family Therapy*, 17, 13–20.

Buchanan, A. (1992). *Children Who Soil. Assessment and Treatment*. Chichester: Wiley.

Buckstein, O. (1995). *Adolescent Substance Abuse. Assessment Prevention and Treatment*. New York: Wiley.

Budd, K., Riner, L. and Brockman, M. (1983). A structured evaluation system for clinical evaluation of parent training. *Behavioural Assessment*, 5, 373–90.

Burgoyne, J. (1984). *Breaking Even: Divorce, Your Children and You*. Harmondsworth: Penguin.

Burrett, J. (1991). *To and Fro Children: A Guide to Successful Parenting after Divorce*. London: Thorsons.

Butler, L., Meizitis, S., Friedman, R. and Cole, E. (1980). The effect of school based intervention programmes on depressive symptoms in pre-adolescents. *American Educational Research Journal*, 17, 111–19.*

Butler, R. (1998a). Annotation: Night wetting in children – psychological aspects. *Journal of Child Psychology and Psychiatry*, 39, 453–63.

Butler, R. (1998b). *Overcoming Bedwetting*. Dr Richard Butler, Leeds Community and Mental Health Centre.

Cairns, E. and Cammock, T. (1978b). Development of a more reliable version of the Matching Familiar Figures Test. *Developmental Psychology*, 18, 555–60.

Caldwell, B. and Bradley, R. (1985). *Home Observation of Measurement of the Environment*. New York: Dorsey Press.

Calhoun, K., Moras, K., Pilkonis, P. and Rehm, L. (1998). Empirically supported treatments. Implications for training. *Journal of Consulting and Clinical Psychology*, 66, 151–62.

Camp, B. and Bash, M. (1981). *Think Aloud: Increasing Social and Cognitive Skills. A Problem Solving Program for Children*. Champaign, Ill: Research Press.

Campo, J. and Fritsch, S. (1994). Somatization in children and adolescents. *Journal of the American Academy of Child and Adolescent Psychiatry*, 33, 1223–35.

Cantwell, D.P. (1994). *Therapeutic Management of Attention Deficit Disorder: Participant Workbook*. New York: Guilford.

Cantwell, D.P. (1996). Attention deficit disorder: A review of the past ten years. *Journal of the American Academy of Child and Adolescent Psychiatry*, 35, 978–87.

Carlson, C., Pelham, W., Milich, R. and Dixon, M. (1992). Single and combined effects of methylphenidate and behaviour therapy on the classroom behaviour, academic performance and self-evaluations of children with attention deficit-hyperactivity disorder. *Journal of Abnormal Child Psychology*, 20, 213–32.*

Carr, A. (1993). Epidemiology of psychological disorders in Irish children. *Irish Journal of Psychology*, 14, 546–60.

Carr, A. (1997). *Family Therapy and Systemic Practice*. Lanham, MD: UPA.

Carr, A. (1999). *Handbook of Child and Adolescent Clinical Psychology: A Contextual Approach*. London: Routledge.

Catalano, R., Hawkins, J., Wells, E., Miller, J. and Brewer, D. (1991). Evaluation of the effectiveness of adolescent drug abuse treatment: Assessment of risks for relapse, and promising approaches for relapse prevention. *International Journal of Addiction*, 26, 1085–140.

Cautela, J. and Groden, J. (1978). *Relaxation: A Comprehension Manual for Adults, Children and Children with Special Needs*. Champaign, Ill: Research Press.

Central Statistics Office (1994). *Social Focus of Children '94*. London: HMSO.

Chamberlain, P. (1990). Comparative evaluation of specialised foster care for seriously delinquent youths: a first step. *Community Alternatives: International Journal of Family Care*, 2, 21–36.*

Chamberlain, P. (1994). *Family Connections: A Treatment Foster Care Model For Adolescents With Delinquency*. Eugene, OR: Castalia Press.

Chamberlain, P. and Reid, J. (1987). Parent observation and report of child symptoms. *Behavioural Assessment*, 9, 97–109.

Chamberlain, P. and Reid, J. (1991). Using a specialised foster care treatment model for children and adolescents leaving the State mental hospital. *Journal of Community Psychology*, 19, 266–76.*

Chamberlain, P. and Rosicky, J. (1995). The effectiveness of family therapy in the treatment of adolescents with conduct disorders and delinquency. *Journal of Marital and Family Therapy*, 21, 441–59.

Chambers, W., Puig-Antich, J., Hirsch, M. *et al.* (1985). The assessment of affective disorders in children and adolescents by semi-structured interview. *Archives of General Psychiatry*, 42, 696–703 (K-SADS).

Chambless, D., Caputo, C., Bright, P. and Gallagher, R. (1984). Assessment of fear of fear in agoraphobics: The Body Sensations Questionnaire and the Agoraphobia Cognitions Questionnaire. *Journal of Consulting and Clinical Psychology*, 62, 1090–7.

Christensen, A., Johnson, S. and Glasgow, R. (1980). Cost effectiveness in behavioural family therapy. *Behaviour Therapy*, 11, 208–26.*

Cicchetti, D. and Toth, J. (1995). A developmental psychopathology perspective on child abuse and neglect. *Journal of the American Academy of Child and Adolescent Psychiatry*, 34, 451–565.

Clark, D. and Donovan, J. (1994). Reliability and validity of the Hamilton Anxiety Rating Scale in an adolescent sample. *Journal of the American Academy of Child and Adolescent Psychiatry*, 33, 354–60.

Clarke, G. and Lewinsohn, P. (1984). *The Coping with Depression Course – Adolescent Version: A Psychoeducational Intervention for Unipolar Depression in High School Students*. Eugene, OR: Peter Lewinsohn.

Clarke, M. and Hornick, J. (1984). The development of the Nurturance Inventory: An instrument for assessing parent practices. *Child Psychiatry and Human Development*, 14, 49–63.

Clayden, G. and Agnarsson, V. (1992). *Constipation in Childhood: Information Booklet for Children and Parents*. In Appendix A of A. Buchanan, *Children Who Soil. Assessment and Treatment*. Chichester: Wiley.

Clum, G., Broyles, S., Borden, J. and Watkins, P. (1990). Validity and reliability of the Panic Attack Symptoms and Cognitions Questionnaire. *Journal of Psychopathology and Behavioural Assessment*, 12, 233–45.

Cohen, L., Blount, R. and Panopoulos, G. (1997). Nurse Coaching and Cartoon Distraction: An effective and practical intervention to reduce child, parent, and nurse distress during immunizations. *Journal of Pediatric Psychology*, 22, 355–70.*

Cohen, N., Sullivan, J., Minde, K., Novak, C. and Helwig, C. (1981). Evaluation of the relative effectiveness of methylphenidate and cognitive behaviour modification in the treatment of kindergarten-aged hyperactive children. *Journal of Abnormal Child Psychology*, 9, 43–54.*

Cohen, P., Cohen, J., Kasen, S., Velez, C., Hartmark, C., Johnson, J., Rojas, M., Brook, J. and Streuning, E. (1993). An epidemiological study of disorders in late childhood and adolescence. 1. Age and gender specific prevalence. *Journal of Child Psychology and Psychiatry*, 34, 851–67.

Cone, J. (1984). *The Pyramid Scales: Criterion Referenced Measures of Adaptive Behaviour in Handicapped Persons*. Austin, TX: Pro-ed.

Conners, C. (1990). *The Conners' Rating Scales*. North Tonawanda, NY: Multi-Health Systems.

Conners, C. (1995). *The Conners' Continuous Performance Test*. North Tonawanda, NY: Multi-Health Systems.

Conners, C. (1996a). *Conners' Abbreviated Symptom Questionnaire*. Odessa, FL: PAR. Available from PAR, PO Box 998, Odessa, Florida, USA. Phone 1-800-331-8378.

Conners, C. (1996b). *Conners' Rating Scales Computer Programme*. Available from PAR, PO Box 998, Odessa, Florida, USA. Phone +1-800-331-8378.

Cooper, P. (1995). *Bulimia Nervosa and Binge Eating: A Guide to Recovery*. London: Robinson Publishing.

Cooper, P., Taylor, M., Cooper, Z. and Fairburn, C. (1987). The development and validation of the Body Shape Questionnaire. *International Journal of Eating Disorders*, 6, 485–94.

Cooper, P., Osborn, M., Gath, D. and Feggetter, G. (1982). Evaluation of a modified self-report measure of social adjustment. *British Journal of Psychiatry*, 141, 68–75.

Cooper, Z. and Fairburn, C. (1987). The Eating Disorder Examination: A semi-structured interview for the assessment of the specific psychopathology of eating disorders. *International Journal of Eating Disorders*, 6, 1–8.

Coopersmith, S. and Gilbert, R. (1982). *Professional Manual: Behavioural Academic Self-Esteem*. Palo Alto: Consulting Psychologists' Press.

Corr, C. and Balk, D. (1996). *Handbook of Adolescent Death and Bereavement*. New York: Springer.

Cowen, E., Huser, J., Beach, D. *et al.* (1970). Parents' perception of young children and their relation to indexes of adjustment. *Journal of Consulting and Clinical Psychology*, 34, 97–103.

Cox, D., Sutphen, J., Borowitz, S. and Dickens, M. (1994). Simple electromyographic biofeedback treatment for chronic paediatric constipation/encopresis: Preliminary report. *Biofeedback and Self-Regulation*, 19, 41–50.*

Cox, D., Sutphen, J., Ling, W. and Quillian, W. (1996). Additive benefits of laxative, toilet training, and biofeedback therapies in the treatment of paediatric encopresis. *Journal of Pediatric Psychology*, 21, 659–67.*

Craighead, E., Craighead, L. and Ilardi, S. (1998). Psychosocial treatments for major depressive disorder. In P. Nathan and J. Gorman (eds), *A Guide to Treatments that Work* (pp. 226–39). New York: Oxford University Press.

Crisp, A. (1980). *Anorexia Nervosa: Let Me Be*. London: Academic Press.

Crisp, A., Joughin, N., Halek, C. and Bower, C. (1996). *Anorexia Nervosa: The Wish to Change. Self-help and Discovery, the Thirty Steps* (Second edition). Hove: Psychology Press.

Crisp, A., Norton, K., Gowers, S., Halek, C., Bowyer, C., Yeldham, D., Levett, G. and Bhat, A. (1991). A controlled study of the effect of therapies aimed at adolescent and family psychopathology in anorexia nervosa. *British Journal of Psychiatry*, 159, 325–33.*

Culp, R., Heide, J. and Richardson, M. (1987). Maltreated children's developmental scores: Treatment versus non-treatment. *Child Abuse and Neglect*, 11, 29–34.*

Culp, R., Little, V. and Lawrence, H. (1991). Maltreated children's self-concept: Effects of a comprehensive treatment program. *American Journal of Orthopsychiatry*, 61 (1), 114–21.*

Cunningham, C., Bremner, R. and Boyle, M. (1995). Large group community-based parenting programs for families of preschoolers at risk for disruptive behaviour disorders: Utilization, cost effectiveness, and outcome. *Journal of Child Psychology and Psychiatry*, 36, 1141–60.*

Cunningham, C., Bremner, R. and Secord-Gilbert, M. (1994). *A School Based Family Systems Oriented Course For Parents Of Children With Disruptive Behaviour Disorders: Leaders Manual.* Unpublished manuscript.

Dadds, M. and McHugh, T. (1992). Social support and treatment outcome in behavioural family therapy for child conduct problems. *Journal of Consulting and Clinical Psychology*, 60, 252–9.*

Dadds, M., Schwartz, S. and Sanders, M. (1987). Marital discord and treatment outcome in behavioural treatment of child conduct disorders. *Journal of Consulting and Clinical Psychology*, 55, 396–403.*

Dale, P. (1986). *Dangerous Families: Assessment and Treatment of Child Abuse.* London: Tavistock.

Dangle, R. and Polstner, R. (1988). *Teaching Child Management Skills.* New York: Pergamon.

Davis, M., Robbins-Eshelman, E. and McKay, M. (1988). *The Relaxation and Stress Reduction Workbook* (Third Edition). Oakland, CA: New Harbinger Publications.

Deblinger, A. and Heflinger, A. (1996). *Treating Sexually Abused Children and their Non-offending Parents: A Cognitive Behavioural Approach.* Thousand Oaks, CA: Sage.

Derogatis, L., Lipman, R. and Covi, L. (1973). SCL-90: An outpatient psychiatric rating scale – preliminary report. *Psychopharmacological Bulletin*, 9, 13–27.

deVeaugh-Geiss, J., Moroz, G., Biederman, J., Cantwell, D., Fontaine, R., Greist, I., Reichler, R., Katz, R. and Landeau, P. (1992). Clomipramine hydrochloride in childhood and adolescent obsessive compulsive disorder: A multicentre trial. *Journal of the American Academy of Child and Adolescent Psychiatry*, 31, 45–9.

Dishion, T. and Andrews, D. (1995). Preventing Escalation in Problem Behaviours with High-Risk Young Adolescents: Immediate and 1-Year Outcomes. *Journal of Consulting and Clinical Psychology*, 63, 538–48.*

Dishion, T. and Kavanagh, K. (1989). *The Adolescents Transition Programme* (manuals and accompanying video vignettes). Eugene, OR: Independent Video Services.

Dishion, T., Kavanagh, K. and Soberman, L. (in press).*The Adolescents Transition Programme. Assessment and Interventions Sourcebook.* New York: Guilford.

Donohue, B., Miller, E., Van Hasselt, V. and Hersen, M. (1998). An ecobehavioural approach to child maltreatment. In V. Van Hasselt and M. Hersen (eds), *Handbook of Psychological Treatment Protocols for Children and Adolescents* (pp. 279–358). Mahwah, NJ: Lawrence Erlbaum.

Douglas, V., Parry, P., Marton, P. and Garson, C. (1976). Assessment of a cognitive training program for hyperactive children. *Journal of Abnormal Child Psychology*, 4, 389–410.

Dowling, E. and Osborne, E. (1994). *The Family and The School. A Joint Systems Approach to Problems with Children* (Second Edition). London: Routledge.

DuPaul, G. (1991). Parent and teacher ratings of ADHD symptoms: Psychometric properties in a community based sample. *Journal of Clinical Child Psychology*, 20, 245–53.

DuPaul, G. and Barkley, R. (1992). Situational variability of attention problems: Psychometric properties of the revised Home and School Situations Questionnaires. *Journal of Clinical Child Psychology*, 21, 178–88.

DuPaul, G. and Eckert, T. (1997). The effects of school-based interventions for attention deficit hyperactivity disorder: A meta-analysis. *School Psychology Review*, 26, 5–27.

Durlak, J., Fuhrman, T. and Lampman, C. (1991). The effectiveness of cognitive behaviour therapy for maladapting children: A meta-analysis. *Psychological Bulletin*, 110, 204–14.

Dwivedi, K. and Varma, V. (1997). *A Handbook of Childhood Anxiety Management*. Aldershot: Arena.

Dyregrov, A. (1992). *Grief in Children: A Handbook for Adults*. London: Kingsley.

D'Zurilla, T. and Goldfried, M. (1971). Problem-solving and behaviour modification. *Journal of Abnormal Psychology*, 78, 107–26.

Edgington, A., Hall, M. and Rosser, R. (1980). *Neglectful families: Measurement of Treatment Outcome*. Paper presented at Tri-regional Workshop for Social Workers in Maternal and Child Health. Raleigh, NC.

Edwards, M., Finney, J. and Bonner, M. (1991). Matching treatment with recurrent abdominal pain symptoms: An evaluation of dietary fibre and relaxation treatments. *Behavior Therapy*, 22, 257–67.*

Egan, K. (1983). Stress management and child management with abusive parents. *Journal of Clinical Child Psychology*, 12 (Winter), 292–9.*

Eisler, I. (1995). Family models of eating disorders. In G. Szmukler, C. Dare and J. Treasure (eds), *Handbook of Eating Disorders* (pp. 155–76). Chichester: Wiley.

Eisler, I., Dare, C., Russell, G., Szmukler, G., Le Grange, D. and Dodge, E. (1997). Family and individual therapy in anorexia nervosa: A 5 year follow-up. *Archives of General Psychiatry*, 54, 1025–30.*

Elliott, C. and Jay, S. (1987). An observational scale for measuring children's distress during bone marrow aspirations and lumbar punctures: A critical review. *Journal of Pain and Symptom Management*, 9, 96–108.

Elliott, D., Huizinga, D. and Ageton, S. (1985). *Explaining Delinquency and Drug Use*. Beverly Hills, CA: Sage.

Ellis, J., Spanos, S. and Nicholas, P. (1994). Cognitive-behavioural interventions for children's distress during bone marrow aspirations and lumbar punctures: A critical review. *Journal of Pain and Symptom Management*, 9, 96–108.

Elmer, E. (1986). Outcome of residential treatment for abused and high-risk infants. *Child Abuse and Neglect*, 10, 351–60.*

Eminson, M., Benjamin, S., Shortall, A. and Woods, T. (1996). Physical symptoms and illness attitudes in adolescents: An epidemiological study. *Journal of Child Psychology and Psychiatry*, 37, 519–28.

Engel, J., Rapoff, M. and Pressman, A. (1992). Long term follow-up of relaxation training for paediatric headache disorders. *Headache*, 32, 152–6.*

Estrada, A. and Pinsof, W. (1995). The effectiveness of family therapies for selected behavioural disorders of childhood. *Journal of Marital and Family Therapy*, 21, 4, 403–40.

Eyberg, S. (1980a). Eyberg Child Behaviour Inventory. *Journal of Clinical Child Psychology*, 9, 29.

Eyberg, S. (1980b). *Eyberg Child Behaviour Inventory*. Portland, OR: University of Oregon.

Eyberg, S. and Robinson, E.A. (1983). Dyadic Parent–Child Interaction Coding System: A manual. *Psychological Documents*, 13, Ms. No. 2582. (Available from Social and Behaviour Sciences Documents, Select Press, PO Box 9838, San Rafael, CA 94912.)

Eyberg, S. and Ross, A. (1978). Assessment of child behaviour problems: The validation of a new inventory. *Journal of Clinical Psychology*, 16, 113–16.

Eysenck, H. (1952). The effects of psychotherapy: An evaluation. *Journal of Consulting Psychology*, 16, 319–24.

Fairburn, C. (1995). *Overcoming Binge Eating*. New York: Guilford.

Fairburn, C. and Wilson, G. (1993). *Binge Eating: Nature Assessment and Treatment*. New York: Guilford.

Fairburn, C., Steere, F. and Cooper, P. (1990). Assessment of the psychopathology of bulimia nervosa. In M.M. Fichter (ed.), *Bulimia Nervosa: Basic Research, Diagnosis and Therapy* (pp. 37–56). Chichester: Wiley.

Fairburn, C., Jones, R., Peveler, R., Hope, R. and O'Connor, M. (1993). Psychotherapy and bulimia nervosa: Longer-term effects of interpersonal psychotherapy, behaviour therapy and cognitive behaviour therapy. *Archives of General Psychiatry*, 50, 419–28.*

Fairburn, C., Jones, R., Peveler, R., Carr, S., Solomon, R., O'Connor, M. and Hope, R. (1991). Three psychological treatments for bulimia nervosa: A comparative trial. *Archives of General Psychiatry*, 48, 463–9.*

Fantuzzo, J., Jurecic, L., Stovall, A. and Hightower, A. (1988). Effects of adult and peer social initiations on the social behaviour of withdrawn, maltreated pre-school children. *Journal of Consulting and Clinical Psychology*, 56, 34–9.*

Fantuzzo, J., Sutton-Smith, B., Atkins, M. and Meyers, R. (1996). Community-based resilient peer treatment of withdrawn, maltreated pre-school children. *Journal of Consulting and Clinical Psychology*, 64 (6), 1377–86.*

Farmer, A. and McGuffin, P. (1989). The classification of depressions: Contemporary confusions revisited. *British Journal of Psychiatry*, 155, 437–43.

Farrell, M. and Taylor, E. (1994). Drug and alcohol use and misuse. In M. Rutter, E. Taylor and L. Hersov (eds), *Child and Adolescent Psychiatry: Modern Approaches* (Third Edition, pp. 529–45). Oxford: Blackwell.

Faschingbauer, T. (1981). *Texas Revised Inventory of Grief (TRIG)*. Houston, TX: Honeycomb.

Feindler, E. and Ecton, R. (1985). *Adolescent Anger Control: Cognitive-Behavioural Techniques*. New York: Pergamon.

Fentress, D., Masek, B., Mehegan, J. and Benson, H. (1986). Biofeedback and relaxation response training in the treatment of paediatric migraine. *Developmental Medicine and Child Neurology*, 28, 139–46.*

Fichter, M., Elton, M., Engel, K. *et al.* (1990). The structured interview for anorexia and bulimia nervosa (SIAB): Development and characteristics of a (semi-)

standardized instrument. In M. Fichter (ed.), *Bulimia Nervosa: Basic Research Diagnosis and Therapy* (pp. 57–70). Chichester: Wiley.

Fielding, D.M. and Doleys, D.M. (1988). Elimination problems: Enuresis and encopresis. In E.J. Mash and L.G. Terdal (eds), *Behavioural Assessment of Childhood Disorders* (Second Edition, pp. 586–623). New York: Guilford Press.

Fine, S., Forth, A., Gilbert, M. and Haley, G. (1991). Group therapy for adolescent depressive disorder: A comparison of social skills and therapeutic support. *Journal of the American Academy of Child and Adolescent Psychiatry*, 30 (1), 79–85.*

Finklehor, D. (1990). Early and long-term effects of child sexual abuse. *Professional Psychology*, 21, 325–30.

Finney, J., Lemanek, K., Cataldo, M. and Katz, H. (1989). Pediatric psychology in primary health care: Brief targeted therapy for recurrent abdominal pain. *Behavior Therapy*, 20, 283–91.*

Firestone, P., Kelly, M. and Fike, S. (1980). Are fathers necessary in parent training groups? *Journal of Clinical Child Psychology*, 9, 44–7.*

Firestone, P., Crowe, D., Goodman, J. and McGrath, P. (1986). Vicissitudes of follow-up studies: Differential effects of parent training and stimulant medication with hyperactives. *American Journal of Orthopsychiatry*, 56, 184–94.*

Fisher, B. (1976). *Fisher Divorce Adjustment Scale. Manual, Scale and Computer Scoring Programme.* Available from Family Relations Learning Centre, 450 Ord Drive, Boulder, Colorado, 80303-4730, USA (Phone +1-303-499-1171).

Fonagy, P. and Target, M. (1994). The efficacy of psychoanalysis for people with disruptive behaviour disorders. *Journal of the American Academy of Child and Adolescent Psychiatry*, 33, 45–55.

Forehand, R. and Long, N. (1996). *Parenting the Strong-Willed Child: The Clinically Proven Five Week Programme for Parents of Two to Six Year Olds.* Chicago, Ill: Contemporary Books.

Forehand, B. and McMahon, R. (1981). *Helping the Non-compliant Child: A Clinician's Guide to Parent Training.* New York: Guilford.

Forgatch, M. and Patterson, G. (1989). *Parents and Adolescents Living Together: Part 2. Family Problem Solving.* Eugene, OR: Castalia Press.

Fournier, J., Garfinkle, B., Bond, A., Beauchesne, H. and Shapiro, S. (1987). Pharmacological and behavioral management of enuresis. *American Academy of Child and Adolescent Psychiatry*, 26, 849–52.*

Frankel, F., Myatt, R., Cantwell, D. and Feinberg, D. (1997). Parent-assisted transfer of children's social skills training: Effects on children with and without attention-deficit hyperactivity disorder. *Journal of the American Academy of Child and Adolescent Psychiatry*, 36, 1056–64.*

Fredrick, C. and Pynooss, R. (1988). *The Child Post-Traumatic Stress Disorder Reaction Index.* Los Angeles: University of California.

Friedman, A.S. (1989). Family therapy vs parent groups: Effects on adolescent drug abusers. *The American Journal of Family Therapy*, 17, 335–42.*

Friedrich, W. (1995). *Psychotherapy with Sexually Abused Boys: An Integrated Approach.* Thousand Oaks, CA: Sage.

Friedrich, W., Beilke, R. and Urquiza, A. (1987). Children from sexually abusive families: A behavioural comparison. *Journal of Interpersonal Violence*, 2, 391–402.

Friedrich, W., Grambsch, P., Damon, L., Hewitt, S., Koverola, C., Lang, R., Wolfe, V. and Broughton, D. (1992). Child sexual behaviour inventory. *Psychological Assessment*, 4, 303–11.

Frielander, M., Wildman, J., Heatherington, L. and Skowron, E. (1994). What we do and don't know about the process of family therapy. *Journal of Family Psychology*, 8, 390–416.

Fritz, G., Fritsch, S. and Hagino, O. (1997). Somatoform disorders in children and adolescents: A review of the past 10 years. *Journal of American Academy of Child and Adolescent Psychiatry*, 36, 1329–38.

Furniss, T. (1991). *The Multiprofessional Handbook of Child Sexual Abuse: Integrated Management, Therapy and Legal Intervention*. London: Routledge.

Futterbunk, B. and Eyberg, S. (1989). Psychometric characteristics of the Sutter-Eyberg Student Behaviour Inventory: A school behaviour rating scale for use with preschool children. *Behavioural Assessment*, 11, 297–313.

Garfield, S. and Bergin, A. (1971). *Handbook of Psychotherapy and Behavior Change* (First Edition). New York: Wiley.

Garfield, S. and Bergin, A. (1978). *Handbook of Psychotherapy and Behavior Change* (Second Edition). New York: Wiley.

Garfield, S. and Bergin, A. (1986). *Handbook of Psychotherapy and Behavior Change* (Third Edition). New York: Wiley.

Garmezy, N. and Masten, A. (1994). Chronic adversities. In M. Rutter, E. Taylor and L. Hersov (eds), *Child and Adolescent Psychiatry: Modern Approaches* (Third Edition, pp. 191–208). London: Blackwell.

Garner, D. (1991). *Eating Disorder Inventory-2 (EDI-2)*. Psychological Assessment Resources, PO Box 998, Odessa, Florida 33556, USA.

Garner, D. and Garfinkel, P. (1997). *Handbook of Treatment for Eating Disorders* (Second Edition). New York: Guilford.

Garner, D., Olmsted, M., Bohr, Y. and Garfinkel, P. (1982). The Eating Attitudes Test, psychometric features and clinical correlates. *Psychological Medicine*, 12, 871–8.

Garralda, M. (1992). A selective review of child psychiatric syndromes with a somatic presentation. *British Journal of Psychiatry*, 161, 759–73.

Garralda, M. (1996). Somatization in children. *Journal of Child Psychology and Psychiatry*, 37, 13–34.

Gaub, M. and Carlson, C. (1997). Behavioural characteristics of DSM-IV ADHD subtypes in a school-based population. *Journal of Abnormal Child Psychology*, 25, 103–11.

Gaudin, J. (1991). Remedying child neglect: Effectiveness of social network interventions. *The Journal of Applied Social Sciences*, 15 (1), 97–123.*

Gelles, F. (1987). *The Violent Home* (Updated Edition). Beverly Hills, CA: Sage.

Gesren, E. (1976). A Health Resources Inventory: The development of a measure of the personal and social competence of primary grade children. *Journal of Consulting and Clinical Psychology*, 44, 775–86.

Gilliam, J. (1996). *Attention Deficit Hyperactivity Disorder Test*. Odessa, FL: PAR. Available from PAR, PO Box 998, Odessa, Florida, USA. Phone +1-800-331-8378.

Glennon, B. and Weisz, J. (1978). An observational approach to the assessment of anxiety in young children. *Journal of Consulting and Clinical Psychology*, 46, 1246–57.

Gontard, A. (1998). Annotation: Day and night wetting in children – a paediatric and child psychiatric perspective. *Journal of Child Psychology and Psychiatry*, 39, 431–51.

Goodman, W., Price, L., Rasmusen, S., Mazure, C., Rappoport, J., Heninger, G. and Chasney, D. (1986). The Children's Yale Brown Obsessive-Compulsive Scale. Reprinted in G. Francis and R. Gragg (1996). *Obsessive Compulsive Disorder.* Thousand Oaks, CA: Sage.

Goodsitt, A. (1985). Self-psychology and the treatment of anorexia nervosa. In D. Garner and P. Garfinkel (eds), *Handbook of Treatment for Eating Disorders* (pp. 55–82). New York: Guilford.

Goodwin, D., Boggs, S. and Graham Poole, J. (1994). Development and validation of the Paediatric Oncology Quality Of Life Scale. *Psychological Assessment*, 6, 321–8.

Gordon, D., Arbuthnot, J., Gustafson, K. and McGreen, P. (1988). Home-based behavioural systems family therapy with disadvantaged delinquents. *The American Journal of Family Therapy*, 16, 243–55.*

Gordon, M. (1995). *How to Operate an ADHD Clinic or Subspecialty Practice.* Odessa, FL: PAR.

Gordon, T. (1977). Parent effectiveness training: A preventative program and its delivery system. In G. Albee and J. Joffee (eds), *Primary Prevention of Psychopathology* (pp. 175–86). Hanover, NH: University Press of New England.

Graziano, A. and Mooney, K. (1980). Family self-control instruction and children's night time fear reduction. *Journal of Consulting and Clinical Psychology*, 48, 2, 206–13.

Greenhill, L. (1998). Childhood attention deficit hyperactivity disorder: Pharmacological treatments. In P. Nathan and J. Gorman (eds), *A Guide to Treatments that Work* (pp. 42–64). New York: Oxford University Press.

Gresham, F. and Elliot, S. (1990). *The Social Skills Rating System.* New York: American Guidance Services.

Grych, J. and Fincham, F. (1992). Interventions for children of divorce: Toward greater integration of research and action. *Psychological Bulletin*, 111, 434–54.

Guerney, B.G. (1977). *Relationships Enhancement: Skill Training Programs for Therapy, Problem Prevention, and Enrichment.* San Francisco, CA: Jossey-Bass.

Gullone, E. and King, N. (1992). Psychometric evaluation of a revised fear survey schedule for children and adolescents. *Journal of Child Psychology and Psychiatry*, 33, 987–98.

Gurman, A. and Kniskern, D. (1978). Research on marital and family therapy: Progress, perspective and prospect. In S. Garfield and A. Bergin (eds), *Handbook of Psychotherapy and Behaviour Change* (Second Edition, pp. 817–901). New York: Wiley.

Gurman, A. and Kniskern, D. (1981). Family therapy outcome research: Knowns and unknowns. In A. Gurman and D. Kniskern (eds), *Handbook of Family Therapy* (pp. 742–76). New York: Brunner/Mazel.

Hageman, W. and Arrindell, W. (1993). A further refinement of the reliable change (RC) index by improving the pre-post difference score: Introducing RC-ID. *Behaviour Research and Therapy*, 31, 693–700.

Haley, J. (1976). *Problem Solving Therapy.* New York: Harper and Row.

Hall, A. and Crisp, A. (1987). Brief psychotherapy in the treatment of anorexia nervosa: Outcome at one year. *British Journal of Psychiatry*, 151, 185–91.*

Halper, G. and Jones, M. (1981). *Serving Families at Risk of Dissolution: Public Preventative Services in New York City.* New York: City of New York Human Resources Administration.

Hamill, P. (1979). Physical growth: National Centre for Health Statistics percentiles. *American Journal of Clinical Nutrition*, 32, 607.

Hamilton, S.B. and MacQuiddy, S.L. (1984). Self-administered behavioural parent training: Enhancement of treatment efficacy using a time-out signal seat. *Journal of Clinical Child Psychology*, 13, 61–9.*

Hanf, C. and Kling, F. (1973). *Facilitating Parent–Child Interaction: A Two-Stage Training Model*. Unpublished manuscript, University of Oregon Medical School, Eugene.

Hansen, D., Hecht, D. and Futa, K. (1998). Child sexual abuse. In V. Van Hasselt and M. Hersen (eds), *Handbook of Psychological Treatment Protocols for Children and Adolescents* (pp. 153–75). Mahwah, NJ: Lawrence Erlbaum.

Harrington, R. (1993). *Depressive Disorder in Childhood and Adolescence*. New York: Wiley.

Harter, S. and Pike, R. (1984). The pictorial scale of perceived competence and social acceptance for young children. *Child Development*, 55, 1969–82.

Hartmann, A., Herzog, T. and Drinkman, A. (1992). Psychotherapy of bulimia nervosa: What is effective? A meta-analysis. *Journal of Psychosomatic Research*, 36, 159–67.

Hawkins, J., Catalano, R. and Miller, J. (1992). Risk and protective factors for alcohol and other drug problems in adolescence and early adulthood: Implications for substance use prevention. *Psychological Bulletin*, 112, 64–105.

Hawkins, R. and Clement, P. (1980). Development and construct validation of a self-report measure of binge eating tendencies. *Addictive Behaviours*, 5, 219–26.

Hechtman, L. and Abikoff, H. (1995). Multimodal treatment plus stimulants v. stimulant treatment in ADHD children: Results from a two year comparative treatment study. Paper presented at the annual meeting of the American Academy of Child and Adolescent Psychiatry, New Orleans.

Henggeler, S. and Borduin, C. (1990). *Family Therapy and Beyond: A Multisystemic Approach to Treating the Behaviour Problems of Children and Adolescents*. Pacific Grove, CA: Brooks Cole.

Henggeler, S. (1991a). The Family and Neighbourhood Services Project. In S. Henggeler, C. Borduin, G. Melton, B. Mann, L. Smith, J. Hall, L. Cone, B. and Fucci (1991). The effects of multisystemic therapy on drug use and abuse in serious juvenile offenders: A progress report from two outcome studies. *Family Dynamics Addiction Quarterly*, 1, 40–51.*

Henggeler, S. (1991b). The Missouri Delinquency Project. In S. Henggeler, C. Borduin, G. Melton, B. Mann, L. Smith, J. Hall, L. Cone and B. Fucci (1991). Effects of multisystemic therapy on drug use and abuse in serious juvenile offenders: A progress report from two outcome studies. *Family Dynamics Addiction Quarterly*, 1, 40–51.*

Henggeler, S., Melton, G. and Smith, L. (1992). Family preservation using multisystemic therapy: An effective alternative to incarcerating serious juvenile offenders. *Journal of Consulting and Clinical Psychology*, 60, 953–61.*

Henggeler, S., Melton, G., Smith, L., Schoenwald, S. and Hanley, J. (1993). Family preservation using multisystemic treatment: Long-term follow up to a clinical trial with serious juvenile offenders. *Journal of Child and Family Studies*, 2, 283–93.*

Henggeler, S., Rodick, D., Borduin, C., Hanson, C., Watson, S. and Urey, J. (1986) Multisystemic treatment of juvenile offenders: Effects on adolescent behaviour and family interaction. *Developmental Psychology*, 22, 132–41.*

Herbert, M. (1987a). *Behavioural Treatment of Children With Problems*. London: Academic Press.

Herbert, M. (1987b). *Living with Teenagers*. Oxford: Basil Blackwell.

Herbert, M. (1989). *Discipline: A Positive Guide For Parents*. Oxford: Basil Blackwell.

Herbert, M. (1994). Etiological considerations. In T. Ollendick, N. King and W. Yule (eds), *International Handbook of Phobic and Anxiety Disorders in Children and Adolescents* (pp. 3–20). New York: Plenum.

Herbert, M. (1996a). *ABC of Behavioural Methods*. Leicester: British Psychological Society.

Herbert, M. (1996b). *Banishing Bad Behaviour*. Leicester: British Psychological Society.

Herbert, M. (1996c). *Separation and Divorce: Helping Children Cope*. Leicester: British Psychological Society.

Herbert, M. (1996d). *Supporting Bereaved and Dying Children and Their Parents*. Leicester: British Psychological Society.

Herbert, M. (1996e). *Toilet Training, Bedwetting and Soiling*. Leicester: British Psychological Society.

Hermann, C., Kim, M. and Blanchard, E. (1995). Behavioural and prophylactic pharmacological intervention studies of paediatric migraine: An exploratory meta-analysis. *Pain*, 60, 239–55.

Hester, N., Foster, R. and Kristensen, K. (1990). Measurement of pain in children: Generalizability and validity of the pain ladder and the poker chip tool. In D. Tyler and E. Krane (eds), *Paediatric Pain. Advances in Pain Research and Therapy* (Vol. 15, pp. 79–84). New York: Raven.

Hetherington, M. (1989). Coping with family transitions: Winners, losers and survivors. *Child Development*, 60, 1–14.

Hildebrand, J. (1988). *Surviving Marital Breakdown. Emotional and Behavioural Problems in Adolescents: A Multidisciplinary Approach to Identification and Management*. Windsor, Berks: NFER Nelson.

Hinshaw, S. (1994). *Attention Deficits and Hyperactivity in Children*. Thousand Oaks, CA: Sage.

Hinshaw, S. and Erhardt, D. (1991). Attention deficit hyperactivity disorder. In P. Kendall (ed.), *Child and Adolescent Therapy: Cognitive Behavioural Perspectives* (pp. 98–128). New York: Guilford.

Hinshaw, S., Henker, B. and Whalen, C. (1984). Self-control in hyperactive boys in anger inducing situations; Effects of cognitive-behavioural training and methylphenidate. *Journal of Abnormal Child Psychology*, 12, 55–77.*

Hinshaw, S., Klein, R. and Abikoff, H. (1998). Childhood attention deficit hyperactivity disorder: Nonpharmacological and combination approaches. In P. Nathan and J. Gorman (eds), *A Guide to Treatments that Work* (pp. 26–41). New York: Oxford University Press.

Hodges, W. (1986). *Intervention for Children of Divorce*. New York: Wiley.

Hoffman-Plotkin, D. and Twentyman, C. (1984). A multimodel assessment of behavioural and cognitive deficits in abused and neglected pre-schoolers. *Child Development*, 55, 794–802.

Holroyd, K.A. and Andrasiks, F. (1978). Coping and the self-control of chronic tension headaches. *Journal of Consulting and Clinical Psychology*, 46, 1036–45.

Horn, W., Ialongo, N. and Pascoe, J. (1991b). Additive effects of psychostimulants, parent training and self-control therapy with ADHD children. *Journal of the American Academy of Child and Adolescent Psychiatry*, 30, 233–40.*

Horn, W., Ialongo, N., Popovich, S. and Peradotto, D. (1987). Behavioural parent training and cognitive-behavioural self-control therapy with ADD-H children: Comparative and combined effects. *Journal of Clinical Child Psychology*, 16, 57–68.*

Horn, W., Ialongo, N., Greenberg, G., Packard, T. and Smith-Winberry, C. (1990). Additive effects of behavioural parent training and self-control therapy with attention deficit hyperactivity disordered children. *Journal of Clinical Child Psychology*, 19, 98–110.*

Horn, W., Ialongo, N., Pascoe, J., Greenberg, G., Packard, T., Lopez, M., Wagner, A. and Puttler, L. (1991a). Additive effects of behavioural parent training, child self-control therapy and stimulant medication with ADHD children. *Journal of the American Academy of Child and Adolescent Psychiatry*, 30, 233–40.*

Hornick, J. and Clarke, M. (1986). A cost/effectiveness evaluation of lay therapy treatment for child abusing and high risk parents. *Child Abuse and Neglect*, 10, 309–18.*

Hornick, J., Patterson, C. and Clarke, M. (1983). *The Use of Lay Therapists in the Treatment of Child Abusers: A Summary Report*. Wilfrid Laurier University, Ontario.

Horowitz, M., Wilner, N. and Alverez, W. (1979). Impact of events scale. A measure of subjective stress. *Psychosomatic Medicine*, 41, 209–18.

Houts, A. and Liebert, R. (1984). *Bedwetting: A Guide for Parents and Children*. Springfield, Ill: Charles C. Thomas.

Houts, A., Berman, J. and Abramson, H. (1994). Effectiveness of psychological and pharmacological treatments for nocturnal enuresis. *Journal of Consulting and Clinical Psychology*, 62, 737–45.

Houts, A., Peterson, J. and Whelan, J. (1986). Prevention of relapse in full-spectrum home training for primary enuresis: A components analysis. *Behavior Therapy*, 17, 462–9.*

Howlin, P. (1998). Psychological and educational treatments for autism. *Journal of Child Psychology and Psychiatry*, 39, 307–22.

Hsu, L. (1990). *Eating Disorders*. New York: Guilford.

Hudson, J., Nutter, R. and Galaway, B. (1994). Treatment foster care programs: A review of evaluation research and suggested directions. *Social Work Research*, 18, 198–212.

Ialongo, N., Horn, W., Pascoe, J., Greenberg, G., Packard, T., Lopez, M., Wagner, A. and Puttler, L. (1993). The effects of a multimodal intervention with attention-deficit hyperactivity disorder children: A 9-month follow-up. *Journal of the American Academy of Child and Adolescent Psychiatry*, 32, 182–9.*

Ingersoll, B. (1988). *Your Hyperactive Child; A Parent's Guide to Coping with Attention Deficit Disorder*. New York: Doubleday.

Ioannou, C. (1991). Acute pain in children. In M. Herbert (ed.), *Clinical Child Psychology* (pp. 331–9). Chichester: Wiley.

Ives, S. and Fassler, D. (1985a). *Changing Families: A Guide for Kids and Grown-ups*. Burlington, VT: Waterfront Books.

Ives, S. and Fassler, D. (1985b). *The Divorce Workbook: A Guide for Kids and Families*. Burlington, VT: Waterfront Books.

Iwaniec, D. (1995). *The Emotionally Abused and Neglected Child: Identification, Assessment and Intervention.* Chichester: Wiley.

Jacobson, N., Follette, W. and Revenstorf, D. (1984). Psychotherapy outcome research: Methods for reporting variability and evaluating clinical significance. *Behaviour Therapy*, 15, 336–52.

James, J. and Cherry, F. (1988). *The Grief Recovery Handbook: A Step-by-Step Programme For Moving Beyond Loss.* New York: Harper Row.

Jay, S., Elliott, C., Katz, E. and Siegel, S. (1987). Cognitive-behavioural and pharmacologic interventions for children's distress during painful medical procedures. *Journal of Consulting and Clinical Psychology*, 55, 860–5.*

Joanning, H., Quinn, W., Thomas, F. and Mullen, R. (1992). Treating adolescent drug abuse: A comparison of family systems therapy, adolescent group therapy, and family drug education. *Journal of Marital and Family Therapy*, 18, 345–56.*

Johnston, C. and Mash, E. (1989). A measure of parenting satisfaction and efficacy. *Journal of Clinical Child Psychology*, 18, 167–75.

Johnson, R. and Shrier, D. (1995). Sexual victimisation of boys. *Journal of Adolescent Healthcare*, 6, 372–6.

Kabacoff, R., Miller, I., Bishop, D., Epstein, N. and Keitner, G. (1990). A psychometric study of the McMaster Family Assessment Device. *Journal of Family Psychology*, 3, 431–9.

Kagan, J. (1966). Reflection-impulsivity: The generality and dynamics of conceptual tempo. *Journal of Abnormal Psychology*, 71, 17–24.

Kahn, J., Kehle, T., Jenson, W. and Clarke, E. (1990). Comparison of cognitive behavioural, relaxation and self-modelling interventions among middle school students. *School Psychology Review*, 19, 2, 196–211.*

Kaiminer, Y., Wagner, E., Plummer, E. and Seifer, R. (1993). Validation of the Teen Addiction Severity Index (T-ASI): Preliminary findings. *The American Journal of Addictions*, 3, 250–4.

Kanfer, F., Karoly, P. and Newman, A. (1975). Reduction of children's fear of the dark by competence-related and situational threat-related verbal cues. *Journal of Consulting and Clinical Psychology*, 43 (2), 251–8.*

Kaplan, S. and Busner, J. (1993). Treatment of nocturnal enuresis. In T. Giles (ed.), *Handbook of Effective Psychotherapy* (pp. 135–50). New York: Plenum.

Karoly, P. and Rosenthal, M. (1977). Training parents in behaviour modification: Effects on perceptions of family interaction and deviant child behaviour. *Behaviour Therapy*, 8, 406–10.*

Kazak, A., Penati, B., Waibel, M. and Blackall, G. (1996). The Perception of Procedures Questionnaire (PPQ). Psychometric properties of a brief parent report measure of procedural distress. *Journal of Pediatric Psychology*, 21, 195–207.

Kazak, A., Penati, B., Boyer, B. and Himelstein, B. (1996). A randomized controlled prospective outcome study of a psychological and pharmacological intervention protocol for procedural distress in paediatric leukaemia. *Journal of Pediatric Psychology*, 21, 615–31.*

Kazdin, A. (1983). Hopelessness, depression and suicidal intent among psychiatrically disturbed inpatient children. *Journal of Consulting and Clinical Psychology*, 51, 504–10.

Kazdin, A. (1988). *Child Psychotherapy: Developing and Identifying Effective Treatments.* New York: Pergamon.

Kazdin, A. (1995). *Conduct Disorders in Childhood and Adolescence* (Second Edition). Thousand Oaks, CA: Sage.

Kazdin, A. (1997). Psychosocial treatments for conduct disorder in children. *Journal of Child Psychology and Psychiatry*, 38, 161–78.

Kazdin, A. (1998). Psychosocial treatments for conduct disorder in children. In P. Nathan and J. Gorman (eds), *A Guide To Treatments That Work* (pp. 65–89). New York: Oxford University Press.

Kazdin, A. and Weisz, J. (1998). Identifying and developing empirically supported child and adolescent treatments. *Journal of Consulting and Clinical Psychology*, 66, 37–52.

Kazdin, A. and Esveldt-Dawson, K. (1986). The Interview for Antisocial Behaviour: Psychometric characteristics and concurrent validity with child psychiatric in-patients. *Journal of Psychopathology and Behavioural Assessment*, 8, 289–303.

Kazdin, A., Colbus, D. and Rogers, A. (1986). Assessment of depression and diagnosis of depressive disorder among psychiatrically disturbed children. *Journal of Abnormal Child Psychology*, 14, 499–515.

Kazdin, A., Siegel, T.C. and Bass, D. (1992). Cognitive problem solving skills training and parent management training in the treatment of antisocial behaviour in children. *Journal of Consulting and Clinical Psychology*, 60, 733–47.*

Kazdin, A., Esveldt-Dawson, K., French, N.H. and Unis, A.S. (1987). Effects of parent management training and problem-solving skills training combined in the treatment of antisocial child behaviour. *Journal of The American Academy of Child and Adolescent Psychiatry*, 26, 416–24.*

Keane, T. (1998). Psychological and behavioural treatments of post-traumatic stress disorder. In P. Nathan and J. Gorman (eds), *A Guide to Treatments that Work* (pp. 398–407). New York: Oxford University Press.

Kearney, C. and Silverman, W. (1993). Measuring the function of school refusal behaviour: The school refusal assessment scale (SRAS). *Journal of Clinical Child Psychology*, 22, 85–96.

Kelly, C. (1996). Chronic constipation and soiling in children; A review of the psychological and family literature. *Child Psychology and Psychiatry Review*, 1, 59–66.

Kendall, P. (1992). *Coping Cat Workbook*. Admore, PA: Workbook Publishing.

Kendall, P. (1993). Cognitive behavioural therapies with youth: Guiding theory, current status and emerging developments. *Journal of Consulting and Clinical Psychology*, 61, 235–47.

Kendall, P. (1994). Treating anxiety disorders in children: Results of a randomised clinical trial. *Journal of Consulting and Clinical Psychology*, 62 (1), 100–10.

Kendall, P. and Braswell, L. (1982). Cognitive-behavioural self-control therapy for children: A components analysis. *Journal of Consulting and Clinical Psychology*, 50, 672–89.*

Kendall, P. and Braswell, L. (1985). *Cognitive Behavioural Therapy for Impulsive Children*. New York: Guilford.

Kendall, P. and Chambless, D. (1998). Special section on empirically supported psychological therapies. *Journal of Consulting and Clinical Psychology*, 66, 1–167.

Kendall, P. and Finch, A. (1978). A cognitive behavioural treatment for impulsivity: A group comparison study. *Journal of Consulting and Clinical Psychology*, 46, 110–18.*

Kendall, P. and Wilcox, L. (1979). Self-control in children: The development of a rating scale. *Journal of Consulting and Clinical Psychology*, 47, 1020–30.

Kendall, P. and Wilcox, I. (1980). A cognitive-behavioural treatment for impulsivity: Concrete versus conceptual training in non self-controlled problem children. *Journal of Consulting and Clinical Psychology*, 48, 80–91.*

Kendall, P., Kane, M., Howard, B. and Siqueland, L. (1990). *Cognitive-behavioural Therapy for Anxious Children. Treatment Manual*. Admore, PA: Workbook Publishing.

Kendall, P., Chansky, T., Kane, M., Kim, R., Kortlander, E., Ronan, K., Sessa, F. and Siqueland, L. (1992). *Anxiety Disorder in Youth: Cognitive Behavioural Interventions*. Needham Heights, USA: Allyn and Bacon.

Kendall-Tackett, K., Williams, L. and Finklehor, D. (1993). Impact of sexual abuse on children. *Psychological Bulletin*, 113, 164–80.

Kendell, R. (1976). The classification of depressions: A review of contemporary confusion. *British Journal of Psychiatry*, 129, 15–88.

Kent, R. and O'Leary, K. (1976). A controlled evaluation of behaviour modification with conduct problem children. *Journal of Consulting and Clinical Psychology*, 44, 586–96.*

Kibby, M., Tyc, V. and Mulhern, R. (1998). Effectiveness of psychological intervention for children and adolescents with chronic medical illness: A meta-analysis. *Clinical Psychology Review*, 18, 103–17.

King, B. and State, M. (1997). Mental retardation: A review of the past 10 years part 1. *Journal of the American Academy of Child and Adolescent Psychiatry*, 36, 1656–63.

Kirgin, K., Braukmann, C., Atwater, J. and Wolf, M. (1982). An evaluation of Teaching-Family (Achievement Place) Group homes for juvenile offenders. *Journal of Applied Behaviour Analysis*, 15, 1–16.*

Klein, M., Alexander, J. and Parsons, B. (1977). Impact of family systems intervention on recidivism and sibling delinquency: A model of primary prevention and programme evaluation. *Journal of Consulting and Clinical Psychology*, 45, 469–74.

Klein, R. (1994). Anxiety disorders. In M. Rutter, E. Taylor and L. Hersov (eds), *Child and Adolescent Psychiatry: Modern Approaches* (Third Edition, pp. 351–74). London: Blackwell.

Klerman, G., Weissman, M., Rounsaville, B. and Chevron, E. (1984). *Interpersonal Psychotherapy of Depression*. New York: Basic Books.

Knapp, M. (1997). Economic evaluations and interventions for children and adolescents with mental health problems. *Journal of Child Psychology and Psychiatry*, 38, 3–25.

Kolko, D. (1996). Clinical monitoring of treatment course in child physical abuse: Psychometric characteristics and treatment comparisons. *Child Abuse and Neglect*, 20, 23–43.*

Kovacs, M. (1997). The Emanuel Miller Memorial Lecture 1994 – Depressive disorders in childhood: An impressionistic landscape. *Journal of Child Psychology and Psychiatry*, 38, 287–98.

Kovacs, M. and Beck, A. (1977). An empirical clinical approach towards definition of childhood depression. In J. Schulterbrandt and A. Raskin (eds), *Depression in Children* (pp. 1–25). New York: Raven.

Krementz, J. (1981). *How it Feels When a Parent Dies*. New York: Knopf.

Krinsley, K.E. (1991). Behavioural family therapy for adolescent school problems: School performance effects and generalisation to substance use (Doctoral dissertation, Rutgers University). *Dissertation Abstracts International*, 52, 1725b.*

Kroll, L., Harrington, R., Jayson, D., Fraser, J. and Gowers, S. (1996). Pilot study of a continuation cognitive behavioural therapy for major depression in adolescent psychiatric patients. *Journal of the American Academy of Child and Adolescent Psychiatry*, 35 (9), 1156–61.*

Kübler-Ross, E. (1983). *On Children and Death*. New York: Macmillan.

Kurdek, L. (1987). Children's beliefs about parental divorce scale. Psychometric characteristics and concurrent validity. *Journal of Consulting and Clinical Psychology*, 55, 712–18.

Kutcher, S. (1997). The pharmacotherapy of adolescent depression. *Journal of Child Psychology and Psychiatry*, 38, 755–67.

Kuttner, L., Bowman, M. and Teasdale, M. (1988). Psychological treatment of distress, pain, and anxiety for young children with cancer. *Journal of Developmental and Behavioural Pediatrics*, 9, 374–81.*

Labbé, E. and Williamson, D. (1984). Treatment of childhood migraine using autogenic feedback training. *Journal of Consulting and Clinical Psychology*, 52, 968–76.*

Labbé, E., Williamson, D. and Southard, D. (1985). Reliability and validity of children's reports of migraine headache symptoms. *Journal of Psychopathology and Behavioural Assessment*, 7, 375–83.

Lander, J. and Fowler, K. (1993). TENS for children's procedural pain. *Pain*, 52, 209–16.*

Lansdown, R. and Sokel, B. (1993). Approaches to pain management in children. *ACCP Review*, 15 (May), 105–11.

Larsson, B. and Carlsson, J. (1996). A school-based, nurse-administered relaxation training for children with chronic tension-type headache. *Journal of Pediatric Psychology*, 21, 603–14.*

Lask, B. and Bryant-Waugh, R. (1992). Early-onset anorexia nervosa and related eating disorders. *Journal of Child Psychology and Psychiatry*, 33, 281–300.

Lask, B. and Bryant-Waugh, R. (1993). *Childhood Onset Anorexia Nervosa and Related Disorders*. Hove: Lawrence Erlbaum.

Lask, B. and Fosson, A. (1989). *Childhood Illness: A Psychosomatic Approach*. Chichester: Wiley.

Lazarus, A. and Abramovitz, A. (1962). The use of 'emotive imagery' in the treatment of children's phobias. *Journal of Mental Science*, 108, 191–5.

Le Baron, S. and Zeltzer, L. (1984). Assessment of acute pain and anxiety in children and adolescents by self-reports, observer reports and a behaviour checklist. *Journal of Consulting and Clinical Psychology*, 52, 729–38.

Le Grange, D., Eisler, I., Dare, C. and Russell, G. (1992). Evaluation of family treatments in adolescent anorexia nervosa: A pilot study. *International Journal of Eating Disorders*, 12, 347–57.*

Lee, C., Picard, M.N. and Blain, M. (1994). A methodological and substantive review of intervention outcome studies for families undergoing divorce. *Journal Of Family Psychology*, 8, 3–15.

Lehmann, P. and Dangel, R. (1998). Oppositional defiant disorder. In B. Thyer and J. Wodarski (eds), *Handbook of Empirical Social Work Practise. Volume 1. Mental Disorders* (pp. 91–116). New York: Wiley.

Leitenberg, H., Yost, L. and Carroll-Wilson, M. (1986). Negative cognitive errors in children: Questionnaire development, normative data, and comparisons between children with and without self-reported symptoms of depression, low self-esteem and evaluation anxiety. *Journal of Consulting and Clinical Psychology*, 54, 528–36.

LeShan, E. (1986). *What's Going to Happen to me: When Parents Separate or Divorce* (Revised Edition). New York: Macmillan.

Levine, M. (1991). Enuresis. In M. Levine, W. Carey and A. Cocker (eds), *Developmental-Behavioral Paediatrics* (Second Edition, pp. 389–97). Philadelphia, PA: Saunders.

Levitt, E. (1957). The results of psychotherapy with children: An evaluation. *Journal of Consulting Psychology*, 21, 189–96.

Lewinsohn, P. and Clarke, G. (1986). *The Coping with Depression Course – Adolescent Version: Parent Manual*. Eugene, OR: Peter Lewinsohn.

Lewinsohn, P. and Gotlib, I. (1995). Behavioural theory and treatment of depression. In E. Becker and W. Leber (eds), *Handbook of Depression* (pp. 352–75). New York: Guilford.

Lewinsohn, P., Clarke, G., Hops, H. and Andrews, J. (1990). Cognitive behavioural treatment for depressed adolescents. *Behavior Therapy*, 385–401.*

Lewis, R., Piercy, F., Sprenkle, D. and Trepper, T. (1989). The Purdue Brief Family Therapy model for adolescent substance abusers. In T. Todd and M. Selekman (eds), *Family Therapy Approaches with Adolescent Substance Abusers*. New York: Gardner.

Lewis, R., Piercy, F., Sprenkle, D. and Trepper, T. (1990). Family-based interventions for helping drug-abusing adolescents. *Journal of Adolescent Research*, 5, 82–95.*

Liddle, H. and Dakof, G. (1995). Efficacy of family therapy for drug abuse: Promising but not definitive. *Journal of Marital and Family Therapy*, 21, 511–43.

Liddle, H., Dakof, G., Parker, K., Diamond, G., Garcia, R., Barrett, K. and Jurwitz, S. (1995). *Multidimensional Family Therapy for the Treatment of Adolescent Drug Abuse. A Controlled Clinical Trial*. Manuscript submitted for publication.*

Loeber, R. and Stouthamer-Loeber, M. (1998). Development of juvenile aggression and violence: Some common misconceptions and controversies. *American Psychologist*, 53, 242–59.

Lukas, C. and Seiden, H. (1987). *Silent Grief: Living in the Wake of Suicide*. New York: Scribners.

Lutzker, J. (1984). Project 12-Ways. Treating child abuse and neglect from an eco-behavioural perspective. In R. Daniel and R. Polster (eds), *Parent Training: Foundations of Research and Practise* (pp. 260–97). New York: Guilford.

McArdle, P., O'Brien, G. and Kolvin, I. (1995). Hyperactivity: Prevalence and relationship with conduct disorder. *Journal of Child Psychology and Psychiatry*, 36, 279–304.

McCarthy, D. (1979). Recognition of signs of emotional deprivation: A form of child abuse, *Child Abuse and Neglect*, 3, 423–8.

McConaughy, S. and Achenbach, T. (1994). Comorbidity of empirically based syndromes in matched general population and clinical samples. *Journal of Child Psychology and Psychiatry*, 35, 1141–57.

McCubbin, H., Patterson, J. and Wilson, L. (1985). FILE: Family Inventory of Life Events and Changes. In D. Olson, H. McCubbin, H. Barnes *et al.* (eds), *Family Inventories*, (pp. 82–114). St Paul, MN: University of Minnesota Press.

McGain, B. and McKinzey, R. (1995). The efficacy of group treatment in sexually abused girls. *Child Abuse and Neglect*, 19, 1157–69.*

McGrath, P. (1987). The multidimensional assessment and management of recurrent pain syndromes in children. *Behaviour Research and Therapy*, 25, 251–62.

McGrath, P. (1990). *Pain in Children: Nature Assessment and Treatment*. New York: Guilford.

McGrath, P. (1995). Aspects of pain in children and adolescents. *Journal of Child Psychology and Psychiatry*, 36, 717–31.

McGrath, P., DeVeber, L. and Hearn, M. (1985). Multidimensional pain assessment in children. In H. Fields, R. Dubner and F. Cervero (eds), *Advances in Pain Research and Therapy* (Vol. 9, pp. 387–93). New York: Raven.

McGrath, P., McGrath, P.J., Cunningham, S., Lascelles, M. and Humphries, P. (1990). *Help Yourself: A Treatment for Migraine Headaches*. Ottawa, Canada: University of Ottawa Press.

McGrath, P., Johnson, G., Goodman, J., Schillinger, J., Dunn, J. and Chapman, J. (1985). CHEOPS: A behavioural scale for rating post-operative pain in children. In H. Fields, R. Dubner and F. Cerveero (eds), *Advances in Pain Research and Therapy* (Vol. 9, pp. 395–401). New York: Raven.

McGrath, P., Humphreys, P., Goodman, J., Keene, D., Firestone, P., Jacob, P. and Cunningham, S.J. (1988). Relaxation prophylaxis for childhood migraine: A randomised placebo-controlled trial. *Developmental Medicine and Child Neurology*, 30, 626–31.*

McNeil, C.B., Eyberg, S., Eisenstadt, T.H., Funderburk, B. and Newcomb, K. (1991). Parent–child interaction therapy with behaviour problem children: Generalization of treatment effects to the school setting. *Journal of Clinical Child Psychology*, 20, 140–51.*

Magid, D. and Schriebman, W. (1980). *Divorce is. . . . A Kid's Colouring Book*. Gretna, LA: Pelican.

Malinosky-Rummell, R. and Hansen, H. (1993). Long-term consequences of childhood physical abuse. *Psychological Bulletin*, 114, 68–79.

Malone, A. (1996). The effects of live music on the distress of paediatric patients receiving intravenous starts, venipunctures, injections, and heel sticks. *Journal of Music Therapy*, 33, 19–33.*

Maloney, M., McGuire, J. and Daniels, S. (1988). Reliability testing of the Children's Version of the Eating Attitudes Test. *Journal of the American Academy of Child and Adolescent Psychiatry*, 27, 541–3.

Mann, B.J., Borduin, C., Henggeler, S. and Blaske, D. (1990). An investigating systemic conceptualisation of parent–child coalitions and symptom change. *Journal of Consulting and Clinical Psychology*, 60, 953–61.*

March, J. (1995). Cognitive behavioural psychotherapy for children and adolescents with OCD: A review and recommendations for treatment. *Journal of the American Academy of Child and Adolescent Psychiatry*, 34, 7–18.

March, J. and Mulle, K. (1994). *How I Ran OCD Off My Land: A Cognitive-Behavioral Program for the Treatment of Obsessive-Compulsive Disorder in Children And Adolescents* (Revision 1.8). Unpublished Manuscript. Department of Psychiatry, Duke University Medical Centre, Box 3527, Durham, NC 27710.

March, J. and Mulle, K. (1996). Banishing OCD: Cognitive behavioural psychotherapy for obsessive compulsive disorders. In E. Hibbs and P. Jensen (eds),

Psychosocial Treatments for Child and Adolescent Disorders (pp. 43–63). Washington, DC: American Psychiatric Association (APA).

March, J., Mulle, K. and Herbel, B. (1994). Behavioural psychotherapy for children and adolescents with OCD: An open trial of a new protocol-driven treatment package. *Journal of the American Academy of Child and Adolescent Psychiatry*, 33 (3), 333–41.*

Martin, B. (1977). Brief family intervention: Effectiveness and the importance of including the father. *Journal of Consulting and Clinical Psychology*, 45, 1002–10.*

Mash, E. and Terdal, L. (1997). *Assessment of Childhood Disorders* (Third Edition). New York: Guilford.

Matson, J. (1989). *Treating Depression in Children and Adolescents*. New York: Pergamon.

Maughan, B. (1995). Long term outcomes of developmental reading problems. *Journal of Child Psychology and Psychiatry*, 36, 357–71.

Mayer, J. and Filstead, W. (1979). The adolescent alcohol involvement scale: An instrument for measuring adolescent use and misuse of alcohol. *Journal of Studies in Alcohol*, 40, 291–300.

Meichenbaum, D. (1977). *Cognitive Behaviour Modification. An Integrative Approach*. New York: Plenum.

Meichenbaum, D. (1985). *Stress Inoculation Training. A Clinical Guidebook*. New York: Pergamon.

Meichenbaum, D. and Goodman, J. (1971). Training impulsive children to talk to themselves: A means of developing self-control. *Journal of Abnormal Psychology*, 70, 117–26.

Milner, J. (1986). *The Child Abuse Potential Inventory Manual (Revised)*. Webster, NC: Psytec Corporation.

Milner, J. and Ayoub, C. (1980). Evaluation of at risk parents using the Child Abuse Potential Inventory. *Journal of Clinical Psychology*, 36, 945–8.

Mindell, J. and Andrasik, F. (1987). Headache classification and factor analysis with a paediatric population. *Headache*, 27, 96–101.

Minuchin, S., (1974). *Families and Family Therapy*. Cambridge, MA: Harvard University Press.

Minuchin, S., Rosen, B. and Baker, L. (1978). *Psychosomatic Families*. Cambridge, MA: Harvard University Press.

Moos, R. (1974). *Family Environment Scale: Preliminary Manual*. Palo Alto, CA: Stanford University, Social Ecology Laboratory.

Moos, R. and Moos, B. (1981). *Family Environment Scale Manual*. Palo Alto, CA: Consulting Psychologists' Press.

Morgan, A. and Hayward, A. (1988). Clinical assessment of anorexia nervosa: the Morgan Russell outcome assessment schedule. *British Journal of Psychiatry*, 152, 367–71.

Morgan, R. and Young, G. (1975). Parental attitudes and the conditioning treatment of childhood enuresis. *Behaviour Research and Therapy*, 13, 197–9.

Morris, R. and Kratochwill, T. (1991). Childhood fears and phobias. In T. Kratochwill and R. Morris (eds), *The Practice of Child Therapy* (Second Edition, pp. 76–114). New York: Pergamon.

Mufson, L., Moreau, D., Weissman, M. and Kerman, G. (1993). *Interpersonal Psychotherapy for Depressed Adolescents*. New York: Guilford.

Mulvey, E., Arthur, M. and Reppucci, N. (1993). The prevention and treatment of juvenile delinquency. *Clinical Psychology Review*, 13, 133–67.

Nathan, P. and Gorman, J. (1998). *A Guide to Treatments that Work*. New York: Oxford University Press.

Nemeroff, C. and Schatzberg, A. (1998). Pharmacological treatment of unipolar depression. In P. Nathan and J. Gorman (eds), *A Guide to Treatments that Work* (pp. 212–25). New York: Oxford University Press.

Newcomb, M. and Bentler, P. (1988). *Consequence of Adolescent Drug Abuse: Impact on the Lives of Young Adults*. Newbury Park, CA: Sage.

Nicol, A., Smith, J., Kay, B., Hall, D., Baslow, J. and Williams, B. (1988). A focused casework approach to the treatment of child abuse: A controlled comparison. *Journal of Child Psychology and Psychiatry*, 29 (5), 703–11.*

Novaco, R.A. (1975). *Anger Control: The Development and Evaluation of an Experimental Treatment*. Lexington, MA: D.C. Heath.

O'Leary, K. and O'Leary, S. (1972). *Classroom Management: The Successful use of Behavior Modification*. New York: Pergamon.

Oates, R. and Bross, D. (1995). What have we learned about treating child physical abuse? A literature review of the last decade. *Child Abuse and Neglect*, 19, 463–73.

Ollendick, T., King, N. and Yule, W. (1994a). *International Handbook of Phobic and Anxiety Disorders in Children and Adolescents*. New York: Plenum.

Ollendick, T., Mattis, S. and King, N. (1994b). Panic in children and adolescents: a review. *Journal of Child Psychology and Psychiatry*, 34, 113–34.

Olness, K. and Gardner, G. (1988). *Hypnosis and Hypnotherapy with Children*. Philadelphia, PA: Grune and Stratton.

Olson, D., Portner, J. and Lavee, Y. (1985). *FACES III*. Minnesota: Family Social Science, University of Minnesota.

Olson, R. and Roberts, M. (1987). Alternative treatments for sibling aggression. *Behaviour Therapy*, 18, 243–50.*

Ordman, A. and Kirschenbaum, D. (1985). Cognitive behaviour therapy for bulimia: An initial outcome study. *Journal of Consulting and Clinical Psychology*, 53 (3), 305–13.*

Ost, L. (1990). The Agoraphobia Scale: An evaluation of its reliability and validity. *Behaviour Research and Therapy*, 28, 697–708.

Oster, G. and Caro, J. (1990). *Understanding And Treating Depressed Adolescents And Their Families*. New York: Wiley.

Osterhaus, S., Passchier, J., Van der Helm Hylkema, H. and de Jong, K.T. (1993). Effects of behavioural psychophysiological treatment on schoolchildren with migraine in a nonclinical setting: Predictors and process variables. Special Issue: Interventions in paediatric psychology. *Journal of Pediatric Psychology*, 18, 697–715.*

Pagliaro, A. and Pagliaro, L. (1996). *Substance Use among Children and Adolescents*. New York: Wiley.

Palmer, R., Christie, M., Cordle, C. and Kendrick, J. (1987). The clinical eating disorder rating instrument (CEDRI): A preliminary description. *International Journal of Eating Disorders*, 6, 9–16.

Papadatou, D. and Papadatou, C. (eds) (1991). *Children and Death*. London: Hemisphere.

Parkes, C. (1975). Determinants of outcome following bereavement. *Omega*, 6, 303–23.

Parsons, B. and Alexander, J. (1973). Short term family intervention: A therapy outcome study. *Journal of Consulting and Clinical Psychology*, 41, 195–201.*

Patterson, G. (1965). An application of conditioning techniques to the control of a hyperactive child. In L. Ullmann and L. Krasner (eds), *Case Studies in Behaviour Modification* (pp. 370–5). New York: Holt Rinehart and Winston.

Patterson, G. (1973). *Living with Children*. Champaign, Ill: Research Press.

Patterson, G. (1975). *Families: Applications of Social Learning to Family Life.* Champaign, Ill: Research Press.

Patterson, G. (1976). *Living with Children: New Methods for Parents and Teachers.* Champaign, Ill: Research Press.

Patterson, G. and Forgatch, M. (1987). *Parents and Adolescents Living Together. Part 1. The Basics.* Eugene, OR: Castalia Press.

Patterson, G., Chamberlain, P. and Reid, J. (1982). A comparative evaluation of a parent-training program. *Behaviour Therapy*, 13, 638–50.*

Patterson, G., Reid, J., Jones, R. and Conger, R. (1975). *A Social Learning Approach To Family Intervention: Volume 1: Families With Aggressive Children.* Eugene, OR: Castelia Press.

Paul, G. (1967). Outcome research in psychotherapy. *Journal of Consulting Psychology*, 31, 109–18.

Pearce, J. and Pezzot-Pearce, T. (1997). *Psychotherapy of Abused and Neglected Children.* New York: Guilford.

Pedro-Carroll, J. (1989). Children of Divorce Intervention Programme (CODIP). Available from Dr Pedro-Carroll, Centre for Community Studies, University of Rochester, 575 Mt Hope Avenue, Rochester, New York 14620, USA.

Pedro-Carroll, J. and Cowen, E.L. (1985). The children of divorce intervention project; An investigation of the efficacy of a school-based prevention program. *Journal of Consulting and Clinical Psychology*, 53, 603–11.*

Pedro-Carroll, J., Alpert-Gillis, L.J. and Cowen, E.L. (1992). An evaluation of the efficacy of a prevention intervention for 4th to 6th grade urban children of divorce. *The Journal of Primary Prevention*, 13, 115–30.*

Peed, S., Roberts, M. and Forehand, R. (1977). Evaluation of the effectiveness of a standardized parent training program in altering the interaction of mothers and their noncompliance children. *Behaviour Modification*, 1, 323–51.*

Pelham, W. (1994). *Attention Deficit Hyperactivity Disorder: A Clinician's Guide.* New York: Plenum.

Pelham, W., Carlson, C., Sams, S., Vallano, G., Dixon, J. and Hoza, B. (1993). Separate and combined effects of methylphenidate and behaviour modification on boys with attention deficit hyperactivity disorder in the classroom. *Journal of Consulting and Clinical Psychology*, 61, 506–15.*

Perry, M. and Gordon, E. (1975). Situation interview. Unpublished manuscript.

Peterson, L. and Shigetomi, C. (1981). The use of coping techniques to minimize anxiety in hospitalized children. *Behavior Therapy*, 12, 1–14.*

Petti, T. (1978). Depression in hospitalized child psychiatry patients: Approaches to measuring depression. *Journal of the American Academy of Child Psychiatry*, 17, 49–59.

Piers, E. and Harris, D. (1963). *The Piers-Harris Self-Concept Scale.* Unpublished manuscript, Pennsylvania State University, University Park.

Piers, E. and Harris, D. (1969). *The Piers-Harris Children's Self-Concept Scale.* Nashville, TN: Counsellor Recordings and Tests.

Pinsof, W. and Wynne, L. (1995). *Family Therapy Effectiveness: Current Research and Theory*. Special Edition: *Journal of Marital and Family Therapy*, 21 (4). Washington, DC: AAMFT.

Pisterman, S., Firestone, P., McGrath, P., Goodman, J., Webster, I., Mallory, R. and Goffin, B. (1992). The role of parent training in treatment of pre-schoolers with ADHD. *American Journal of Orthopsychiatry*, 62, 397–408.

Polansky, N., Chalmers, M., Buttenwieser, E. and Williams, D. (1981). *Damaged Parents: An Anatomy of Neglect*. Chicago, Ill: University of Chicago.

Porteus, S. (1955). *The Maze Test: Recent Advances*. Palo Alto, CA: Pacific Books.

Pozanski, E., Grossman, J., Buchsman, Y., Banegras, M., Freeman, L. and Gibbons, R. (1984). Preliminary studies of the reliability and validity of the Children's Depression Rating Scale. *Journal of the American Academy of Child and Adolescent Psychiatry*, 23, 191–7.

Protinsky, H. and Kersey, B. (1983). Psychogenic encopresis: A family therapy approach. *Journal of Clinical Child Psychology*, 12, 192–7.*

Puig-Antich, J. and Chambers, W. (1978). Schedule for Affective Disorders and Schizophrenia for school aged children. New York State Psychiatric Institute: unpublished interview schedule.

Putnam, F., Helmers, K. and Trickett, P. (1993). Development, reliability and validity of a child dissociation scale. *Child Abuse and Neglect*, 17, 731–42.

Quay, H. and Peterson, D. (1975). *Manual for the Behaviour Problem Checklist*. Unpublished manuscript.

Quay, H. and Peterson, D. (1987). *Manual for the Revised Behaviour Problem Checklist*. Coral Gables, FL: University of Miami, Department of Psychology.

Quinn, W., Kuehl, B., Thomas, F. and Joanning, H. (1988). Families of adolescent drug abusers: Systemic interventions to attain drug-free behaviour. *American Journal of Drug and Alcohol Abuse*, 14, 65–87.

Quinn, W., Kuehl, B., Thomas, F., Joanning, H. and Newfield, N. (1989). Family treatment of adolescent substance abuse: Transitions and maintenance of drug free behaviour. *American Journal of Family therapy*, 17, 229–43.

Radloff, L. (1977). The CES-D: A self-report depression scale for research in the general population. *Applied Psychological Measurement*, 1, 358–401.

Rae, W., Worchel, F., Upchurch, J. and Sanner, J. (1989). The psychosocial impact of play on hospitalized children. *Journal of Pediatric Psychology*, 14, 617–27.*

Rainbow Collection Catalogue gives up-to-date lists of literature and audio-visual aids to help children, families and schools deal with grief-related problems. Available from 447 Hannah Branch Road, Burnsville, NC 28714, USA. Phone 704-675-5909.

Rando, T. (1991). *How To Go On Living When Someone You Love Dies*. New York: Bantam.

Rapoport, J. (1989). *Obsessive Compulsive Disorder in Children and Adolescents*. New York: American Psychiatric Press.

Raschke, H. (1987). Divorce. In M. Sussman and S. Steinmetz (eds), *Handbook of Marriage and the Family* (pp. 597–624). New York: Plenum.

Reddy, L. and Pfeiffer, S. (1996). Effectiveness of Treatment Foster Care with children and adolescents: A review of the outcome studies. *Journal of the American Academy of Child and Adolescent Psychiatry*, 36, 581–8.

Reeker, J., Ensing, D. and Elliot, R. (1997). A meta-analytic investigation of group treatment outcomes for sexually abused children. *Child Abuse and Neglect*, 21 (7), 669–80.

Rehm, L. (1977). A self control model of depression. *Behaviour Therapy*, 8, 787–804.

Reid, J. (1978). *A Social Learning Approach To Family Intervention. Volume 2. Observation In Home Settings.* Eugene, OR: Castalia Press.

Reid, J. (1985). Behavioural approaches to intervention and assessment with child abusive families. In P. Bornstein and A. Kazdin (eds), *Handbook of Clinical Behaviour Therapy with Children* (pp. 772–802). Homewood, Ill: Dorsey Press.

Reynolds, C. and Richmond, B. (1978). What I think and feel: A revised measure of children's manifest anxiety. *Journal of Abnormal Child Psychology*, 6, 271–80.

Reynolds, H. and Johnson, F. (1994). *Handbook of Depression in Children and Adolescents.* New York: Plenum Press.

Reynolds, W. (1987). *Reynolds Adolescent Depression Scale.* Odessa, FL: Psychological Assessment Resources, Inc.

Reynolds, W. (1991). Development of a semistructured clinical interview for suicidal behaviour in adolescents. *Psychological Assessment: A Journal of Consulting and Clinical Psychology*, 2, 382–90.

Reynolds, W. and Coats, K. (1986). A comparison of cognitive-behavioural therapy and relaxation training for the treatment of depression in adolescents. *Journal of Consulting and Clinical Psychology*, 54, 653–60.*

Rice, J. and Rice, D. (1985). *Living Through Divorce: A Developmental Approach to Divorce Therapy.* New York: Guilford.

Richter, I., McGrath, P., Humphreys, P., Goodman, J., Firestone, P. and Keene, D. (1986). Cognitive and relaxation treatment of paediatric migraine. *Pain*, 25, 195–203.*

Richters, J., Arnold, L., Jensen, P., Abikoff, H., Conners, C., Greenhill, L., Hechtman, L., Hinshaw, S., Pelham, W. and Swanson, J. (1995). The National Institute of Mental Health Collaborative Multisite Multimodal Treatment Study of Children with Attention Deficit Hyperactivity Disorder (MTA): 1. Background and rationale. *Journal of the American Academy of Child and Adolescent Psychiatry*, 34, 987–1000.

Robin, A. and Foster, S. (1989). *Negotiating Parent–Adolescent Conflict: A Behavioural Family-Systems Approach.* New York: Guilford.

Robin, A., Siegel, P. and Moye, A. (1995). Family versus individual therapy for anorexia: Impact on family conflict. *International Journal of Eating Disorders*, 17, 313–22.*

Robinson, E. and Eyberg, S. (1981). The dyadic parent–child interaction coding system: Standardization and validation. *Journal of Clinical Child Psychology*, 29, 245–50.

Rolland-Cachera, M., Cole, T., Sempé, M., Tichet, J., Rossignol, C. and Chaurrand, A. (1991). Body mass index variations: Centiles from birth to 87 years. *European Journal of Clinical Nutrition*, 45, 13–27.

Ronen, T., Wozner, Y. and Rahav, G. (1992). Cognitive intervention in enuresis. *Child and Family Behavior Therapy*, 14, 1–1.*

Roseby, V. and Deutsch, R. (1985). Children of separation and divorce: Effects of social role-taking group intervention on forth and fifth graders. *Journal of Clinical Child Psychology*, 14, 55–60.*

Roth, A. and Fonagy, P. (1996). *What Works for Whom. A Critical Review of Psychotherapy Research.* New York: Guilford.

Russell, G., Szmukler, G., Dare, C. and Eisler, I. (1987). An evaluation of family therapy in anorexia nervosa and bulimia nervosa. *Archives of General Psychiatry*, 44, 1047–56.*

Russell, R. and Sipich, J. (1974). Treatment of test anxiety by cue-controlled relaxation. *Behaviour Therapy*, 5, 673–6.

Rutter, M., Tizard, J. and Whitmore, K. (1970). *Education, Health and Behaviour*. London: Longman.

Rzepnicki, T., Schuerman, J., Littell, J., Chak, A. and Lopez, M. (1994). An experimental study of family preservation services: Early findings from a parent study. In R. Barth, J. Berrick and N. Gilbert (eds), *Child Welfare Research Review* (Vol. 1, pp. 60–82). New York: Elsevier.*

Saigh, P. (1989). The development and validation of the Children's Post Traumatic Stress Disorder Inventory. *International Journal of Special Education*, 4, 75–84.

Salk, L. (1978). *What Every Child would Like His Parents to Know about Divorce*. New York: Harper and Row.

Sanders, M. and Dadds, M. (1993). *Behavioral Family Intervention*. New York: Pergamon Press.

Sanders, C., Maugher, P. and Strong, P. (1985). *Grief Experiences Inventory*. Palo Alto, CA: Consulting Psychologists' Press.

Sanders, M., Rebgetz, M., Morrison, M. and Bor, W. (1989). Cognitive-behavioural treatment of recurrent non-specific abdominal pain in children: An analysis of generalization, maintenance, and side effects. *Journal of Consulting and Clinical Psychology*, 57, 294–300.*

Sanders, M., Shepherd, R., Cleghorn, G. and Woolford, H. (1994). The treatment of recurrent abdominal pain in children: A controlled comparison of cognitive-behavioural family intervention and standard paediatric care. *Journal of Consulting and Clinical Psychology*, 62, 306–14.*

Santisteban, D., Szapocznik, J., Perez-Vidal, A., Kurtines, W., Murray, E. and LaPerriere, A. (1996). Efficacy of intervention for engaging youth and families into treatment and some variables that may contribute to differential effectiveness. *Journal of Family Psychology*, 10, 35–44.*

Sarafino, E. (1994). *Health Psychology. Biopsychosocial Interactions* (Second Edition). New York: Wiley.

Sarason, I., Johnson, J. and Siegal, J. (1979). Assessing the impact of life change: Development of the life experiences survey. *Journal of Consulting and Clinical Psychology*, 46, 932–46.

Saunders, B. and Becker-Lausen, E. (1995). The measurement of psychological maltreatment: Early data on the Child Abuse and Trauma Scale. *Child Abuse and Neglect*, 19, 315–23.

Schafer, D. and Moesch, M. (eds) (1981). *Developmental Programming for Infants and Young Children*, Vols 1–5. Ann Arbor, MI: University of Michigan Press.

Scherer, D., Brondino, M., Henggeler, S., Melton, G. and Hanley, J. (1994). Multisystemic Family Preservation Therapy: Preliminary findings from a Study of Rural and Minority Serious Adolescent Offenders. *Journal of Emotional and Behavioural Disorders*, 2, 198–206.*

Schinke, S., Botvin, G. and Orlando, M. (1991). *Substance Abuse in Children and Adolescents: Evaluation and Intervention*. Thousand Oaks, CA: Sage.

Schwartz, J., Kaslow, N., Racusin, G. and Carton, E. (1998). Interpersonal family therapy for depression. In V. VanHasslet and M. Hersen (eds), *Handbook of Psychological Treatment Protocols for Children and Adolescents* (pp. 109–51). Mahwah, NJ: Lawrence Erlbaum.

Scopetta, M., King, O., Szapocznik, J. and Tillman, W. (1979). Ecological structural family therapy with Cuban immigrant families. *Report to the National Institute on Drug Abuse*, Grant No. H81DA 01696.*

Seligman, M., Peterson, C., Kaslow, N., Tanenbaum, R., Alloy, L. and Abramson, L. (1984). Attributional style and depressive symptoms among children. *Journal of Abnormal Psychology*, 93, 235–8.

Selman, R. (1980). *The Growth of Interpersonal Understanding*. New York: Academic Press.

Selvini Palazzoli, M. (1978). *Self-starvation: From Individual To Family Therapy In The Treatment Of Anorexia Nervosa*. (Translated by A. Pomerans.) New York: Jason Aronson.

Serketich, W. and Dumas, J.E. (1996). The effectiveness of behavioural parent training to modify antisocial behaviour in children: A meta-analysis. *Behaviour Therapy*, 27, 171–86.

Shackleton, C. (1983). The psychology of grief: A review. *Behaviour Research and Therapy*, 6, 153–205.

Shadish, W. (1990). *Manual for Calculating Effect Sizes*. Unpublished manuscript. Psychology Department, Memphis State University.

Shadish, W. (1993). *Effect Size Coding Manual*. Memphis, TE: Memphis State University.

Shadish, W., Montgomery, L., Wilson, P., Wilson, M., Bright, I. and Okwumabua, T. (1993). The effects of family and marital psychotherapies: A meta-analysis. *Journal of Consulting and Clinical Psychology*, 61, 992–1002.

Shaffer, D. (1994). Enuresis. In M. Rutter, E. Taylor and L. Hersov (eds), *Child and Adolescent Psychiatry: Modern Approaches* (Third Edition, pp. 505–19). Oxford: Blackwell.

Shaffer, D., Gould, M., Brasic, J., Ambrosini, P., Fisher, P., Bird, H. and Aluwahlia, S. (1983). A Children's Global Assessment Scale (C-GAS). *Archives of General Psychiatry*, 40, 1228–31.

Shain, M., Suurvali, H. and Kilty, H. (1980). *The Parent Communication Project: A Longitudinal Study Of The Effects Of Parenting Skills On Children's Use of Alcohol*. Toronto: Addiction Research Foundation.

Shepard, M. and Soldma, G. (1979). *Divorced Dads. Their Kids, Ex-wives and New Lives*. New York: Berkeley.

Shirk, S. and Russell, R. (1996). *Change Processes in Child Psychotherapy*. New York: Guilford.

Silberman, L. and Wheelan, A. (1980). *How To Discipline Without Feeling Guilty: Assertive Relationships With Children*. New York: Hawthorne.

Silverman, P. and Worden, J. (1993). Children's reaction to the death of a parent. In M. Stroebe, W. Stroebe and R. Hansson (eds), *Handbook of Bereavement: Theory, Research, and Intervention* (pp. 300–16). New York: Cambridge University Press.

Silverman, W. (1987). *Anxiety Disorders Interview Schedule for Children (ADIS-C) and Parents (ADIS-P)*. State University of New York at Albany: Greyhound Publications.

Silverman, W. and Albano, A. (1996). *The Anxiety Disorder Interview Schedule for Children-IV-Child and Parent Version*. Albany, NY: Greywind Publications.

Silverman, W. and Kurtines, W. (1996). *Anxiety and Phobic Disorders: A Pragmatic Approach*. New York: Plenum.

Silverman, W. and Nelles, W. (1988). The Anxiety Disorders Interview Schedule for Children. *Journal of the American Academy of Child and Adolescent Psychiatry*, 27, 772–8.

Silverman, W. and Rabian, B. (1994). Specific phobias. In T. Ollendick, N. King and W. Yule (eds), *International Handbook of Phobic and Anxiety Disorders in Children and Adolescents* (pp. 87–110). New York: Plenum.

Silverman, W., Fleisig, W., Rabian, B. and Peterson, R. (1991). Childhood anxiety sensitivity index. *Journal of Clinical Child Psychology*, 20, 162–8.

Skinner, H. (1982). The drug abuse screening test. *Addictive Behaviour*, 7, 363–71.

Skitka, L. and Frazier, M. (1995). Ameliorating the effects of parental divorce: Do small group interventions work? *Journal of Divorce and Remarriage*, 24, 159–79.*

Slade, P. (1982). Towards a functional analysis of anorexia and bulimia nervosa. *British Journal of Clinical Psychology*, 21, 167–81.

Slade, P. and Dewey, M. (1986). Development and preliminary validation of SCANS: A screening instrument for identifying individuals at risk of developing anorexia and bulimia nervosa. *International Journal of Eating Disorders*, 5, 517–38.

Slade, P., Dewey, M., Kiemle, G. and Newton, T. (1990). Update on SCANS: A screening instrument for identifying individuals at risk of developing an eating disorder. *International Journal of Eating Disorders*, 9, 583–4.

Smith, M. and Glass, C. (1977). Meta-analysis of psychotherapy outcome studies. *American Psychologist*, 32, 752–60.

Smith, M., Glass, C. and Miller, T. (1980). *The Benefits of Psychotherapy*. Baltimore, MD: Johns Hopkins University Press.

Smith, S. and Pennell, M. (1996). *Interventions With Bereaved Children*. London: Kingsley.

Spaccarelli, S. (1994). Stress, appraisal and coping in child sexual abuse: A theoretical and empirical review. *Psychological Bulletin*, 116, 340–62.

Spaccarelli, S., Cotler, S. and Penman, D. (1992). Problem-solving skills training as a supplement to behavioural parent training. *Cognitive Therapy and Research*, 16, 1–18.*

Spence, M. and Brent, S. (1984). Children's understanding of death: A review of three components of a death concept. *Child Development*, 55, 1671–86.

Spielberger, C. (1973). *Preliminary Manual of State-Trait Anxiety Inventory for Children*. Palo Alto, CA: Consulting Psychologists' Press.

Spielberger, C., Gorusch, R. and Luschene, R. (1970). *Manual for the State Trait Anxiety Inventory*. Palo Alto, CA: Consulting Psychologists' Press.

Spivack, G. and Shure, M. (1974). *Social Adjustment of Young Children*. San Francisco, CA: Jossey-Bass.

Spivack, G. and Swift, M. (1967). *Devereux Elementary School Behaviour Rating Scale Manual*. Devon, PA: The Devereux Foundation.

Stambrook, M. and Parker, K. (1987). The development of the concept of death in childhood. A review of the literature. *Merrill-Palmer Quarterly*, 33, 133–57.

Stanton, M. and Heath, A. (1995). Family treatment of alcohol and drug abuse. In R. Mikeselle, D. Lusterman and S. McDaniel (eds), *Integrating Family Therapy: Handbook of Family Therapy and Systems Theory* (pp. 529–41). Washington, DC: APA.

Stanton, M. and Shadish, W. (1997). Outcome, attrition and family-couples treatment for drug abuse: A meta-analysis and review of the controlled comparative studies. *Psychological Bulletin*, 122, 170–91.

Stanton, M. and Todd, T. (1982). *The Family Therapy of Drug Abuse and Addiction.* New York: Guilford.

Stark, J., Opopari, L., Donaldson, D., Danovsky, M., Rasile, D. and DelSanto, A.F. (1997). Evaluation of a standard protocol for retentive encopresis: A replication. *Journal of Pediatric Psychology*, 22, 619–33.*

Stark, K. (1990). *Childhood Depression: School-based Intervention.* New York: Guilford.

Stark, K. and Kendall, P. (1996). *Treating Depressed Children: Therapists Manual for ACTION.* Ardmore, PA: Workbook Publishing.

Stark, K., Reynolds, W. and Kaslow, N. (1987). A comparison of the relative efficacy of self-control therapy and behavioural problem solving therapy for depression in children. *Journal of Abnormal Child Psychology*, 15, 91–113.*

Stark, K., Kendall, P., McCarthy, M., Stafford, M., Barron, R. and Thomeer, M. (1996). *A Workbook for Overcoming Depression.* Ardmore, PA: Workbook Publishing.

Stark, L., Owens, S., Judy, S., Anthony, S. and Lewis, A. (1990). Group behavioural treatment of retentive encopresis. *Journal of Pediatric Psychology*, 15, 659–71.*

State, M. and King, B. (1997). Mental retardation: A review of the past 10 years, part 11. *Journal of the American Academy of Child and Adolescent Psychiatry*, 36, 1664–71.

Stolberg, A. and Garrison, K.M. (1985). Evaluating a primary prevention program for children of divorce. *American Journal of Community Psychology*, 13, 11–124.

Stolberg. A. and Mahler, J. (1994). Enhancing treatment gains in a school-based intervention for children of divorce through skill training, parental involvement and transfer procedures. *Journal of Consulting and Clinical Psychology*, 62, 147 56.*

Stolberg, A., Zacharias, M. and Complair, C. (1991). *Children of Divorce: LeadersGuide, KidsBook and ParentsBook.* Circle Pines, MN: American Guidance Service.

Straus, M. (1979). Measuring Intrafamilial conflict and violence: The Conflict Tactics (CT) Scale. *Journal of Marriage and the Family*, 41, 75–88.

Stroebe, M. (1993). Coping with bereavement: A review of the grief work hypothesis. *Omega Journal of Death and Dying*, 26, 19–42.

Stroebe, M., Stroebe, W. and Hansson, R. (1993). *Handbook of Bereavement: Theory, Research, and Intervention.* New York: Cambridge University Press.

Stuart, R., Jayaratne, S. and Tripodi, T. (1976). Changing adolescent deviant behavior through reprogramming the behaviour of parents and teachers: An experimental evaluation. *Canadian Journal of Behavioural Science*, 8, 133–43.*

Sullivan, P. and Scanlan, J. (1987). Therapeutic issues. In J. Garbarino, P. Brookhouser and K. Authier (eds), *Special Children-Special Risks: The Maltreatment of Children with Disabilities* (pp. 127–59). New York: de Grutyer.

Sullivan, P., Scanlan, J., Brookhouser, P. and Schulte, L. (1992). The effects of psychotherapy on behaviour problems of sexually abused deaf children. *Child Abuse and Neglect*, 16, 279–307.*

Sutter, J. and Eyberg, S. (1984). *Sutter-Eyberg Student Behaviour Inventory.* (Available from Sheila Eyberg, Department of Clinical and Health Psychology, Box J-165, HSC, University of Florida, Gainesville, FL 32610, USA.)

Sweitzer, M. and Boyd, A. (1979). Parent performance checklist: A behavioural assessment of parenting skills. Unpublished manuscript, Florida Mental Health Institute.

Szapocznik, J. and Kurtines, W. (1989). *Breakthroughs In Family Therapy With Drug Abusing Problem Youth*. New York: Springer.

Szapocznik, J., Kurtines, W., Foote, F., Perez-Vidal, A. and Hervis, O. (1983). Conjoint versus one-person family therapy: Some evidence of the effectiveness of conducting family therapy through one person. *Journal of Consulting and Clinical Psychology*, 51, 889–99.*

Szapocznik, J., Kurtines, W., Foote, F., Perez-Vidal, A. and Hervis, O. (1986). Conjoint versus one-person family therapy: Further evidence for the effectiveness of conducting family therapy through one person with drug-abusing adolescents. *Journal of Consulting and Clinical Psychology*, 54, 395–7.*

Szapocznik, J., Perez-Vidal, A., Brickman, A., Foote, F.H., Santisteban, D. and Hervis, O. (1988). Engaging adolescent drug abusers and their families in treatment: A strategic structural systems approach. *Journal of Consulting and Clinical Psychology*, 56, 552–7.*

Szmukler, G. and Patton, G. (1995). Sociocultural models of eating disorder. In G. Szmukler, C. Dare and J. Treasure (eds), *Handbook of Eating Disorders* (pp. 177–94). Chichester: Wiley.

Szmukler, G., Dare, C. and Treasure, J. (1995). *Handbook of Eating Disorders*. Chichester: Wiley.

Target, M. and Fonagy, P. (1996). The psychological treatment of child and adolescent psychological disorders. In A. Roth, A. and P. Fonagy (eds), *What Works for Whom. A Critical Review of Psychotherapy Research* (pp. 263–320). New York: Guilford.

Tarter, R. (1990). Evaluation and treatment of adolescent substance abuse: A decision tree method. *American Journal of Drug and Alcohol Abuse*, 16, 1–46.

Taylor, E. (1994). Syndromes of attention deficit and overactivity. In M. Rutter, E. Taylor and L. Hersov (eds), *Child and Adolescent Psychiatry: Modern Approaches* (Third Edition, pp. 285–307). London: Blackwell.

Thapar, A., Davies, G., Jones, T. and Rivett, M. (1992). Treatment of childhood encopresis: A review. *Child Care, Health and Development*, 8, 343–53.

Tonge, B. (1994). Separation anxiety disorder. In T. Ollendick, N. King and W. Yule (eds), *International Handbook of Phobic and Anxiety Disorders in Children and Adolescents* (pp. 145–68). New York: Plenum.

Touyz, S., Beumont, P., Glaun, D., Phillips, T. and Cowie, I. (1984). A comparison of lenient and strict operant conditional conditioning programmes in refeeding patients with anorexia nervosa. *British Journal of Psychiatry*, 144, 517–20.

Treasure, J. (1997). *Anorexia Nervosa. A Survival Guide for Families, Friends and Sufferers*. Hove: Psychology Press.

Treasure, J. and Schmidt, U. (1993). *Getting Better Bit(e) by Bit(e): A Survival Kit for Sufferers of Bulimia Nervosa and Binge Eating*. Hove: Lawrence Erlbaum (Self-help).

Ullmann, R., Sleator, E. and Sprague, R. (1984). A new rating scale for diagnosis and monitoring of ADD children. *Psychopharmacology Bulletin*, 20, 160–4.

Vahlquist, B. (1955). Migraine in children. *International Archives of Allergy*, 7, 348–55.

Van Hasselt, V. and Hersen, M. (1998). *Handbook of Psychological Treatment Protocols for Children and Adolescents*. Mahwah, New Jersey: Lawrence Erlbaum.

Van Londen, A., Van Londen, B., Monique, W., Van Son, M., Mulder, J. and Guido, A. (1995). Relapse rate and subsequent parental reaction after successful treatment of children suffering from nocturnal enuresis: A 21/2 year follow-up of bibliotherapy. *Behaviour Research and Therapy*, 33, 309–11.*

Vandereycken, W., Kog, E. and Vanderlinden, J. (1989). *The Family Approach to Disorders: Assessment and Treatment of Anorexia Nervosa and Bulimia*. New York: PMA.

Varni, J., Thompson, K. and Hanson, V. (1987). The Varni-Thompson Paediatric Pain Questionnaire: 1. Chronic-musculo-skeletal pain in juvenile rheumatoid arthritis. *Pain*, 28, 27–38.

Vaughn, C. and Leff, J. (1976). The influence of family and social factors on the course of psychiatric illness: A comparison of schizophrenic and depressed neurotic patients. *British Journal of Psychiatry*, 129, 125–37.

Vessey, J., Carlson, K. and McGill, J. (1994). Use of distraction with children during an acute pain experience. *Nursing Research*, 43, 69–372.*

Vostanis, P. and Harrington, R. (1994). Cognitive behavioural treatment of depressive disorder in child psychiatric patients: Rationale and description of a treatment package. *European Child and Adolescent Psychiatry*, 3, 111–23.

Wahler, R., House, A. and Stambaugh, E. (1976). *Ecological Assessment of Child Problem Behaviour. A Clinical Package for Home, School and Institutional Settings*. New York: Pergamon.

Waldron, H.B. (1996). Adolescent substance abuse and family therapy outcome: A review of randomised trials. *Advances in Clinical Child Psychology*, 19, 199–234.

Walker, C., Bonner, B. and Kaufman, K. (1988). *The Physically and Sexually Abused Child: Evaluation and Treatment*. New York: Pergamon.

Walker, J. (1993). Co-operative parenting post-divorce: Possibility or pipe dream? *Journal of Family Therapy*, 15, 273–92.

Wallerstein, J. (1991). The long term effects of divorce on children: A review. *Journal of the American Academy of Child and Adolescent Psychiatry*, 30, 349–60.

Wallerstein, J. and Kelly, J. (1980). *Surviving the Break-up*. London: Grant McIntyre.

Walsh, F. and McGoldrick, M. (1991). *Living Beyond Loss: Death in the Family*. New York: Norton.

Ward, B. (1993). *Good Grief: Exploring Feelings of Loss and Death*. (Vol. 1: With under elevens. Vol. 2: With over elevens and adults.) London: Kingsley.

Warr, P. and Jackson, P. (1985). Factors influencing the psychological impact of prolonged unemployment and of re-employment. *Psychological Medicine*, 15, 795–807.

Webb, N. (1993). *Helping Bereaved Children: A Handbook for Practitioners*. New York: Guilford.

Weber, G. and Stierlin, H. (1981). Familiendynamik und Famlientherapie der Anroresxia Nervosa Familie (pp. 108–22). In R. Merman (ed.), *Anorexia Nervosa*. Hamburg, Germany: Ferdinand Enke.

Webster-Stratton, C. (1981). Videotape modelling: A method of parent education. *Journal of Clinical Child Psychology*, 10, 93–8.

Webster-Stratton, C. (1984). Randomized trial of two parent-training programs for families with conduct-disordered children. *Journal of Consulting and Clinical Psychology*, 52, 666–78.*

Webster-Stratton, C. (1986). *Parent And Children Series Videocassette Program*. Eugene, OR: Castalia Press.

Webster-Stratton, C. (1987). *Parents And Children: A 10 Program Videotape Parent Training Series With Manuals*. Eugene, OR: Castalia Press.

Webster-Stratton, C. (1990). Enhancing the effectiveness of self-administered videotape parent training for families with conduct-problem children. *Journal of Abnormal Child Psychology*, 18, 479–92.*

Webster-Stratton, C. (1991). *Dinosaur Social Skills And Problem-Solving Training Manual*. Unpublished Manuscript.

Webster-Stratton, C. (1992). Individually administered videotape parent training: 'Who Benefits?'. *Cognitive Therapy and Research*, 16, 31–5.*

Webster-Stratton, C. and Hammond, M. (1997). Treating children with early-onset conduct problems: A comparison of child and parent training interventions. *Journal of Consulting and Clinical Psychology*, 65, 93–109.*

Webster-Stratton, C., Kolpacoff, M. and Hollinsworth, T. (1988). Self-administered videotape therapy for families with conduct-problem children: Comparison with two cost-effective treatments and a control group. *Journal of Consulting and Clinical Psychology*, 56 (4), 558–66.*

Weisz, J. and Weiss, B. (1993). *Effects of Psychotherapy with Children and Adolescents*. London: Sage.

Wells, K. and Egan, J. (1988). Social learning and systems family therapy for childhood oppositional disorder: Comparative treatment outcome. *Comprehensive Psychiatry*, 29, 138–46.*

Wender, P. (1987). *The Hyperactive Child, Adolescent and Adult. Attention Deficit Disorder Through The Lifespan*. New York: Oxford University Press.

Wesch, D. and Lutzker, J. (1991). A comprehensive 5 year evaluation of Project 12-Ways: An eco-behavioural program for treating and preventing child abuse and neglect. *Journal of Family Violence*, 6, 17–35.*

West, R. (1994). *Eating Disorders: Anorexia Nervosa and Bulimia Nervosa*. London: Office of Health Economics.

Whitehurst, G. and Fischel, J. (1994). Early developmental language delay: What, if anything should the clinician do about it. *Journal of Child Psychology and Psychiatry*, 35, 613–48.

Whiteman, M., Fanshel, D. and Grundy, D. (1987). Cognitive-behavioural interventions aimed at anger of parents at risk of child abuse. *Social Work*, Nov.–Dec., 469–74.*

Wilkinson, G. (1993). *WRAT-3: Wide Range Achievement Test* (Third Edition). Wilmington, DE: Wide Range Inc.

Williamson, D. (1993). Advances in paediatric headache research. In T. Ollendick and R. Prinz (eds), *Advances in Clinical Child Psychology* (Vol. 15, pp. 275–304). New York: Plenum Press.

Wilson, T. and Fairburn, C. (1998). Treatments for eating disorders. In P. Nathan and J. Gorman (eds), *A Guide to Treatments that Work* (pp. 501–30). New York: Oxford University Press.

Winters, K. (1989). *Personal Experience Screening Questionnaire*. Los Angeles, CA: Western Psychological Services.

Winters, K. and Henly, G. (1989). *Personal Experience Inventory*. Los Angeles, CA: Western Psychological Services. Phone +1-310-478-2061.

Wisniewski, J., Genshaft, J., Mulick, J., Coury, P. and Daniel, L. (1988). Relaxation therapy and compliance in the treatment of adolescent headache. *Headache*, 28, 612–17.*

Wolchik, S., Sandler, I., Braver, S. and Fogas, B. (1985). Events of parental divorce: Stressfulness ratings by children, parents and clinicians. *American Journal of Community Psychology*, 14, 59–74.

Wolchik, S., West, S., Westover, S., Sandler, I., Martin, A., Lustig, J., Tein, J. and Fisher, F. (1993). The children of divorce parenting outcome evaluation of an empirically based program. *American Journal of Community Psychology*, 21, 293–330.*

Wolfe, D. and Werkerle, C. (1993). Treatment strategies for child physical abuse and neglect: A critical progress report. *Clinical Psychology Review*, 13, 473–500.

Wolfe, D., Sandler, J. and Kaufman, K. (1981). A competency-based parent training program for child abusers. *Journal of Consulting and Clinical Psychology*, 49, 633–40.*

Wolfe, D., Edwards, B., Mannion, I. and Koverola, C. (1988). Early intervention for parents at risk of child abuse and neglect: A preliminary investigation. *Journal of Consulting and Clinical Psychology*, 56, 40–7.*

Wolfe, V. and Birt, J. (1995). The psychological sequelae of child sexual abuse. In T. Ollendick and R. Prinz (eds), *Advances in Clinical Child Psychology* (Vol. 17, pp. 233–63). New York: Plenum.

Wolfe, V., Gentile, C., Michienzi, T., Sas, L. and Wolfe, D. (1991). Child Impact of Traumatic Events Scale. A measure of post-sexual-abuse PTSD symptoms. *Behavioural Assessment*, 13, 359–83.

Wood, A., Harrington, R. and Moore, A. (1996). Controlled trial of brief cognitive-behavioural intervention in adolescent patients with depressive disorders. *Journal of Child Psychology and Psychiatry*, 37 (6), 737–46.*

Woodside, B. and Shekter-Wolfson, L. (1991). *Family Approaches in Treatment of Eating Disorders*. Washington, DC: APA Press.

Worden, J. (1997). *Children and Grief: When A Parent Dies*. New York: Guilford.

World Health Organization (1992). *The ICD-10 Classification of Mental and Behavioural Disorders*. Geneva: WHO.

World Health Organization (1996). *Multi axial Classification of Child and Adolescent Psychiatric Disorders: ICD 10*. Geneva: WHO.

Wortman, C. and Silver, R. (1989). The myths of coping with loss. *Journal of Consulting and Clinical Psychology*, 57, 349–57.

Yule, W. (1994). Posttraumatic stress disorder. In M. Rutter, E. Taylor and L. Hersov (eds), *Child and Adolescent Psychiatry: Modern Approaches* (Third Edition, pp. 392–406). London: Blackwell.

Zangwill, W. (1983). An evaluation of a parent training program. *Child and Family Behaviour Therapy*, 5, 1–16.*

Zennah, C. (1996). Beyond insecurity: A reconceptualization of attachment disorders of infancy. *Journal of Consulting and Clinical Psychology*, 64, 42–52.

*Studies reported in references marked with an astrix were selected for review.

Index